Dak To and the Border
Battles of Vietnam,
1967–1968

ALSO BY MICHAEL A. EGGLESTON
AND FROM McFARLAND

*The 5th Marine Regiment Devil Dogs
in World War I: A History and Roster* (2016)

*Exiting Vietnam: The Era of Vietnamization and American
Withdrawal Revealed in First-Person Accounts* (2014)

*President Lincoln's Recruiter: General Lorenzo Thomas and the
United States Colored Troops in the Civil War* (2013)

*The Tenth Minnesota Volunteers, 1862–1865:
A History of Action in the Sioux Uprising and the
Civil War, with a Regimental Roster* (2012)

Dak To and the Border Battles of Vietnam, 1967–1968

MICHAEL A. EGGLESTON

McFarland & Company, Inc., Publishers
Jefferson, North Carolina

LIBRARY OF CONGRESS CATALOGUING-IN-PUBLICATION DATA

Names: Eggleston, Michael A., 1937– author.
Title: Dak To and the border battles of Vietnam, 1967–1968 / Michael A. Eggleston.
Description: Jefferson, North Carolina : McFarland & Company, Inc., Publishers, 2017. | Includes bibliographical references and index.
Identifiers: LCCN 2016059002 | ISBN 9781476664170 (softcover : acid free paper) ∞
Subjects: LCSH: Dak To, Battle of, Vietnam, 1967. | Vietnam War, 1961–1975—Campaigns.
Classification: LCC DS557.8.D33 E35 2017 | DDC 959.704/342—dc23
LC record available at https://lccn.loc.gov/2016059002

BRITISH LIBRARY CATALOGUING DATA ARE AVAILABLE

ISBN (print) 978-1-4766-6417-0
ISBN (ebook) 978-1-4766-2699-4

© 2017 Michael A. Eggleston. All rights reserved

No part of this book may be reproduced or transmitted in any form or by any means, electronic or mechanical, including photocopying or recording, or by any information storage and retrieval system, without permission in writing from the publisher.

Front cover: 3rd Battalion, 12th Infantry on Hill 1338 (U.S. Army)

Manufactured in the United States of America

*McFarland & Company, Inc., Publishers
Box 611, Jefferson, North Carolina 28640
www.mcfarlandpub.com*

Acknowledgments

I would like to thank my wife, Margaret, for her endless patience and efforts to comment on and edit this book. I would also like to express my gratitude to all who contributed to this book or helped in its preparation: Billy E. Boedeker from Granbury, Texas, Sa Won Chang, Stanley S. DeRuggiero, Paul A. Donahue, John Eggleston, John L. Feagin, Jr., Charles L. Gove, Dennis Hale, Gary Luoma, Tom Means, Irvin "Bugs" Moran, Ed Placencia, David Plum, Dante' M. Puccetti, Juan Alex Quintanar, John R. Robinson, Frances Rogers, Cliff Stoval, Mercer "Nick" Vandenburg, Steve Vorthmann, Gary F. Walls, and Professor Robert Wilensky.

Table of Contents

Acknowledgments	v
Preface	1
Introduction	3
1—Background	5
2—The U.S. at War	16
3—Dak To	26
4—Last of the Border Battles	99
5—Aftermath: Tet '68—31 January 1968	122
Biographical Sketches	157
Appendix A: Names, Acronyms and Terms	165
Appendix B: Vietnam Chronology	169
Appendix C: Unit Organization	172
Appendix D: The Wall	174
Chapter Notes	193
Bibliography	201
Index	209

Preface

Several books, television programs and magazine articles describe the battle of Dak To minute-by-minute in the words of the soldiers who fought there. It is a very gripping human story. But, there is something missing: how did we get to Dak To, how did decisions elsewhere affect the battle, and what happened after. Written half a century after the fighting, this history answers these questions.

This book is focused on Dak To and a series of decisive battles called the "Border Battles" in Vietnam that had a major impact on the war. At Dak To, a small village in the Central Highlands, battles in the French War through the fall of Saigon in 1975 are described. The focus is on the Vietnam War in 1967–1968. This history is important because it describes in detail the Border Battles and explains how they were interrelated and how they affected the battles that followed. The book relies on my records and letters from two tours in Vietnam as well as memoirs of Vietnam veterans of Dak To, many of which have not previously been published. Other important sources that I relied on include the memoirs, letters, and books written by the key leaders during this period, such as Haig, Kissinger, Nixon, Westmoreland, Ho Chi Minh, and General Vo Nguyen Giap, the North Vietnamese commander. Unit combat after-action reports were invaluable, since they were written immediately after the battle, when facts were fresh in the minds of the participants. I studied Edward F. Murphy's book on Dak To. It is perhaps the best of those that describe this battle. I used it frequently to fact-check my history.[1]

Some may call this book a hybrid, because it merges the official history of the war with the oral history of people who were there. There are hundreds of memoirs of Vietnam—U.S. infantry soldiers who describe slogging through the jungle, ambushes, and all of that, but this book also inserts what was going on elsewhere in Saigon, the Pentagon, and the White House. Other books provide the official history, while still others are memoirs. This book includes both. Some of the memoirs are brutal; others may appear mundane; while still others are humorous. Gallows humor among soldiers is legendary. It kept us sane. In all cases, we have done our best to tell what we saw.

This book is written for the veterans who fought at Dak To and for people who want to learn more about the war in Vietnam. It goes into detail to recognize the accomplishments of soldiers who served there. A number of veterans reviewed the draft of this book and wrote back that I needed to give credit to their units for the roles each played in various fights. They wanted to make sure that I got the history right. They gave me their photographs and memoirs. These compose a significant part of this book. Half a century after the battle,

I have endeavored to complete the record of what happened at Dak To. I also summarize some of the background and history of the war beyond the time frame of the Border Battles. Chapter 5 describes events on the home front, the U.S. withdrawal, and the war's end after the Border Battles. The appendices provide background, including definitions of the acronyms, chronology of the war, organizational structure, and, most important, in Appendix D, a listing of U.S. people who died in the battle of Dak To. Several soldiers were posthumously awarded the Medal of Honor for their actions at Dak To, and they are identified in Appendix D.

I have written half a dozen histories, including one on Vietnam that was my memoir as well as the memoirs of fifteen other soldiers. I served two tours in Vietnam, located at Pleiku, not far from Dak To. On my second tour, long after this battle, I had detachments located near Dak To, so I visited there and know the terrain. This triggered my interest in the Border Battles.

Introduction

> *The fight at Dak To was the third engagement during the fall of 1967 that collectively became known as the "Border Battles." ... Dak To was possibly the greatest portent if it was the opening round in "a concentrated offensive effort" throughout South Vietnam.*[1]—General William C. Westmoreland

This book is formatted to provide a historical account of events, including the memoirs of the soldiers who served in the Vietnam War. Dak To was the turning point of the war, when major battles called the Border Battles were fought in 1967–1968. To fully document the Border Battles, it was necessary to explain what was happening in Saigon, the Pentagon, and the White House. I have also identified the U.S. intelligence information available during the battles, the units involved (173d Airborne Brigade, elements of the 4th Infantry Division, 1st Infantry Division, and the 1st Air Cavalry Division) and the opposing enemy forces. Appendix C provides a complete listing of the units.

This book starts with the occupation of Indochina by the French more than 100 years ago and explains the involvement of the French until their final defeat by Viet Minh nationalists in 1954. It then turns to the deepening involvement of the U.S. and its allies, from military aid to advisors, and finally to the commitment of U.S. ground forces in 1965. The focus of U.S. involvement is the Border Battles, from early 1967 through the Tet Offensive of 1968. What follows is the period of Vietnamization, the withdrawal of U.S. forces from Vietnam, ending in 1973, and finally the fall of the Saigon regime in 1975.

Throughout the entire Vietnam conflict, I consider the veterans' accounts as the best judgment of what happened. U.S. government and South Vietnamese accounts are often self-serving. The members of the Army of the Republic of Vietnam (ARVN) tended to blame the U.S. for their defeats and seldom acknowledged the corruption in Saigon and incompetence of many Republic of Vietnam Armed Forces (RVNAF) commanders in the field. This is tragic and very unnecessary, since there were many outstanding RVNAF accomplishments. There are many RVNAF accounts that are scrupulously accurate. Among the best is Major General Nguyen Duy Hinh's *Lam Son 719*.[2]

The U.S. press reports were at times exaggerated. Many members of the Saigon press corps later wrote books about the Vietnam War. Stanley Karnow's is one of the best.[3] He won the Pulitzer Prize for his history. Neil Sheehan was also a correspondent, and his history provides a complete summary of the U.S. involvement in the Vietnam War.[4] These two books are in a category of "must read" for those interested in learning more about the war in Vietnam.

Recollections written by soldiers after the war are the best source. Many times these recollections are limited in scope (most soldiers served one year) and lack context, but when compared with and integrated into the history of the war, they reveal details of what happened. Letters home are always a great source of information but are often less than candid.

Casualty numbers are frequently quoted with the knowledge that they are questionable but are often the only measure of success (or failure) used by the U.S. commander, General Westmoreland, during the war. Shelby Stanton, in his book *The Rise and Fall of the American Army U.S. Ground Forces in Vietnam 1965–1973*, summarized.

> Accurate assessments of North Vietnamese Army and Viet Cong losses were largely impossible due to lack of disclosure by the Vietnamese government, terrain, destruction of remains by firepower used, and the fact that allied ground units were often unable to confirm artillery and aerial "kills." The entire process of accumulating valid casualty data was also shrouded by the shameful gamesmanship practiced by certain reporting elements under pressure to "produce results." American losses were subject to statistical manipulation as well. For instance, dying soldiers put aboard medical evacuation helicopters were often counted as only wounded in unit after-action tables.[5]

This is a memoir for all of the Vietnam veterans who are quoted within this book. I also captured quotes and testimony of many key people such as Henry Kissinger, Alexander Haig, Richard Nixon, William Westmoreland, Bruce Palmer, and others who participated in the war. Sometimes the comments are brutally frank, such as those of Tom Marshall, who was a helicopter pilot in 1971, moving RVNAF out of Laos during Lam Son 719. He wrote a book about it:

> I'm not saying it's the ARVN's fault as much as it is the command's fault. The command doesn't even know what the hell it's doing. I mean, it throws them out there on the damn mountaintop and expects them to do damn wonders. It's just like throwing a bunch of dinks—eight hundred dinks—can you imagine, eight hundred RVNAFs being attacked by six thousand NVA. I mean, you can see why they're getting their asses kicked. It's just that plain and simple. It's the United States' advisors and the Vietnamese higher-ups who don't know what in the hell they're doing. They're just dicking around with people's lives …[6]

1

Background

French Indochina

At the close of World War II in 1945, the Japanese, who had occupied Indochina[1] during the war, were on their way home, while the French sought to reclaim their colonial empire. This was not what the Vietnamese had in mind. After having fought the Japanese through a long war, the Vietnamese wanted independence. Ho Chi Minh, the Vietnamese leader, summarized: "If they [the French] force us into war, we will fight. The struggle will be atrocious, but the Vietnamese people will suffer anything rather than renounce their freedom."[2] Ho's words were prophetic, as would be proven thirty years later when North Vietnamese tanks rumbled through the gates of the South Vietnamese palace in Saigon, ending the war.

French involvement in Vietnam started in August 1883, when a French fleet arrived at the mouth of the Perfume River near the imperial capital of Vietnam, Hue, and demanded the surrender of the government. Before the Vietnamese could respond, the fleet opened fire, killing thousands of unarmed Vietnamese.[3] The French seized Vietnam and turned it into a colony of France. There were many riches that France wanted to exploit, as most colonial powers do. Rubber, tea, and rice were not the least of these. Vietnam had been invaded and occupied several times in the past, but the French occupation was the most recent. As a result of the slaughter in Hue in 1883, the Vietnamese capitulated. The French took over and declared that Vietnam was now their protectorate. They sent in troops. What followed was over seventy years of French exploitation of Vietnam that ended in 1954.

Along the way, there were some strange occurrences. At the World War I peace conference at Versailles in 1919, a very young man attempted to see U.S. President Woodrow Wilson. The young man wanted to argue for self-rule in Vietnam. His name was Ho Chi Minh,[4] but Wilson refused to see him.[5] Had he done so, the history of Vietnam might have been different, but that is very unlikely. Most say that Ho was a communist, while others argue that he was a nationalist. It appears that he was a nationalist when he sought to see Wilson, but his political leanings changed to communism after he visited Moscow in 1925. Dean Acheson, secretary of state, put it another way in 1949: "Question whether Ho [Chi Minh] as much Nationalist as Commie is irrelevant. All Stalinists in colonial areas are nationalists."[6] Today, it does not really matter, given the outcome of the war, but his political leanings did change over time.

A very strange situation emerged in Vietnam during World War II. The Japanese left

French Indochina in 1945 (Wikipedia).

the French bureaucratic colonial administration intact to rule Vietnam while they directed its activities.[7] This was a decisive period of time. The Vietnamese realized that the French were defeated and incompetent and could not fight (as seen in the World War II Fall of France in 1940). During World War II, while the Japanese exported their plunder from Vietnam, nearly twenty percent of the population in the North died from starvation.[8] The reason for the starvation was crop failures in the South. The North was not self-sustaining and suffered the most since it was relying on crops from the South. Years later, the mayor of Hanoi described the scene:

> Peasants came in from the nearby provinces on foot, leaning on each other, carrying their children in baskets. They dug in garbage piles, looking for anything at all, banana skins, orange peels, discarded greens. They even ate rats. But they couldn't get enough to keep alive. They tried to beg, but everyone else was hungry, and they would drop dead in the streets. Every morning, when I opened my door, I found five or six corpses on the step. We organized teams of youths to load the bodies on oxcarts and take them to mass graves outside the city. It was terrifying—and yet it helped our cause because we were able to rally the nation.[9]

In August 1945, after the U.S. Army Air Corps incinerated the Japanese towns of Hiroshima and Nagasaki with nuclear weapons, the Japanese decided to surrender unconditionally.[10]

Bao Dai was the titular leader of Vietnam throughout the war. He resided in Hue, the traditional capital of Vietnam, and also spent time at his hunting lodge at Ban Me Thuot. When World War II ended, he moved to Hanoi and became the pawn of the Vietnamese nationalist movement under Ho Chi Minh. He was a playboy who did nothing, but the

Top: Ho Chi Minh in 1946 (Library of Congress). *Bottom:* **Bao Dai (1913–1997) (Wikipedia).**

Viet Minh, the nationalist group led by Ho Chi Minh, used him to their advantage. They appointed him "Supreme Advisor" and manipulated him for their own purpose.[11]

By the fall of 1945, it was clear that a war between the French occupiers and the Viet Minh was imminent. As the French general Etienne Valluy summarized, "If those gooks want a fight, they'll get it."[12]

The French got their fight. At the same time, Ho appealed to the United States to recognize his cause. At this time, the U.S. president, Harry Truman, was not inclined to support an avowed communist such as Ho against a very weak ally: France.

In the postwar period, the French strengthened their control of Vietnam without regard to the Vietnamese people. Atrocities were committed by both sides, including the massacre of about one hundred and fifty French civilians in Saigon.[13] The war with the French would drag on for nine years. At one point, General Leclerc, the French commander, declared victory and would learn otherwise, as General Westmoreland would learn twenty years later. The French historian Philippe Devillers summarized:

> If we departed, believing a region pacified, the Vietminh would arrive on our heels.... There was only one possible defense, to multiply our posts, fortify them, arm and train the villagers, coordinate intelligence and police. What was required was not Leclerc's thirty-five thousand troops but a hundred thousand—and Cochinchina was not the only problem.[14]

Bao Dai was lured back by the French and served as chief of state until the final French defeat and withdrawal in 1956. Bao Dai was the last emperor of Vietnam. Among the people in Bao Dai's cabinet before the war was a bureaucrat named Ngo Dinh Diem. Diem would play a key role in the history of Vietnam.

There was much bad news for the West in the 1949–1950 time frame, all of which influenced Vietnam. Chairman Mao defeated the Nationalist government in China and stationed his troops along the border of Vietnam. They were ready to provide support to the Viet Minh in spite of the fact that the Chinese had been traditional enemies of the Vietnamese. Soul-searching in the U.S. revolved around who lost China. With Senator Joseph McCarthy initiating a red witch hunt in the United States, there was no sympathy for anyone such as Ho who could be viewed as a Communist. Although Ho Chi Minh wrote at least eight letters to President Truman, Truman had no interest in initiating any contact with or negotiating with Ho. This was also a Cold War issue. The U.S. would support the French in Vietnam, and in return, the French would support the U.S. doctrine in Europe for containment.

The Soviet Union had constructed and detonated its first nuclear weapon, thanks to input from traitors in the U.S. and the U. K. The U.S. had lost its sole possession of nuclear technology, and with that went enormous leverage. This could have been used to negotiate a settlement in Vietnam if Truman had wished to do so.

The French continued to drain their military resources fighting a losing war in Vietnam. By 1950, French losses exceeded 50,000, and the Viet Minh were killing French officers at a rate faster than they could be graduated from officer schools in France.[15] This reduced France's ability to meet its NATO requirements in Europe. By late 1952, French casualties (dead, wounded, captured, and missing) were up to more than 90,000.[16] By this time, the U.S. was funding forty percent of the cost of the French war, but France did not ask for the commitment of U.S. ground forces.[17]

In the meantime, the war in Korea had an effect on Vietnam. When the North Koreans invaded South Korea in June 1950, the U.S. responded by moving thousands of troops to defend its ally, South Korea, and this was one of the most curious wars in recent history.

It was called a "Police Action" by the U.S. Some background is relevant. In 1950, Dean Acheson, the U.S. secretary of state, announced that Korea was outside the U.S. "Defense Perimeter." This occurred during his Press Club speech on 12 January 1950. The North Koreans believed what Acheson said and viewed his statement as a green light for them to invade the South. They should not have believed Acheson's statement. The U.S., as it turned out, would fight to defend its ally. Acheson would later deny his statement and indicated that his Press Club speech was "grossly distorted."[18] This was symptomatic of the U.S. view of Asia during the 1950s. Korea and Vietnam were sideshows that did not deserve much thought or time until major conflicts there erupted. The focus was on the Soviet Union and Senator Joseph McCarthy.[19] These two were the major threats to our democracy. U.S. troops were tied up in Korea, and the U.S. had a reduced capability to assist France in Vietnam, except for funding and some air support missions.

Ngo Dinh Diem (1901–1963) (Department of Defense).

The French sought a "set piece battle" with the Viet Minh. This meant a conventional fight in which both sides faced off and fought it out in a battle, one side winning and the other side losing. The Viet Minh did not fight that way. It came down to guerrilla warfare, with ambushes on the French, and the Viet Minh would then fade away. Ho made it clear to the French: "You can kill ten of my men for everyone I kill of yours, but even at those odds, I will win."[20]

The Last French Defeat

The best example of the Viet Minh "hit and run" tactics was the destruction of the French Groupement Mobile 100 (G.M. 100) that Doctor Bernard Fall described in his book *Street Without Joy*. G.M. 100 was one of the best units of its type. Its troops had fought in Korea as a part of the U.S. 2nd Infantry Division, and the French troops were seasoned fighters. It was an elite force. In December 1953, G.M. 100 moved into Vietnam's Central Highlands, in an area that would later be called Corps Tactical Zone 2 (CTZ2) and still later Military Region 2 (MR2), not far from Ban Me Thout. When the Viet Minh attacked the French at Kontum near Dak To and further south at Cheo Reo, G.M. 100 was ordered to reinforce Cheo Reo on New Year's Day, 1954. The G.M. 100 assembled at Cheo Reo and performed road clearance of Route 7 to the coast. By 1 February 1954, the threat to Kontum had become clear, and G.M. 100 was ordered north to Kontum, where the civilians were in panic over Viet Minh activities. The Viet Minh were transitioning from guerrilla warfare to a full-scale conventional war. Thirteen years later, this same transition occurred at the same place—Dak To—during the Border Battles. It was perfect for this purpose due to terrain and proximity to nearby border safe havens. Dr. Fall described the action.

To the north and northeast of the town [Kontum], the mountain tribesmen partisans had either withdrawn into the jungle or, undermined by Communist propaganda, had murdered their French NCOs and this time, the enemy did not avoid contact. A strong patrol from the 2d Korea [these were French veterans of the Korean War] to Kon Brai, led by Lieutenant de Bellefont, fell into a well-laid ambush, in which the whole platoon was nearly wiped out, leaving seven dead (including the lieutenant) and thirteen wounded, while the Viet Minh lost five dead.

At 1300, on February 2, all the posts to the northwest of Kontum, including the important post of Dak-To, were simply submerged by enemy troops in battalion strength attacking in several waves. Air support, called in from the fighter-bomber airfields in NhaTrang and Seno, continued strafing missions around Dak-To until nightfall, but only a handful of survivors succeeded in reaching the outposts of Kontum. The 2d Korea continued its patrol activities in the direction of Kon Brai and suffered casualties from mines and booby traps.

Slowly, the 803d Viet-Minh Regiment continued to narrow its stranglehold around the G.M. In a wide sweep beyond the city it attacked the post of Dak Doa, 28 kilometers to the southeast of Kontum, which suffered 16 casualties but continued to hold. On February 5, the enemy blew up several bridges to the north of Kontum, thus prohibiting any jeep-borne patrolling north on highway 14. It was only a matter of hours before the G.M. would be totally encircled in Kontum, but the High Command decided not to defend Kontum; the evacuation of the town by all troops, European civilians and Vietnamese civil servants was completed without major incident by February 7, and the G.M. now grimly dug in around Pleiku for a last-ditch defense of the central region of the Southern Mountain Plateau.[21]

Dien Bien Phu

The French decided that they would establish a base camp west of Hanoi in a valley called Dien Bien Phu. This was intended to block the return of Viet Minh General Vo Nguyen Giap into Laos, which he had easily accomplished in 1953, but withdrew because of the rains.[22] In this way, the French hoped to entice the Viet Minh to attack them. The French got their wish. Giap marshaled his forces around the French garrison. By 13 March 1954, Giap was prepared to attack. He had assembled 50,000 troops at Dien Bien Phu. The French had 13,000, and about half of these were fighters.[23] One of Giap's soldiers recalled:

> We had to cross mountains and jungles, marching at night and sleeping by day to avoid enemy bombing. We sometimes slept in foxholes, or just by the trail. We each carried a rifle, ammunition, and hand grenades, and our packs contained a blanket, a mosquito net, and a change of clothes. We each had a week's supply of rice, which we refilled at depots along the way. We ate greens and bamboo shoots that we picked in the jungle, and occasionally villagers would give us a bit of meat. I'd been in the Viet Minh for nine years by then, and I was accustomed to it.[24]

The French battle plan was a soldier's nightmare. The French established their camp in a valley, which meant that any force on the surrounding hills could destroy the French. If the Viet Minh closed in, the French would have to rely on air resupply and had limited assets, although the U.S. agreed to provide some airlift capability. The French thought that this would be a perfect "set piece battle." The Viet Minh would be cut to pieces by air support and artillery as they attacked. This would defeat the Viet Minh and end the war. This was similar to the situation experienced by the ARVN/U.S. and NVA in other later battles such as Khe Sanh and Lam Son 719.

The French commander, Colonel Christian de Castries, had established strong points on the hills surrounding Dien Bien Phu. He named these for his French mistresses (Huguette, Claudine, Dominique, and Eliane). Perhaps like his mistresses, it was a French fantasy: the outposts could easily be overcome by the Viet Minh, and they were. The greatest miscalculation was artillery. The French concluded that since the Viet Minh had no artillery

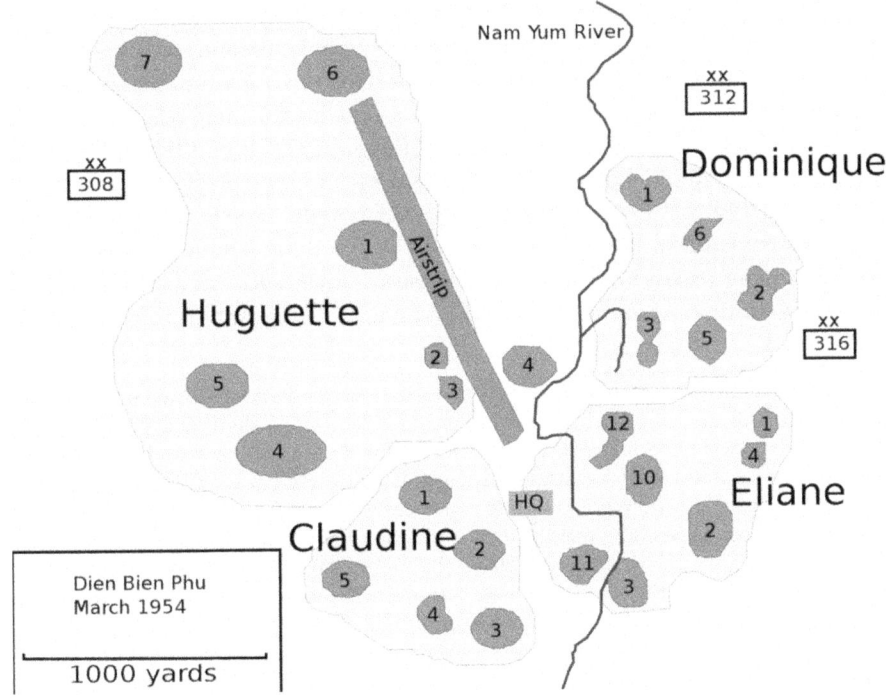

Map of Dien Bien Phu in spring 1954, showing position numbers (Wikipedia).

at Dien Bien Phu and the French had air support, Dien Bien Phu could survive an attack by the Viet Minh.[25] Giap solved the problem for the Viet Minh. The troops dismantled their artillery pieces and humped them up the mountains to overlook Dien Bien Phu. Viet Minh artillery overlooking Dien Bien Phu fired at will. It was a "turkey shoot." Giap's battle plan was simple:

> By launching a big offensive with fresh troops, we could have foreshortened the duration of the campaign, and avoided the wear and tear of a long operation.... [But] we saw that these tactics had a very great, basic disadvantage. Our troops lacked experience in attacking fortified entrenched camps. If we wanted to win swiftly, success could not be assured.... Consequently, *we resolutely chose to strike and advance surely ... strike to win, strike only when success is certain. If it is not, then do not strike.*[26]

Initially, Giap lost heavily and changed his battle plan. A veteran of the battle recalled:

> General Giap changed the entire plan. He stopped the attack and pulled back our artillery. Now the shovel became our most important weapon. Everyone dug tunnels and trenches under fire, sometimes hitting hard soil and only advancing five or six yards a day. But we gradually surrounded Dien Bien Phu with an underground network several hundred miles long, and we could tighten the noose around the French.[27]

It was a hard fight. Giap's infantry moved through the tunnels and trenches to the French line while his artillery pounded the French position. Bad weather limited air support for the French. Two U.S. Air Force officers were killed at Dien Bien Phu: Captain James McGovern and his copilot, Wallace Buford, died when their supply aircraft was shot down by the Viet Minh. These were among the earliest U.S. casualties in the Vietnam War. Over 58,000 U.S. dead would follow after the French war.[28]

The French artillery commander, faced with defeat, committed suicide. The French defenses were easily overcome. On 7 May 1954, the French surrendered at Dien Bien Phu, and thousands of the surviving French soldiers became what was known as "pearls." This meant that they were hostages until France paid a ransom for their release.

This had become a conventional war rather than a guerrilla conflict. As the Viet Minh activity continued around Pleiku, rain, mud, and mosquitoes plagued the French. Next, G.M. 100 was ordered east to An Khe, the town that would later become the home of the 1st Air Cavalry Division in 1965. After spending weeks at An Khe, on 24 June 1954, G.M. 100 received orders to abandon its defensive positions at An Khe and withdraw to Pleiku, moving west on Route 19. At road marker "Kilometer 15," Sergeant Li-Som's unit was in the lead and stopped.

> Within a few moments, the whole column fell completely silent. Nothing could be heard now save the slight rustling of the wind in the top of the grass blades—and a slight knacking: knackknack-kna-a-ack. This was what Li-Som had been listening for: the slight knacking sound which high jungle grass makes a few minutes after the passage of a large body through it, as the long, resilient strands return to their normal position; the knacking continues even a few minutes after the strands have returned to their normal position, making the ear (as often in the jungle) a more precious auxiliary than the eye. To Li-Som, the message was clear. The Viets were here. The big, the final ambush to engulf all of Mobile Group 100, was ready to be sprung.... The main Communist striking force was already in place, its weapons poised, while the French were strung out along a road where their heavier firepower could hardly come into play. Two Communist machine guns opened up at a range of about 30 yards, but Li-Som had not stopped; as soon as he had realized what was happening, he had stormed forward—as much as one can "storm" in tall grass which has the consistency and stopping power of as many feet of water.[29]

It was a massacre. The column was ambushed by the Viet Minh and suffered heavy losses. The survivors of G.M. 100 managed to break through the ambush and finally reached Pleiku on 29 June, after days of fighting on Route 19. The destruction of G.M. 100 was the last battle of the French War.

While Giap and the French were fighting at Dien Bien Phu, a peace conference was scheduled in Geneva, Switzerland. The peace conference started on 7 May 1954, the same day that the French surrendered at Dien Bien Phu. The French would soon be out of Vietnam, and the forces left behind would be Ho in Hanoi and Bao Dai enjoying the life of a playboy in Paris. Bao Dai appointed Ngo Dinh Diem, the nationalist, as his prime minister for South Vietnam. Diem would reside in Saigon. Diem had an inflexible personality and was a Catholic in a predominantly Buddhist country: two items that would haunt the U.S. years later.

The peace conference was short as most conferences go and was concluded on 21 July 1954. One observer at the peace conference had stated: "You cannot expect to negotiate at the conference table what you have lost on the battlefield." This was proved wrong. The French had been beaten, but Vietnam would be partitioned at the 17th parallel (North of Khe Sanh) with the Viet Minh controlling the North and Bao Dai in the South. The 17th parallel became the Demilitarized Zone (DMZ), separating North and South Vietnam. Author Shelby L. Stanton described South Vietnam.

> Vietnam's southern half was officially the Republic of Vietnam, a thin 1,500-mile crescent-shaped country more commonly known as South Vietnam. Its long outer coasts are washed by the Pacific Ocean, and its interior mosaic of mountains, jungles, plains, and swamps are hedged in by the spine of the Chaine Annamitique, a western mountain range, which fades south into a vast alluvial plain created by the delta of the Mekong River.

Palm-lined white sand beaches fringe coves and bays where coral reefs can be clearly seen through the glassy sea. A vibrant green mantle of rice paddies extends inland. These stretch almost endlessly across the flat delta, crisscrossed by ribbons of canals. At the time of the war, many areas of South Vietnam remained a wild and exotic wilderness. Mountain slopes dropped deep into luxurious growths of tropical flora, bracken, tuft-twisted bamboos, and majestic jungle trees. Silver rivers and waterfalls laced the deep rain forests. These were steeped in a wonderful variety of folklore and legend. Large rubber and coconut plantations stretched across rolling plains, and tigers stalked pine-forested plateaus.

Tropical monsoons allowed only two seasons; hot and dry and hot and rainy, and the alternation of the monsoons and dry seasons determined the pattern of life. The majority of the eighteen million inhabitants lived in the open lowland plains and rice-bearing deltas. Their hamlets and villages were generally self-governing. An old proverb states that the Emperor's law stops at the village gate. The people had existed through the centuries by cultivating rice on lands irrigated by primal pumps and sluices. The rugged uplands region was left to the ethnically alien and primitive mountain tribes.[30]

The plan was for free elections to be conducted two years after the treaty to reunify Vietnam. The Soviet Union and China had dominated the discussions. The Viet Minh would leave the South, and the French would leave the North. Few participants were happy with the outcome. The Viet Minh were outraged. After winning Vietnam on the battlefield, the Viet Minh now had to settle for a divided country. Pham Van Dong, the Viet Minh representative, speaking about China's representative, Zhou Enlai, simply said, "He has double-crossed us."[31] Zhou supported the partition of Vietnam. The migration of people between the North and the South had started. Added into the mix were Vietnamese nationalists and Catholics who fled south rather than live in Ho's communist regime. Diem ousted Bao Dai in 1955 and consolidated his power in the South, while Ho did the same in the north. The planned elections to reunify the country in 1956 never occurred. In April 1956, the last French soldiers left South Vietnam. The U.S. inherited Diem's anti-communist regime in the South. At the same time, Cambodia and Laos achieved independence as the French departed.

In the years that followed the Geneva Accords, the U.S. increased aid to Diem, while Ho infiltrated more troops into South Vietnam. In December 1960, Hanoi established a new organization in the South: the National Liberation Front. Its purpose was to unify the various groups opposing Diem.[32] At that time, the U.S. was involved in a major effort to train the South Vietnamese Army.

Counting Dominos

Until the French defeat, the U.S. had provided funds and hardware, including aircraft to help the French fight their war against the Viet Minh. Ngo Dinh Diem, governing the South, was an unpopular leader hated by both the North Vietnamese and the Buddhists in the South. As Secretary of State John Foster Dulles put it: "Americans had underwritten Diem because we knew of no one better."[33] The Joint Chiefs opposed any support of Diem until he proved that he had a stable government, something that never occurred. Eisenhower embraced the regional domino theory and explained it with this metaphor: "You have a row of dominoes set up, you knock over the first one, and what will happen to the very last one is that it will go over very quickly."[34] In other words, if South Vietnam fell to the Communists, so would Southeast Asia. This would lead to a global bandwagon

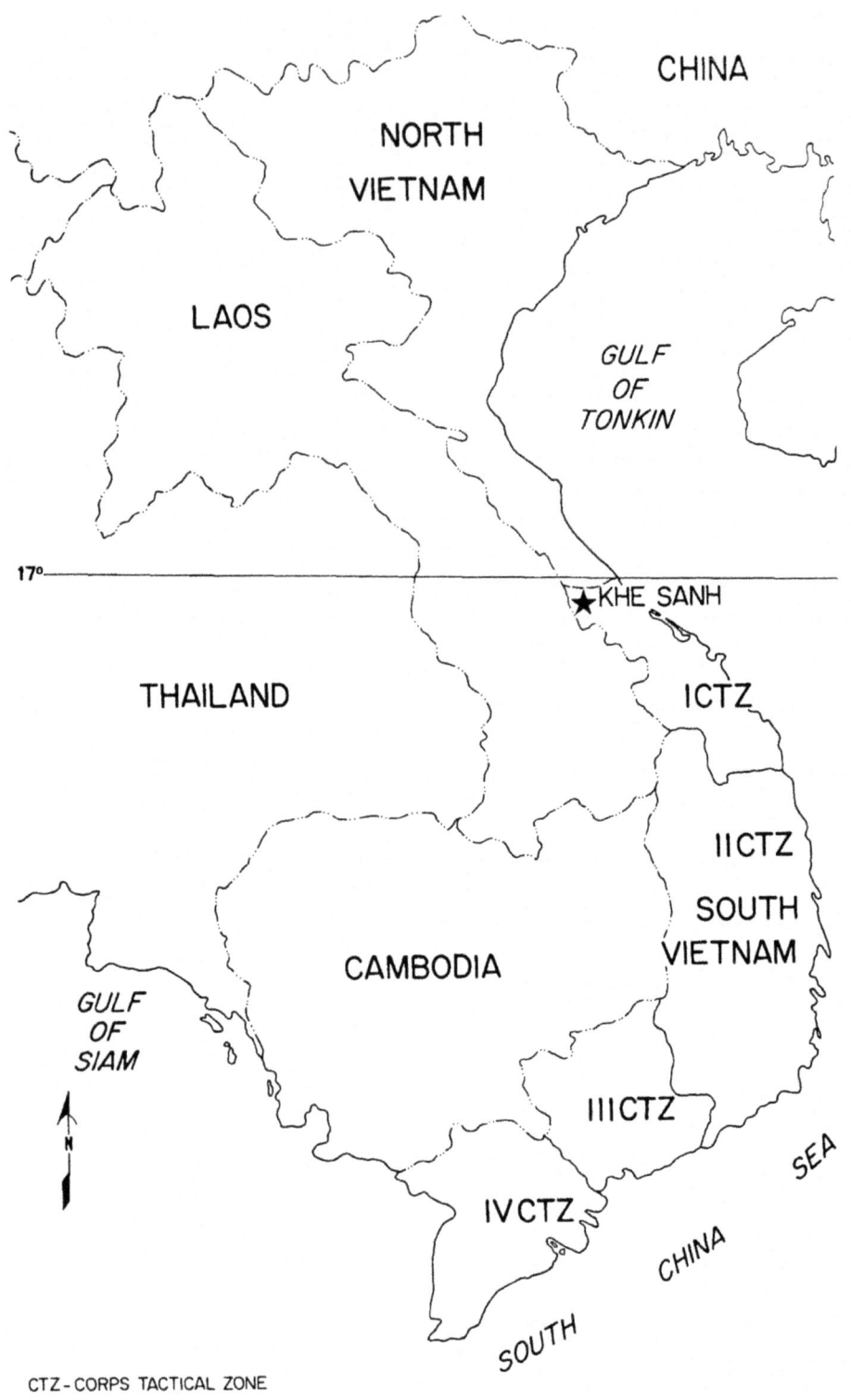

Vietnam divided—1954 (courtesy Moyer S. Shore).

effect, with countries appeasing and joining the Soviet Union, since the U.S. could not be trusted.³⁵

Each president following Eisenhower embraced the domino theory, which was flawed. It assumed that all nations had the same culture, background, and aspirations, which they did not. The Vietnam, Laos, and Cambodia dominoes fell, but others such as Thailand did not. With the defeat of the French, the conclusion was that the U.S. would need to shore up the Diem regime to prevent the South Vietnam domino from falling to the North.

Unit crest of the Military Assistance Command, Vietnam (author's collection).

2

The U.S. at War

The Advisors

After Ngo Dinh Diem took over as president of South Vietnam in 1954, there were a few years of peace while Ho rearmed in the north and Diem cleaned out stay-behind enemies of his regime, now known as the Viet Cong. Diem ran a corrupt, autocratic regime and operated similarly to a Chinese mandarin. His regime had many problems, such as lack of popular support and his repression of the Buddhist majority, which did not trust him because he was a Catholic.

> By the time President John F. Kennedy took office in January 1961, the Viet Cong in South Vietnam had already rebounded from a decimated, apparently moribund handful in the late 1950s to some 14,000 fighters. They waged a combination guerrilla war and campaign of terror and assassination, successfully targeting thousands of civil officials, government workers, and police officers. The new president commissioned a study in the spring of 1961, which concluded that South Vietnam had entered "the decisive phase in its battle for survival." Accordingly, on April 29, 1961, President Kennedy authorized an additional 100 MAAG [Military Assistance Advisory Group] advisors as well as the creation of a combat development and test center in South Vietnam. He also asked for increased economic aid. Less than two weeks later, on May 11, the president committed 400 U.S. Special Forces troops to raise and train a force of South Vietnamese "irregulars" in areas controlled by the Viet Cong, particularly along the border.
> The Special Forces, an elite army organization trained in small unit tactics—guerrilla warfare—had been in existence since the U.S. Army created the Rangers in 1942. President Kennedy would give the soldiers a higher profile, new status, and a new item of uniform: the Green Beret. For their part, these "Green Berets" soon came to respect the skill, courage, and determination of the Viet Cong.[1]

The advisors' mission statement sounded very high-minded and noble, but things never seemed to work that way:

> To represent the United States of America in South Vietnam; to perform assigned and implied duties in such a way as to further the best interest of the United States of America; to advise and assist officials of the Government and/or members of the Armed Forces of South Vietnam in performance of their duties and in the defense of this Country against communism; and to conduct one's self personally in such a way as to bring respect for and credit to the Armed Forces of the United States of America.[2]

Lieutenant John Loving was assigned as an advisor to Regional Forces in MR3. He summarized the environment and his duties.

Ben Cau was located in an area of Vietnam called the "Angel's Wing" because it stuck out into Cambodia, looking like the wing of an angel on the map. The village was very close to the Cambodian border in an area that was notorious as a VC stronghold. The infamous Ho Chi Minh Trail, which originated in North Vietnam and ran south through Laos and Cambodia, actually terminated in this area of Tay Ninh Province. Most of the men, material, and supplies that fueled the Vietcong insurgency came down this trail from the north to the south.

Ben Cau was actually made up of three small villages, or hamlets, with the seat of control, group headquarters, in the middle hamlet next to the bridge. The headquarters building was a crude, wooden structure with a tin roof, which, I noted from the air, was full of holes caused by mortar rounds or rockets. The other two villages also had a South Vietnamese company assigned to each for security. This was an effective method of securing the rural areas against the activities of the VC in the countryside, working very well as a defense against small VC forces and occasional attacks from North Vietnamese Army units passing through the area. The government troops were called Regional Forces but were manned with soldiers from all over, especially Saigon. Mobile Advisory Team 66 was assigned with the Regional Forces to provide support and advice. The support, I would discover, amounted mostly to calling in firepower from artillery and helicopter gunships, as well as bringing in medical helicopters called "dust-offs" or "medevacs" to evacuate the wounded. Another, unofficial support activity was helping the Vietnamese troops obtain certain supplies and munitions. At first, the advisory function seemed a bit presumptuous to me since our counterpart Vietnamese officers had generally been fighting for years and had more experience with war than I would ever have. However, I would soon learn that the thing that we could never give our counterparts was the will to fight. They fought because they had to, while their enemies, the VC and the North Vietnamese regulars, fought with a burning desire, fueled by nationalism, to unite their country and rid it of foreign influence.[3]

While the U.S. was sending more advisors, the ARVN appeared to be losing, while the Viet Cong were gaining confidence and increasing their numbers. By the end of 1962, the U.S. had 11,300 people in South Vietnam.[4] They were advisors to the South Vietnamese.

Ap Bac

David Halberstam was a journalist in Saigon during the early years of the Vietnam War. His book, *The Making of a Quagmire*, was published in 1964, before many of the significant events of the war had occurred. Halberstam covered the battle of Ap Bac, January 2, 1963. Lieutenant Colonel John Paul Vann was advisor to the South Vietnamese 7th Division. A force of 2,500 members of Republic of Vietnam Armed Forces (RVNAF), supported by U.S. helicopters, ARVN armored personnel carriers (APCs), and advisors were defeated by three hundred Viet Cong. As the ARVN force moved in on the VC, the VC opened fire. One VC leaped up and tossed a grenade at the advancing APCs, which did no harm but encouraged other VC to do the same.[5] This stopped the ARVN advance. Nothing could persuade the ARVN officers to move forward. The ARVN under Ngo Dinh Diem, the South Vietnamese president, were accustomed to avoiding combat and faking operations. The battle was a disastrous defeat, and it demonstrated that the war was rapidly being lost, something that few in the Kennedy administration wanted to hear. After briefings and efforts to get official recognition of the problem without success, John Paul Vann went public about the situation in discussions with David Halberstam and reporter Neil Sheehan. It made news in the States. Halberstam received the Pulitzer Prize for reporting after he returned to the U.S. in December 1963.

Ap Bac was a turning point in the war. Until then, it had been a war on the cheap for the Kennedy administration. U.S. aid and advisors were sent, but the war was well down on Kennedy's list of priorities and received little press coverage. Earlier, Kennedy had

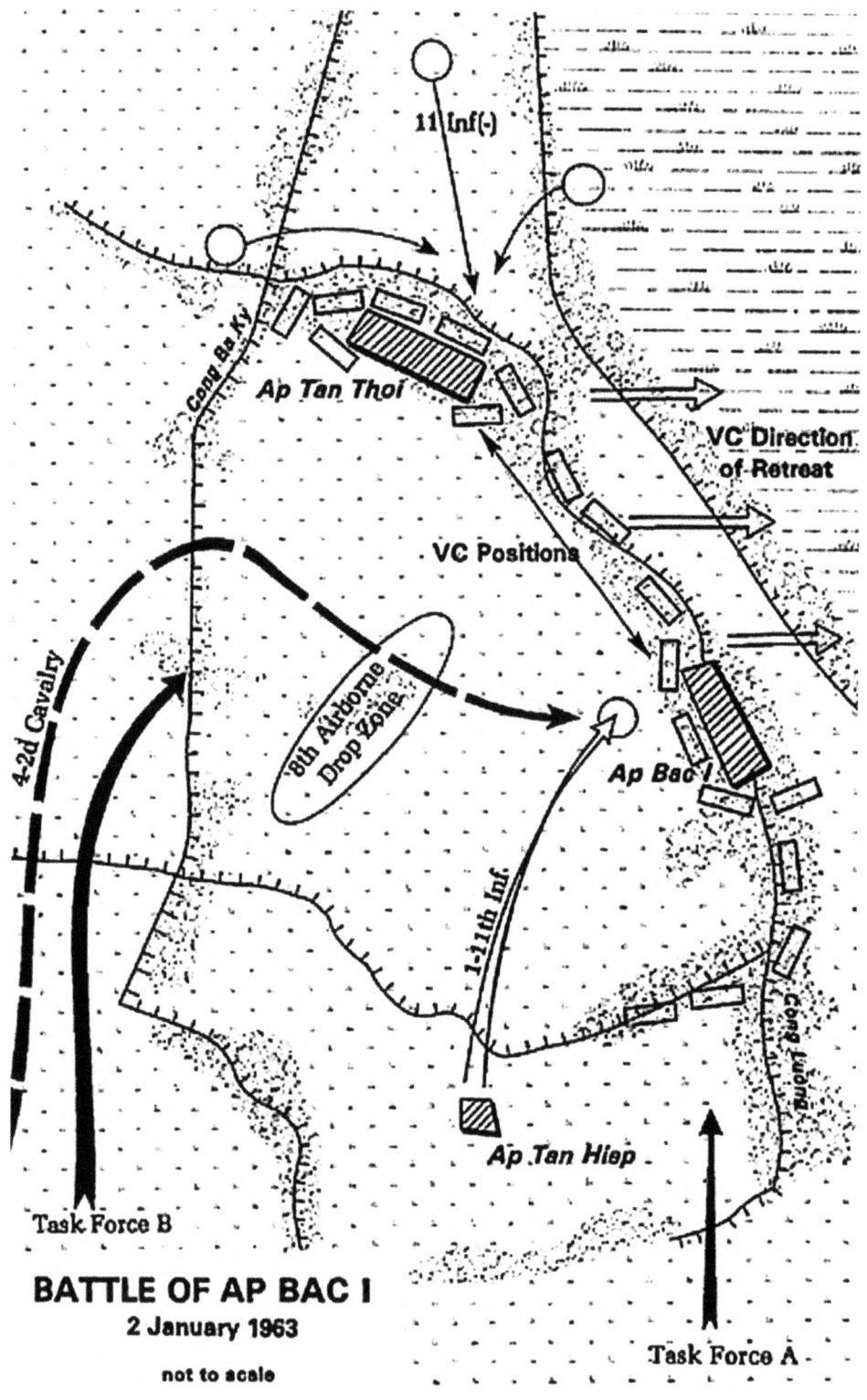

Battle of Ap Bac (courtesy U.S. Army Center for Military History).

decided to let Robert McNamara, the secretary of defense, "handle the war." This was not working. McNamara knew nothing about Ap Bac until he read about it in the *New York Times* (Halberstam's article). Now, people, Vann and others, were publicly stating the war was being lost. "*New York Times* ... headline noted that five helicopters had been downed and another nine hit. The subhead was uncompromising: 'Defeat Worst Since Buildup Began—Three Americans Are Killed in Vietnam.'"[6]

At first the U.S. military shrugged off the results of Ap Bac. General Paul D. Harkins, MACV commander, called the Viet Cong "those raggedy-ass little bastards."[7] In a comment worthy of Diem, Admiral Felt, CINCPAC, stated: "The Viet Cong left the battlefield, didn't they?" It was apparent to Kennedy that the military (and perhaps McNamara as well) had become detached from reality: General Harkins was still claiming victory. "Yes, I consider it a victory. We took the objective. We've got 'em on the run." What Harkins did not say was that the ARVN occupied Ap Bac two days after the victorious Viet Cong had conducted an orderly withdrawal.[8]

Kennedy had always liked and trusted journalists. He told his friend in the press corps, Charles Bartlett: "We don't have a prayer of staying in Vietnam. Those people hate us. They are going to throw our asses out of there at almost any point. But I can't give up a piece of territory like that to the Communists and then get the people to reelect me [in 1964]." To his aide, Kenny O'Donnell: "If I tried to pull out completely now from Vietnam we would have another Joe McCarthy red scare on our hands, but I can do it after I'm reelected. So we better make damn sure that I *am* reelected."[9] Kennedy was getting input from many sources after Ap Bac. While the military argued for more advisors, helicopters, weapons, and generals, the Harriman group argued against a purely military solution. Nation-building and civic action programs were the answer: "What was needed was a consuming motive to lead South Vietnamese to fight for Saigon. Why, for example, should peasants die for a government which, when it recovered territory from the Viet Cong, helped the landowners collect back rent?" In the end, Kennedy settled for a modest increase in the number of advisors while he waited for his second term, which would never arrive.[10]

The era of charm and easy deceit by the U.S. government was coming to an end. In the long term this may have been one of the most significant outcomes of Ap Bac. It started a trend in the press and later in the entire nation that government could not be trusted to tell the truth: a fact that subsequent events would prove correct. Newspapers were now pressing for answers and MACV continued to blame correspondents for bad press. If there was a time for the U.S. to abandon Diem and leave Vietnam it was now. Diem's actions after Ap Bac further condemned him and his regime. Journalist Deborah Shapley explained what had happened.

> The officers of the Seventh Infantry Division who performed so ignominiously at Ap Bac—[and] were later decorated by Diem, for they seized the Viet Cong radio transmitter that afternoon—had been chosen by Diem for their loyalty to him, for coup insurance, not courage or proficiency in war. Neil Sheehan, the young UPI reporter in Saigon at that time [Sheehan would later write a history of the Vietnam War and John Paul Vann], would later learn that Diem had promulgated a secret order to his trusted officers the previous fall: they were not to take casualties on their own side. Casualties would make army service unpopular, and Diem needed a loyal army so that his family could stay in power.[11]

Stanley Karnow's history of the war was published in 1983 and is considered by many to be the most complete description of the war. It won the Pulitzer Prize and was the basis for the public television series *Vietnam: A Television History*. Karnow served as chief correspondent for the series. He claimed that he had no cause to plead in writing this book,[12] but he had biases that became apparent in reading his history. He demonstrated that the U.S. made every mistake possible in fighting this war; he said that Ho Chi Minh was a nationalist who should be admired and the Nixon administration was self-serving (this last may be due to the fact that Nixon had Karnow on his "enemies" list).[13] In 1959 Karnow wrote the dispatches on the first U.S. deaths in Vietnam.[14] "The outcome at Ap Bac aggravated the friction then growing between the American government and the news media. Neither Kennedy nor his successors would impose censorship, which would have required them to acknowledge that a real war was being waged. Instead, they wanted journalists to cooperate by accentuating the positive."[15]

That did not happen. Correspondents simply told the truth, with their own twist, which is their privilege. Just after the Ap Bac battle, when Peter Arnett of the Associated Press asked him a tough question, Admiral Felt shot back: "Get on the team."[16] Sheehan's coverage of the battle of Ap Bac is quite lengthy, possibly because of Vann's involvement. Vann was in and out of Vietnam a number of times before he was killed in a helicopter crash in 1972. Sheehan's thesis is that Vietnam was a wrongful war, and he uses military reports to prove his point. Sheehan quotes a story that made the rounds after Ap Bac. "A Viet Cong porter spends two and one half months toting three mortar shells down the mountain and rainforest tracks of the Ho Chi Minh Trail. He finally reaches a battle and hands them to a mortar man, who fires them off faster than the porter can count and says: 'Now go back and get three more.'"[17] Sheehan always captured humor, and this makes his history very readable.

Francois Sully (a correspondent for *Newsweek*) clashed with U.S. Ambassador Nolting over the Hamlet program. The Strategic Hamlet Program was designed to concentrate rural populations into camps, where they could be isolated from the Viet Cong. The problems were that it uprooted the rural populations from their traditional lands where their ancestors were buried, and there was no way of knowing how many of the people in the camps were VC.[18] Nolting asked, "Why, Monsieur Sully, do you always see the hole in the doughnut?" Sully replied "Because, Monsieur l'Ambassadeur, there is a hole in the doughnut."[19] To the relief of Nolting, Diem expelled Sully.[20]

The result was changes by Kennedy, including the removal of General Harkins and his subsequent retirement. It appears that Harkins and Admiral Felt were the only U.S. persons of any rank who believed that the South Vietnamese had won a victory at Ap Bac. After Harkins returned to the U.S., a common phrase in the army upon screwing up was "I just pulled a Harkins."[21]

The battle of Ap Bac was a decisive event. Most scholars agree that it proved that Diem was losing the war. The defeat was so bad that the ARVN left their dead and wounded behind and fled in panic. General Robert York, R&D Field Unit, Vietnam, later visited Ap Bac and found that the ARVN dead still littered the battlefield. U.S. advisors loaded about twenty ARVN dead on a vehicle and departed. General York was the only U.S. general who visited Ap Bac after the battle.[22] It got worse. When Harkins and Diem trumpeted victory, the Viet Cong commander challenged the ARVN to a rematch and returned to Ap Bac with his battalion. The ARVN took no action on the VC challenge.[23]

The Fall of Diem

Following Ap Bac, the situation did not improve for the ARVN. Faking operations and promotions of ARVN generals based upon loyalty to Diem and not military competence took its toll. For Diem, it was a family experience. His brother Nhu was a good organizer and expert at intrigue, which helped the regime remain in power.[24] Worse, Diem's repression of the Buddhists had caused a violent reaction. The world press saw the self-immolation of Buddhists in the streets as a means of protest. Madam Nhu, the wife of Diem's brother, in her best style offered that if they needed more gasoline to kill themselves, she would be happy to provide it. "Let them burn!" she exulted. "And we shall clap our hands."[25] Some ARVN generals, perhaps motivated by hope of promotion or a realization that the war could not be won by Diem, planned a coup. The U.S. cooperated. Henry Cabot Lodge, the U.S. ambassador in Saigon, summarized. "We are launched on a course which there is no respectable turning back: the overthrow of the Diem government.... There is no possibility, in my view, that the war can be won under a Diem administration."[26]

Kennedy had hoped for a sort of "bloodless coup" in which Diem would be deposed and given an airplane ticket to live elsewhere and a military junta would replace him. The ARVN military was not that stupid: if you depose someone, you want to make sure they do not return later and depose you. Their concern was well founded. In a previous coup, Diem had regained power and punished those who had ousted him. The coup was executed on 2 November 1963. Diem and Nhu fled to a Catholic church in Saigon and hoped to escape from there, but they were trapped and surrendered to the insurgents, who offered them some sort of safe-conduct. Diem and Nhu were loaded into the back of an armored vehicle and were murdered there. Photos of their riddled corpses circulated around the world.

Kennedy was horrified.[27] He had not expected this. Less than three weeks later, Kennedy was killed in Dallas, and Vice President Lyndon B. Johnson (LBJ) assumed the presidency. In less than a month, two heads of state had been murdered. The war in Vietnam was now under new management. What followed was a succession of ARVN generals who took over the government and were in turn replaced by other ARVN generals. The first to lead the military junta was General Duong Van Minh, called "Big Minh." He lasted only a few months before he was replaced. This was not helpful to the war effort.

Following the death of JFK, Vietnam appeared to be the last priority of the new president. LBJ was more concerned about civil rights and economic issues. He continued Kennedy's policies in Vietnam. It soon became apparent that the situation in South Vietnam had been degenerating since the death of Diem. The Strategic Hamlet Program was in shambles, started by Diem and hated by the peasants who were forced to live in the camps. Many of the ARVN in the field were pulled back to Saigon to participate in coups attempts and other activities that made it more difficult to defend the hamlets. By December, in one area, three quarters of the hamlets had been destroyed by the VC or the inhabitants themselves.[28] Word finally reached Washington that all was not well in South Vietnam. LBJ sent Secretary of Defense McNamara to South Vietnam for an assessment. He blamed poor U.S. leadership (no surprise: Harkins) and also indicated that the situation should be monitored. If no improvement, stronger measures should be taken. The Joint Chiefs of Staff (JCS) argued for stronger measures. General Curtis "Bombs Away" LeMay, the air force chief, argued for bombing North Vietnam, as one might expect. He said: "We are swatting flies when we should be going after the manure pile."[29] By early 1964, the JCS proposed a plan to LBJ. The most extreme measure was the introduction of U.S. troops to take over the war. The U.S. would guide the direction of the war. The war would become "Americanized." LBJ did not approve the plan at that time. It was before the election. LBJ thought that "wars are too serious to be entrusted to generals." He also knew that the armed forces "need battles and bombs and bullets in order to be heroic."[30] This is not far from President Eisenhower's warning when he left office about the threat of the military-industrial complex.

Several things happened that forced LBJ's hand. The effectiveness of the South Vietnamese regime continued to plummet, and it was clear that South Vietnam would soon lose the war. In August 1964, Hanoi handed the U.S. a gift that provided the U.S. with an excuse to intervene in a major way in the war in Vietnam. Many of the details have been contested ever since. North Vietnam torpedo boats attacked a U.S. destroyer in international waters in the Gulf of Tonkin. U.S. warships returned fire. There were claims that a second attack followed, but these were false. Also, a separate, unrelated RVNAF operation was ongoing at that time, and it is possible that the North mistook U.S. ships for a part of that operation.[31] McNamara lied to the U.S. Congress on this point, maintaining that both attacks were genuine. Both the U.S. and North Vietnam contested the events, but this was an election year for LBJ, so he needed to appear as a firm leader. The U.S. retaliated with air strikes, which blew up some boats and did other damage, but further actions by the U.S. were more serious. LBJ presented to Congress what has been called the Gulf of Tonkin Resolution. It was approved by Congress on 7 August 1964 and gave LBJ the authority to deploy troops without declaring war. LBJ ordered the deployment of U.S. troops to rescue the South Vietnamese regime in Saigon. Over ten years later, in 1975, the fantasy ended when NVA tanks rolled into the government palace grounds in Saigon and ended the war. Between the two dates, over 58,000 U.S. citizens and over a million Vietnamese people perished.

McNamara's War

Robert S. McNamara was secretary of defense from 1961 to 1968. He is best known for bringing systems analysis to the Pentagon, which helped balance resources against needs. While he was in office, army staff officers had a saying that if McNamara had it figured out correctly, the last rifle bullet in the inventory would be fired as the peace treaty was being signed. The fact is that war is the most wasteful enterprise on the face of the earth. The best one can do is control it a bit, and McNamara did that.

If any single person can be blamed for precipitating our full involvement in the war in Vietnam, it was Robert McNamara. Based upon McNamara's comments to Congress, the Tonkin Gulf Resolution gave LBJ broad powers to wage war on North Vietnam. At the start, this involvement was based upon deceit. Much of McNamara's involvement in the war was revealed when he testified in court in General Westmoreland's 1984 libel suit against CBS.[32] He was very clever in avoiding responsibility for his decisions and actions throughout his long career. During his testimony at the Westmoreland trial, McNamara gave the CBS attorneys an opportunity to question him on broader issues. The testimony below is a remarkable example of the use of semantics to deceive. David Boies (CBS) believed he had a historic opportunity to show the world that McNamara had deceived the public. In evidence was McNamara's pessimistic memo to the president of May 19, 1967, which was declassified for the trial and of which the Pentagon Papers had quoted only excerpts. Boies's grilling aimed to show, as Judge Leval correctly interpreted the line of questioning, that "the witness is not a truth-teller."

> The listing figure in the witness box [McNamara] said he did not believe in 1967 that they had reached the "cross-over point" and were winning, as Westmoreland claimed. He said the tables attached to his May 19 memo showed this. Boies protested: But you say in the memo's text that "we reached the

cross-over point." "No," McNamara shot back, "the sentence you have quoted ... quotes General Westmoreland." He said he had put the statement in quotation marks in the memorandum to show it was Westmoreland's, not his own. McNamara had pulled up the blind on his semantic game, the key to the riddle.

Boies showed him an article from *Newsweek* from September 1967. In it McNamara was asked if "the war" was "stalemated"; he had said, "Heavens, no." To Boies and the jury McNamara now claimed he had been talking about the two tracks, not just the shooting war, he said. The courtroom was hushed; he was coming to life, assuming some of his old authority.

I did say it's a no-win militarily.... I said it cannot be won by military action. We had a two-track approach, one political and the other military, and the military was designed to move us along the political track.

His subtext was: *Therefore, I was being ethical. I was working for a resolution with probes to Hanoi as the carrot and military punishment as the stick.* So *the fighting was not in vain.* Yet it was hard to grasp, between his own digressions and the lawyer's verbal pounding. "I admit these seem like hairline distinctions," he said at one point, as Boies hung over him with body language that said, *Aren't you a damn liar, sir?*[33]

Author Deborah Shapley summarized: "Most of the lessons drawn from McNamara's life have been negative: that management by numbers ruined America's manufacturing know-how; that the [World] Bank's lending left the poorest countries with crippling debt; that the deceits and subterfuges of Vietnam disillusioned a generation with government. David Halberstam has called McNamara a 'dangerous figure' because of his 'special skill to fool people,' to 'seem better than his official acts,' whereas 'the real McNamara' is 'someone who says one thing in public and always follows the mandate of his superiors in private.'"[34]

Build-Up

Until Ap Bac, U.S. forces were composed of advisors and Special Forces units. That changed in 1965 when the Saigon regime was losing the war and the U.S. committed combat units to shore up the South Vietnamese. Marines landed in March 1965 at China Beach, Da Nang, to protect the airbase. The marines were followed by the Army's 173rd Airborne Brigade in May to the Bien Hoa area, and in September, the 1st Air Cavalry Division arrived in Vietnam and set up a base camp in the Central Highlands near the town of An Khe. In November 1965, U.S. forces received intelligence that the North Vietnamese were assembling troops in the Ia Drang valley southwest of Pleiku, and a strike was planned using the advantage of the helicopters to move troops to surprise and defeat the enemy. Lieutenant Colonel Hal Moore's 1st battalion of the 7th Cavalry (which had a heritage back to Custer's outfit) was airlifted in to trap the North Vietnamese. The result was a major battle described in a book entitled *We Were Soldiers Once...and Young*, as well as the Mel Gibson film based on it.[35] From 1965 forward, U.S. military strength increased steadily. Appendix B provides a year-by-year tally of the increases and the growing number of those killed in action.

As U.S. Forces were deployed to South Vietnam, a logistical expansion of enormous proportions was needed to support the war. Stanley Karnow described the transformation that started in the summer of 1965.

American army engineers and private contractors labored around the clock, often accomplishing stupendous tasks in a matter of months. Their giant tractors and bulldozers and cranes carved out roads and put up bridges, and at one place in the Mekong delta they dredged the river to create a six-hundred-acre island as a secure campsite. By 1967, a million tons of supplies a month were pouring

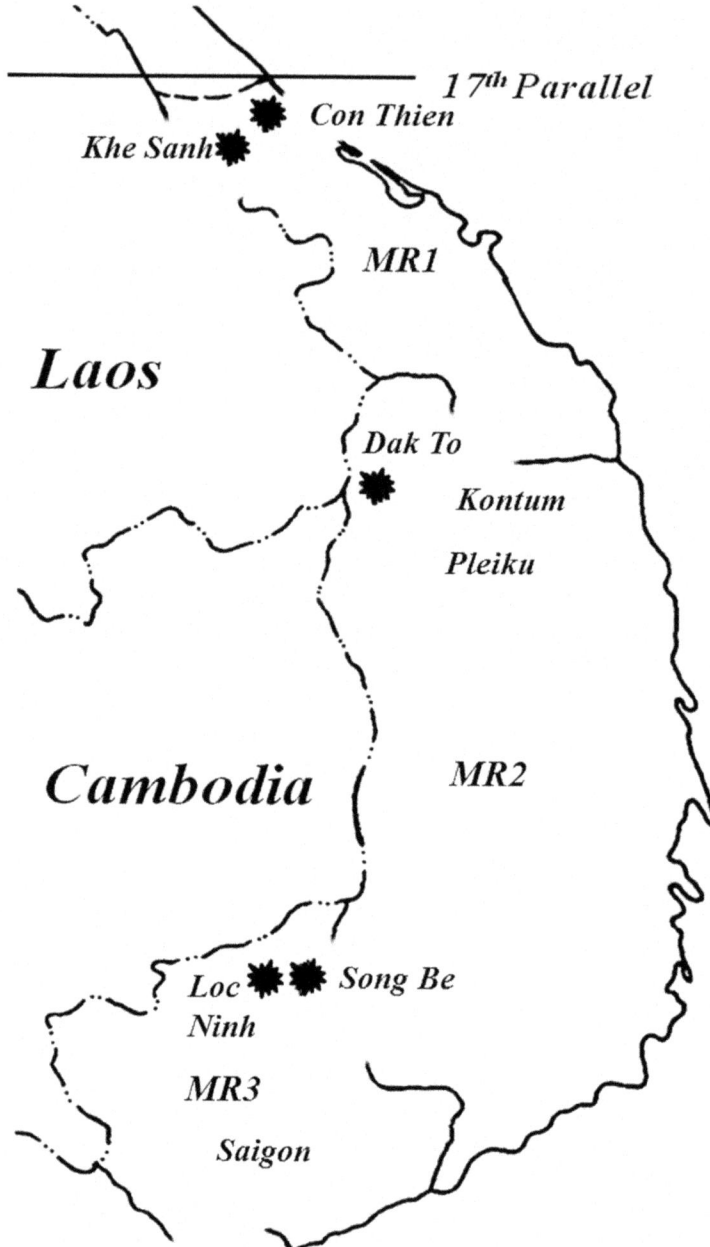

The NVA border attacks (author's collection).

into Vietnam to sustain the U.S. force—an average of a hundred pounds a day for every American there.[36]

Author Shelby Stanton described the equally enormous problems.

President Lyndon B. Johnson announced on July 28, 1965, that United States forces in Vietnam would be expanded immediately to 125,000 men. The administration made it clear that it intended to meet these growing overseas requirements without mobilization. New soldiers would be gained through more drafting and increased enlistments. This political decision engaged the military in a major war without any of its anticipated National Guard or Reserve component assistance. The peacetime standing Army had a very thin crust of engineers, signalmen, logistics supervisors, and service units. Soon a crisis developed in supply and support of the combat formations going to Vietnam. The adverse consequences were legion, but this basic governmental policy never really changed. The ammunition situation was so chaotic that the 173d Airborne Brigade arrived in Vietnam with only fifteen days' worth of bullets. Daily cargo flights from Okinawa were instituted just to keep rifle magazines full. Ammunition for other deploying units was being sent on ahead and off-loaded, a good practice which was undone whenever the units were diverted from their original destinations. As a result, ammunition crates and stacks of shells were piled up all over the beaches at Cam Ranh Bay and aboard leased sampans and barges floating on the Saigon River. The lack of transportation truck companies, another type of basic logistical unit, prevented ready transfer of such stockpiles to where they were needed.

A number of mad scrambles typified early logistical experiences in Vietnam. One of the worst happened during the summer deployment of the 2d Brigade, 1st Infantry Division, from Fort Riley, Kansas, to Vietnam. The unit was directed to secure the coastal town of Qui Nhon, where a natural harbor promised an ideal enclave site. Supplies were loaded by truck and aircraft at Saigon and hauled 250 miles north. Two days before arrival in Vietnam, the ships were diverted so that the brigade could secure the Saigon area. A battalion was offloaded to defend Cam Ranh Bay until the programmed American garrison (the 1st Brigade of the 101st Airborne Division) could get there, and the rest of the brigade then proceeded to Bien Hoa. A frantic last-minute relocation of supplies was made in an effort to get the tons of materials back south. The 1st Infantry Division's 2d Brigade arrived at Bien Hoa, located on the banks of the Dong Nai River outside Saigon, on July 16, 1965, minus large quantities of its supplies. The only port worth its name in Vietnam was the bustling commercial dock fifty miles inland at Saigon.... Viet Cong sappers were having a field day destroying massive quantities of supplies, but no one could measure the losses. Without inventory control no one knew what was where.[37]

America Takes Over the War

As 1965 ended, the U.S. build-up was in full swing, and U.S. units were taking the war to the enemy in what became known as "search-and-destroy" operations. The measure of success used was the number of enemy killed, wounded, or captured. The term "body count" entered reports, indicating the number of enemy dead bodies found on the battlefield. By the end of 1965, the number of U.S. troops in Vietnam had increased to 184,300, up from 23,000 at the end of 1964. As 1966 opened, the air war continued. Operation Rolling Thunder (1965–1968) included the heavy bombing of targets in North Vietnam, but there was no indication that it was reducing Hanoi's support for the war in the south.[38] Infiltration of NVA troops to the south increased from 1,500 per month in 1965 to 4,500 in 1966.[39] That year also saw an endless stream of U.S. combat operations in South Vietnam. These search-and-destroy operations were not designed to clear and hold ground, but only to attack the enemy, roll up an impressive body count, and move on. Very often, the enemy moved back in as the U.S. departed, as described in the account of the French war. It had become a war of attrition. General Westmoreland had a point to what seemed like a pointless exercise in blood. He called it the "cross-over point," or the point at which the rate of enemy losses exceeded the rate at which the enemy could replace its losses. To LBJ's frustration, there was no way of telling when the cross-over point would be reached, and as the rate of coffins sent back home increased, opposition to the war also increased. There was no end in sight. As 1966 closed, U.S. forces in Vietnam had increased to 385,300.[40] The total of U.S. dead stood at 8,694 as 1967 opened.

3

Dak To

Hanoi's Plan[1]

In 1967, controversy reigned in Hanoi. Should the NVA continue guerrilla warfare, or should a conventional military attack be launched? The decision was to launch a conventional military offense in the South, with the goal of causing a South Vietnamese uprising to reject their government. In the early spring of 1967, the Vietnamese communists were losing the war due to the massive influx of U.S. troop units. Ho and his advisors convened a plenum to consider a new strategy to win the war. Clearly, the anti-war movement in the U.S. and the friction the war caused with our European allies[2] were very encouraging to Hanoi, but a brilliant stroke was needed to win the war. The new strategy that emerged from the 13th Plenum was "to cause a spontaneous uprising in order to win a decisive victory in the shortest possible time."[3] This meant the abandonment of guerrilla warfare, with a general offensive to win in a single stroke. Work started to develop a plan that would become known as Tong Cong Kich, Tong Khai Nghia, "General Offensive, General Uprising," shortened to TCK-TKN.[4] The concept appeared very promising. The RVNAF troops were deserting at a high rate. At times the numbers deserting exceeded the rate of U.S. arrivals during the massive U.S. build-up. Second, and possibly more important, was the fact that the South Vietnam regime lacked the support of its people. A single stroke could cause the collapse of the RVNAF and the regime, as it ultimately did in 1975.

Hanoi's Phase I (September–December 1967) would include an NVA invasion in South Vietnam's border areas with Cambodia and Laos. This would draw U.S. units out of the populated areas. The infiltration into South Vietnam had already been increasing from two battalions per month in 1964 to fifteen battalions in 1966.[5] The VC would then attack in the cities, hoping to cause a popular uprising (Phase II). The plan was well known and even appeared in the U.S. press. Nevertheless, General Westmoreland moved elements of the 173rd Airborne Brigade, 1st Air Cavalry Division, the 1st Infantry Division, the 4ID, and other U.S. and ARVN units to the western border areas. The marines would defend the DMZ in MR1. As always, North Vietnam wanted to isolate and annihilate entire U.S. units in order to have an impact on the American public. Hanoi's dogma of little regard for their own casualties remained unchanged. North Vietnam would always counter its heavy losses with a flow of replacements sent south. North Vietnam would also test its concept of mass attacks and command and control of large formations.[6]

A high rate of U.S. casualties was expected, and this would enhance the flow of U.S.

coffins back home in order to fuel the anti-war movement. General Giap, North Vietnam's commander, knew that he would pay a high price in blood for this campaign, but it could end the war. The decision-makers in Hanoi had in mind Dien Bien Phu, the great victory over the French in 1954. In that battle, the loss of the equivalent of a single French division had caused the collapse of the French in Vietnam. Giap's plan was based upon four assumptions.

1. The ARVN would collapse and desert in large numbers.
2. The people would rally to support the VC.
3. The ARVN and the people would turn on the Americans.
4. The tactical situation at Khe Sanh would parallel that at Dien Bien Phu in 1954.[7]

The assumptions appeared to be unrealistic, and events that followed would prove them to be invalid. The problem was that the clique in Hanoi that had managed the war were the same people since 1954. They were not in touch with reality. For example, their belief that a war-weary South Vietnamese population would suddenly switch sides was clearly unrealistic. Giap's entire plan hinged upon success in the cities (Phase II). With success in the cities, Phase III, the general offensive to end the war, could proceed. It was a soft plan that assumed that the allies would do nothing, especially at Khe Sanh. U.S. air power and the ability to move forces quickly over long distances seemed omitted from consideration. The planning did not mention the impact on the American home front, e.g., causing the American public to lose heart and trigger the withdrawal of U.S. forces. It did not need to. The impact on the U.S. home front was built into the dogma of the Vietnamese communists. From switching dog tags on dead U.S. troops[8] to confuse the identification of the dead to wiping out entire units, the propaganda value of actions was always considered.

The U.S. had problems of its own at that time. General Westmoreland pursued a strategy of attrition even though Ho Chi Minh promised, "You can kill ten of us to one of you and still we will win." The measure of success that was used was the body count, which led to false reporting and even the deaths of innocent civilians.

> Actually, the My Lai massacre itself reflected the stark terror of a war of attrition, in which military success, for lack of terrain objectives, was measured statistically by counting corpses. While casualty counts are valid measurements of war, in Vietnam they unfortunately became more than yardsticks used to gauge the battlefield. Rather than means of determination, they became objectives in themselves. The process became so ghoulish that individual canteens were accepted as authorized substitutes if bodies were too dismembered to estimate properly. Guidelines were even issued by MACV on factoring additional dead based on standard percentages by type of encounter and terrain. This appalling practice produced body counts that went largely unquestioned, and were readily rewarded by promotions, medals, and time off from field duty. For example, General Westmoreland had issued a special commendation to the 11th Infantry Brigade based on its claim of 128 enemy killed at My Lai.[9]

Other programs, such as pacification, offered a better chance of success. The U.S. Marines from the commandant down supported pacification and opposed General Westmoreland's strategy of attrition. Furthermore, bad tactics were used. General Westmoreland's reaction to an enemy force was to attack with massive U.S. forces. This produced massive U.S. casualties. Colonel William J. Livsey, (the 4th Infantry Division operations officer during the Dak To fight), promoted a different approach: use small patrols to locate the enemy and massive air strikes and artillery to destroy it.[10] Or, in the words of Napoleon: "Artillery kills and infantry occupies." The U.S. had ample forces to counter the NVA. At the start of 1967, the U.S. strength was 385,300 in Vietnam. This was approaching the all-time high for U.S. forces during the Vietnam War (536,300 in 1968). Elements of four U.S. divisions would ultimately be deployed to the border regions during these battles. Additionally, local ARVN battalions were committed as well as the ARVN strategic reserve (airborne and rangers) and local forces such as the Civilian Irregular Defense Group (CIDG).[11]

The fact that there would be a major attack by Hanoi in the Central Highlands and in the cities was widely known. The problem was that the exact time, location, and strength of the enemy attacks were not known. The Hanoi timeline of Phase I was to start with attacks in the border regions in September 1967 by four NVA regiments. This would surprise the U.S. infantry, since they were accustomed to fighting poorly equipped and trained VC units. Instead, mainline well-disciplined NVA regiments with brand-new equipment were committed to the fight. More importantly, they would attack in force, sometimes in waves—a far cry from the hit-and-run guerrilla tactics of the past. In one incident that followed at Loc Ninh, the NVA attacked an artillery position in waves. The artillerymen lowered their howitzer tubes to the horizontal and fired "beehive" rounds that were similar to firing a mass of ball bearings. The result was devastating. The VC soldiers fell in heaps. A total of 852 lay dead.[12] General Westmoreland got his coveted body count.

Phase I would start with assaults on Con Thien and Dak To, followed by others, with the final attack at Khe Sanh in January 1968. It did not turn out that way.

Dak To

The town of Dak To is located in the Central Highlands, thirty miles from the Laotian and Cambodian borders. "It lies on a valley floor with surrounding hills covered by tall, thick trees capped by triple-canopy jungle soaring a hundred feet off the ground. These peaks and ridges slope steeply up to elevations of four thousand feet."[13] Weather and terrain favored the enemy. This was similar to Dien Bien Phu in 1954, but with a different outcome. Dak To was being used as a forward operations base by the U.S. Studies and Operations Group (SOG),[14] which launched reconnaissance teams to monitor the Ho Chi Minh Trail in Laos. Battles occurred nearly every year starting in 1966, but the greatest fight was in 1967.

The U.S. 4th Infantry Division (4ID) was commanded by MG W.R. Peers, who launched Operation Sam Houston in the Central Highlands on 1 January 1967. The purpose of the operation was to interdict the movement of NVA troops and equipment into South Vietnam from communist sanctuaries in Cambodia and Laos. The operation did not really get started until mid–February, and much of the fighting was in the border areas of Pleiku province and further north in Kontum province. Since the NVA tactic was to attempt to surround and annihilate small U.S. units, General Peers ordered companies to stay within mutual supporting distance. This meant that one company could quickly move to support another that was under attack. The distance/time factor varied but was usually considered to be one hour.[15] Operation Sam Houston resulted in many contacts with the NVA in the border areas, and General Peers reported a body count of 733 NVA with friendly losses of 155 when the operation ended on 5 April 1967. He noted that terrain favored the enemy and that friendly firepower could not be used to its full advantage. This would continue in the engagements that followed, and the concept of mutual support became increasingly important.

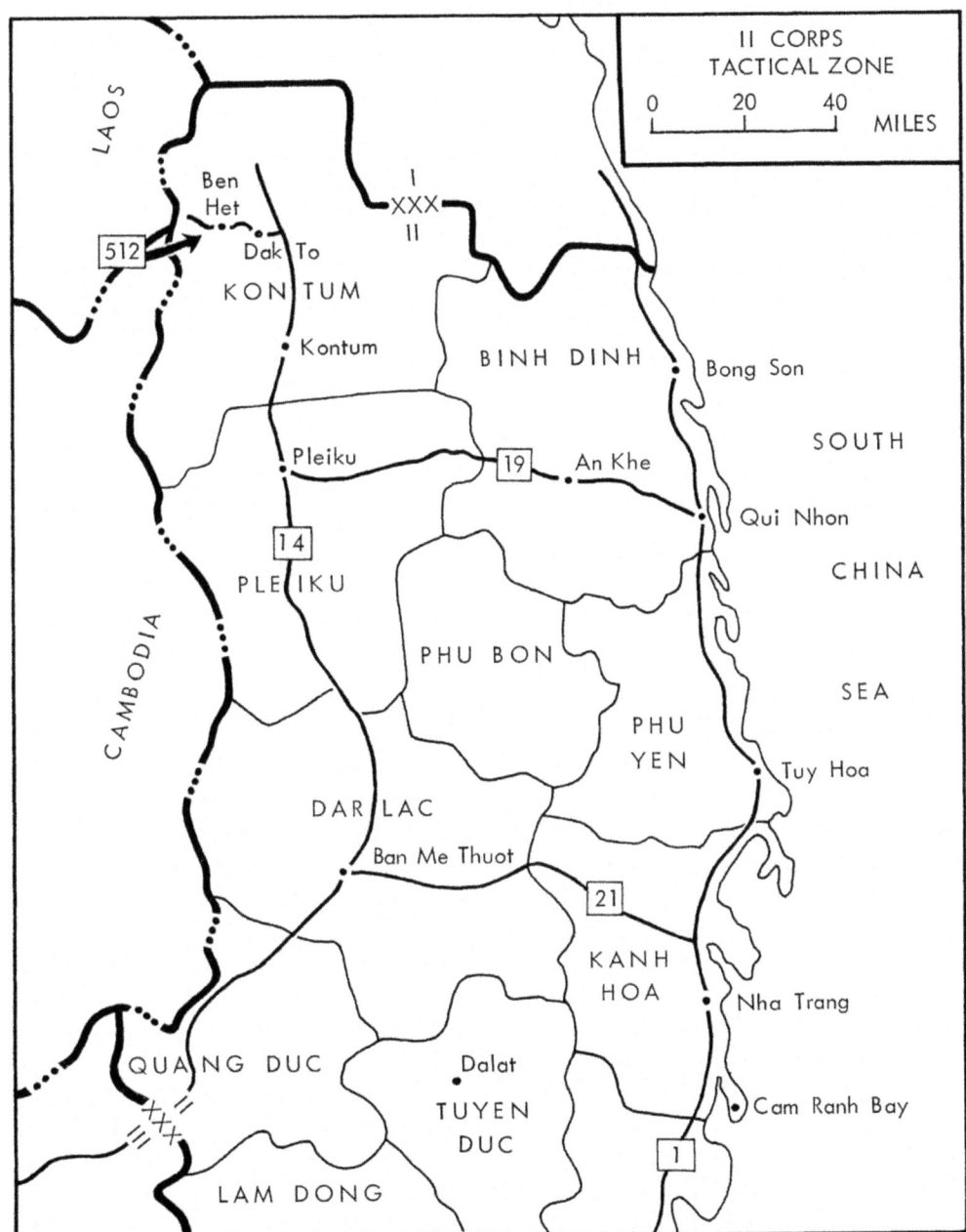

The road to Dak To (from John Albright, John H. Cash and Allan W. Sandstrum, *Seven Firefights in Vietnam* [Washington: Office of the Chief of Military History, United States Army, 1970]).

NBC News reported on the fighting in Kontum.

BILL RYAN, ANCHOR: Last week in Kon Tum Province, in the central highlands, elements of the 4th Division took part in Operation Sam Houston. Enemy units, perhaps two regiments thought to have crossed from Cambodia during the Lunar New Year's Truce, were in the area. The 1st Platoon, C Company, 2nd Battalion, 8th Infantry Regiment, engaged the enemy in Kontum. Lieutenant Conrad Braun spoke with correspondent Howard Tuckner.

HOWARD TUCKNER REPORTING: What'd you lose?

2ND LT. CONRAD BRAUN: I had thirty-six when I started. We got twenty-one killed, fourteen wounded, and one man not a scratch on him.

TUCKNER: Did they try to overrun you at any time?

BRAUN: First two assaults they made, they made two assaults in the platoon perimeter just coming at us screaming and yelling. We knocked them down with small arms fire and M79 fire. Then they stopped assault and we could hear their officers down there. We were trying to get them to come out again and come at us. Then they didn't assault us anymore. They just tried this sneaky stuff. They crawled out one, two men at a time, threw grenades inside the perimeter, then crawled back. We killed quite a few of them doing this. One time, one dink crawled up on the platoon perimeter and Owen Mapes shot him, shot him in the leg and just left him out there. And dink's two buddies came up to help him out and Mapes just emptied a magazine automatic fire and killed all three of them.

TUCKNER: What were you thinking about?

BRAUN: I was thinking of getting support in there, and I was thinking of the company that was coming to help us, and I was thinking of—Like, I was talking on the radio trying to get help, but I was thinking of my wife, and my baby that I haven't seen, I guess. I got a baby coming in June and that was on my mind. I was—I just knew we were going to get overrun. I didn't think the company—the company was so far away, I didn't think we could hold long enough to be relieved in time, and I knew we were getting hit with a couple companies, of course the mortars were all over us, and well, when we did get relieved, Sergeant Brown had six rounds left and I had a hand grenade.[16]

As soon as Operation Sam Houston ended, a new operation called Francis Marion commenced on 6 April 1967. For all intents and purposes it was basically a continuation of Sam Houston and consisted of search-and-destroy operations in the border areas. The NVA purpose was to draw U.S. forces from the populated regions to the border areas. As many as six NVA regiments were ready to fight and had replaced losses incurred during Sam Houston. Battalions of the 8th and 22nd Infantry Regiments as well as tanks from the 10th Cavalry of the 4ID became involved in the operation. Much of the action centered around the Duc Co Special Forces Camp in Pleiku Province, near the border. Initial contacts occurred in late April. The 8th Infantry, reinforced with tanks, struck an NVA battalion that had moved into an area near Duc Co and had constructed bunkers. In a two-day fight, these were destroyed and the NVA lost 133 people, while U.S. losses included wounded and one KIA. Fighting continued along the border for weeks, with a pattern of NVA moves into South Vietnam followed by contacts with the 4ID, withdrawal into the Cambodian sanctuary, and return. This was carried out during the southwest monsoon season (May-October), which limited mobility and air support. This became known as the NVA monsoon offensive. It was also during this period that the 4ID base camp, Camp Enari, was completed south of Pleiku.[17] This appeared to demonstrate that the U.S. had taken the bait and was moving its forces from the populated areas to the border regions, but the 4ID had been laagered (set up in a defensive campsite) there for nearly a year and could quickly move to the populated areas when required.

With NVA incursions across the border near Dak To increasing, Operation Greeley was launched in June 1967, and General Peers was reinforced with the 173d Airborne Brigade, commanded by General John R. Deane. Operation Greeley continued for months in the Dak To area, while Operation Francis Marion further south ended on 12 October 1967 as fighting at Dak To reached its peak. Francis Marion and Greeley were consolidated and became Operation MacArthur.

Camp Enari with Dragon Mountain in the background (courtesy James Allan Long).

The 173d Airborne Brigade that would fight at Dak To had three battalions (the 1st, 2nd and 4th) and was under the command of the 4ID. Each battalion had 750 men and was composed of four companies with about 150 troops each. Each company had three or four platoons of thirty each, a weapons platoon, and staff. The squad is the building block of the infantry and consists of five to ten soldiers. There were usually four squads in each platoon. All units were usually under strength. Other details of organization are at Appendix C.

In the Central Highlands, the Allies were supported by Montagnard tribes. John Ketwig of the 4ID described the Montagnards in October 1967.

> The population of Vietnam consisted of three groups: the haves, the havenots, and the Montagnards. The Montagnards lived in Stone Age seclusion in the highlands. They had been nomadic until the war. Now they had become our only true allies. Trained by the Green Berets, a Montagnard warrior never ran under fire. He might forsake his M-16 for his crossbow, but he never forsook a friend. He didn't steal, and he didn't beg. He asked nothing, but offered a sense of family and community found nowhere else in Vietnam. The Montagnards suffered horribly. Despised by the Vietnamese, they had been banished into the mountains, where they had developed a culture not unlike that of the American Indians before Columbus. As European weapons had spelled doom for the North American Indian, helicopter gunships and jet fighter air-support missions signaled the end of the Montagnard civilization. Regardless, they embraced the Americans.
>
> Drinking Montagnard wine requires a ceremony. It sits, uncovered, in the tropical sun, fermenting in heavy crocks. A slender bamboo is notched and laid across the opening of the jug with a tiny bamboo

sliver dangling down into the liquid. The chief adjusts this sliver, to half or three quarters of an inch. You kneel at the jug, and it is filled to overflowing. You drink through a huge bamboo straw, and it is an insult to your hosts if you rise before the liquid falls below the dangling sliver. A quart of this rich brew, the hundred-degree sun, and the motion of rising caused many GIs to pass out.[18]

The monsoon starts in the Central Highlands in May and continues into October. In the words of today's Vietnamese weather forecaster: "Adventure activities are unadvisable [in July-August]." Double- and triple-canopy jungle covers the hills surrounding Dak To with trees as high as forty-five meters. In the few open areas, bamboo with stalks as thick as eight inches reside. It would be very difficult to cut a landing zone (LZ). The trees and bamboo limited the effectiveness of artillery and air support, since targets could not be seen and air support such as resupply and medevac helicopters had difficulty in landing. There was a high probability of friendly-fire casualties, since the enemy used the "grab them by the belt buckle" tactic. This meant that they closed with U.S. units to within a few meters to make air support difficult. The jungle was a very spooky place. The high trees blocked out the sun. One existed in eternal twilight. Ground visibility was sometimes less than ten to fifteen meters. The humidity and monsoon kept the troops soaked. It was like a sauna, but at night temperatures could drop into the fifties. Happiness was a small ray of sunlight that also made you a target for a sniper, who always seemed to be waiting. In summary, the U.S. troops found themselves with bad strategy, bad tactics, nasty terrain and bad weather. John L. Leppelman, C/2/503d, recalls:

> We moved through the hills of Dak To, not keeping track of time. It was an endless search for Charlie and occasionally taking sniper fire with no head-on contact. These hills were actually mountains,

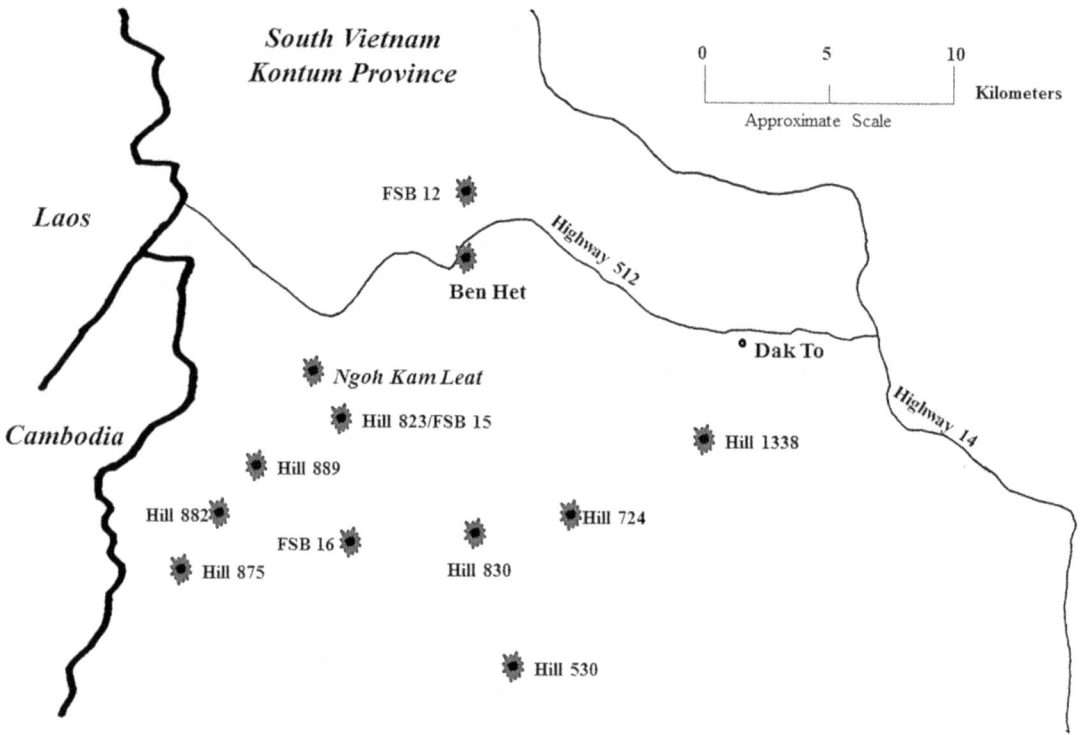

The hills of Dak To (author's collection).

steep, muddy and leech infested. We were usually under triple canopy jungles which made it appear dark and dreary.[19]

As April 1967 ended, heavy contact with NVA units was increasing in the Central Highlands. The 4ID was located at Camp Enari near Pleiku, while the 1st Air Cavalry Division had its base camp at An Khe on Highway 19 east of Pleiku. The 173rd Airborne Brigade was chasing small bands of VC near its base camp at Bien Hoa Airbase. The troops had no idea what they would run in to after chasing small, irregular VC units. They had never been up against NVA main force regiments, and they would be going to the Central Highlands. Colonel James B. Adamson, commander of the 4ID's 2nd Brigade, tried to warn the 173rd Brigade commander, General Deane, and his staff that they would be fighting a different war in the Central Highlands. He told them, "First you must realize that up here in the highlands you are fighting the NVA, not the VC. They're professionals who know how to fight. Second, don't let a company get out by itself where it will be easy pickings for the NVA. They'll wipe it out."[20] Adamson could tell that he was not getting through to the 173rd. In spite of his warnings, they remained overconfident with a superior attitude: a fatal flaw that would be paid for in blood.

In May, intelligence information indicated that the NVA planned a major offensive across the Laotian border in the highlands. On 24 May, two battalions of the 173d were ordered to suit up for a move from Bien Hoa to Cateka, a tea plantation, near Pleiku. The 173rd would be under the operational control of the 4ID. As the hurry-up-and-wait routine persisted at Bien Hoa Airbase, the troops waiting for the lift were a bit anxious over their new environment.

The Elephant Soldiers

Each soldier carried a lot of gear. Most carried 500 rounds of ammunition for their M-16s. As one veteran said, "Never get caught without: carry extra.... Don't worry, the load will be gone, soon." Canteens of water, six grenades, two anti-personnel claymore mines, 100–200 rounds of M-60 ammunition, one or more rounds for the company mortar, shovel, and sometimes a chainsaw for cutting trees for the LZ.[21] Total weight was up to one hundred pounds, plus personal items like letters and rations. Most cargo was carried in a rucksack, which gave birth to a new verb, "hump"—the noise made when one lifted the rucksack.[22] Humping through the woods had a clear meaning. Gary Walls, a grenadier (his M-79 weapon fired grenade rounds), described the load he carried. It was similar to that carried by others.

> Into my rucksack I added to the few personal items: my rolled up air mattress, poncho and liner. Several days' worth of C-rations went on top of that and about twenty rounds of high-explosive 40mm grenades in an old Claymore bag occupied some space as well. Everyone carried about ten sandbags that, when dry, were lightweight; when wet, it was different. On my LBE (load bearing equipment, or the web belt and suspenders) were ammunition pouches in which I carried the 12-gauge shotgun adapter, shotgun shells, and an oily rag for wiping down the launcher.
>
> Two canteens were clipped on the belt, and a "fat rat" on my rucksack contained a total of a gallon of water. Trip flares, smoke grenades, and fragmentation grenades were stuffed into pouches. The rucksack was mounted on a frame, and onto the lower half of the frame I strapped a 150-round box-like "can" of 7.62mm machine gun ammunition. Nearly everyone carried gun ammo, and I think there must have been close to fifteen hundred rounds for each machine gun. And on top of this went a bagged Claymore mine, tied into place.

I thought I was done, but the weapons platoon (mortars) people started passing out 60mm mortar rounds, usually several to a customer. Later, the 60mm mortars were exchanged for 81mm mortars, which had a longer range and a bigger punch. The downside of this was the 81mm rounds weighed much more than the 60s, about 15 pounds each.

All in all, it was a very heavy and awkward weight topped off by a steel helmet that one wasn't to casually take off: I lived in it. I have learned since that the NVA soldiers referred to American troops as the "elephant soldiers" because of all the equipment we lugged around, making it difficult to move quickly and quietly through the jungle. Mobility on the ground largely belonged to the enemy, as he traveled light and could choose when to engage or elude, but then, he didn't have the luxury of air

Gary Walls in the field, August 1967 (courtesy Gary F. Walls).

support (and artillery fire, for the most part). Or helicopter transport, always their bane. American forces could mass quickly, another new advantage in the deadly game of jungle war.

I'm not sure what it all weighed in at: possibly 80 to 100 pounds, depending upon how many C-rations we might carry at any given time, among other factors. My shoulders began to hurt almost immediately. I also wore a sort of vest with twelve 40mm grenade rounds in pouches on the front of it. We traded off carrying a D-handled shovel, which sometimes helped while humping up the side of a muddy hill. Just as often, it became tangled up in the *damn it* or *wait-a-minute* vines. LAWs were carried, too. This light, anti-tank weapon, a bazooka-like, one-shot, disposable rocket launcher, managed to get caught on nearly every vine but was fairly light and good for destroying bunkers. It was our RPG: *rocket-propelled grenade*.[23]

The NVA

The 173rd would be facing a well-trained, equipped, and indoctrinated NVA force.

Recruits [NVA] were often told by their veteran cadre that Americans killed and tortured prisoners and that American soldiers were cannibals who ate children. Many of the naive, uneducated recruits believed what they heard. The message received was that a horrible fate worse than death awaited them if they ever surrendered to the Americans. The indoctrination worked well, because few NVA soldiers ever gave themselves up unless wounded and unable to continue fighting.[24]

The core NVA unit was a three-man cell. The cell members shared everything and were responsible for medical treatment and evacuation of those KIA. Three or four cells composed a squad, led by a sergeant. Squad morale and discipline were maintained by sessions of self-criticism that included performance critiques by peers and leaders.

The combat uniform was light green (sometimes blue, brown, or khaki) cotton shirt and trousers. Web harnesses and straps provided for ammunition, canteens, and medical supplies. Canvass boots or sandals were used as footgear. A soft cloth cap or sun helmet kept the sun or rain off but provided no protection against bullets or shrapnel. The backpack was of light-weight canvass that quickly dried out when wet. It carried grenades and supplies. A six-inch-wide entrenching tool was also carried. The Soviet 7.62mm AK-47 assault rifle was the most common infantry weapon. This weighed 10.58 pounds and used a thirty-round magazine. The weapon had an effective range of 300–400 meters. Some carried the Soviet 7.62mm SKS semi-automatic rifle that had a range of up to 400 meters. Officers and senior NCOs carried pistols of various types.

Unit weapons included the Soviet 7.62mm Ruchnoy Pulemyot Degtyaryova (RPD) light machine gun that used a 100-round drum. Some units also had the 12.7mm wheel-mounted heavy machine gun used most commonly as an anti-air weapon. Mortars were 60 and 82mm, with the 82mm capable of reaching targets up to 3000 meters. One of the most common weapons was the rocket-propelled grenade (RPG). The RPG was a shoulder-fired weapon used against armor and other targets. Its 40mm missile could penetrate up to ten inches of armor at ranges of 100 meters.[25]

Battle of the Slopes 15–23 June 1967

Vietnam's bloodiest campaign started on 15 June, when the 24th NVA Regiment annihilated a CIDG[26] patrol led by two U.S. Special Forces advisors near Dak To. On 17 June, the 173rd battalions, 1/503d and 2/503d, were ordered to move from Catecka to Dak To.

The objective was Hill 1338, about five kilometers south of Dak To. The bodies of two Americans were discovered, mutilated. They were cut from groin to head, with internal organs exposed. One person who saw the bodies said that they looked like a page from an anatomy book.

> A particularly grisly aspect of this fighting involved the constant discovery of human skeletons from past battles. On June 20th, the 173rd Airborne Brigade paratroopers found the osseous remains of two Special Forces, eight of their indigenous CIDG strikers, and one NVA soldier. Three days later, the bones of a missing radioman from one of their own patrols was found. Still more skeletal corpses of Army Special Forces and their CIDG soldiers were discovered throughout the period. Ghosts seemed to haunt every tropical mistshrouded sepulcher, and the unnerved parachutists freely admitted the whole area "spooked them out."[27]

Sa Won Chang, A/1/503rd, reported the discovery of remains.

> In mid–June 1967, I was a point man on that steaming hot day. Moving up a ridgeline, I smelled rotting human flash and notified our platoon leader, Lieutenant Gerald Quinn. I found a CIDG body lying in middle of trail. The body wore the regular OD green uniform, not tiger fatigues. The remains were skull and bones, except for the very end of the fingers that had flesh left. Then our squad leader, Sergeant Eugene Porter, moved while I was still on point and moving westerly on the ridgeline. I caught something in the corner of my right eye, like a white balloon by a big tree. I immediately turned to my right side and readied my weapon to fire. I then moved toward what appeared to be the white balloon. Instead I found the body of a U.S. Special Forces soldier. The body had puffed up while under the shade of that big tree. The body didn't have a shirt or boots. The head was gone and there was a big hole in the chest, but it had OD green pants on. The next day, we brought in body bags, and Sergeant Porter and I put his body into a body bag. We also found four or five other CIDG bodies and put them in plastic body bags to be flown out. When we found them, they were all scattered in every direction as they tried to run from a large NVA force. We also found many hand grenade explosion sites.[28]

On 20 June, the 2/503d started its move up Hill 1338. Alpha Company, led by Captain David H. Milton, was in the lead. His orders were to cut an LZ for resupply helicopters and sew CS (tear gas) crystals[29] around it to prevent the enemy from encircling the LZ. This was a bad decision, as seen by the account of one survivor.

> On the morning of 6/22, my squad had the unenviable "gas" detail. Our early-morning task was to saturate our laager site with CS crystals. If Charlie had notions of a rear assault, he was in for a stinging surprise. None of us were aware that CS came in a solid compound, and [we] were unfamiliar with its protocol. We hadn't checked our gas masks since who knows when, and at stand down, all who needed to were ordered to shave before saddling up for the airstrip. I remember vividly the immediate, unrelenting excruciating pain when the gas contacted our open pores, not only on our faces, but under arms, and sweaty crotch areas as well.[30]

Charlie Company, commanded by Captain Ronald R. Leonard, moved through Alpha Company on its way farther up Hill 1338. At about 1700 hours, Milton was ordered to return to Dak To the next day to take over security at the battalion CP, relieving Bravo Company. As night fell, the 2/503d had two companies on Hill 1338, with Charlie Company about fifteen hundred meters farther up the hill than Alpha. The troops dug into their night firing position. The next morning, Charlie Company continued its move up Hill 1338, while Alpha Company started its return to Dak To. To this point, not a shot had been fired, but elements of the 24th NVA Regiment had had ample time to prepare a welcome for the 2/503rd. Charlie Company had a platoon of CIDG with it to act as guides. By mid-afternoon, 21 June, Captain Leonard halted Charlie Company and started looking for a night laager position (a fortified campsite). As the troops settled, a night listening post (LP) moved out beyond the perimeter of the camp. A CIDG soldier with them stopped dead. "Beaucoup [many] VC, no go!" He was forced forward as troops moved out. The stillness was shattered by an exchange of gunfire. The point man had run into an NVA soldier, and the two exchanged fire. Both missed, but a nearby CIDG soldier was killed as the NVA soldier escaped. The dead CIDG was placed in the center of the perimeter to be airlifted out the next day.

The rest of the night was uneventful, and dawn, 22 June, found both companies in thick fog and low clouds. People were jumpy after waiting all night for an NVA attack that did not happen. At Charlie Company, a new guy, PFC Jimmy Lee Cook,[31] made a new-guy mistake. He left the camp to urinate and forgot to tell his buddies. As he returned in the poor light, his buddies thought he was NVA, and he was shot dead. Captain Leonard now had two dead bodies to be evacuated. Farther downhill, Alpha Company prepared for its return to Dak To, and Lieutenant Judd, second platoon leader, started downhill in the lead at 0625. Rifle fire broke the morning calm as Judd's point squad collided with the NVA, and a firefight followed. Milton called the battalion tactical operations center (TOC) at Dak To to report the encounter, but the TOC seemed unconcerned. Judd pulled back up the hill a bit as Milton sent him another platoon, led by Lieutenant Hood, to help. The NVA was closing in on the platoons, which were starting to lose people very quickly. Milton called in his position to the TOC, requesting artillery support, which followed. Because of the high trees and fog, the artillery fire was ineffective. The heavy volume of fire could now be heard all the way to the TOC, and everyone realized that something big was happening. The NVA had launched a series of frontal attacks to overwhelm and destroy the two platoons. So far the platoons were holding, but they would not last long. Close air support was called in, but when the troops threw smoke to mark their position, the trees and bamboo dissipated the smoke and the aircraft could not determine where the friendly troops were located. Much worse, on the ground, the smoke marked friendly positions for the NVA, and they converged on the smoke.

Farther up the hill, Captain Leonard heard the firing and was ready to move his Charlie Company down to support Alpha Company. The TOC for some reason told Leonard to hold his position, and it was not until 0900 hours that the TOC ordered Leonard downhill.[32] Critical time had been lost in supporting Alpha Company. Charlie Company moved very slowly, fearing an NVA ambush. As time passed, the TOC became agitated by the slow progress. "Charlie Six, [Leonard], you've got to move faster. Get down that hill!"[33] Meanwhile, Milton held his position as he sent a third platoon under Lieutenant Sexton to reinforce the other two. Milton had no further help that he could send. The situation had become desperate. An M-60 machine gunner changed the red-hot barrel with his bare hands as their position was being overrun. The three platoon leaders were now dead, and most of their troops were dead or wounded. The platoons were being surrounded.[34] It was the end of the line, and a move back up to Milton's command post (CP) seemed prudent, but this presented a horrifying dilemma. It would mean leaving most of the wounded behind, and most knew the fate of the two Special Forces advisors killed with their CIDG troops. In the end it was every man for himself, and everyone who could crawled out in an effort to reach Milton's CP. As they fled, they heard the screams of the wounded being executed by the NVA. Milton sent men down to help the wounded crawling up, but only a few reached the CP. Milton called in artillery support at about 1130 hours, as Leonard continued his slow movement down to Alpha Company. John Leppelman was in C/2/503rd and recalled his sliding effort to reach Alpha Company.

Frenchy slowly slid over the edge and then slid about ten feet, where he stopped by digging his heels into the thick mud. The rest of us quickly followed. We moved almost silently as we slipped and slid down the dark side of the mountain. It took us about fifteen minutes to get about midway down the steep slope to where we could look into the valley. I peered over the edge and could see part of the valley floor below us. Several bodies were scattered around. None were moving. The valley floor was quiet; then Flynt pointed, and we saw several NVA moving through some bamboo. Before we had a chance to do anything, bullets started splattering in the ground around us. In the panic mode, we ran zigging and zagging back up where men were offering us hands to pull us over the top. The LT and K were demanding to know what we had seen. "They're all dead," Flynt gasped.[35]

The fog had cleared, making the artillery support more effective. Bravo Company was airlifted into a position below Alpha but was too late to do any good. Close Air Support (CAS) arrived at 1335 hours to support Bravo Company's move. Five-hundred-pound bombs and napalm added to the din of the battle. One survivor stated nearly half a century later that the noise of all of the exploding ordnance and small-arms fire was so intense that he could not hear commands shouted next to him or even think.

As Captain Leonard's Charlie Company approached Alpha, the folly of spreading CS crystals become apparent. As his troops approached the old LZ, the protective masks of the troops were found to be ineffective due to the moisture. Soon half of the company was on the ground, temporarily disabled by the CS.[36] At 1420 hours, Leonard arrived at Milton's CP, and the two briefly conferred before sending a team down to check on the fate of the three platoons. The team was driven back by NVA fire, and at that point it was too late in the day to launch a rescue mission, so Charlie Company dug in to spend the night. Helicopters were brought in to evacuate the wounded and the Alpha Company survivors. Captain Milton, who was wounded, was among the first out. Later he explained that he had been ordered out by the TOC. Through the night, artillery ringed the friendly positions as the troops waited for dawn. The battle was over, and the NVA had abandoned the field. Paul Donahue was nearby as the battle ended.

I had pulled a 12P.M. to 6A.M. switchboard shift, went to bed and awoke about 4 hours later, too hot to sleep long. Upon awakening, I stepped outside my tent to see an F-100 diving out of the sky and thought to myself, "What the hell is this?" When he dropped a bomb, I watched the bomb fall through the fog hanging on to the hill behind us; it exploded with a dull thud. Upon looking up, I saw a group of my friends gathered around a radio on the back of a Jeep. I went over and asked "what's up," and they told me a company of infantry had been ambushed up on the hill. This was June 22, the day A Co. 2/503 was ambushed, suffering 75 KIA and 35 WIA. We listened to the battle on the radios and knew they were in a world of shit, as every time a mike was keyed, all you could hear was automatic weapons and screams. They started to bring in the dead and wounded, and we walked over to the B-Med area and saw about fifty bodies wrapped in ponchos laying all over the ground with doctors and medics attending them. It was hard to believe that just a few months ago I was in Jump School with a lot of these men.[37]

At 0700 hours, 23 June, Bravo Company, which had taken no part in the battle, started up the hill, while Charlie Company moved, down looking for Alpha Company survivors. They found a clearing where the three platoons had attempted to hold the NVA. It was a scene from hell, with dead bodies stacked everywhere. Only three survivors were found. Most of the dead had been executed with a single gunshot to the back of the head. John Leppelman, C/2/503d, described what he saw.

In the early dawn, as the first light started to seep through the canopy, the brush started moving directly in front of my position. Several of us took aim on the foliage as a man staggered out, yelling at us in English not to shoot him. He was a survivor from the disaster below. As he made his way through our line, we saw that a large chunk of his skull was missing, and we could actually see his brain. He told us that after the NVA had overrun Alpha's position, they started executing all the survivors by shooting them in the head. Many men had begged for mercy but were executed. He had lain in a pile of American bodies while a gook had placed a rifle barrel against his head and pulled the trigger. By some miracle the bullet had glanced off his head, taking a big chunk of skull, hair, and flesh. He had been stunned but recovered and, once it was dark, escaped back up the mountain. We were furious, and the word quickly was passed around among the enlisted men that we would take no prisoners. The gooks had executed Americans who were wounded and out of ammunition. When we reached the valley floor, we spread out on line and moved forward slowly. When we stepped from the bamboo cover, we saw about ten American bodies stacked like cordwood in front of us. They were dead, with bullet holes in their heads. They had been stripped of weapons and gear. Welch and I moved around the bodies and moved down the trail slowly to where another eight of our men were scattered in various positions of death. Suddenly one of the bodies moved and stood up. He had multiple wounds but, to our amazement, was still alive. I called the CO and told them we had found a survivor and needed a medic at our location.

Paul Donahue in Tuy Hoa (courtesy Paul Donahue).

American bodies were scattered all through the bullet-scarred jungle. Welch and I came to another group. Welch whispered, "Look, his hand's moving." I looked at the pile of bodies and saw a man clenching and unclenching his fist. I got back on the horn, described what we had, and told the company to hurry. We needed medics fast. My God, I thought, these men lay here, out of ammo, waiting to die. They didn't have a prayer. As I moved, I found several men with weapons jammed, and a couple had died with their M-16s broken down, trying to fix the malfunction. As I moved among the men, I got madder and madder until I wanted to turn around and go back and shoot Alpha Company's CO [Milton]. He had definitely fucked up by not being with his men. He had stayed top and sent one platoon after another to their death as the battle had raged on below him; he had called artillery in on top of the besieged troops, as well as runs from gunships. This had almost no impact on the situation because of the triple canopy overhead.[38]

As the bodies arrived back at Dak To, Captain Milton started the grisly task of identifying the dead. This was made more difficult for those executed, because the exit wound often destroyed facial features. The number of Alpha Company casualties was staggering. Of the 137 men who started up Hill 1338, 76 were killed and 23 wounded.[39] Forty-three of those killed had been executed by the NVA. Alpha Company earned the nickname "No DEROS Alpha."[40] Similar nicknames were added later. When other 173d, ARVN, CIDG, and air support casualties are added, the total number of friendly killed, missing, and wounded was much higher. The enemy body count was meager considering the number of friendly casualties. After patrolling the area looking for dead NVA and digging up graves, a total of twenty dead NVA were found. It was reasonable to add some to represent those dead and wounded carried, away so a reasonable estimate would be fifty.[41] The chain of command immediately started to inflate the body count, and by the time it reached Saigon it stood at 513.[42] General Larsen at Nha Trang, the I Field Force Vietnam (IFFV) commander, called General Westmoreland to warn him of the excessive body count and was told that it was too late. The numbers had been released.[43]

As soon as the smoke cleared, the search for the guilty started. The blame was pushed down below brigade and battalion. Captain Leonard was blamed for not moving faster to reinforce Alpha Company, while Captain Milton was blamed for not reinforcing his platoon earlier. Everyone knew that the fault lay at a higher level. Sending in troops against an enemy force of unknown strength was unwise. Further, the bad weather and triple canopy forest negated the significant U.S. advantage of overwhelming fire superiority. Colonel Adamson, 4ID, recommended that General Deane, Commander of the 173d Airborne Brigade, be relieved of his command, but that did not happen.[44] Some said that would get unwanted media attention on a disastrous defeat.

John Leppelman summarized:

> I sat back and listened as Flynt said, "We were too far apart to do any good for anybody. We can't get artillery or choppers into this AO because of the canopy, so we don't have any support to speak of. What happened to Alpha could just as easily have happened to us or Bravo Company. Higher-higher has got us so far apart that we can't even provide support for each other, and to top it all off, the intelligence people gave us a bum fucking steer." Flynt was right. The upper quagmire of command had set the situation up because of its ignorance of what was in the mountains and also by splitting our elements up so that we could be of no use to each other when the shit hit the fan. In most of the officers' minds, we were just dumb enlisted men, and we were not supposed to know battlefield tactics. They were the experts.[45]

Alpha Company Commander David H. Milton, was interviewed in 2011, and his recollections are recorded below.

> I want to make it very clear. When C Company men came single file through my company location, they were crying because they didn't get there sooner but instead they sat on the trail for hours because the C Company 1st sergeant convinced the C Company commanding officer we were in an ambush. It's 40 years later and too late to argue the point. However, if C Company had arrived in a more timely manner, the NVA could not [have] continued executing my remaining wounded men…. As I remember, the terrain between C Company and A Company was relatively flat. We had reconnoitered the area several days before; that's why this area was selected for C Company's first operation…. C Company men were some of the bravest men I worked with. The problem with C Company was with the 1st sergeant and the CO. They, in my opinion, made a very poor decision—they remained on the trail way too long because they thought we were in an ambush. That is why they didn't arrive until the firing had stopped or quieted down.[46]

Also on 23 June 1967, General Westmoreland visited Dak To and congratulated the troops for "kicking ass!" This was a monstrous lie. All the troops had to do was recall the stacks of body bags. As one listening soldier asked: "Wonder what he's been smoking?"[47]

The first round of the Border Battles was a mixed result. New U.S. and ARVN units were rushed to reinforce Dak To. For Hanoi, the Allies had been lured from the cities to the border areas as planned, but the schedule was off. The move from the cities was far too soon for Phase II, the Tet Offensive, planned for late January 1968. The Dak To campaign would continue, but not according to Hanoi's plan.

Hill 830, 10 July

On 23 June 1967, reinforcements started to arrive at Dak To. 1st Battalion, 12th Cavalry, 1st Brigade of the 1st Air Cavalry Division was followed by the ARVN 1st Airborne Task Force (the 5th and 8th Battalions) and the 3rd Brigade of the 1st Air Cavalry Division. These units were sent on search-and-destroy operations[48] north and northeast of Dak To. The 173d went south and southeast of Dak To in search of the 24th NVA Regiment.[49] The 4th Battalion of the 503d Regiment was commanded by Lieutenant Colonel Lawrence Jackley. He had created a fourth company in his battalion by moving people from other companies. This gave him a fourth maneuver element, Delta Company. Delta Company was small, sixty-five to seventy people. On 7 July, C/4/503d left the other companies to provide security for a fire support base. That same day, based upon specific intelligence, Jackley was ordered 2500 meters southeast to engage what was thought to be an NVA regiment near Hill 830, twelve kilometers south of the village of Ben Het. Jackley was reinforced by eleven CIDG troops who would act as trackers and guides. It was an impossible mission. General Deane sent Jackley against an NVA regiment several times his unit's size and entrenched, on high ground, in bad weather that negated air support. Colonel Jackley sent his S-3 (the operations officer), Major Walter D. Williams, to accompany the column. It was raining incessantly. On 10 July, the battalion reached Hill 830, where the NVA regiment was supposed to be located. The order of march was Alpha Company, led by Captain Alan Phillips, followed by Delta Company, under Lieutenant John M. Deems, with Bravo Company, under Captain Daniel Severson. This looked like it could be a repeat of the battle at Hill 1338. The sky was overcast, and visibility had dropped to a dozen meters.

At 1530 hours, Captain Phillips started to look for a bivouac or laager site near the top of Hill 830. Soon after, Alpha Company's lead platoon, under Lieutenant Vandenburg, reported hitting a big trail, and a firefight erupted. Enemy fire engulfed Vandenburg's platoon, and soon it appeared that Alpha Company was surrounded. It had run into NVA bunkers. Vandenburg recalled:

> I remember 830 quite clearly. I was the lead platoon with my 1st squad (Sgt. Allen) as point. He was probably 20 meters to my front. I called in the fresh footprints we had found, and within a minute, we started receiving fire from our right front at approximately 2:00 o'clock position. Initially the fire was sporadic (Cpt Phillips even thought it might be us firing). As I started to move my men up, Danny [Lieutenant Jordan] was moving up his platoon on my left when we received intense fire from multiple locations to our front (12:00 o'clock). I do not know where Danny was located for sure, but he was most likely parallel to me. I was able to get both my M-60s working until a round hit John Borowski's gun. He is the one I tossed my M-16 to and whose 45 I ended up using. He was also, as mentioned in my letter home, one of my men that was killed. Also incoming rounds ripped holes in my RTO's radio (Tom Walker) and rendered it useless. That is why we had to low-crawl to issue and get orders.[50]

One of Delta Company's platoons was also soon engaged, and artillery support was called in. Meanwhile, Bravo Company fell back a few meters to a more defensible position. Unlike the Hill 1338 fight, the three companies were in close proximity and could support each other. To everyone's annoyance, Colonel Jackley orbited overhead, could see nothing, and did little good. Major Williams was with Delta Company and was now directing the battle. He entered Bravo Company's perimeter and directed Captain Severson to attack the right side of the bunker complex. Bravo Company's 4th platoon, under Master Sergeant Lawrence Okendo, stayed behind to prepare defensive positions, while Severson and Williams moved forward.

Captain Severson, his three platoons, and Major Williams didn't have to advance very far before beginning their attack. About a hundred meters from Okendo's reserve position they descended into a shallow saddle. Before them the side of Hill 830 rose steeply, covered by a confusion of bamboo, trees, and thick underbrush. Severson paused briefly to put his platoons on line. Lieutenant Ligon was on the right with his RTO, Specialist Owens, at his side. The paratroopers started up the slope. It was so steep they were forced to half-crawl as they climbed hand over hand. Halfway up, Severson ordered Ligon to echelon to the left. By the time he had done so the center platoon, in the lead, had made it to within thirty meters of the slope's summit. Then the NVA opened up.[51]

As Okendo worked, a CIDG soldier came out of the jungle carrying one wounded trooper from Alpha Company on his back with six M-16 rifles in his arms. An incredible load for a very small person. Okendo relieved him of the load, and the CIDG soldier went back into the jungle to get another wounded Alpha Company soldier. Sergeant Okendo watched:

> In the LZ, a new replacement was seriously cut in the head with a machete. He got in the way of a trooper feverishly swinging his machete to clear the LZ. A bad loss. I had one hectic job, clearing the LZ, defending the small perimeter and trying to restrain my men from splitting to get into the firefight. Some of the near tragedies in the heat of battle can be viewed with a lot of laughs when the smoke clears. I knew we were facing a full-size NVA Battalion with heavy weapons, and judging from the area and the news from the wounded coming into my perimeter, the NVAs were dug in, while our troops were attacking in the open.
>
> The cold of Dak To mountains started settling in, coupled with soft drizzling rain. Several of the wounded were being evacuated from Bravo Company's area.... We could hear the Dustoff helicopter over the tremendous amount of mortar and small-arms fire. Slowly the wounded dribbled into our perimeter; Cpl Jackson, our medic, had his work cut out for him. A small defilade near the center of the perimeter was used for the wounded, to protect them from sniper and small-arms fire.[52]

As Severson and Williams led the attack, a mortar round landed between them. Severson was badly wounded, and Williams received a fatal wound. His right side was blown away. Lieutenant Ligon was the one of two Bravo Company officers still uninjured. Ligon's courage under fire and cool head prevented a panic among the troops. The other officer was hiding in a hole with the company first sergeant back at Okendo's position. Okendo was furious because he couldn't get the two to leave the safety of their hole. Alpha Company was still in the lead but bogged down. Colonel Jackley could now see the action as the fog lifted, and he ordered Phillips to fall back to Bravo Company. Delta was already moving to that position. With three companies concentrated at one position, this would not be a rerun of the Hill 1338 massacre. Enemy fire was tapering off. When Captain Phillips arrived, Okendo told him of the lieutenant and first sergeant cowering in a hole. Phillips ordered them out, and they refused. A court-martial for the two seemed appropriate. The number of wounded was beyond the capability of the medics to treat, and there was no adequate LZ for medevac choppers, so the wounded were removed using baskets lowered on cables by the helicopters through the jungle canopy. Sergeant Okendo described the scene.

> Military gear was strewn all over the battle area and covered with mud. I had a cowboy (our helicopter support company)[53] overhead trying to evacuate the wounded in my area; as he started descending, his props started hitting the branches around the perimeter. The area was too small. I immediately signaled the cowboy to back up. He sent down an extraction line.
>
> One of the new officers from Bravo company was wounded and talking incoherently. I checked him out, lifted his jacket, and found a bullet wound just below his shoulder blades and a leech sucking up the blood below the wound. I got the extraction line around him; his moans and incoherency could cause me more problems than the gooks.

> Dusk was setting in fast, along with a heavy mist that was now drifting up the treetops and covering the area with a thick blanket of dense fog. What more can occur to a bunch of wounded paratroopers? Soon after dusk, Doc Jackson told me that we lost Sgt Beach; he led the point element up Hill 830 and had a bullet wound in the head.
>
> It was a night the Sky Soldiers will never forget. It was wet, cold, and one of the wounded was moaning. It was impossible to keep him quiet. Then keeping the other wounded dry and as comfortable as possible was a tremendous task; every trooper did their part to aid the wounded.[54]

As the sun went down, it was clear that the 4/503d would spend another night in the jungle.

At dawn, 11 July, Lieutenant Deems ordered Lieutenant Allen to send a patrol out to check for the enemy.

> Allen repeated the order to Sergeant Dunston. Dunston replied almost immediately "Six, we don't have to recon the hill. I'm right in the middle of the gooks' positions." It was true. Just meters from where Dunston and his squad had spent a watchful night, the abandoned NVA bunkers began. Allen took his platoon on a sweep to their immediate front. The paratroopers counted more than sixty bunkers and foxholes ringing the base camp; many were covered with a twofoot-thick layer of logs and dirt for overhead protection. Abandoned equipment and ammo were scattered about. But there were no NVA to be found.[55]

Meanwhile, an LZ was completed to allow the evacuation of the casualties. Colonel Jackley ordered the removal of the cowardly lieutenant and platoon sergeant. The troops favored courts-martial for the two, but that would not happen. They were simply transferred out of the 173d.[56] A search of Hill 830 revealed two more NVA base camps and NVA bodies. Total body count was nine, with one NVA medic captured. The 4/503d suffered twenty-two dead and sixty-two wounded. A call went out to base camp for volunteers to fill the ranks. Many cooks, military policemen (MPs), engineers, and others responded, keeping up the strength in infantry units.

July 12 was spent searching the hill, and the companies were lifted out in order to continue the search for NVA on 13 July. The battalion had fought well, and there were many valor awards. At the top of Hill 830, near what appeared to be an NVA command post, a dead trooper of the 173d had been respectfully laid out under a poncho by the NVA. It was a tribute to his bravery.[57] Clashes with the NVA were occurring across western Kontum province and were not restricted to a few hill sites.

> North Vietnamese pressure against CIDG outposts at Dak Seang and Dak Sek, 20 and 45 kilometers north of Đắk Tô respectively, was the impetus for dispatching the 42nd ARVN Infantry Regiment into the area while the ARVN Airborne battalion moved to Dak Seang. On 4 August, the 1st of the 42nd encountered the North Vietnamese on a hilltop west of Dak Seang, setting off a three-day battle that drew in the South Vietnamese paratroopers. The 8th Airborne, along with U.S. Army advisors, was airlifted into a small unimproved air field next to the Special Forces camp at Dak Seang. The camp was under sporadic fire and probing ground attack by PAVN forces. This occurred when its Special Forces commander and a patrol failed to return and the camp received what appeared to be preparatory fire for a full-scale ground attack by PAVN. The terrain was high mountains with triple canopy jungle. The importance of the Dak Seang camp was that it lay astride the Ho Chi Minh Trail, the main infiltration route of the PAVN into the South.[58]

Paul Donahue was sent to Dak Seang, a CIDG camp advised by U.S. Special Forces north of Dak To where Highway 14 peters out.[59] He recalled the fighting.

> I was assigned to go to with about ten other signal guys to a Special Forces Camp called Dak Seang to set up a radio relay station, as communications in the mountains were very spotty. Not long after

arriving, a patrol from the camp was ambushed right outside the perimeter. Two Green Berets were KIA, and a number of Montagnards were also KIA. One night we were mortared, and a couple of days later the NVA tossed a grenade into a village about a click from the camp, killing a baby and wounding a lot of civilians who then came to the camp for medical help. Shortly after that, an ARVN Airborne unit was inserted outside the camp and went on a search-and-destroy mission up a large mountain that overlooked the camp. Soon they were in a large firefight up on the mountain that lasted about two days. It was an NVA base camp, and within the camp they found a mockup of the special forces camp, indicating that they were preparing to attack the camp within days. I was replaced at the camp about a week later and returned to the Dak To base camp. We then left for Tuy Hoa, only to return to Dak To in November.[60]

Tuy Hoa

While the 4/503d trained replacements, the 1/503d and 2/503d continued the search for the NVA. Intelligence indicated that the K-101D Battalion, Doc Lap Regiment, 24th NVA Regiment, 174th Regiment, and others were lurking in the tri-border area of Cambodia, Laos, and Vietnam. It appeared that the NVA could cross the border leaving Vietnam at any time and end the fighting (temporarily). Patrols continued, as did bad weather and eternal discomfort. The leeches were the worst. They could crawl into troopers' mouths, noses, and ears while they were asleep.[61] Search-and-destroy operations continued through July and into August. By mid–August, U.S. intelligence concluded that the NVA had crossed over into Laos, so forces at Dak To could be replaced. General Peers's 4ID was now at full strength, and most of the 173d (less 2/503d) could be withdrawn.

General Deane, commander of the 173d, was replaced by General Leo H. Schweiter on 23 August 1967. Three weeks later, the 1/503d and 4/503d would move to Tuy Hoa on the coast. The relocation started on 17 September. The 173d would provide protection for the rice harvest around Tuy Hoa to prevent the local VC from extorting rice from the farmers. The VC operated in small groups, lobbing occasional mortar rounds and ambushing patrols. After Dak To, it was light duty for the 173d, and the Tuy Hoa beach was a delight. On 11 October, 2/503d joined the rest of the 173d at Tuy Hoa. In late October a fourth battalion, the 3/503d, was added to the 173d, increasing its combat power. It had been formed in the U.S. six months earlier.[62]

A.T. Lawrence was a lieutenant in 2/8th of the 4ID, which replaced the 2/503rd after it departed Dak To for Tuy Hoa. He summarized the operations of his battalion.

> Although my battalion was the first unit to conduct search-and-destroy missions into the hills to the south of Dak To, where we stumbled upon some of the enemy bunker complexes, the NVA were not yet ready to engage in battle, as they were still in the process of bringing in more regiments, and so they simply permitted us to walk back down the steep jungle slope, unmolested, back to the village of Dak To.
>
> I can only surmise that the NVA were intent upon assembling a divisionsize force of five full regiments and that most likely only their lead regiment had arrived on the scene, while their strategic plan called for an entire division to be in place so they could tie up two or three American brigades, rather than just our small undersized battalion.[63]

Meanwhile, back in the states, October 1967 was the month of large anti-war demonstrations. Tens of thousands converged on the Pentagon in Washington, D.C. Campuses also had their share of protests, but the majority of Americans took no part in demonstrations. According to Gallup, 53 percent of America still supported the war.[64]

Battle in the Hills—Operation MacArthur

By 28 October 1967, Allied intelligence was convinced that the NVA would again attack the Special Forces camp at Dak To. Operation MacArthur was launched in early November to accomplish search-and-destroy missions around Dak To.

Lieutenant Colonel James H. Johnson had replaced Lieutenant Colonel Jackley as commander of 4/503d. The 4/503d arrived at Dak To from Tuy Hoa on 1 November. There were new faces. Captain James J. Muldoon had taken command of Alpha Company, while Bravo Company was now commanded by Captain George Baldridge. Newly promoted Captain William Connolly commanded Charlie Company, while Captain Thomas Baird commanded Delta Company. Delta was a small provisional company that had only two infantry platoons instead of four. Total strength was three officers and eighty-five men. Colonel Johnson was ordered to move his battalion from Dak To about twenty kilometers west to Ben Het, where Fire Support Base (FSB) 12 was being constructed.

Sergeant Lawrence Okendo, B/4/503d, explained the use of the FSBs, which would become crucial during the Border Battles.

> Each infantry unit had its own area of operations, called an AO, where search-and-destroy missions were conducted by rifle companies under a canopy of artillery cover and other supporting elements that was conducive to the needs of the infantrymen.

Setting up the Fire Support Base (courtesy John L. Feagin).

The areas for selective AOs were assigned to the infantry brigade or battalion. In turn, the commander would make a visual reconnaissance by air, then selecting an area that could support a fire support base (FSB). This would be an area best suitable to support his infantry units in their operations of search-and-destroy missions.

The selected area for the FSB, once selected, one infantry company would air-assault the selected site, clear the area by patrols. Soon as the area is secured, a perimeter large enough to support an artillery battery is staked out by the assaulting company; fighter positions and foxholes are dug, forming a firm perimeter.

Chinook CH-47 helicopters, capable of carrying 44 troops and one field artillery 105mm howitzer with ammunition pallet slung beneath, start bringing in the artillery battery and other supporting elements. The artillery personnel will start digging emplacements for their guns immediately.[65]

Intelligence indicated that the 1st NVA Division planned a major attack at Dak To.

While the Sky Soldiers settled in at FSB 12, the 4th Infantry Division stumbled upon information revealing the NVA's full plans. In the early morning hours of 2 November, at the hamlet of Bak Ri west of Ben Het, an ARVN outpost accepted the surrender of a North Vietnamese NCO. Sergeant Vu Hong claimed to be an artillery specialist with the NVA 66th Regiment. His regiment was one of four infantry regiments and one artillery regiment forming the NVA 1st Division.[66]

Skirmishes occurred around Dak To, where 4ID battalions encountered the NVA as early as 3 November. Since the NVA threat was mounting, two more battalions of the 173d were committed to Dak To. The 1/503d, 2/503d, and supporting artillery arrived at Dak To from Tuy Hoa on 5–6 November. The 3/503d remained at Tuy Hoa because it was too new to be committed to major fighting. Additional ARVN forces were also sent to Dak To. The 3d ARVN Airborne Battalion replaced the 9th Battalion and was joined by the 2d Battalion and the 3/42d Infantry Regiment. The ARVN units would try to find and engage the 24th NVA Regiment.

Hill 724

East of Dak To, old battlefields would be revisited. On 7 November 1967, in search-and-destroy operations, 4ID battalions were attacked. Near Hill 830, the 3/8th Infantry (called the Dragoons) was hit while the 3/12th Infantry was attacked at Hill 1338. Engagements continued at Hill 724.

On 7 November 1967, three companies of the 3/8th Infantry, 4ID, moved on Hill 724. The battalion, commanded by Lieutenant Colonel Glen D. Belnap, had a strength of five hundred troops, and each company had about 120 men. They started taking casualties before they reached the hill, including the A Company commander, Captain John Taylor, who was killed. They had walked into an NVA ambush and were outnumbered 10–1. The NVA were very well equipped, and for two days the fighting went on before the fifty survivors of Alpha Company were evacuated, following air strikes that caused the NVA to withdraw. On 11 November, three companies of 3/8th Infantry assembled for an attack on Hill 724. C/3/8th was the first to reach the summit, followed by Bravo and Delta Companies. When they reached the summit, it became clear to the troops why this hill was important: they had a perfect field of view of the surrounding terrain. The NVA launched an attack that started with a thirty-minute mortar barrage that rained down on the three companies, and this was followed by North Vietnamese troops that attacked out of the jungle. Air support, including napalm, forced the NVA to withdraw. By the time the action ended that

Soldiers of the 8th Infantry descending from Hill 724 (U.S. Government).

evening, eighteen Americans were dead, including Captain Falcone, the commander of B Company, and another 118 were wounded. The 4ID claimed that 92 North Vietnamese had died in the clash.[67] Juan Alex Quintanar was on Hill 724 in D/3/8 and provided the following record of the fighting.

> October 28, 1967. A and D company of the 3/8 Infantry were the first U.S troops to arrive at the Dak To airstrip. Wasting no time, D Company made a combat assault west and behind the advancing enemy. Contact was made with well-entered and well-equipped North Vietnamese Army (NVA) troops. Dak To was considered an NVA fortress with base camps around the rugged mountains.
>
> November 8, 1967. We fought over two to three NVA Battalions. The body count was 286 NVA.
>
> November 9, 1967. This day will burn in my head for the rest of my life. D Company 3/8 Infantry received orders to load up two cargo nets. The bodies were stacked 2 ft. high, a total of about 29 bodies. The first helicopter arrived, along with a young news reporter by the name of Peter Arnett. I helped load up the first cargo net. As it lifted up in the air it was gruesome site. Arms, legs and heads were hanging out. The second cargo net lifted up and hit four to five trees and almost crash-landed, arms, legs, and heads falling back to the ground. I thought myself "Damn it, I'm not going out this way." An hour later we were hit with the 3rd human wave attack.
>
> November 11, 1967. C Company was 1st. D Company would be the 2nd to advance to Hill 724. The Dragoons, who didn't have a chance to dig in and secure their new position atop Hill 724, fought from behind tree stumps and clumps of bamboo. On the other hand, NVA had snipers positioned in trees while launching a human wave attack against C and D Companies that opened a section for B Company to move up Hill 724.[68]

Many reporters made the scene on Hill 724, as they did later on Hill 875. Juan Alex Quintanar recalled his meetings with the press.

> During the Battle of Dak To in November 1967, a total of 52 reporters and photographers were screened by the 1st Brigade, 4th Infantry Division Military Press Office. All press conferences were out of Saigon. Peter Arnett was the only reporter who would fly daily by helicopter back to Pleiku near Signal Hill. He would send out by Morse code to Saigon for approval to cover combat actions at Dak To. Mr. Arnett learned Morse code when he joined the New Zealand Army during the Korean Conflict. The next morning Mr. Arnett would drive to camp Holloway near Pleiku and fly directly to Dak To with the 52nd Aviation Group, called the Flying Dragons. Back at Dak To there would be a 5:00 p.m. military briefing. Mr. Arnett would already have the news in hand, because he flew daily to the field and got firsthand accounts of the combat actions. The Morse code was still being used in Vietnam in late 1967.
>
> During the Battle of Dak To, I would meet six reporters. The first group would be a news crew consisting of a reporter, cameraman, and soundman. They were near Hill 724. They interviewed Pvt. Howe, Pvt. Jackson, Pvt. Walker, Pvt. Williams, and myself, Pvt. Quintanar. They told us to write home because our families were worried about us and that we were making front-page news. He said the "4th Infantry Division was locked in battle with a large force of enemy troops." Twenty minutes later, the sound of gunfire was heard on the other side of the ridgeline.
>
> All three news men moved to the top of the hill. Soon after they reached the top, 10–12 mortar rounds landed directly on them. Pvt. Howe went up the hill only to come back and say that the news group was torn up pretty bad. I took a look for myself. I found a camera with shrapnel holes and sound equipment badly damaged. All three newsmen were hanging on [for] dear life! I helped load one of the guys on to the helicopter that was waiting. I don't think this one was alive. I returned to look at the damaged camera and sound equipment. There were 8–10 videotapes hit by shrapnel all over the field. Which tape was ours, I'll never know.
>
> On November 9, I would see Peter Arnett. He arrived in a helicopter. Pvt. Ostherloth said to me, "That's Peter Arnett, the news reporter." I said, "So what, we're here to pick up 2 cargo nets and help load the dead Americans, so they can go home. I wish I could go home! But not in a cargo net." After being wounded on top of Hill 724 on November 11, I had to wait for the next day for medevac. On November 12, I would see the battalion commander, LTC Glen Dean Belnap, and CSM Herbert Roberts. They landed on Hill 724. I was sitting near the only tree on the hill. They were looking for the body of Capt. John Falcone, which was found near two bomb craters before they both left. CSM Roberts got down on one knee and made the sign of the cross for the dead soldiers. I was airlifted that afternoon and saw the 1st Air Cavalry join us on the hill. On November 15, I was released from the mash unit, or field hospital. I then came to work at the Brigade HHQ Company on the command radio with Major Stiner, Assistant S-3. I would meet the 3rd group of news reporters at the military briefing, Peter Kann and Chislain Bellorget, on the afternoon of November 15. The word was out that the men of D Company 3/8 Infantry were ordered to pull out of Hill 724. As D Company 3/8 Infantry landed at the Dak To airfield, I heard, "Here come the Dak To warriors." Pvt. Walker and Pvt. Williams looked like war-torn soldiers. I embraced them with a big hug. They told me, "We got our asses kicked." I said, "I know, but we were able to stop the enemy from advancing and holding any part of the Dak To region." They both walked away. I never saw them again after that day.[69]

In several days of fighting in these areas, the U.S. lost over thirty KIA and nearly 160 wounded. Some units were down to less than half strength. One chopper pilot recalled that the units had lost so many NCOs that they were instantly promoting SP4s to E5. They called them "Shake and Bake" NCOs. The NVA lost over one hundred KIA. It was clear that the NVA had no plans to leave.

Ngok Kom Leat

While the 3/8th Infantry was fighting on Hill 724, the 4/503rd Infantry was ordered to secure Hill 823 so that a new fire support base (FSB 15) could be established at its peak.

On 4 November, Colonel Johnson ordered three companies of his 4/503d to leave FSB 12 and move to Hill 823. The fourth company, Bravo, would stay at FSB 12 to secure it. Each of the three companies would be reinforced by a CIDG platoon to act as guides. Artillery would then be lifted on to the summit. Once again, three companies would move against an NVA regiment or perhaps a larger force. The Alpha, Charlie, and Delta Companies were moving on a parallel axis through hilly terrain known as Ngok Kom Leat. Lawrence Okendo recalled:

> As Bravo company constructed their perimeter on Fire Base #12, A, C, and D companies 4/503rd moved out on a search-and-destroy mission, moving on parallel axis to the southwest and west of Ben Het. A contingent of Montagnards were assigned to the 4th battalion task force. The commanders were told that they were confronting up to two North Vietnamese battalions. This assignment was not the best military situation for the Sky Soldiers; their formation was such that they could not assist each other in the event of an ambush. Since each unit was in an independent formation, the great distance between them was a critical factor.[70]

On 6 November, Johnson ordered Alpha Company to fall in behind Captain Baird's Delta. They were moving on the lower ridgelines of Ngo Kom Leat. Second Platoon, commanded by Lieutenant Michael D. Burton, was in the lead and moved out at 0845. Burton's point man soon noticed that NVA communications wire ran along the trail. They followed the wire, while Burton ordered sweeps around the platoon as they quietly moved forward. Soon they could hear the sound of NVA talking, and word was sent back.

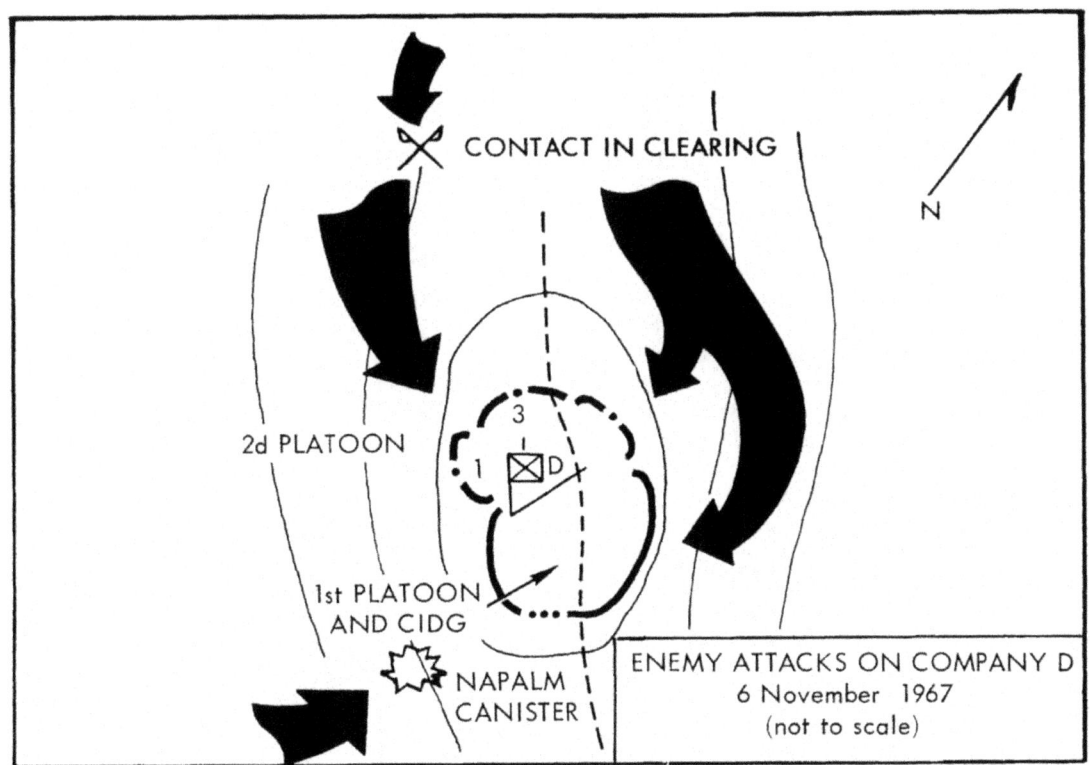

Delta Company defense (from John Albright, John H. Cash and Allan W. Sandstrum, *Seven Firefights in Vietnam* [Washington: Office of the Chief of Military History, United States Army, 1970]).

A feeling of tense expectation that already permeated the column heightened as the men reached the knoll. Fresh prints of bare feet in the soft ground, a bamboo reel for wire, newly dropped human feces all pointed to the nearness of the enemy. Baird first drew his force into a defensive perimeter, then began to advance by bounds, at each halt sending four squads out on cloverleaf sweeps in an effort to circumvent any possible enemy ambush. 1st Lt. Michael D. Burton, 2d Platoon, sent his two lead squads forward to conduct the initial sweep up the ridge. As S. Sgt. Jimmy R. Worley's 1st Squad began to move out of the 2d Platoon defensive position, the hairraising chatter of automatic weapons fire sounded from less than fifty meters up the hill. In an instant, four days of slogging in search of the enemy were forgotten in the shock of combat.[71]

Colonel Johnson ordered Bravo Company to leave FSB 12 and move to Hill 823. He then ordered air strikes ahead of Delta Company and on Hill 823 to help clear the summit for the planned LZ. As explosions rocked the area, Baird concluded that they were in the midst of the NVA, but he couldn't tell exactly where the enemy was located. Contact was imminent. At about 1300, one of Burton's men saw an NVA soldier and fired. The NVA opened fire. The heavy fire ripped through the thick bamboo, showering the troopers with its water. Delta Company formed a defensive perimeter, and the CIDG fled. They didn't stop until they reached Lieutenant Robert Allen's platoon in the rear. Captain Baird had been wounded in the exchange but remained in command of Delta Company.

Lieutenant Burton pulled his 1st Squad back, then sent it around to the left flank and up the ridge again. From the right, the 2d Squad supported the move, attempting to suppress enemy fire with its M-60 machine gun and M-79 grenade launcher. As the 1st Squad moved up the hill in an attempt to flank enemy gunners, it came upon a small clearing. There Spec. 4 Charles E. Moss spotted a green-uniformed North Vietnamese soldier carrying an AK-47. When the man turned away, Moss cut him down with a short burst from his M-16. A firefight ensued.

Baird then ordered Burton to pull his platoon back along the trail into a company perimeter. To disengage would not be an easy matter, but it was preferable to the possible piecemeal destruction of a company strung out in column. While Worley's men fell back, the 2d and 3d Squads continued to lay down covering fire. As if on cue, intense automatic weapons fire from up the trail rained down on the 2d Squad and spilled over into the company position. Two assistant M-60 gunners and a rifleman were wounded. Subsequent events crowded together with lightning rapidity.

Although the company for the moment still lacked its engaged 2d Platoon, other elements were forming a defensive position with Captain Baird. The platoon of Vietnamese irregulars, because of its central position in the column, at first occupied the forward edge and flanks of the perimeter, but as the tide of combat drew closer they drifted away from Sergeant Ky, back along the trail toward the rear of the perimeter. Baird moved his 1st Platoon up to cover the exposed flanks, while his first sergeant, Sfc. William Collins, began to reorganize the irregulars to cover the rear.

A little later additional assistance to stiffen the Montagnard troops would come from another source: Sergeant Terrazas and his squad from Company A were coming up on the rear of the perimeter. The men had unsuccessfully attempted to follow the trail of their parent unit. Now they homed in on the sounds of combat.

With his rear taken care of and his flanks secured by the 1st Platoon, Baird faced the pressing problem to his front. Although Sergeant Worley's squad successfully pulled back through the 2d and 3d Squads, Burton's entire platoon became locked in a tight firefight with what the men estimated to be a company of North Vietnamese. Burton's men needed assistance to disengage in order to close the short gap between platoon and company.

Baird called for a tactical air strike, but found all the fighters in his area momentarily unavailable. Helicopter gunships moved in to do what they could to relieve the pressure, and the 105mm howitzers of Battery B, 3d Battalion, 319th Artillery, lent their weight from the fire support base six kilometers away. With this help, the 2d Platoon broke away.[72]

NVA fire intensified as the enemy moved in on Delta. Air strikes slowed the NVA attack, but it continued after the air force departed. The heavy bamboo and high trees limited the

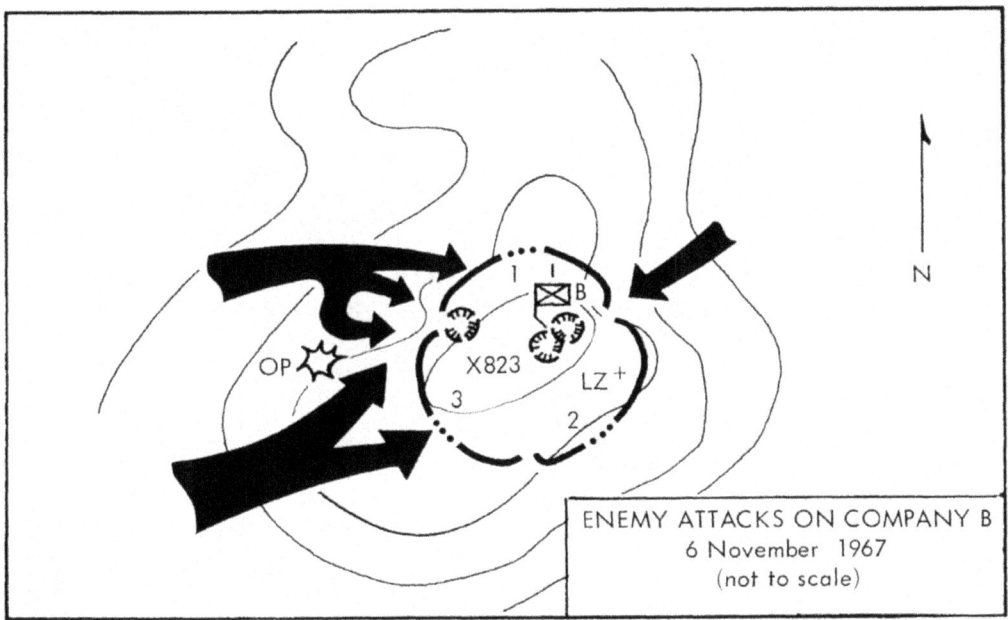

Defense of Hill 823 (from John Albright, John H. Cash and Allan W. Sandstrum, *Seven Firefights in Vietnam* [Washington: Office of the Chief of Military History, United States Army, 1970]).

effectiveness of the strikes. Lieutenant Allen's platoon, in the rear, had not been engaged, but at about 1500, hours one of the troopers yelled, "Here they come!"[73] The NVA was surrounding Delta, and Colonel Johnson ordered Alpha and Charlie Companies to move to Delta's assistance. As Alpha moved to Delta's aid, the results of the air strikes could be seen. The blackened bodies of fifteen NVA soldiers holding charred rifles were found.[74]

Sporadic attacks against Delta continued throughout the afternoon, and more air strikes were called in. Enemy fire subsided, and evacuation of the wounded was completed by 2200 hours. Throughout the night the NVA fired occasional shots, but by dawn, 7 November, it was clear that the NVA had departed. Alpha Company checked the battlefield. The body count was twenty-eight NVA dead and many weapons recovered, included six machine guns. Friendly losses were six KIA and twenty wounded.[75] The caution exercised by Baird during the advance and his quick action to call in air support saved the 4/503d from heavy losses.

The Fight for Hill 823

While fighting continued at Ngok Kom Leat, Bravo Company was relieved of its security mission at FSB 12 and would make a combat assault on the summit of Hill 823. Once again, a single company was moving against the NVA without mutually supporting units close by. This would not end well. Bravo would be ready to move at 0900, 6 November 1967.

Lieutenant Colonel Johnson surveyed Hill 823 from the air on 5 November. To Johnson's experienced eye the easiest approaches for an enemy counterattack would be along the wide fingers running from the summit to the west and northwest. Bravo Company would have to carefully secure that area to prevent an NVA attack. With the combat assault (CA) scheduled to begin at 0900, Johnson had

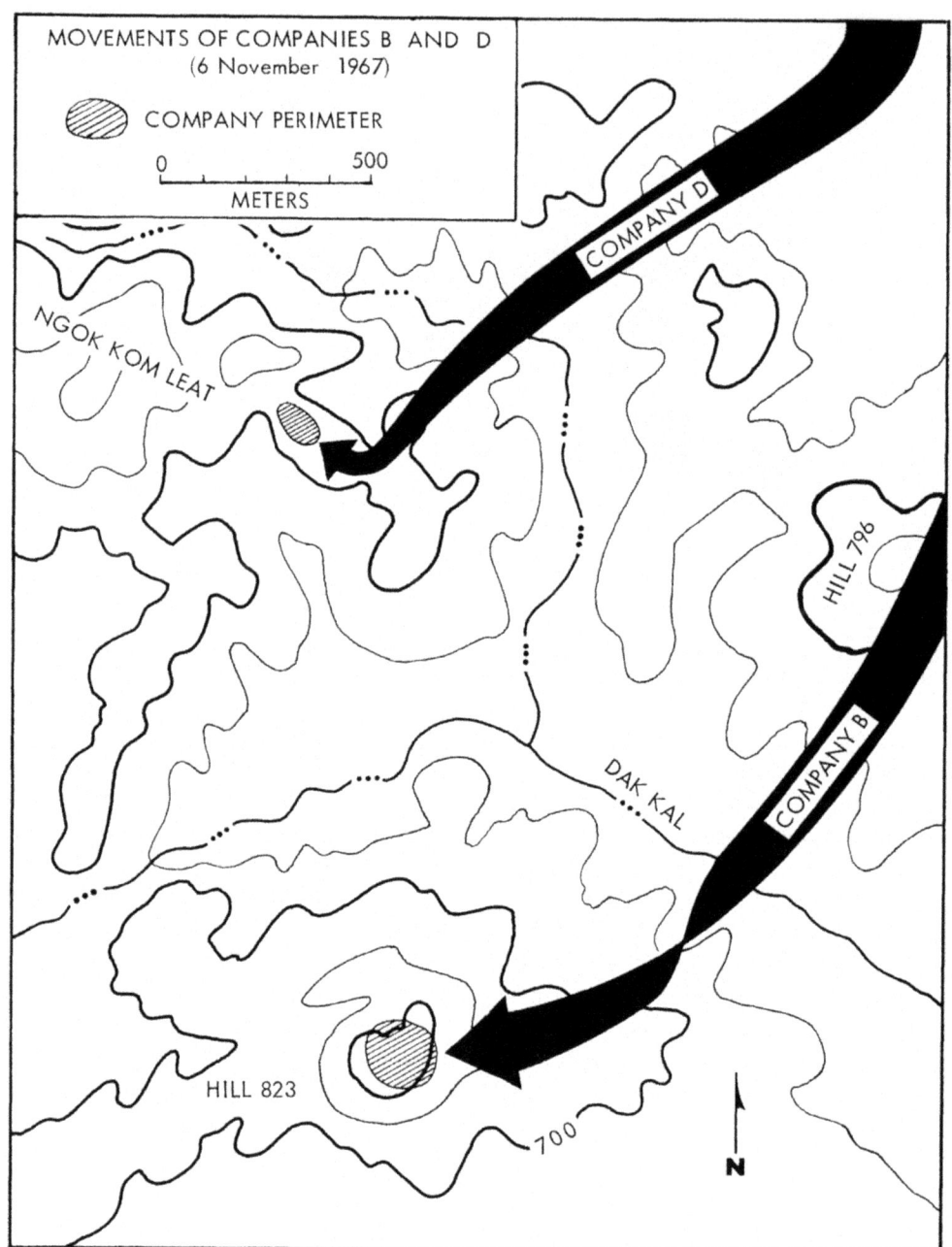

Attack of the 4th Battalion, 503rd Infantry (from John Albright, John H. Cash and Allan W. Sandstrum, *Seven Firefights in Vietnam* [Washington: Office of the Chief of Military History, United States Army, 1970]).

ordered early morning air strikes to blast an LZ onto the top of Hill 823. Because his surveillance flight the previous day had failed to reveal any sign of an NVA presence, Johnson limited the air strikes to five. They should be enough to clear an LZ. Just before 0900 Johnson again had his C-and-C chopper hover above Hill 823. It was readily apparent the aerial bombs had not sufficiently cleared the summit for an LZ. He ordered up more air strikes with larger ordnance.[76]

Since another air strike was needed, the lift from FSB 12 to Hill 823 was delayed. Room for one helicopter on the LZ was needed, and the additional air strikes blasted down enough timber to allow for this landing space. By 1430, Bravo was finally on Hill 823. Evidence of the NVA was found. Scattered equipment indicated that the NVA had been on the hill and were caught in the air strikes.

> It was a deserted hilltop now as Capt. George T. Baldridge, the company commander, surveyed his new domain. Hill 823 dominated the ground to nearly all points of the compass. A lush valley separated the hilltop from the ridge where Company D was hanging on. The west and northwest slopes would provide the enemy with comparatively easy approaches to the summit of Hill 823, but the southern slope was too steep for organized assault. Observation was clearest down the southeast slope—fifty meters. Movement on the hill would be hampered severely by broken tree limbs and piles of bamboo. Captain Baldridge positioned his 1st Platoon where it could defend the northern and northwestern slopes. He disposed his 2d Platoon along the eastern and southern portions of his projected perimeter and in its rear he placed his mortar platoon. Turning to Lt. Robert H. Darling, Baldridge directed him to move the men of his 3d Platoon up over the crest and a short distance down the hill (about 150 meters from the landing zone), in order to secure the western portion of the perimeter. Darling was to establish a two-man observation post a hundred meters farther down the hill to provide early warning of an attack along that likely avenue of approach. When his platoon reached its assigned position, Darling sent PFC. Clarence A. Miller and Spec. 4 Louis C. Miller (they were not related) down the slope to set up the observation post. Ten minutes later, the two Millers were dead. Darling himself was supervising the distribution of his men along the perimeter when his two-man observation post was struck by a violent fusillade of small arms fire, delivered at close range. With his radio operator and three other hastily designated riflemen, he raced headlong down the slope toward the now silent post. An enemy ambush force of platoon size caught them from their right before they had covered half of the distance.[77]

Baldridge heard the firing and called Darling on the radio. Darling's RTO made a gasping reply that Darling was hurt bad, and the radio then went dead. All were caught in the open and killed except for SSG Robert J. Bickel, who tried to crawl back, but he also was shot and killed before he could reach safety.

> Baldridge later recalled his actions as the attack developed: "I moved forward to the 3d Platoon.... At that point I could hear the gooks laughing and shouting down below. Lieutenant Darling and his men had been hit 30 or 40 meters down from the perimeter." Realizing that his western perimeter was in trouble, Baldridge radioed S. Sgt. Johnnie R. Riley for 60mm mortar fire at 100 meters and 81mm mortar fire at 250 meters in front of the 3d Platoon. Some mortar men were moved to positions left by members of the 2d Platoon who were being shifted to fill gaps in the 3d Platoon line. Artillery strengthened the developing cordon of fire in front of the beleaguered platoon. Riley's mortars saved the lives of three men who had belatedly followed Lieutenant Darling's party down the hill. Having made its kill, the NVA ambush party turned its fire on these three soldiers, wounding all of them. Taking cover in a bomb crater, the wounded men exchanged fire with the enemy until two of them ran out of ammunition and the third was about to expend his last magazine. As enemy soldiers closed in, 60mm mortar rounds erupted in front of the crater. While their would-be exterminators worried about their own survival, the Americans made it back to the company perimeter and were later evacuated.
>
> Following their initial success, the North Vietnamese pressed the attack up the slope, the NVA tide cresting a few meters in front of the 3d Platoon, near its juncture with the 2d Platoon. Some fifteen determined enemy soldiers made it that far. One of them got near enough to shoot at close range a paratrooper struggling with a jammed M-79. The Americans delivered continuous fire on their attackers for twenty minutes before the enemy survivors reeled back down the hill. For some reason, at least thirty North Vietnamese soldiers hiding in heavy, broken bamboo farther down the hill had failed to join in the assault.
>
> During a lull that followed, SFC John L. Ponting moved from his position as platoon sergeant, 1st Platoon, to take command of the 3d Platoon. Other men throughout the company also shifted to fill gaps that had opened as a result of the first attack. Reorganization was accomplished swiftly, and

fortunately so, for a second attack came at 1515. It was launched from the same direction as the first. Although the attack was quickly repulsed, four more men of the 3d Platoon were wounded. From a bomb crater at the junction of the 1st and 3d Platoons, men manning a machine gun and a 90mm recoilless rifle slammed flanking fire into the second thrust. Reacting to the effectiveness of these fires, enemy soldiers moved in around the crater and harassed it with grenades during the rest of the day and into the night.

The worst of the fight was over in fifteen minutes, leaving Company B with seven men dead and thirteen wounded. In the next hour all wounded were evacuated by medical helicopters, but the North Vietnamese were still much in evidence in the vicinity of Hill 823, just as they continued to threaten the company over on the slopes of Ngok Kom Leat.[78]

In the second attack, a mortar round landed at Captain Baldridge's CP, wounding him and seven others. Bravo Company had thirteen wounded, and these were quickly evacuated by medical helicopter. Captain Ronald R. Leonard was flown in to replace Baldridge. As dusk approached, Bravo Company prepared for a long night of firing. In the darkness, small teams of NVA slipped closer to the perimeter. Some got close enough to cut the Claymore mine activation wires. Muldoon's Alpha Company and Captain Connolly's Charlie Company would join up and move to reinforce Leonard. Charlie Company was about a kilometer

Soldiers laying down covering fire (from John Albright, John H. Cash and Allan W. Sandstrum, *Seven Firefights in Vietnam* [Washington: Office of the Chief of Military History, United States Army, 1970]).

from Alpha and could not get there before dark, so Connolly stopped where he was. The two companies would join up the following day.

> Sergeant Leo Hill had taken up a position with a buddy, Specialist 4th Class Diaz, and an engineer. Several times during the long night Hill could hear the NVA moving furtively on the slope below him. In response, Diaz would point his M-79 nearly straight up, then they'd all duck as the missile landed and exploded only fifteen to twenty feet away. Aerial protection for the paratroopers came from Puff the Magic Dragon and its vicious array of miniguns. The C-47 flew fire support missions for Bravo Company as well as Dog. Grunts at both locations took great comfort in the neon light-like streams of tracer rounds that poured out of the miniguns. Thousands of rounds per minute chewed up the ground around the base of Hill 823. Sometimes the rounds came frighteningly close to the Sky Soldiers. Sergeant Hill was pelted with clods of dirt several times as the bullets carved furrows in the ground in front of his bunker. He was terrified that the friendly fire would find him in his hole. The flare ship Spooky droned overhead throughout the night, too. One-million-candlepower flares were dropped every fifteen minutes, bathing the surrounding landscape in an eerie glow.[79]

At dawn, swarms of helicopter gunships and fighters arrived to dump ordnance as close as two hundred meters from the perimeter. This brought an end to the fighting. As the NVA faded from the scene, patrols were sent out to get an NVA body count and collect weapons. The area around the perimeter was littered with NVA equipment and bodies. Carefully prepared bunkers were also found, indicating that the NVA had been there for quite some time.

Although occasional harassing fire reminded Company B's men that remnants of the North Vietnamese force remained around Hill 823, the fight for that promontory was at an end. The Americans had prevailed.

> The enemy on Ngok Kom Leat had in the meantime disappeared with the coming of daylight on 7 November. Captain Muldoon's men [A and D Companies] spent most of the day searching the area, bringing in supplies, and moving wounded comrades to waiting helicopters. Muldoon's two companies linked up with Company C that morning as it came up from the west.
>
> Although Colonel Johnson had intended to consolidate all companies of his battalion during the day on the new, hard-won fire support base, the crash of a resupply helicopter as it was leaving Ngok Kom Leat and the requirement to secure its radios, machine guns, and other equipment forced him to delay the move. But now reinforcements for Company B were available from another source. The commander of the 173d Airborne Brigade, newly arrived in Dak To, made another company available. At midday helicopters brought Company C, 1st Battalion, 503d Infantry, to Hill 823. The next day, 8 November, Colonel Johnson at last got his entire 4th Battalion, 503d Infantry, together again on the hill. Although he intended pursuing the enemy toward the west, his superiors deemed it time the battalion had a short rest. That afternoon and the following day the 1st Battalion, 503d Infantry, phased in to replace Johnson's men.
>
> The fights on the Ngok Kom Leat and Hill 823 were but opening rounds in a battle that was to continue in the vicinity of Dak To for two and a half weeks, but in those rounds the 4th Battalion, 503d Infantry, had driven at least a portion of the North Vietnamese 66th Regiment back toward the Cambodian border and materially lessened the threat to Dak To.[80]

U.S. losses were 15 KIA and 48 wounded. The NVA 66th Regiment lost 117 KIA, and one prisoner was taken. Hill 823 was redesignated FSB 15.

Task Force

The 1/503d battalion was commanded by Lieutenant Colonel David J. Schumacher, who was well known for putting his career ahead of everything else.

Captain McElwain [C/1/503rd] took an instant disliking to Colonel Schumacher. He, too, felt Schumacher epitomized the ticket puncher so prevalent in the army's officer corps. He viewed his battalion commander as an opportunist, far more interested in furthering his career and accumulating combat glory than in caring for his men. After one particular action at Tuy Hoa, for example, Schumacher had ordered his staff to prepare a recommendation awarding him the Silver Star. McElwain knew the award was a sham and was openly pleased when brigade rejected the recommendation.[81]

Schumacher was ordered to pursue the NVA after the fight on Hill 823. Against the admonitions of Colonel Livsey, he divided his battalion into two small task forces from his companies to accomplish the mission. TF Black would be commanded by Captain Thomas McElwain. His Charlie Company received two platoons from Delta Company. TF Blue would be commanded by Captain David Jesmer. It would include his Alpha Company and the remaining platoon of Delta. B/1/503 would remain on FSB 15 to provide security.[82] TF Black would move 2 KM west of FSB 15 (Hill 823) and would then turn south toward Hill 889. TF Blue would depart FSB 15 moving southeast and then turn back to the west. The two TFs would rendezvous at Hill 889. The task forces started down Hill 823 on 10 November. As they neared the base of the hill, NVA occupation of the area appeared. NVA contact was expected, but TF Blue moved a kilometer from Hill 823 and laagered without incident. TF Black continued to move but ran into an NVA communications line on the trail. McElwain tapped into the line and got a ring back: the line was hot and the NVA were close by. He called the info in to the battalion S-3, who warned him "Be careful, Tom. The little people are all over the place."[83] TF Black laagered about two KM from Hill 823. After an uneventful night, the two TFs would move out on 11 November to link up near Hill 889.

Task Force Blue was led by Lieutenant Ed Robertson's platoon. Blue was slowed down by the scout dog and handler. The dog frequently alerted as it detected the NVA. Captain Jesmer, commander of TF Blue, soon came to disregard the dog's alerts, which was a mistake. At two hundred meters from Jesmer's starting point, the jungle exploded in front of him with NVA fire. In response, Jesmer pulled back and ordered his mortars to provide covering fire. This was followed by close air support. The fighters unloaded five-hundred-pounders on the NVA. Sa Won Chang was leading the point squad for Alpha Company and described the action.

> Our squad (only six or seven men, due to shortage of personnel) moved out with me on point, PFC Herbert right behind me, the RTO, and four other members, with one patrol dog and his handler, following [a] trail westerly all morning, encountering NVA's bloodied bandages and cooked rice thrown on the trail.
> Every time we stopped for rest of the company to catch up, our platoon leader, 1LT Kennemer, was calling me to be extra careful, because NVAs were around with a PRC 25. If the scout dog alerted, then I'd send out a clover leaf patrol to check out the immediate area of interest.
> On or about 1430 hours or 1500 hours, I saw a lone rucksack about fifty or seventy-five meters ahead of my location. So we moved and got to the rucksack and found that the rucksack was soaked with blood. So I motioned squad members to come forward and sent them out on another clover leaf patrol and to look out for a grave or graves for intelligence purposes. While the clover leaf patrol was out, myself and PFC Herbert right behind me moved forward, following the trail that was bending toward north. We had moved about fifty or so meters when I encountered an NVA soldier standing in his foxhole in middle of the trail, looking, smiling at me.
> I brought up my M-16 and started firing at him; at same time, PFC Herbert threw a grenade and blew up the foxhole. At same time, NVA heavy machine guns were firing all around us. Then I saw an NVA with bandages wrapped around his head get up right behind the just-blown foxhole and run across the trail diagonally from where I was kneeling. He was so close that I forgot about the M-16 in my hand; instead I was pulling my bayonet. At the same time, he was running into the woodline,

where heavy MGs were firing. Then I lifted up my M-16 and fired after him. Then I got up, running and firing at the same time at the blown foxhole and surrounding area. With running momentum, I jumped and rolled over the small bushes. To my surprise, I was facing a newly dug foxhole. Without thinking, I pulled my last grenade and tossed. It hit loose dirt around the foxhole. I hugged ground and counted for three thousand (3 seconds); it was a dud. Then I looked to my right and saw PFC Sam Charmichael. I told him to throw me a hand grenade. I threw the hand grenade and heard an explosion. I ran fifty or so meters where we had first encountered the first foxhole and found 1LT Kennemar telling me to pull back, because PFC Herbert was dead. I looked at lying PFC Herbert and saw his feet were moving, so told the lieutenant that Herbert wasn't dead and ran out and grasped his pistol belt and dragged him back to platoon line (by then the rest of the platoon had set up a perimeter). Medics and other squad members carried PFC Herbert further back to the safe area.

The 3rd Platoon linked up with the point squad of D/1/503rd on the late afternoon of 12 November 1967, and then we swept the NVA-held ground and found many shallow NVA graves and fox holes. A Company moved on to the D/1/503rd area. We found many shallow graves throughout the area. An NVA unit had had a run-in with Delta Company, 1/503rd, the day before, and they were licking their wounds when our squad stumbled on them.

The 1st SGT Sam Duckett went to the first foxhole and pulled an NVA soldier out of the hole and took out a large radio from the foxhole. I went to the second foxhole and found the dud hand grenade still lodged on newly dug loose dirt with NVA's right hand.

We stayed two or three days in and around area between Hill 823 and Hill 889. A company had an award ceremony for the gallant soldiers by the 173rd Brigade commanding general, BG Schweiter. I believe it was on 13 or 14 November 1967. I also received a Bronze Star medal for the actions on 12 Nov. 1967.

In 1994, Dave Herbert came and visited with us. He is paralyzed and living in Salt Lake City area, Utah.[84]

By 1100 hours, the TF Blue fight was over. Jesmer surveyed the scene and was impressed by the NVA dead. They were well-equipped with brand new uniforms and weapons. These were fresh NVA arrivals from North Vietnam. While the fight was temporarily over for TF Blue, it was just starting for TF Black.

As the day started for TF Black on 11 November, Captain McElwain followed the NVA communications wire found the day before. A platoon was sent in each direction at 0800 hours. One platoon had traveled less than 150 meters when the point man saw an NVA trail-watcher and fired, wounding the NVA soldier. The platoon was inching down a fifty-meter-wide finger that was narrowing as they moved. A second trail-watcher was seen and killed: another new arrival from North Vietnam. As Lieutenant Gerald Cecil's platoon was following the wire, he sensed that they were about to be hit and pulled back his platoon into a defensive position. His sixth sense saved his platoon, because as they moved back, NVA fire exploded to their front. Had they moved any farther forward, the platoon would have been wiped out by the NVA ambush. As fire on Cecil increased, Captain McElwain sent another platoon forward to reinforce Cecil. As the volume of NVA fire increased around him, Captain McElwain ordered all of his troops to assemble on him. TF Black's 170 troops were now completely surrounded by an NVA battalion.

TF Black was now in dire straits. TF Blue was still tied up but could move to reinforce TF Black later. Bravo Company, 1/503d, was still back at Hill 823, guarding FSB 15, and could not be moved, so General Schweiter, commander of the 173d, ordered 4/503d to rush a company to TF Black immediately. An LZ less than a kilometer from TF Black was located, and the rescue attempt was in progress by 1115. Ammunition was running out, and the resupply failed, as the helicopters, under heavy fire, kicked the ammunition crates out the door and watched them tumble down the hill, out of TF Black's reach. The battle raged until 1300, as troopers searched their dead to retrieve ammunition.

Captain Bill Connolly, C/4/503d, had just returned from Ben Het when he was ordered to reinforce Task Force Black. Charlie Company troops were ready and eager for the rescue attempt, but the lift helicopters did not arrive to pick up the company at FSB 12 until 1300. They started delivering C/4/503d a short time later. Gary Walls remembered the action.

> We sat, waiting for the Hueys. Over the radio handsets, heavy gunfire could be heard when the trapped companies transmitted. Stomachs were light, and everyone seemed preoccupied with their silent thoughts. The prospects of wading into a vicious, close-up firefight had finally materialized. The warm earth and blue sky suddenly seemed more intense, more *alive* and worldlier to me—then the Hueys skimmed over the distant hilltops and ridgelines. Our ride had arrived.
>
> The line of slicks approached and set down near us. We automatically moved towards them through the warm, churning air and climbed aboard. The rotors whirled harder, that familiar *whop-whop-whop* sound, and the helicopter lifted off the ground, blasting dust into the air. Gunships preceded the Hueys, and the fleet of helicopters flew over the green jungle in the general direction of the border area where we'd been earlier. After a few minutes, the gunships pulled ahead and began firing rockets into a section of jungle not far from a hilltop. The bamboo exploded in brief flashes of bright yellow light followed by flying chunks of earth and spinning fragments of bamboo. The mini-guns raked the heavy foliage, slashing at the jungle. The pilot set our Huey down quickly, hovering over the shattered and still smoking ground. We poured out of the slick and took up positions around our part of an LZ blown out of the jungle with rockets. Before the choppers had all taken off, Sgt. Goins motioned us to follow and gave a directional arm signal. We climbed through the broken bamboo and started up a ridge, dense with growth, as the Hueys were pulling up.[85]

At nearly the same time, TF Blue was ordered to move to reinforce TF Black. TF Black now had two separate rescue parties on the way to them, but TF Blue was soon blocked and had to call in artillery support. TF Blue would not reach Black by nightfall and was ordered to laager until the next morning. PFC Steven C. Vorthmann, C/4/503rd, had been in country a month and recalled the situation.

> Dak To was in the very northwest corner of II Corps, several kilometers from the borders of Laos, Cambodia, and I Corps. The North Vietnamese Army (NVA) was very active in the area. C Company was involved in three firefights in my first month in the field—November 6, 11, and 20–24. I thought, "Well, I guess this is what it's going to be like, so get used to it." On November 11, I received a very minor RPG shrapnel wound in the leg, for which I received a tetanus shot and a Purple Heart. I believe two or three guys to my immediate left were killed.[86]

At 1330 the NVA volume of fire increased as C/4/503d moved to TF Black's perimeter. Gary Walls recalled:

> Speed and silence were of the essence, and we pushed up the ridge until the ground leveled off to where we knew we were on top of the ridge. Pausing for several minutes, we caught our breath and crouched behind cover, waiting for the others to close up. The crackle of automatic weapons started up several hundred meters away and swelled into a roar that crashed and echoed across the jungle: the 1st Battalion's companies were being subjected to another ground attack. The deeper-sounding machine guns joined in; then the intensity fell off and gradually became a series of scattered shots. We had continued to move up the ridge once the second platoon came up. I lost all awareness of the weight of my rucksack or how far we had traveled. We silently moved along the ridge top towards the captured harbor [laager] site, and all at once we were there and I could see a small hammock strung between two trees ahead of me and several bunkers in front of us. There was not any movement, and I rapidly moved along to my left, watching our flank, while getting up to the line of bunkers.
>
> Miles, who was also a grenadier, quickly rushed up on the one bunker that turned out to be occupied. Two young North Viets were inside the hole and evidently had not been paying any attention. It was utterly fantastic, what with all the firing just several hundred meters away, but they were talking and only noticed Miles at the last moment. One made a move for his AK, but Miles was right on top

of them and pushed the ominous snout of his 40mm grenade launcher into their faces while shaking his head. Two mouths dropped open and four hands rose into the air, and they were dragged from the bunker, terrified, as C Company reoccupied the lost harbor site without firing a shot. (Miles's reward was the standing three-day pass for each prisoner, or six days' furlough for him.) I had nearly caught two litter-bearing enemy soldiers who had been carrying one of their severely wounded men up the trail (to my left) to the harbor site. They must have seen our people moving within the perimeter, for I only heard the momentary sound of feet fleeing and brief movement before coming across the badly wounded North Viet lying on a litter and twitching with a fatal head wound.

Down the ridge before me, from where the litter bearers had come, the sound of firing was beginning again and swelled into a massive roar. The tempo increased rapidly, and only the heavier sounding M-60s were distinct from the M-16s and AK-47s, and grenades exploded loudly, adding to the cacophony. Another ground attack was under way. Sgt Goins quickly swung the squad around to the left. A photographer, who had hitched a ride along, was right up front with us. Miles became impatient, though, feeling that the man was only in the way. I grinned and whispered to the photographer not to pay any attention to Miles, who then complained, "Well, shit, man, those fuckers are *shooting* at us and *this* guy wants to take pictures!"[87]

PFC John A. Barnes, an M-60 machine gunner in 1/503d, had been badly wounded and was at the aid station when an enemy grenade landed among the wounded. Barnes threw himself on the grenade to save his buddies and was killed. Barnes was awarded the Medal of Honor for his actions that day in spite of Colonel Schumacher's attempt to stop the award. Schumacher did not think that medals should be given to people who committed suicide.[88] The wounded did their best to help each other. Sergeant Wooldridge had a shattered left knee and hobbled along with another trooper who lost his right foot. They supported each other as NVA fire continued to hit around them. C/4/503rd linked up with TF Black, and the enemy fire subsided at 1530 as the NVA departed. Gary Walls recalled more:

> Having made contact on our right with our own people (not our point element, though, but those coming from behind), we quickly pressed ahead, crouching over as we moved ahead. Acrid powder smoke drifted through the jungle. Suddenly a whooshing explosion blasted from my left and something, most likely a B-40 rocket-propelled grenade, went past me, flaming. I hit the ground again and looked ahead in time to see little holes starting to appear in the bamboo and accompanied by the loud popping sounds like firecrackers. The 1st Battalion's guys were shooting at us, the NVA, and the North Viets were firing rocket-propelled grenades as well. Fladry quietly asked me if I was all right. I said, yes, I was, and we both got up and continued.
>
> Around some thick bushes we came into view of the ambush site. Several dead Americans lay on the ground in a small clearing. The living were behind the bodies, using them for cover. Rifle barrels wiggled and faces appeared. Some were crying from the release of the immense tension, but all were smiling beneath the dirt and bloody bandages. They had believed, basically, that they had *had* it. Bodies of North Vietnamese soldiers lay crumpled where they had fallen, their weapons still clutched in their dead hands. In some places their dead and ours were mingled together. The fighting was desperate and to the death. The foliage down the slope began moving and the rapid firing of AKs began again, the bullets popping overhead. The American perimeter promptly raked the jungle in return, and the firefight seemed to start anew. But the shooting did not seem to be as heavy as before. I heard the banging sound of three or four mortar rounds being fired. Fladry whispered, "Mortars!" and we pressed ourselves on the ground, as if we could get lower than we were. The terrible seconds ticked by as the 82mm rounds arced high and plunged to earth, "walking" almost methodically across our perimeter. The beat of explosions swept over our largely unprotected positions. One round landed near us, and there was an ear-splitting explosion. Something hit my right leg hard. I had the peculiar mental image of being struck in the leg with a hammer. The feeling quickly faded as my lower right leg went semi-numb and I could feel the wet, bloody pant-leg clinging to my skin. My first fear was that my shinbone was broken and, if the North Vietnamese pressed a mass attack and broke through our perimeter, I would be in a nearly impossible situation. I felt along my right shin while still lying flat and was relieved that the tibia was untouched; a fragment of steel had gone into the flesh next

to the bone. I told Fladry I had been hit, and he crawled around and tore my pant leg to have a look. "Well, it looks like you've got a Purple Heart," he said.[89]

Resupply helicopters arrived and dropped supplies, but attempts to evacuate the wounded failed. Walls continued:

The morning of November 12th dawned cold, and many were wrapped in poncho liners. I clutched my scrap of vinyl [picked up from a dead NVA soldier] like an alley bum, shivering, until the sun warmed up the air. I looked around the perimeter and was happy to see my rucksack piled up with a few others. Someone had been thoughtful enough to bring them back up after all. My C-rations were gone, but I expected that—1st Bat's men had not eaten for most the entire day. My few personal belongings were untouched. I fished out my little camera and took several pictures, but the light was poor and the photographs didn't turn out. Those of us who were wounded were tagged by the medics and put in a group to await the arrival of the medevac flights once they resumed. The clearing patrols silently reentered the perimeter (after an icy stand-to). I understand that they saw maybe two dozen NVA dead littering the jungle beyond where we were, possibly killed by artillery fire or when the weapons platoon had defended the perimeter, but I cannot state that as a fact. I turned my equipment over to the other grenadiers, chiefly to Miles, and whatever else I had that might be useful to them, or anyone else, although I thought I would be back in a couple of days. Several medevacs had come in and left with a load of wounded, and I was scheduled to go out on the next flight. The firefight had cost numerous lives, as I remember, and forty or more wounded, and the enemy's casualties were unknown but may have been around seventy dead altogether. It is difficult to say. Their facilities for treating their wounded were limited and Spartan; the firefight could have put the better part of two enemy companies out of action.[90]

At dawn on 12 November, the grisly task of recovering the dead and counting enemy bodies started. Total U.S. casualties were heavy. Twenty were KIA, nearly 190 wounded, and two missing. Captain McElwain's initial body count was between seventy and eighty NVA dead. Schumacher was outraged by the low count, "Goddamnit, Captain, you lose twenty people and you expect me to accept a body count of seventy? You go back there tomorrow and find me some more bodies."[91] The two argued some and settled on a body count of 175. Intelligence later determined that the companies had fought against the 8th and part of the 9th battalions of the 66th NVA Regiment.

173rd Airborne Brigade Long Range Reconnaissance Platoon (LRRP) at Dak To, 1967

Irvin (Bugs) Moran tells the story of the LRRP at Dak To:

The 173rd LRRP first arrived in the tri-border area of Dak To in June of 1967. The brigade's three parachute infantry battalions were engaging North Vietnamese Army (NVA) units in the mountains surrounding the Dak To base camp at this time, and LRRP teams were needed for reconnaissance patrols. Our platoon at this time consisted of 35 to 38 enlisted members and one officer. The teams consisted of five or six men who conducted long-range missions that could last for five to seven days.

Infiltrations were done at either first or last light via choppers. These LRRP missions in the Dak To area that summer of 1967 were extremely dangerous and exhausting. The jungle terrain in this mountainous tri-border area has been described as some of the wildest and most rugged jungle environment in the entire Southeast Asia region. Attempting to move silently through these unforgiving mountain ridges and ravines was extremely difficult. The trees were double and sometimes triple canopy, which gave the entire area a very dark and dreary appearance. In addition to the North Vietnamese, LRRP teams ran into just about every species of animals that called this godforsaken place

A 173rd LRRP Team at Dak To. Left to right: Ray Freeman, Rick Brooks, Art Silsby, Freddie Williams, and McLaughlin (courtesy Irvin "Bugs" Moran).

home. Open areas that allowed for ingress and egress by choppers were very hard to find, and if a team was compromised and pursued by NVA units, extraction by ropes (McGuire rigs) was the only way out.[92]

Our 173rd LRRP teams located and observed numerous NVA units moving both in and out of the Dak To area that June, July, and August of 1967, and some teams were compromised, resulting in very up-close and personal engagements. Teams located both old and fresh bunker complexes in all four compass directions surrounding the Dak To basecamp. Some missions intended for five to seven days ended abruptly, such as my first mission just west of the Dak To base camp in July. As our five-man team exited the chopper, we immediately received intensive fire from a size-undetermined NVA unit that was located right next to the LZ. The choppers were able to successfully extract us, resulting in a mission of roughly 15 minutes. Our goal of locating the NVA had been accomplished!

To the relief of most LRRP members, we were taken out of the Dak To area during the first part of September 1967. These Dak To missions had been exceedingly difficult, and everyone was looking forward to easier missions in the mountains west of the coastal area of Tuy Hoa. The 173rd LRRP had no desire to return to that death-shrouded place called Dak To.

Fate intervened. During the first week of November 1967, our platoon was alerted for a move from the beaches of our base camp in Tuy Hoa back to Dak To. The 173rd parachute battalions had already returned to Dak To and were being hit hard. We arrived back at the Dak To base camp around November 7th, and virtually all six to seven teams were immediately inserted by choppers into the mountains surrounding the Dak To airstrip. Most teams observed heavy NVA activities in this entire tri-border area.

While on these missions, our teams were kept apprised of all the enemy contacts being made by the three 173rd battalions. All teams were extracted and returned to the Dak To base camp as the battle for Hill 875 developed. When LRRP teams were out on missions, major air assets were held in standby for immediate extraction of a team in trouble. At this time, these assets were needed for aid and relief of the embattled 173rd line companies on Hill 875. The LRRP members were extremely frustrated. We knew we could get onto that hill faster than any other unit, but brigade headquarters would not allow it. Our commanding officer at the time, Lt. Jim Parkes, took three team leaders down to the chopper pads at the Dak To airstrip and volunteered to rappel onto the hill with LZ clearing kits, ammo, and medical supplies. Saner minds prevailed, and this plan was also denied. Lt. Parkes was allowed to board a chopper headed to Hill 875 on November 20th with the plan of kicking out LZ clearing kits over the makeshift command post. This chopper received horrendous small arms fire while over the hill, and Lt. Parkes received career-ending wounds. His extreme valor that day is not known to many.

When Hill 875 was taken on November 23th, our teams were again inserted on missions surrounding Dak To, with the intent of locating the NVA units retreating back into Laos and Cambodia via the infamous Ho Chi Minh trails. On December 1st, a large NVA unit was located just east of the area where the borders of Laos and Cambodia join Vietnam. I was point man on this mission. We ran headlong into the NVA point element and were able to eliminate it. We had no doubt that this NVA unit was retreating back into either Laos or Cambodia after the heavy fighting of the past few weeks. It quickly became apparent that this NVA unit knew it had run into a small reconnaissance team, and they immediately started pursuing us through the steep mountainous terrain. We succeeded in finding a very small opening in the triple canopy jungle, and three choppers snatched six of us out via McGuire rig ropes. Two team members dangled 120 feet below each of the three choppers as we flew 20 minutes at 5,000 feet back to a 4th Division fire support base. This panoramic view of the Dak To mountains was priceless, but not one that anyone wanted to see again. Our 173rd LRRP left the Dak To area in the middle of December. These 1967 missions in Dak To tested the abilities and perseverance of every platoon member. The memories of these missions of almost 50 years ago are still with us today.[93]

The FSB 16 Fight

While TF Black was fighting for its life near Hill 889, other contacts with the NVA were occurring in the vicinity of Dak To. The 173d Long Range Reconnaissance Platoons (LRRPs) were constantly combing the area and finding signs of the NVA. Four separate NVA regiments were located: the 32d moving west, the 24th northeast of Dak To, and the 174th that was moving south of Ben Het in order to screen for the 66th, so that it could escape across the Cambodian border. The 66th had been badly mauled by the 173d around Hill 823. What was needed was a good location where the 66th could be blocked to prevent its escape. The search for a new fire support base was launched. It would be named FSB 16. A location used during a previous operation was selected. It was five kilometers southwest of Hill 823 and only seven kilometers from the Cambodian border. On 10–11 November, the site was pounded by B-52s and close air support aircraft. The air assault of two companies from the 2/503d into the new fire support base was scheduled for 0900, but it had to be slipped to 1430 because helicopter lift was still supporting the fighting near Hill 889. The two companies, Bravo and Delta, landed unopposed shortly after their liftoff. Engineers started expanding the LZ in preparation for the arrival of the rest of the battalion the next day.

On 12 November, A/2/503, commanded by Captain Michael J. Kiley, was on the ground and ordered to search the nearby high ground for the NVA. C/2/503rd under Captain Kaufman also landed. Alpha Company departed FSB 16 at 0930, 12 November. Four hundred meters west of FSB 16, the dog alerted. Sergeant Lance D. Peebles was leading the point squad and ordered the dog released. Before that could happen, the surrounding jungle exploded with heavy NVA fire concentrated on Sergeant Peebles's squad. Peebles's platoon leader moved down the slope to support as Kiley ordered another platoon to reinforce. The two platoons joined and laid down a heavy volume of fire as Peebles rejoined his platoon. NVA fire subsided, and Kiley moved to continue his mission. Soon the entire company was engulfed in fire, and casualties started to mount. The meaning of the company nickname, "No Return Alpha," became apparent to the FNGs.[94] Alpha Company pulled back near Bravo Company, but it was evident that the NVA was between the two companies and firing heavily on both. Colonel Steverson ordered Charlie Company to reinforce, while artillery and close air support rained down on the NVA. By 1400, the NVA fire subsided, and work started to evacuate the wounded. A prisoner revealed that the 2/503d was attacked by the 174th NVA Regiment, the unit ordered to assist the withdrawal of the 66th NVA Regiment.

Dusk arrived by 1730, and 13 November was a quiet night. The companies returned to FSB 16 the next morning. Colonel Steverson ordered two companies to move out to secure an unnamed hill nearby, less than one hundred meters away. It was a long go-round to get there, and at 1545 hours, Bravo Company halted to look for a good laager site. At that time, the point man observed two bunkers and came under fire. Lieutenant Phillip Bodine moved his platoon together. Lieutenant C. Allen McDevitt's platoon nearby was also under attack. Captain James P. Rogan, B/2/503d commander, called in artillery and close air support, but the NVA was too close, less than twenty meters, to effectively adjust fire without hitting his own troops.

The fight had been going on for over an hour when Rogan ordered a withdrawal, but it was easier said than done. He needed to push the NVA back so that he could recover his wounded. To do that, he sent in two more platoons, and they were ordered to counterattack. It worked, and most of the wounded were recovered.

Medevac helicopters were brought in but were driven off by heavy NVA fire. The wounded would spend the night within the perimeter, and during the night, several died. At dawn, the NVA had disappeared, and Rogan ordered patrols out to find the remaining wounded. They were successful. One NVA soldier was shot dead while going through the pockets of a wounded trooper. By 0900, medevac helicopters started the lift of wounded back to FSB 16. Bravo Company was hard hit during the battle, losing twenty-one KIA and seventeen wounded. During the morning of 14 November, artillery fire, close air support, and mortars pounded the area, followed by sweeps that found thirty-four NVA bodies. Bravo Company was replaced by Charlie Company and returned to FSB 16. Search-and-destroy operations in the area continued.

Meanwhile, back at Dak To, an event occurred that would have a major impact upon Operation MacArthur. On the night of 12 November, the NVA launched the first of what would become a series of rocket attacks on Dak To airfield. On 15 November, three C-130 transport aircraft were in the turn-around area of the runway when three rounds landed on them, destroying two. Gary Luoma was an MP assigned to the 173rd. He remembered that several crew members were killed. "One of my assignments was to pick up people from the C-130 that got hit. I took the pilot, copilot, and engineer back to the 4ID or 173rd. The four-engine plane, one of the largest planes over there, burned to the ground."[95] The aircraft, with full fuel tanks, were burning furiously when additional rounds set ammunition and fuel tanks afire. Shelling continued into the night, when a lucky (for the NVA) round hit two C-4 (plastic explosives) containers, and they both detonated. This sent a fireball into the sky that could be seen for miles.[96]

One account said that people a mile away were knocked down by the blast. One soldier near the detonation said that the blast lifted him off of his feet and tossed him into a bunker. He was not injured. Two craters over forty feet deep were found in the clean-up after the fire. It was said to be the biggest explosion of the Vietnam War and destroyed over 1,100 tons of munitions. Miraculously, there were no fatalities, but there were several injuries. Lieutenant Fred Dyerson witnessed the event and later said, "It looked like Charlie had gotten hold of nuclear weapons."[97] Major General William B. Rosson, at IFFV headquarters in Nha Trang, now had a major task ahead of him. Replacing the massive loss of ordnance

The burning C-130s at Dak To airstrip (4th ID tents in the foreground), 15 November 1967 (courtesy Charles L. Gove).

in the middle of a major campaign became his top priority. By pulling and lifting resources from all over the theater, he was able replace items needed without slowing down the campaign.

Fight for Hill 882

While Dak To airfield was burning on the morning of 15 November, the 1/503 moved out from the area near Hill 889, where they had just finished the fight against the NVA 66th Regiment. Captain Jesmer's Alpha Company was in the lead, followed by Delta Company under Captain Thomas Needham's command. Captain McElwain's Charlie Company was in the rear. They were looking for NVA survivors of the TF Black fight and were following up on intelligence reports of NVA in the area. Signs of NVA were found on the first day, but there was no contact. They moved out the next morning in the same order of march. Lieutenant Ed Robertson's platoon was in the lead, and at 1145 hours, his point man saw an NVA soldier and fired. Heavy return fire sent the troops diving for cover. Captain Jesmer assembled his platoons and called in artillery and air support. Robertson's platoon was on the right, and he was frustrated because he could not force the NVA out of their positions. He called Captain Jesmer. "Captain, the fucking gooks are in trenches and nothing we do gets to them." At first Jesmer didn't believe Robertson about the trenches. Then 1st Sgt Duckett got his attention and pointed uphill. Through a break in the bamboo and trees, they could see an enemy soldier appear out of a trench and toss grenades at four of Lieutenant John Robinson's men lying behind a log. "I'll be damned," Jesmer said.[98] John Robinson recalled:

> 1st Sgt Duckett then came to the 1st Platoon sector of the perimeter. All the platoons were in contact, and we were trying to figure out how and where their trench system tied in with the bunkers. Rounds were routinely coming in over our heads; then one cracked much closer, missing us by inches. We hit the dirt, and the 1st Sgt. said, "A damn sniper; check the trees." Seeing nothing, we returned to our kneeling position. Moments later, another round; this time it went between us. I said, "I didn't see a thing in the trees." Top exclaimed, "He's not in the trees; that one came straight at us, so the son of a bitch must be in that huge stand of bamboo to our right front." "Well, these damn pee shooters won't penetrate that bamboo, and I can't pull a 60 off the line, so I'll get an M-79," I replied. "Wait, maybe we can do something else. Do you still have that white phosphorus grenade that you've been humping all over the AO?" he asked. "Yeah," I responded. "Let me have it; I think I have a better angle than you. Cover me, and I'll try to lob it between those two large stocks just right of center," he said. On his signal, I emptied a magazine as he slung the Willie Pete in a high arch. At first it sailed like a perfect forward pass, then started to tumble end over end, and landed exactly as he had envisioned. It exploded just as it disappeared in the bamboo, and the sniper came out screaming, covered in the burning liquid. He ran at a 45-degree angle from the 1st Sgt., who stitched him from his butt to his head. "Damn, Top, you should have played pro ball," I exclaimed in admiration.[99]

Artillery and air support pounded the NVA positions, and they left at about 1400. Alpha Company moved into the NVA positions and were surprised by the extent of the abandoned trench system. Large command bunkers were well entrenched into hillsides that provided overhead cover. A 12.7mm antiaircraft gun was found and quickly evacuated back to Dak To.[100] This sort of weapon would be deadly against assault helicopters. To complicate his life, Jesmer received correspondents, who arrived on resupply helicopters. The distraction of non-combatants when contact was expected was something that he did not need. Sa Won Chang in A/1/503rd provided his account of the action:

> A Company moved out in a southwesterly direction. Our platoon was in the rear on 16 November 1967, and we were moving toward Hill 889. Early in the afternoon, the point platoon started receiving enemy fire, and soon after, the point platoons returned fire. From the enemy shouting, we knew where the NVA soldiers were. The NVA soldiers were firing and tossing hand grenades at the point platoon. Then our 105mm artillery rounds started pounding the enemy locations on Hill 889. Our Platoon was securing the rear, and I told my squad members to dig in. We started digging ground as fast as we could and found very soft dirt, so with the D-handle shovels that we had, we didn't have much trouble digging.
>
> Then fast movers [U.S. close air support jet aircraft] came in pairs, flying low, and strafed with their 20mm cannons. We stopped digging and jumped into the holes we had just been digging. We could feel the 20mm rounds hitting all around us, thunderous jets screaming right over us, and big explosions as 500-pound bombs detonated on enemy positions. We yelled for them to drop more bombs. Then we continued digging foxholes in case we might have to stay in this location longer. With the artillery barrage and close air support, A Company started to move up the hill. Our squad came up the hill and found neatly dug deep trenches interlocked with each other. We ran clearing patrols all around the trenches, and NVA deserted the area, but we found many bloodied objects in the area that indicated many wounded and perhaps KIA enemy soldiers.
>
> I have to mention what kind of combat-related items were carried by combat soldiers on load-bearing harness: pistol belt, two ammo pouches with six magazines filled with ammunition, two or three hand grenades, two water canteens, one or two smoke grenades, a bayonet with scabbard, and a lensatic compass w/case. Items to be carried in rucksack: 600 rounds of M-16 ammunition (30 or

35 loaded magazines) in an empty claymore mine bag, one M-72 LAW, ten empty sandbags for foxhole sides and overhead cover, one claymore mine, one stick of C4 explosive, one machete (jungle sword) to break trail or cut trees down for overhead covers, a trip flare w/wire, three days of C-rations, one poncho, one poncho liner, one waterproof bag, one air mattress, one round of 81mm mortar round (rotating basis within squad) from the weapons platoon, personal items: toothbrush (rarely used), razor and blade, writing tablet. Steel helmet w/liner. Items to be carried by hand: M-16 rifle. Other items: Pick and wooden handle, D handle (regular construction shovel). The pick and D-handle shovels were rotated within fire teams. We never used entrenching tools (it takes too long to dig a hole chest-deep and four men wide). Total weight of the rucksack is about 60 to 70 pounds.

A Company also had many news reporters and motion picture producers join us on or about 16 November 1967. Hot chow was flown in, and serving stations were set up. While we were going through the chow line, news reporters and motion picture producers were taking pictures. I heard news reporters were from NBC and Army Information Agencies. Also there was a young, courageous female reporter, whom I would never forget because of brave actions shown by her on Hill 882.[101]

At dawn on 17 November, the 1/503d moved in pursuit of the NVA. By nightfall, they were approaching Hill 882. Still no enemy contact. After a quiet night, Jesmer broke camp and moved forward on Hill 882 at 0730, 18 November. The 1st Platoon was in the lead. Sergeant Thomas Means was in A Company, Lieutenant John Robinson's 1st platoon. He recalled the scene.

We arrived in the central highlands in the fall of '67. Our first day there, we were all given five-gallon cans for a shower, issued new jungle boots and clothing (everything we had was rotted out). Quite a few us got whiskey and beer and then commenced to get drunk. Second day, next AM, they called assembly and had a chaplain speak to all of us. Next, they had hot food. It was really rare to get hot food, not to mention that we were allowed to eat all that we wanted. We all knew that something was up. After that, we all loaded our rucksacks up with C's [C rations] and ammo. We were choppered out on search-and-destroy missions to various locations around Dak To. We stayed in the mountains for a long time with no going back—we had no base camp like we had at Bien Hoa. We had small fights until we hit Hill 882 in November 1967. We'd been on Hill 875 before second battalion [503rd] had their big encounter and had found lots of trenches and spider holes. November 17–18, '67 were my last days with A Company.

We began on November 18th, and I was pulling point [lead soldier] heading to Hill 882. We found that the NVA had carved steps in the mountainside up Hill 882. Our platoon leader, Lieutenant Robinson (a great person—one of a kind) radioed me to take the finger (ridge) up the hill instead of the steps. I remember a lot of booby traps along the way.

Once on top, Lieutenant Robinson sent out a small patrol. Wayne Hughes was point man on that patrol. They ran into an NVA patrol (which turned out to be more than just a patrol). Wayne and his team ran back firing. Sergeant Douglas Bruce Baum and I opened fire from each side of that trail. Doug and I stayed in our positions firing while our company made ready. There were two NVA machine guns that kept Doug and me pinned down. We were only ten meters apart when Doug was hit by machine gun fire. Ten fucking meters and I couldn't reach him to help. I tried twice. When I was able to fall back to the company, Lieutenant Robinson yelled and asked about Doug. I said he was dead—shortly after that Lieutenant Robinson shot a tracer round through the head of an NVA soldier that had a bead on me. Once I was back, I saw a medic working on Wayne Hughes. He was hit in the head. Wayne was extremely religious and was always combing his hair (Wayne is still religious, but a lot less hair now).

Shortly after, I was wounded by shrapnel from an RPG in my leg. That night I was back with the other wounded under my poncho, and James Powers asked me to go out and try to bring in Doug. I found out the next morning that Doug bled out from his wounds while trying to get back. I heard that Medic Dyer was killed upon reaching Doug. Just a week earlier I'd convinced Doug to send home a short-timer's letter (less than thirty days to go).

I got out of hospital in January '68 and was under Lieutenant Rosen in the rear. I pulled point and ran patrols for him. At the end of my time, I had to help graves registration and unload bodies from

A Company that were hit in another fight in the central highlands. The first body I was responsible for was Richard Wagner, my cousin.

I left the Republic of Vietnam in February 1968—not one day or night goes by that I don't think about it. You can't erase anything from that place: the smell, the screams, the firefights, the sounds of choppers, nothing—it's all intact in our memories. I must say that if it wasn't for my wife of forty-eight years, I'd be dead or incarcerated. I love you, Lana.[102]

By noon, Alpha Company was on a finger (a spur that juts out from high ground) leading to the top of the hill. Robinson's platoon started up the finger at 1315, and as Jesmer waited for a progress report, a B-40 rocket hit his CP. Meanwhile, Robinson reached the summit and prepared defensive positions, sending a squad out to recon the area. The squad ran into an NVA soldier and fired. When Jesmer heard the firing, he immediately moved Alpha toward the summit, followed by Delta and Charlie Companies. Robinson recalled:

> This quick action by Captain Jesmer may very well have prevented another "Battle of the Slopes" type action. "Big Dave," as we fondly called him (but not to his face), made exactly the right decision and made it quickly. He understood NVA tactics; fix, double envelop, encircle & annihilate. A platoon by itself could not survive. A platoon leader engaged in a firefight does not have the time or the assets to call in artillery, gunships, and/or Tac Air. That is the CO's job, and he has the tools. Caught in a situation like this, the CO has two choices: either have the platoon pull back to the company or reinforce. If the CO orders a pull-back, then the platoon leader has a double problem. He has to retrieve his point, which is in contact, or worse, the whole platoon and then retreat under fire, with the wounded. This makes his men an easy target and signals the enemy to increase their efforts. This option is not really an option at all, because even a seemingly light encounter can escalate in minutes to a life-or-death struggle. If the CO decides to reinforce, which should be SOP, he must do so quickly and in force. If he piecemeals, then the predictable result is disaster, as each reinforcing element becomes engaged and ultimately surrounded. To protect what is left of the Command Group, the CO must then call in supporting fire on the location of his already embattled troops. When making this decision, time is critical; mere minutes can make the difference between success or total disaster. The old adage "he who hesitates is lost" was never truer.[103]

The three companies took positions on the summit. The NVA attack was signaled by a sniper shot that killed one of the Alpha troopers. Heavy NVA fire exploded around the summit of Hill 882. Robinson counted at least a dozen machine guns firing on his position.[104] This was a major event; the NVA was making platoon-sized human-wave attacks. Snipers were taking their toll on the defenders, since they were in treetops looking down on the troops. One trooper was hit in the head, blowing part of his skull off. The medic calmly replaced the skull section and wrapped a bandage around the soldier's head. Many of the troops were firing skyward, trying to take out the snipers. One sniper was hit and landed on an M-60. The gunner's comment: "That scared the shit out of me."[105] At Captain Thomas Needham's position, he became concerned about the safety of the correspondents, and moving around his perimeter, he found a correspondent manning an M-60 that he had taken over from a wounded gunner. Other correspondents were helping the wounded.[106] When air support arrived, five-hundred-pounders and napalm landed within two hundred meters of Alpha Company, where most of the fighting was going on. Dust, smoke, and debris from the impacts helped the NVA, since it masked their attacks. After three hours of fighting, Robinson's 1st platoon had three unwounded members remaining, and Alpha Company's strength was down by a third. With casualties piling up, Jesmer called for medevac helicopters. Schumacher refused, ordering correspondents to be evacuated first. Apparently Schumacher was concerned about his career. A dead correspondent would cause negative media attention that could reflect unfavorably on Schumacher. Jesmer refused and Schumacher backed off, so the wounded were evacuated, while the correspondents stayed behind.[107] Two medevac lifts were accomplished before dark settled in. The correspondents and most of the wounded would spend the night on Hill 882. Sa Won Chang, A/1/503rd, related his experience on Hill 882.

> A Company moved out, and our 3rd Platoon was bringing up the rear. We knew the NVA was somewhere on Hill 882 because we found many bloodied bandages along the trail, but didn't run into the NVA. The male reporter approached me and asked me, "Do you think we'll see some actions today?" I told him we might and moved on toward Hill 882.
>
> Next day, our platoon was still bringing up the rear, moving up the ridge line to Hill 882, when we heard shots fired by point platoon. We stopped and took up secure positions. Adjacent to where I was, I saw cut-up trees lying around a ditch. So I went to the ditch and found it looked familiar to me. I jumped into the ditch and found it was not a ditch, but it was a foxhole that PFC Jones and I had made four months earlier when we didn't run into any NVA soldiers.
>
> Then someone yelled "saddle up." As soon as we put rucksacks on our shoulders, I saw a platoon in file start running, I mean running, up the ridge line. We were all running up toward crest of Hill 882. We didn't quite make it up there. Firefights were going on, and someone yelled "SNIPER UP ON TREES!" With that warning, I jumped over to a man who had an M-60 MG. I pulled the trigger and held the handle of the M-60. I started spraying bullets at the top of trees all around us until 1st Sergeant Duckett shouted "cease fire." I gave back the M-60 to the gunner, but firefights were going strong in direction of the point platoon.
>
> Moving up the ridge line, I found three or four male news reporters sitting on their rears. They had a dazed look on their faces. I walked up to the news reporter who asked me about having action. I said, "You wanted action and here you are, don't sit on your duff, cover yourselves." As we came up to the crest of the hill, we took off our rucksacks. At about same time, Fast Movers were flying over us, strafing with 20mm guns near where we were. We were popping smoke to let the FAC pilot know where we were, but that was impossible since we were all mixed up together with the NVA. About that time, the NVA opened up with all they had. At same time, I saw NVA mortar rounds hitting treetops all around us. I assumed that the NVA was firing at us with small arms to pin us down, while killing mortar shots were fired to finish us off. About the time I moved around and located the rest of my squad members, I designated an area to dig in to set up a perimeter and tie in to the left and right of rest of the 3rd Platoon.
>
> I heard someone yelling, saying, "Platoon Leader got hit!" My squad's perimeter was being shaped up, so I went back to find my platoon sergeant but couldn't find him. I did find Lieutenant Kennemer sitting with a bandage wrapped around his chest in a pit that we had dug in July. Lieutenant Kennemer didn't have his rucksack. So I asked him where his rucksack was, and he told me that it was in front of where my squad was. I ran to my squad area and looked forward and saw the lieutenant's rucksack. I retrieved the rucksack and took it Lieutenant Kennemer. I took out his poncho so he could lay down and also took out his canteen so he could drink water. When I came back to the squad area, I ordered members to be ready to fix bayonets in case of an NVA attack. At this time, I saw the female reporter running around taking pictures and talking to soldiers in the midst of explosions of NVA mortar rounds and small arms fire. I didn't see any male reporters doing that. Finally, things were calmed down and I went looking for my rucksack. I found it and discovered that a 20mm round went through one of pockets and demolished my can of peaches. I had saved it for a special deal to be made with a member of my squad to inflate my air mattress. I heard CO's RTO Sandstrom from Minnesota had lost both of his legs from a B-40 rocket attack. I met him again in Fitzsimmons General Hospital in May 1968. PFC Sam Carmichael died when his own hand grenade's pin was pulled accidentally by a tree branch; he was the soldier who threw me the hand grenade to destroy my second encounter with an NVA foxhole on 12 November 1967. In total we lost about 30 to 40 troopers [see Appendix D for listing of those killed]. Luckily, 1st squad didn't lose any soldiers that day.
>
> During the night of 18 November 1967, medevac choppers flew in to attempt to take all reporters to the rear; due to heavy enemy fire, the medevacs were aborted. We spent the night in our foxholes, ready to shoot at any moving human being. Wounded or dazed NVA soldiers were walking around within the perimeter. I heard sporadic rifle fires throughout the night. All of the reporters, the WIAs, and KIAs were flown out on 19 November 1967.[108]

General Westmoreland (left) awarding the Distinguished Service Cross to 2nd Lt. John Robinson. To Lt. Robinson's right is Cpt. Ronald Leonard, who also received the Distinguished Service Cross (courtesy John R. Robinson).

By dawn, 19 November, the NVA were gone. The wounded and the correspondents were airlifted out. The 1/503rd had clashed with the 66th NVA Regiment. The 1/503d had lost 7 KIA and 34 wounded. A sweep of the area found fifty-one NVA bodies. John Robinson recalled further:

> Jesmer. He made quick, sound decisions and never hesitated to use Artillery and Air assets. His insistence on letting "the heavy stuff" do its job, "then we'll go in" was sometimes questioned and even criticized by some, but never by his "grunts," who knew the consequences and thanked God that Big Dave was in command.[109]

And Sa Won Chang recalled:

> Early morning of 19 November 1967, our platoon went out on clearing patrol and found many dead NVA soldiers from our artillery and close air support, along with A Company's small arms fire. I'll

never forget about the two dead bodies of NVA soldiers. One with just the back of the skull left, which was covered with moving bugs and flies, and the other's face was purple in color, with his eyes looking right at me. We conducted the patrol without further incidents. On the night of 19 November 1967, we were lying near our foxholes when we heard the explosions of bombs and could feel the explosions through the ground. We were saying to each other: "Hey man, that's B-52 carpet bombing near Hill 875." We never went out for that night's bomb damage assessment patrol. A Company, 1/503rd, stayed around Hill 882 and conducted more patrols, but that was uneventful.[110]

Sp4 Gene Boedeker from Lieutenant John Robinson's 1st Platoon provided a minute-by-minute account of the battle.

I arrived in Vietnam in late May 1967. After two weeks of jungle training, I was assigned to A Company, 1st Battalion, 503rd Regiment. I spent 5½ months with the 173rd, all in the jungle. I'm proud to say that I had the best officers: Captain Jesmer and Lieutenant Robinson. We had the best 1st Sergeant, Samuel Duckett. All were liked and very respected by the men. The troops that I served with were very dependable in the worst situations; people like John Barthelemy, Tom Riley, James Coker, and many more.

We had been sent from Dak To to Tuy Hoa in September. When word got to us that we were going back to Dak To, there weren't too many smiles. It meant high mountains and many NVA. We had taken the hills around Dak To in June, and we returned in November to claim them back.

Gene Boedeker (left) with a visitor at Fort Hood, Texas, hospital in 1968 (courtesy Billy E. Boedeker).

The battles for Dak To raged for nearly the whole month of November, with some units of the 173rd in nearly constant contact somewhere. On November 15th, we made contact after being told to fill in a gap to our right. In the process, I exposed myself to an NVA soldier, and by some very good luck, he missed 10–12 times at approximately 20–30 feet. God only knows. On the 16th, while approaching Hill 889, our platoon was on point when rifle and machine gun fire broke out. John Barthelemy (Bart) was being shot at and came running down to where I was. As he retreated down the hill, he slid close to me, smiled, and said, "There's a bunch up there and they're pissed." We moved up the hill to a bomb crater that was possibly created in June. There were four of us in the crater: Bart, Tom Riley, Blackman, and I. As I peered up the mountain out of the bomb crater, a bullet narrowly missed my ear. I turned to Blackman and said be careful, you almost shot me in the ear. He informed me that it wasn't him. As I raised my head to look up the hill, again, I looked right up at the barrel of an NVA as he fired at about thirty feet. He missed, again. After a lot of tossing hand grenades, we retreated. Artillery and jets pounded the positions.

On the second day, the NVA let us get to the bomb crater: more grenades. While in the grenade-throwing contest, a grenade came by me and bounced toward Bart. I hollered, he rolled the wrong way, and landed squarely on top of it. He rolled, looked up, and smiled: "It's a dud." Lucky Bart. The general kept calling down to the captain and Lieutenant Robinson, telling them to attack. Tom Riley was behind a big log to the left of the bomb crater. Bart was behind a big mound of dirt from the bomb crater. To the right, Blackman and I were in the crater. I looked up: Tom was running up the hill to the left while Bart was running on the right, so I tried to catch up. The NVA retreated. We had the hill.

Lieutenant Robinson put us in the old NVA positions. The positions seemed shallow, so we started to dig and hit metal. We dug slowly, thinking that it was a booby trap. We uncovered a 12.7mm anti-aircraft gun and lots of ammo. There were weapons and ammo buried around the hill. They had planned to come back after we left.

On the morning of the 18th, Lieutenant Robinson took point, followed by Lieutenant Robertson's platoon. We were in the fight so fast that I thought that we were on point. We crossed Hill 882 to the saddle between Hills 875 and 882. Captain Jesmer told us we would have turkey and dressing on top of Hill 875. Our point man reported communications wire and steps cut into the ridge ahead of us and some bloody bandages scattered around the trail, possibly from the Hill 889 encounter. We were told to take up positions. Blackman and I took up positions on the left edge of the ridge. As soon as we were in position, the fight exploded: a steady volume of fire and explosions occurred. Leaves, dirt, debris and smoke filled the air. The volume of noise was intense. As the fight worked its way across the ridge, Blackman fired on movements. He concentrated on one clump of bushes that kept moving. Every time he would shoot, they would return fire. Then I notice that when he would shoot, someone above us would shoot. I rolled over on my back to see if I could pick the sniper out of the trees, above. When I rolled back over, there were two NVA firing a machine gun down the ridge toward Bart and the rest of the platoon. There was a tree in front of me and I couldn't bring my rifle around, so I took out a grenade, popped it [pulled the pin and released the lever] and rolled it down the hill to them. An NVA raised up and shot me in the mouth, knocked out my teeth and busted my lips. At first I lay there for a few seconds, and then realized that I wasn't dead. I started feeling for an exit wound and then bumped Blackman. He looked at me and said "Oh, shit." I wasn't really sure if the sniper, the gunner, or the one Blackman was shooting at had hit me.

We lay there for a few minutes and noticed how close the artillery and air support were hitting. The aircraft fire was impacting a few meters in front of us. I looked back and noticed the smoke marking friendly positions was about thirty meters behind us. We had not gotten the word to pull back and were hanging out there in front of the rest. Blackman and I started back to the perimeter with Sanders on my left. As the three of us started back, Sanders was shot in the back. He turned and fired at the NVA and I grabbed him as we headed back to the perimeter. We found a hole with one guy in it, so Sanders joined him. Blackman and I found a hole in the center of the ridge. There were two guys in the hole to our right. As soon as we were in our hole, a rocket came in and blew up right next to the two soldiers. I thought it had killed them, but didn't. While Blackman was linking up the gun, I looked to the front and saw several NVA pushing through the bushes. I fired several times and they fell 15–30 feet in front of us. One was only 10–15 where he fell.

Things started to slow down, and a sergeant told me to go to the medics. He brought a new young guy by name of Garcia. I went back and got treated, and while waiting, some soldiers brought Garcia in and started treating his wounds.[111] I asked who was with Blackman and they didn't know, so I started back to Blackman. A sergeant said to stay put, he'd get someone up there to check on Blackman. I told him that he wasn't my sergeant, and I took off to see how Blackman was doing.

I wasn't there long, and the firing had slowed to a few shots at movements here and there. Then that sergeant came back and told me to go back to the medics, since he had a replacement for me, so I started back. I must have veered to my left a little as I crawled when I noticed movement on my left. I thought that it might be an NVA soldier, so I turned and finally got a look. It was a soldier coming from the bomb crater. I asked him if there was anyone else out there and he said no. I told him where I thought the center of the perimeter was and he took off. I started that way and noticed some movement from where the soldier had come from. I readied myself for what I knew would be the enemy.

As I started to fire, a soldier raised up and smiled, not knowing how close he was to getting shot. He crawled to me, and we started to the center of the perimeter. As we did we found a dead soldier. He had two grenades on his pistol belt, so we each took one, and the soldier with me stood up and took off running. I waited a few seconds to see if he was followed and then stood up. I had only taken a few steps when I was hit in the back of the leg by a bullet. It was a numbing feeling, but didn't hurt. They fixed me up and I sat for a while when I heard 1st Sergeant Duckett tell Captain Jesmer he needed some help to take the bomb crater back. We needed it for extractions [lifting the troops out by helicopter]. I said "I'll go with you, top [1st Sergeant]." He said "No, you're hurt." I said that it wasn't as bad as it looked. I just looked like crap. Anytime I saw someone I knew, I'd stick my tongue out at them to see their reaction. Top said if I thought I could to come along.

When we got to the crater, Top went low and I went across the middle. I had one grenade and tossed it to Top as I shot a clip of ammo over the edge. Some people replaced me and I started back. When I thought that I had stumbled, I looked down and my leg was behind me. They doctored me for a while, and Tommy Riley came and sat beside me. He had been wounded in his left arm, and he asked if my rifle was still shooting full automatic. I said yes and he said his would only shoot semi-automatic. Would I trade? I said yes. A sergeant came up to my right and asked Tommy if he wanted a .45 automatic pistol. I reached back to get it from him for Tommy when a large explosion blew me into the air. I remember seeing leaves go by. When I landed, I looked at Tommy. He had taken a bad hit and was dead.[112] I was glad to have known Tommy. It was an honor to call him my friend.

They carried me to another location, where the dead and wounded were collected. As I lay there, I started to realize that I had lost several friends and more were wounded. After a while, some soldiers came over and said they were taking me to be extracted. I asked them to take Sanders first since I thought that he was worse off. He was gut-shot. As I lay there, no more soldiers were removed. After about an hour, Lieutenant Robinson came by and told me that Tommy wasn't dead. He tried to be uplifting by saying he had just talked to Tommy. I told him I was with Tommy when it happened. Shortly after that, Top came over and said that there would be no more choppers that night. He said that they would get the rest of us out tomorrow. I told him that there would be no tomorrow for me. He asked if there was anything that he could do for me, and I said two favors. He asked me what they were. I said say the Lord's Prayer with me and he said he would and asked what the other favor was. I replied, "Get me a gun." He said my fight was over, and my reply was that the NVA didn't know the fight was over. I had no intention of being captured, since I had seen what they did with captured soldiers. In a short time, I said another prayer for my family and friends. Top came back with the rifle, saying the clip's full, one in the chamber, and the safety's on. He laid the rifle across my chest.

Later that night, I was awakened by soldiers dragging me to the bomb crater. The pilots came in total darkness and extracted more of us. As it lifted off, the NVA bullets pelted the chopper. I wondered if we were going to crash and burn, but as we lifted off I thought that we might just make it.

The next thing I remember was someone pounding on my chest and hollering at me. They said that they had almost lost me, twice. I remember I was cold and the lights were bright. They got me stable and flew me to Tuy Hoa. The doctor told me that they might have to take my leg. I begged him not to. I faded out as they worked on me. When I awoke, I had two bullets taped to my chest, I had four teeth shot out, my left leg was two and a quarter inches shorter, I had more than two hundred holes in my body, and both eardrums had holes in them from several very close explosions. I was flown to Japan, where I underwent several surgeries. I was sent home to the U.S. after two months in Japan.

I came home and received the Bronze Star. In March, I was given notice that I was going to receive the Distinguished Service Cross (DSC). Two weeks later, the colonel said someone was coming to talk to me about receiving the Medal of Honor. He did come. I told him I just did what everyone else was doing. I just looked like crap while doing so [Gene's DSC was not upgraded to the Medal of Honor].[113]

Distinguished Service Cross Citation:

The President of the United States of America, authorized by Act of Congress, July 9, 1918 (amended by Act of July 25, 1963), takes pleasure in presenting the Distinguished Service Cross to Private First

Class Billy E. Boedecker (ASN: US-54440175), United States Army, for extraordinary heroism in connection with military operations involving conflict with an armed hostile force in the Republic of Vietnam, while serving with Company A, 1st Battalion (Airborne), 503d Infantry, 173d Airborne Brigade (Separate).

Private First Class Boedecker distinguished himself by exceptionally valorous actions in close combat on 18 November 1967 as acting assistant machine gunner of an airborne infantry company conducting search-and-destroy operations on Hill 882 near Dak To. His unit was moving toward the crest of the hill when it was subjected to savage automatic weapons, rocket and small arms fire from an estimated two companies of North Vietnamese Army soldiers. Private Boedecker unhesitatingly raced to the point of heaviest contact, set up his machine gun and placed devastating fire on the hostile force, killing six of the enemy. He was wounded by small arms fire and taken to the center of the perimeter. After receiving first aid, he quickly moved back to his machine gun, shouting words of encouragement to his fellow soldiers as he ran toward the forward position. During the ensuing action, Private Boedecker was struck six more times by enemy bullets. He was evacuated to the rear, treated and told to remain with the other seriously wounded men. Although weak from loss of blood, he got to his feet and courageously returned once more to his exposed position, repelling furious North Vietnamese assaults with a heavy volume of fire. While fighting fiercely against the advancing hostile force, Private Boedecker was wounded yet again by an enemy rocket and evacuated from the battlefield to a hospital. Private First Class Boedecker's extraordinary heroism and devotion to duty were in keeping with the highest traditions of the military service and reflect great credit upon himself, his unit, and the United States Army.

General Orders: Headquarters, U.S. Army, Vietnam, General Orders No. 1419 (March 29, 1968)
Action Date: 18-Nov-67 Service: Army
Rank: Private First Class Company: Company A
Battalion: 1st Battalion (Airborne)
Regiment: 503d Infantry Regiment, 173d Airborne Brigade (Separate)

Boedeker recalled:

I gave my medals and stuff to my mother. I never saw the stuff until years later. People ask me if I ever gave a thought to the lives I may have taken. I said I wondered some about their families, but it was their job to take my life and mine to take theirs. That's what soldiers do. Airborne![114]

And Robinson added:

The battle for Hill 882, while not the major action in the "Battle of Dak To," was of sufficient magnitude that it produced the unusual situation where the DSC was awarded to 2 members of the same platoon, for the same action, on the same day. Sp4 Gene Boedeker and 2nd Lt John Robinson were so honored.[115]

Hill 875

In late spring, 1967, the NVA prepared an elaborate defense system on Hill 875. On the crest, a series of interconnecting bunkers were dug in with up to eight feet of dirt and teak logs. These could only be penetrated by the heaviest of bombs.[116] The battle for Hill 875 lasted five days and would be the costliest fight of the Vietnam War. It ended the Border Battles in the MR2. The weather and terrain were typical of that experienced in the earlier battles around Dak To. By mid–November the monsoon had passed and, the mornings were clear and bright.[117] Earlier on 3 November 1967, Sergeant Vu Hong, an artillery specialist assigned to the 66th NVA Regiment, surrendered to South Vietnamese Popular Forces near Dak To. He explained that the mission of his division was to annihilate a major U.S. unit in order to force the Allies to send additional units to the border region from the populated areas. General Peers, Commander of the 4th ID, later wrote, "The Enemy had

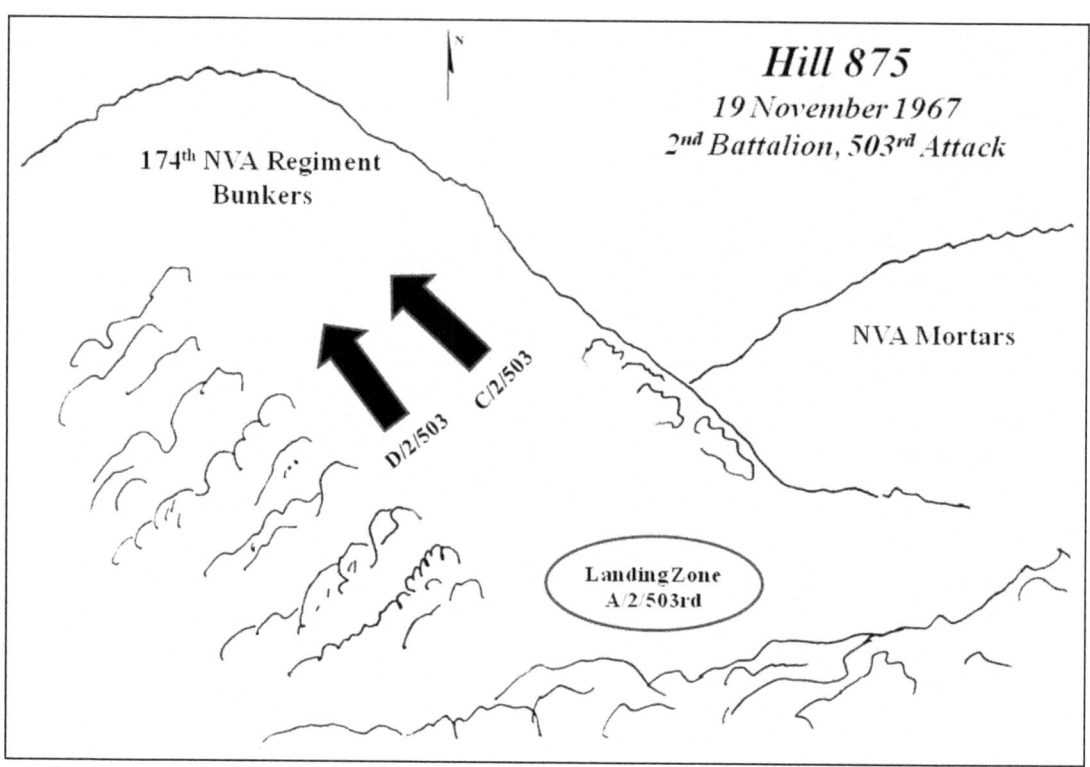

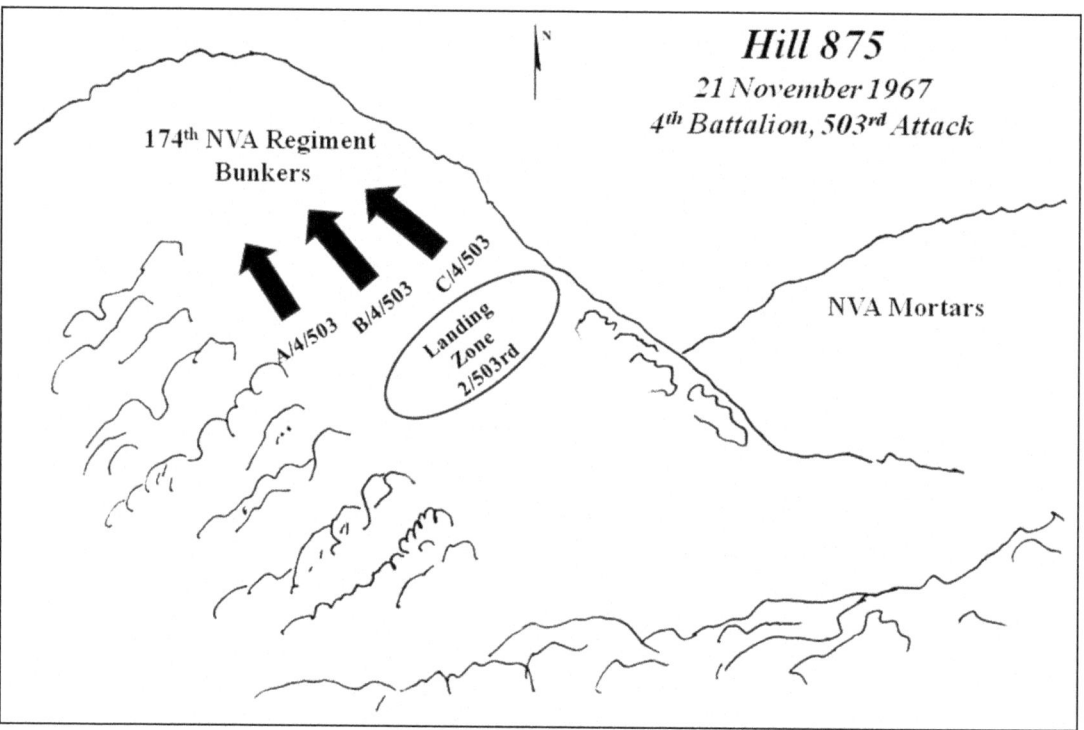

Top: The fight for Hill 875 (from Leonard B. Scott, LTC, *The Battle for Hill 875, Dak To, Vietnam, 1967* [Carlisle Barracks, PA: U.S. Army War College, 1988]). *Bottom:* 4/503rd Attack (from Leonard B. Scott, LTC, *The Battle for Hill 875, Dak To, Vietnam, 1967* [Carlisle Barracks, PA: U.S. Army War College, 1988]).

prepared the battlefield well. Nearly every key terrain feature was heavily fortified with elaborate bunker and trench complexes. He had moved quantities of supplies and ammunition into the area. He was prepared to stay."[118] Sergeant Lawrence Okendo of the 4th Battalion, 503rd, explained the background.

> On 17 November, 1967, units of the 2nd battalion, 503rd Airborne Infantry, 173rd Airborne Brigade (Sep.) located an abandoned enemy encampment that was used as a hospital area by the NVAs. The treatment area was large, with bed-like clusters and extensive land lines in place. CHICOM field medical dressing and other medical paraphernalia littered the area, indicating the area was used very recently. This area was proof that the NVA suffered heavy casualties in prior battles with the Sky Soldiers in the nearby hills of 830, 815, 823, and 882.[119]

Saturday, 18 November 1967

On 18 November, while fighting continued on Hill 882, a small Special Forces group collided with the NVA 174th Regiment in bunkers on the slopes of Hill 875. The Special Forces and Montagnards pulled back. The 2/503d got the mission to clear Hill 875. Lieutenant Colonel Steverson, commander of 2/503d, assigned the mission of planning and executing the attack to his senior company commander, Captain Harold J. Kaufman of Charlie Company. Colonel Steverson would be airborne, circling above. The other two company commanders were Captain Kiley of Alpha Company and Lieutenant Bart G. O'Leary commanding Delta Company. Bravo Company had sustained heavy losses in earlier battles, was therefore combat ineffective, and would not participate in the battle. Fortunately, the intelligence about the enemy bunkers was carefully considered as the attack was planned. Total strength of three companies should have been 450 troops, but due to earlier heavy losses, the attacking force would be only 290 troopers. By 1430, the three companies started their move to the base of Hill 875. Steverson ordered the companies to laager near the northern base of Hill 875 and prepare for the attack the following morning. During the night, artillery and air pounded the hill in preparation for the attack in the morning. Rayburn C. "Cliff" Stovall's battery provided artillery support at the battle of Hill 875 and at other battles in the region. He recalled:

> In November 1967 I commanded Battery C, 3-319 Field Artillery. Although my battery was the direct support battery for the 1/503rd, we also supported other battalions as well. We fired for everyone, it seemed, during November 1967 in the area around Dak To.
> My battery fired approximately 18,000 rounds of 105mm ammunition during the battle of Hill 875 alone. Our battery was on a hill just a little north and west of Hill 875 (I believe that was the direction). We were on the same hill as the Headquarters, 1/503, overlooking Dak Pek (I believe it was Dak Pek) to the north. Cambodia was several miles further west. We fired in that direction, supporting the 1/503rd, and often south and east in support of other units.[120]

Sunday, 19 November 1967—The First Day

At 0800, the troopers checked their equipment in preparation for the attack as they waited for the last air strikes to finish up. At 0930, the troops moved forward. SP4 Tom Brock recalled that Major Charlie Watters, the 2nd Battalion chaplain, moved past him, remarking "Tom, I'm getting too old for this." Brock replied "Father, that makes two of us."[121] Father Watters was well known to the battalion because he was always with the troops in the field, regardless of foul conditions. He was famous for his camouflage parachute vestments and his Sunday announcements: "Church call and no excuses!"[122]

Delta Company moved out with Charlie Company on its right, while Alpha Company worked on an LZ in the rear. The 2/503 would be moving up a ridge line to the summit of Hill 875. They were moving into a trap. The artillery and air had created a tangle of fallen timber. At 1030 hours, Lieutenant O'Leary, D/2/503rd, moved closer to his point squad and saw his point man, SP4 Kenneth Jacobson, climb over a tree limb, motioning that the he could smell the NVA. As he turned around, Jacobson was shot[123] and all hell broke loose around Delta Company. Kaufman received the report, and as he did, firing broke out in front of his Charlie Company. Both companies had come under heavy fire after moving only a few meters. Kaufman pulled the companies back about twenty meters to establish a perimeter and called in artillery and air support. He pulled his pistol and fired several times in the air to prevent the withdrawal from turning into a rout. The troops dug in with knives and helmets used as shovels.[124]

At 1300, the 2/503rd resumed the attack. Charlie and Delta Companies had moved forward about fifteen meters when they were hit again by heavy fire. First Sergeant Deeb of Delta Company was able to get to a bunker firing port and tossed in a grenade that killed the crew. Delta Company moved on, only to find themselves under heavy fire from the same bunker. It was apparent that the bunkers had interconnecting tunnels that allowed them to replace crews. Taking Hill 875 would take some time. Friendly artillery hit the troops as they moved forward, and the attack lost momentum. Captain Kaufman halted the attack and fell back to the perimeter.

In the rear, Captain Kiley was making progress on the LZ and in collecting the wounded. He had sent two platoons forward to follow Delta and Charlie Companies. A small observation post (OP) was twenty-five meters in front of the platoons, and it included SP4 Carlos Lozada with his M-60 machine gun.

An NVA company attacked the OP, and Lozada cut down about twenty NVA before the OP was ordered to withdraw. Lozada stayed behind and continued firing to cover the withdrawal of the troops. Having done so, he rose to follow them but was killed by heavy enemy fire. Carlos Lozada was posthumously awarded the Medal of Honor for his valor that day. Ed Placencia, A/2/503rd, was SP4 Lozada's squad leader, and he recalled what happened.

> As we started up hill 875, we had rotated so that my platoon was the rear platoon and my squad was the trail squad. When the lead element was hit, our company had not even started moving. As word came down that the lead element was in full contact, my platoon sergeant instructed me to set up a perimeter for rear security. He assigned five additional soldiers to my squad to get us up to full strength. I deployed my squad, setting up to face the rear. We could hear the battle farther up the hill; after about thirty minutes, we started taking heavy fire. I radioed my platoon sergeant, informing him we were under heavy fire.
>
> I tried calling several times but got no response. Realizing we would be overrun if we stayed put, I put a fire team leader in charge and proceeded up the hill to find out what was going on. Before leaving, I instructed my fire team leader to hold the position until I got back. I finally came across a second lieutenant, who, as I discovered later was a forward observer for the artillery. I asked him what was going on. He informed me that we were supposed to pull in so we could form a battalion perimeter. As I started back down the hill, he asked me where I was going. I informed him that my men were still waiting for me and I promised them I would not leave them. He told me he would wait ten minutes, then he and the six men who were with him would leave. As I retreated down the hill, I was bypassed by several NVA soldiers who had infiltrated behind my men's position. Finally arriving at my men's position, I found that they were under heavy fire. I went to each position, informing them that we needed to leave immediately. All my men gathered except my M-60 gunner. I rushed to his position to let him know we needed to pull out. He let me know that he wouldn't

leave or we would be overrun. He insisted that I take the rest of the squad to join the rest of the battalion. As we left, we could hear his machine gun firing. His machine gun firing went on for several minutes, then came to a sudden stop. My machine gunner, Carlos Lozada, was awarded the Medal of Honor. If he hadn't stayed, I don't believe the rest of us would have made it off the Hill.[125]

The NVA had sent men down from the crest on the west side of the hill and around to the rear of Alpha Company. Incredibly, steps had been carved into the side of the hill to facilitate movement. Some say that there were even hand rails.[126] Realizing that the LZ was in trouble, Kiley ordered his platoons that were moving up the ridge to turn and support those fighting near the LZ. As they moved down the ridge, one platoon was ambushed and overrun by a large NVA force. They fought in place, and many were shot or bayoneted by the NVA, while the other platoon was able to fight off the enemy attack and raced back up the ridge. Survivors sought to reach the Charlie and Delta perimeter, dragging along their wounded. Having wiped out the two platoons, the NVA turned down the ridge to attack what remained of Alpha Company. Captain Kiley was killed, and his company was overrun. Survivors crawled up the ridge, and some were able to reach the perimeter. Ed Placencia continued his account.

As we proceeded up the Hill, we passed several of our wounded. We reached the point where the lieutenant was waiting for us. I had my fire team take the rest of my squad on up into the perimeter. I informed the lieutenant that we had several wounded farther down the hill and thought we could save many of them. I continued on down, and three of his own men accompanied me. I instructed these men to get any men that were not leg shot. We would not be able to carry anyone and didn't have time to tend any wounds. As we rounded up the wounded, we just told them to run uphill, following the sound of shooting. We were able to move twenty-five to thirty men before we could see and hear the NVA approaching us from downhill. I instructed the guys to head uphill, and as we approached the place where we thought the lieutenant and his men were waiting on us, and someone opened fire on us. We quickly dropped to the ground, thinking it was our own men; we began yelling "friendly, friendly!" We low-crawled forward, then realized it was the enemy firing at us. We opened fire and moved forward till they were on one side of the tree and we were on the other. I realized we couldn't stay there. I jumped around the tree and fired my weapon, not realizing I only had one round in the chamber.

There I stood with an empty M-16, facing three armed NVA, all with AK-47s. I had plenty of ammunition in my ammo pouches but knew if I tried to rearm myself, they would open fire. Instinctively I raised my rifle as if to open fire. All three soldiers started running off. I fell back around the tree and loaded another magazine into my weapon. As I jumped around the tree, an NVA soldier, crouching behind a felled log, fired a B-40 rocket. As the rocket exploded, it hit me in the head and knocked me backwards to the ground. After clearing my head, I got up and once more jumped out around the tree. Unfortunately, the NVA soldier had reloaded and fired another B-40 rocket, which exploded and once again struck me in the head. The first rocket struck me in the head and blew my helmet off my head and struck me in the face. The second rocket struck me in the face, severely cutting my face. Getting up off the ground again, I asked the lone remaining soldier with me if he had any grenades. He had five and I had three. I told him to start arming and throwing grenades. After the eighth explosion, I ran forward to the position from where the gook was firing the B-40 rockets. As I approached, he began rising from behind the log. I had a full magazine and caught him head-on as I approached his position; dropped him dead. I jumped on the log, and lying on the ground were the three soldiers who had run from the tree. The concussion from the grenades exploding had them disoriented and unable to function. I unloaded my magazine, reloaded, and emptied another magazine. Once again I reloaded another magazine and unloaded.

As I was firing, I was hit in the shoulder from downhill, knocking me off the log. I ran back down to the tree. By this time I had only one man left with me and told him we had to move. He was scared and was afraid to advance. We could see The NVA coming up the hill, but he refused to move. I finally grabbed him and started pulling him up the hill after me. I was suddenly struck behind the head: he had hit me with his weapon and run back to the tree, laid on the ground crying for his mother. I had to leave him. At this point I knew I had to proceed uphill. I was having trouble seeing as blood continued to blind me. All I could do was continue to advance and follow the noise of the battle. As I struggled moving through the jungle, half blinded, wounded, and becoming exhausted, I began to wonder if I would get to the rest of the battalion.

Suddenly someone grabbed me. I didn't know who it was and turned to fire when that person said "Ed, it's me, it's me." As I turned, I realized it was a staff sergeant I was stationed with in Germany. The staff sergeant had someone help me into the perimeter to see a medic. At that time my body shut down and was unaware that the medic had been working on me. When I woke up, the medic was about to administer a shot of morphine. When I stopped him, he insisted it was just for the pain. I would be awake, but it would take care of the pain. I told him that I didn't hurt and didn't need or want any morphine. I can't say why, but I never did feel any pain. For some reason I was spared that. We had established a perimeter, but the NVA were determined to overrun us. They constantly probed our perimeter, trying to find a weak spot. What the NVA realized is that they were up against the 173rd Airborne. The courage that was displayed in this battle by the American troopers was something to behold. I am proud to have been a part of such a prestigious outfit.[127]

The NVA trap had been sprung, and by 1435, the 2/503d was surrounded by a large NVA force. While the NVA continued to pour heavy fire on the 2/503rd from the crest of Hill 875, scores of NVA troops swirled around the U.S. position. The 2/503rd was now two-thirds up Hill 875, where the ridge line was gradual but sharply pitched off on both sides. Captain Kaufman moved his CP to a huge lone tree where the wounded were collected. Ammunition and water were running out, and six helicopters were shot down trying to resupply the battalion. Supplies that were dropped fell outside the perimeter. Finally, at 1735, two pallets fell within the perimeter. Supplies were distributed, but the troops were still short of what they needed. As night fell, artillery and air continued to ring the battalion with ordnance to prevent an NVA breakthrough. At 1835, the airborne Forward Aircraft Controller (FAC) that had been directing the airstrikes was low on fuel and would be replaced by another that would soon arrive. As he departed, he provided the new FAC with a reference point that he had been using: a signal fire on the side of the hill. What he did not know was that the fire had gone out and a new one was started farther down the hill. Captain Kaufman had assembled his officers to issue orders for the next day. The large tree was nearby. SP4 Robert Fleming, the Delta Company radio operator, was there and noticed a single fighter coming in to deliver its ordnance on the NVA. This one was different. It flew directly over the perimeter, something not done earlier. Something was wrong. Fleming saw the aircraft bank and come in on its bombing run. He was fascinated as he watched the release of the two bombs and thought that they would land within the perimeter. One five-hundred-pounder landed just outside the perimeter and killed at least twenty-five NVA soldiers. The second detonated as it hit a branch of the lone tree. The five-hundred-pound bomb rained shrapnel down on Kaufman's command group and the wounded. Fleming was knocked unconscious by the blast, and when he woke, fires were burning and bodies and body parts were all around him. Chaplain Watters, Captain Kaufman, and many of the wounded were dead. Chaplain Watters would later receive the Medal of Honor, posthumously, for his valor that day. When the bomb exploded inside the perimeter, SP4 Brock recalled a brilliant flash of light. He remembered a soldier kneeling near his foxhole when the bomb detonated. He reached up, felt the soldier's boots after the blast, and thought that the guy was okay until he felt blood gushing on his hand and realized that the soldier's legs had been sheared off. His boots were still laced. Nearly everyone was killed or wounded.[128] The blast had killed forty-two and wounded another forty-five. Of the 290 soldiers of 2/503d that started up the hill, only 73 were unscathed. Had the NVA attacked at that time, they could have walked through the 2/503d unopposed. The NVA troops were also in shock from the blast just outside the perimeter. Placencia recalled:

> We had called in for some medevac choppers, but the first few were shot down, so no more were allowed to try to get us out. We were in a really bad way, as we were low on ammunition. Our officers got together and called for an emergency air strike. A nearby pilot heard our distress call and agreed to drop a couple five-hundred-pound bombs at our position. I don't know what went wrong, but one bomb hit the tree at the center of the command post, where all the wounded had been gathered so the medics could get to them. Those bombs killed most of the wounded and killed and wounded scores more. Those bombs killed most of our officers, medics, and radio operators. When the bombs dropped, Father Watters was killed. That news devastated me, as I had watched him time and again expose himself to enemy fire to help our wounded. I watched him comfort his men, hear confessions, administer last rites and help the medics. Father Watters was also declared a Medal of Honor winner.[129]

Although badly wounded, Lieutenant O'Leary took command of the battalion. The location of the 2/503d battalion commander, Colonel Steverson, is not clear, but apparently he was still orbiting somewhere over the battlefield or at the battalion CP four miles away.[130] O'Leary started reorganizing the defense of the perimeter. It was now dark, and some of the wounded would die that night before medical aid could reach them. Of the thirteen medics who started up the hill, eleven were dead, and the other two were wounded. It would be a long night on Hill 875. Placencia described the difficult period:

> Making it through another night seemed like a miracle; having our perimeter probed all night with little ammunition was an ordeal. The following morning, a couple helicopters were able to drop much-needed firepower. If the NVA had known how little ammunition we had, they surely would have overrun us. The resupply with ammo seemed to raise everyone's spirits. We were out of water, with a merciless sun baking us; we surely were in dire straits. On the third day, the 3rd Battalion finally hooked up with us, bringing with them much-needed water and medical supplies. What a godsend. When we cut a new LZ, the higher-ups decided to try to get a helicopter in to evacuate the wounded. I was told I would be on the first chopper out. Each bird could take two litters and three ambulatory patients. As the bird started to rise, the NVA had a 20mm canon mounted in the jungle and opened fire on us. We were hit several times, but the pilot managed to get us back to base camp. I heard later that the helicopter never flew again. That was the last that I saw of Hill 875. I had been hit six times, and my eardrums were perforated. They treated me in three different hospitals in Vietnam, then transferred me to Okinawa, then to Valley Forge General Hospital in the States for a couple more months. I finished my Army career in Fort Bragg, NC. My heart goes out to all the troopers who fought, were wounded, and died in the battle for Hill 875. It was my honor to serve my country in battle and I would do it again in a minute.[131]

Sp4 Dennis Hale, D/2/503rd, also recalled the battle nearly half a century later.

> I spent three tours over there. My first was with the 173rd. Airborne Brigade. The other two, I was a helicopter door gunner on helicopter gunships with the 1st Aviation Brigade at Soc Trang in the Delta. Honestly, when the first shot was fired, I was scared half to death. I hit the prone position like a dead drop, my heart was racing and pounding in my chest, my breathing was shallow but my eyes were rapidly scanning in front of me looking at where the firing was coming from. I somehow came to my senses, knowing I had a fire team to think about. I was an SP/4 fire team leader—there were two fire teams per squad. As we assaulted the hill on the first day, less than two hours after Father Watters's mass, an immense volume of automatic firepower and mortars rained down on us. The NVA were extremely accurate with their rocket and mortar attacks. We hit the ground and scrambled for what cover we could find. I was on point that day. Behind me I saw an officer shouting "move forward"—while we were under mortar attack. I stayed where I fell, firing my M-16 indiscriminately, listening to the automatic fire ahead of me maybe 25 yards away. There was an enormous noise of

shouting, soon guys were screaming for a medic—all the while, rocket, mortar, and automatic fire was going on. Three, maybe four feet away from me, my assistant gunner for the M-60 was hit in his stomach by scrap metal, badly. A medic soon got to him—both he and I could do nothing but watch him die.

I'm not sure if it was the first night or early morning the second day, but an order was given for us up front to pull back because jets were called in to bomb the top. We didn't sleep at night and rarely fired our weapons in fear of giving away our positions. We threw every grenade we could get our hands on. The intense firefight seemed to diminish a little on the second day—a black trooper was equipped with flamethrower some helicopter dropped to us. Platoon Sergeant Charles Brown saw him take a direct hit on his tanks, and it blew him up. In the evening, just as some of the fighting quieted down, it took us by complete surprise—we got hit by two 500lb bombs [one landed outside of the perimeter]. The screaming and shouting was the loudest I've ever heard—it lasted most of the night, and the mortar fire kept coming. The blast was so loud, it caused an immense head pressure and ringing in our ears. Thirty-five paratroopers died in an instant.[132]

Lieutenant Colonel James Johnson, commander of the 4/503d, was on a search-and-destroy mission west of Ben Het when he received a call late that night from brigade. He was ordered to break off his mission and prepare to be lifted back to FSB 16. FSB 16 was only three kilometers from Hill 875. Colonel Johnson's battalion would rescue what remained of the 2/503d. Alpha and Bravo Companies would relieve 2/503d, while Charlie Company would link up and act as reserve. Delta Company would secure FSB 16.

Monday, 20 November 1967—The Second Day

By 0600, 2/503d was in a desperate situation. Ammunition and other items were short, especially water and medical supplies. The soldiers were reusing bandages taken off the dead in order to treat the wounded. It had been a cold night, with temperatures dropping into the fifties, as they often did in the highlands. The 4/503d was struggling through the jungle to the LZ so that it could be lifted to FSB 16. Only two helicopters were available to lift the troops to FSB 16, since the others were lost or damaged in the battle thus far. By 0900, Bravo Company had assembled at FSB 16. Captain Ron Leonard, commander of Bravo Company, was ordered to move to Hill 875 immediately without waiting for the rest of the 4/503d. By 1000, he was moving through the jungle toward 2/503d. Steve Vorthmann, C/4/503rd, recalled the fight on the second day.

> Elements of the 2nd Battalion encountered a dug-in superior NVA force and were hit hard on Hill 875. Then their Command Post (CP) was hit with a friendly air strike, which killed many officers and the wounded that were assembled there. On the evening of Monday, 20 November, C Company, commanded by Captain Connolly, started the march to reinforce them. It was very dark, and we were unable to see three feet as we walked and stumbled through the jungle over hills and through valleys. I have never understood how Captain Connolly got us to Hill 875 in the dark and to the friendlies that were nearly surrounded by the enemy! As we were going to our assigned positions, we were stumbling over things which by the light of dawn we discovered were dead GIs. It was late and we were tired, so we just dug spider holes that night: 4' × 4' × 2' deep.[133]

By 1730 hours, Bravo Company had reached the base of Hill 875 and finally linked up with the survivors of 2/503d farther up the hill. A helicopter managed to reach the perimeter and dropped off Major William Kelly, the 2/503d battalion executive officer, the battalion surgeon, Captain Grosso, and others officers to replace those killed and wounded. The helicopter was able to load five of the most critically wounded before it lifted off under fire. A follow-on helicopter was driven off by heavy ground fire. Major Kelly took command of the forces on the ground. As the sun set, 4/503d attempted to cut an LZ, but heavy NVA fire drove them to cover. Alpha Company of the 4/503d reached the perimeter at 2100 and dug in. By then, the better part of the two battalions were concentrated into the small perimeter. It would be another cold night before the wounded could be evacuated. Correspondent Peter Arnett recalled what he found when he arrived on Hill 875.

> By nine we reached the slopes of Hill 875 and began using the thick vines that hung from the trees to pull our way up. Ahead the jungle had been seared by bombing and shelling; the splintered tree trunks stood stark in the moonlight.
>
> We began to see the shapes of dead bodies in the shadows around us, and a soldier near me cried out, "Ah, look at the gooks, they're all killed," but after a few moments it became clear they were not Vietnamese but American dead, victims of the previous day's battle left lying there, their uniforms, boots and weapons stolen by their attackers. At ten o'clock our advance company reached the remnants of the Second Battalion, and we covered the last few hundred yards even more cautiously and in silence, all aware we were in the killing zone on a forsaken hill.
>
> We moved further on and gasped at what we found: mounds of dead paratroopers spread-eagled where they had fallen, and behind pitiful barricades of tree branches, the wounded. There were scores of them, some with head and chest wounds crudely bandaged and others with untended arm and leg wounds, the blood seeping through their sleeves and trousers. One made a whispered request for water and I handed him a bottle. He told me he had been there for thirty six hours, lying on a carpet of leaves waiting to be evacuated, that he had seen the errant bombing that killed thirty of his buddies, that eleven of the twelve battalion medics had been killed trying to help the wounded. He was sure he would die.[134]

Tuesday, 21 November 1967—The Third Day

By morning, more wounded had died during the night, and it was not until noon that medevac helicopters could start evacuating the wounded and bringing in supplies. The 4/503d was to attack the summit of Hill 875 at 1100, but this was delayed until 1430 to allow more time for artillery and air to soften up the target.

This was a tough mission. By this time, the strength of 4/503d was down to slightly more than a company. The troops would be going up against an NVA battalion, the 2/174th. The 2/174th was dug in on the top of the hill with three lines of trenches that included interconnecting bunkers. At the top, within the last line, were two tunnels leading down the hill on each side. These could be used to resupply, reinforce, or escape.

It was a phenomenon that started in Vietnam. Battalion and higher commanders exercised command while airborne and circling the battlefield. They would designate someone on the ground to lead the battalion. In effect these senior commanders had changed from being leaders with their troops to battle managers, but the troops called them "Flying Squad Leaders."[135] Colonel Steverson had done this. Now Colonel Johnson designated Captain Leonard to be the ground commander of 4/503d during the attack. In this case, the advantage of this arrangement was not clear. Most of the battlefield was obscured by triple-canopy forest, so when airborne, the commander had limited vision. Further, the arrangement added another link to the chain of command.

The 4/503d was to attack with three companies abreast. Bravo Company was in the center, with Charlie on the right and Alpha on the left. There was no reserve. Captain Leonard led Bravo Company forward. Alpha Company, commanded by Captain Muldoon, moved forward and was soon in difficulty. Captain Bill Connolly commanded Charlie Company, and he had one hundred men available for this task. Steve Vorthmann was in Connolly's company and recalled that day.

We got mortared every morning and other times too. On Tuesday morning as we were receiving mortar rounds, the rounds were being walked closer and closer to us. Three or four of us tried to squeeze into our hole and get as low as possible. The last round hit nearby, and the highest point in our hole was Dennis White's butt, which received a piece of shrapnel. I thought if they had fired one more round it would have landed in our hole. Tuesday, 21 November, was mostly spent enhancing our positions and trying to create a Landing Zone (LZ) for Hueys to bring in supplies and carry out the wounded and dead. Besides the regular trees and bamboo, there were many mature trees that were from one to one and a half feet in diameter. Engineers would affix C4 to the trunks and blow them. The five-foot-high horizontal crisscrossed trees looked like matchsticks. (I don't remember when the LZ was completed or if there was an assault attempt before Thanksgiving.) Some guys put the KIAs (killed in action) into body bags. I was one of those who loaded them onto the Hueys. The guys on the ground would lift the body bags five feet onto the trees. We would balance on the trees and attempt to load them onto the wavering, hovering choppers. Physically, and probably psychologically, that was the hardest job I have ever had to do. I estimated we loaded eighty bodies that day. From documents I believe there were approximately 120 Americans killed in action on Hill 875.[136]

The NVA were waiting for artillery and air support fires to lift. They planned to wait until all U.S. units cleared the perimeter and would then open fire. It worked perfectly. Mortar and small arms raked the attacking force. Thus 4/503d got pinned down as the battle raged all afternoon. The troops were able to reach the first line of trenches, but losses were heavy. The 4/503d had lost a third of its strength; twenty-one were killed and 119 were wounded.

Stanley J. DeRuggiero in C/4/503rd was on the right side of the advance.

On 21 November 1967, we arrived at Dak To at night. The next morning, we were notified that A Company [2/503rd] was surrounded, and we quickly moved out. A man on point would chop with a machete through the very thick jungle. When he was exhausted, he was replaced by a man with fresh energy. I don't know how many clicks we were away from Hill 875, but it took all day and we didn't get there until about 10:00 pm. We were exhausted because we had not gone on any trail for fear of ambush. When we were near, I could see the hill about two hundred yards away. The air strikes and artillery had cleared the triple canopy jungle and I could see the dead bodies all over the place: enemy soldiers with swollen stomachs and burned from napalm. There were hundreds of them.

We finally reached the bottom of the hill and were merged into the perimeter with A/2/503rd. We were very tired and hungry since we hadn't eaten all day. We didn't dig our holes as usual since we thought that we were done fighting the enemy.

That morning we focused on eating and casually digging our holes for cover. Then, the mortar rounds started coming in on everyone on the hill. It seemed like they had four or five mortar tubes going at once. I immediately hit the ground next to a large tree that had fallen. It was three feet in diameter. A mortar round landed on the other side of the fallen tree. The mortar tubes went silent and we started digging in, frantically. Then, the mortar tubes started again, and by chance I jumped on the other side of the log. A mortar round hit the opposite side.

After a lull in the bombing, I started digging again. The hole was incomplete when mortar rounds started coming in again. I hit the ground and a mortar round hit a large branch of a tree near me about twenty feet above my head. The branch came slamming down, nearly killing us.

The night before we arrived, they had called in an air strike. They instructed the marine pilot that they would mark the enemy position by shooting a flare over their position. Tragically, a breeze blew the flare over the position of our men where they had gathered all of the wounded and had a command post. The huge bomb landed there [other accounts indicate that the cause was a signal fire that had been moved]. I don't know if the count is accurate, but I was told that sixty men died.[137]

Lieutenant Mercer "Nick" Vandenburg, in Alpha Company, was on the left side of the advance.

I had arrived as part of the relief battalion: Company A, 4/503d, 173d Airborne Brigade. There were a few holes; some had been scratched out by the men of the 2nd Battalion, but most had been made by mortar rounds, artillery, and air strikes. As the weapons platoon leader, I was positioned in the middle of the perimeter where some of the dead had been collected. I knocked the reddish dirt from my chest and looked back down the hill to my right. The rounds had landed in the area covered by 1st Platoon, the unit I had lead for more than five months.

I had returned to my company a week earlier after fighting a bout with malaria. As the senior platoon leader, I was given the weapons platoon, which simply meant my platoon was always third in the line of march, and we didn't have to pull point or set up night ambushes: a privilege only a grunt infantryman could appreciate. But now it didn't seem to matter. Carnage was everywhere. Many of the dead had been blown to pieces, more than a few from an errant friendly air strike. What I thought was a mound of dirt near my head during the night turned out to be the partial torso of a man. Still others seemed physically OK, until I realized they were dead. One, a dog handler, lay with an arm stretched towards his German shepherd; neither showed any outward sign of injury. The men from the 2nd Bat. had been here for two days, and a few near me tried to make light of the situation, but it didn't work. We knew they had caught hell, and nobody knew what might happen next.

The mortar rounds landed uncomfortably close. The ground shuddered and debris from the trees showered down amidst the whine of shrapnel. Finally the shelling stopped, and I knew I was safe for another few minutes. The NVA had our position nailed

Lieutenant Mercer "Nick" Vandenburg at Dak To (courtesy Mercer [Nick] Vandenburg).

down and were sporadically walking rounds across the perimeter. You could hear the dull whump of incoming rounds from at least two different positions. There was time to scramble but not a decent place to hide. We had arrived on the hill the night before and had moved into positions without digging in.

Quickly the word passed that 1st Platoon had taken a number of casualties. Despite the noise made by digging (making you a target), everyone started bunkering in. I crept over to the company command post to see Captain Muldoon. He told me that Smith and Arnold were killed and that Sgt. Mays and Abner were badly wounded. I went over to where they were. I had known them since the beginning of my tour and felt close to both of them. Sgt. Abner was the strongest man in the platoon: a champion boxer who had a singing voice as smooth as he was strong. We used him on point when the foliage was thick and a strong arm with a machete was needed. Sgt. Mays was one of the few people in Viet Nam who could make you laugh. He was well liked and would regale us with stories about his life in the Detroit ghetto. He always had a smile and would often murmur to me, "Hey sir, I'm not supposed to be here. I can't use this in my business." I'd say, "What's your business?" He'd respond, "Living."

Sgt. Abner was unconscious, his head cracked wide open. Mays was being held, bleeding profusely through the bandages pressed tightly to his neck. There was only a blank stare in his eyes.[138]

Captain Muldoon asked me to take over the 1st Platoon. The new platoon leader had been wounded and was unable to command. We were to attack the hill later that day, and I would make the assault with my old platoon. I went back to my position and let Sergeant Thornton know he was in charge. I said "later" to Greenfield, my RTO. Although I had been with weapons platoon for only a short time, I had found Greeny to be top-notch, and I would have liked him to be my RTO for the attack. To some extent, I was pleased to be back with 1st Platoon. After all, I regarded the first as mine, and the platoon sergeant was still Sgt. Terrazas, the meanest and luckiest E-6 in the unit. If I was going to assault a hill with dug-in NVA, I liked the idea of Sgt. "T" being there. Checking my rucksack and ammunition, I positioned myself next to Sgt. T to give him the ops order. Suddenly, mortar rounds came sailing in. I buried myself as best I could as they exploded. I looked over towards Sergeant T. He was grinning. He looked at me and said, "I'm too God damn mean to get killed, right L.T.?" I thought he might be right, even though I had learned some time ago that bullets and shrapnel don't care who or what you are.

We were to attack at 1300. It was classic Benning 101. Bravo Company was going straight up the hill, while we were to move as best we could and come up a ridge line on their flank. The reality was that we really didn't know just where the NVA positions were (other than they were damn close), so moving outside the perimeter made no difference to me. There was no safe place.

We moved quickly but quietly along the slope of the hill. No one spoke. We moved and stopped, trying to maneuver into position. The word came for us to hold. The attack was delayed until 1515 for more artillery and air strikes. Suddenly, more mortar rounds rained in on us out of nowhere. I scrambled for a crevice in the hillside, and PFC Nicholson dove on top of me. I could feel his body shiver. I tried to be calming. In an earlier firefight, a grenade had ricocheted off a tree and had hit him in the back without exploding. We were both well aware of the chaos of combat. The mortar attack was brief, and we both sat up. Nicholson was fine. He was a good trooper, and I knew he would move out when the time came. I cracked open a can of C-ration. I had not eaten in a day. I took one bite of the fruitcake and stopped. Why I ever thought to eat something before an attack, I'll never know.

Then the air strikes came. The strikes were so close the impact of the rounds lifted you off the ground. The noise was so intense, it made one feel completely isolated. I prayed we'd only find pulverized dirt on top of the hill. The time came for us to move out. No one hesitated; we just started moving. We were in single file when the order came to drop rucks, fix bayonets, and move on line. I looked around. Visibility was a lot better than I had expected; ten to fifteen meters on each side of me. We moved more quickly. I gave the order to start moving on line. Radio check—all safeties off—we kept moving. I was scared but elated; everything seemed to be OK. We started to catch some rifle and automatic weapons fire, but it seemed distant and overhead. Our luck was holding. We kept moving, crouched over, no screaming of "airborne kill" just yet. More incoming fire, I couldn't tell from where, but it didn't seem close; it wasn't stopping us. My RTO handed me the handset; I radioed the message, "Moving on line, we're looking good, Lima out." They were my last words.

I cannot say for certain, but at least three mortar rounds hit near me. The first landed towards my right front (the ridge line sloped down on my left side), one landed behind me, and one landed just to the left side of my front. The impact felt as if a white-hot anvil had been swung like a pendulum and had caught me in the pit of my stomach. I had been running, leaning forward, but the next moment I was lying on my back. I might have been unconscious for a while, but I doubt it. I knew instantly that I was badly wounded. The hot searing pain expanded into a strange tingling sensation. I was in utter disbelief. "Oh God, I'm hit" screamed over and over in my mind. I lifted my head and noticed that most of my clothing had been blown away. I looked like dirty raw hamburger, and there was blood pumping out from my left thigh. I had been fileted from my left leg to my sternum. I cried for help. The only thing I knew for certain was that I didn't like it, that I was probably dying, and I wanted the whole thing to not be true. I tried to lift my left arm and noticed my hand faced at a 90 degree angle. Tendons and bone protruded forward from my forearm, and I could see that my hand was attached by only muscle and skin. Strangely, there was little bleeding, only large spots of blood on the remaining skin, which looked like wax.

I screamed for help. Shock, pain, and disbelief gripped me. Had I bought the farm? I didn't want a slow painful death but a quick one. Sergeant Ferrin stumbled up to me. He was dazed and held a bleeding right arm. He stared and saw the futility of my situation. He cried, "Oh Jesus, I'm sorry—" and he told me he'd go for help. Perhaps a chambered round would end the agony? But my rifle had been shattered with my arm. I realized it was fear and pain to think such stupid thoughts. Maybe I was destined to slowly bleed to death, but I wasn't going to go willingly.

I laid back down and noticed how strangely silent it seemed. I could not hear any sound of battle, and everything seemed almost peaceful. Perhaps I had been deafened, but then I heard crying. I leaned backwards and could see a man behind me. There was blood running down from his face, but I couldn't see any other wounds. I tried to get his attention, but he did not respond. I tried to survey my surroundings. I could see two more bodies. One was lying over a tree limb, and I could tell that the body was swelling. I couldn't tell who it was. I looked back at my mangled arm and became fascinated by the tendons and protruding bone. I felt no pain in the arm, and it did not seem to be a part of me. I noticed my wristwatch had disintegrated along with my wrist. I had no idea how much time had passed: perhaps minutes, maybe hours. Most of the pain now seemed to be coming from my right hip. I thought I was leaning against a canteen, and I tried to figure how to shift my body to alleviate the discomfort. I then noticed there was no canteen. It was gone. The pain was from a gaping wound.

The pain felt somewhat controllable, due probably to shock and nerve damage, but pain became secondary to thirst. Thirst became overwhelming. I knew it was due to loss of blood. My skin was discolored, and even the fingers on my good hand looked shriveled, like I had been swimming too long. I thought of an ice-cold soda, the ones the "goody wagons" would sell at Ft. Benning. I was not much of a sweet soda drinker, having acquired a preference for beer, but now all I could think about was a large cold soda. I wanted to pass out. I began to get angry about the pain and thirst. I could not understand why it was taking so long to die. I shifted my thoughts from anger and thirst to prayer. I also worried about possible NVA in the area. I had no idea what happened to my unit, and I knew I might be mutilated by enemy troops roaming the hill looking for survivors to kill. I shifted my thoughts back into prayer and felt a tremendous calm. I harbored no hatred, nor fear of death. I worried about family, but not for myself. I felt the presence of God, and I knew I would be safe in death as well as life. If I died, it was OK, but I also felt that if I willed it, I could live.

Thirst and prayer were interrupted by movement. One of the bodies near me slowly moved and tried to raise up. It was Sgt. David West. I could tell he had been badly hit. What was he trying to do? He started to walk, and I could see his face. He was completely dazed. He moved up to my right side about five meters away. I yelled to him, but he didn't respond. His clothes were blackened; his arm was dangling limp. He fell, tried to rise up again, and then collapsed with a moan and stopped. Silence reigned again.

Thirst and prayer continued to dominate. I could tell it was beginning to get dark, and I wondered what was going on. I glanced down towards my feet and saw a small creature scamper up to me. A jungle rat was my guess. He sniffed and started to climb up my leg. I thought of my exposed intestines and wondered what he wanted to nibble on. Maybe that bite of fruitcake. "Get going, little guy, I'm not dead yet." He scampered off. I looked at the trooper lying over the tree limb. He was now bloated beyond recognition. Was I presumed dead? I noticed the strong pungent odor of death and wondered if it was me.

Voices and movement! I tried to push myself up. It was friendlies, about 15 meters away, putting someone on a litter. "Hey, here, over here." It was Greenfield. "Greeny, Greeny!" "Quiet, LT, we're coming ... please, there are gooks all over the place." A team of men came and placed me on a litter. It was noticeably darker, but not quite night. We moved slowly and quietly. The terrain was rugged, but not as steep as some of the other hills around Dak To. It was still treacherous, and there was the danger of the unknown. The slightest noise could trigger weapons fire. We stopped often, and it was getting darker. Moving again, a litter bearer must have stumbled, and I fell and started to roll down the hill. I must have cried out, because the next thing I noticed was a hand clasping my mouth. "Don't scream, there are gooks around, please…" I not-so-quietly whispered, "Well, it hurts, damn it." We moved again.

I don't know how long it took, but we made it back to the perimeter. Once inside the perimeter, I caught a glance of Cpt. Muldoon on the radio. He seemed sullen. I was placed in a collection point near the LZ for a doc and evacuation, which I knew wouldn't be before morning. The doc checked on me, but there was little he could do. No morphine, no plasma, no albumin; all of it gone, except for a single unit of saline. I craved water but knew that with a stomach wound I probably could not have any. I was given a very small swallow that was wonderful. I tried to relax and not move. The shock was wearing off, and the pain became more severe. I laid as still as possible, and stared at the sky through the limbs of the few remaining large trees.

The night seemed to last forever. Lt. Billy Atkins (our FO) stayed with me and provided comfort. Artillery fire was called in throughout the night, and when rounds would hit, small debris would shower down. There was no danger, but the impact of the rounds scared the hell out of me. Lt. Atkins stayed with me and kept saying, "You are going to make it. I'm going to make sure you are on the first chopper out of here." He did.

In the prior few days we had lost over eight choppers to enemy fire, so I knew that when the choppers came in at first light, we would be rushing like mad. I do not think we received any fire, but we were quickly loaded and took off faster than any liftoff I could remember. It would be my last chopper ride in Vietnam.[139]

The 2/503d was not in the attack, but was in the rear. The 2/503rd was reorganizing and collecting their dead, but continued to be attacked. The 4/503d pulled back to their perimeter and prepared to attack again. If a poll had been taken that night, the troops would have undoubtedly voted to continue the attack. They had scores to settle and an amazing fighting spirit. Dennis Hale, D/2/503rd, was in the rear while the 4/503rd was engaged further up the hill, and he recalled the events of the third day.

The third day was hell on earth. It merits mention—the smell of dead bodies, the smell of bombed-out trees, bushes, earth were a real stench smell day and night. Many of us felt scared, empty, thirsty, hungry, but we had a life-and-death determination to kill every enemy NVA and take the hill. Unfortunately, when we pulled back and dug foxholes so the jets and artillery could pound the crest, unfortunately several dead lay exposed in front of us. I did what I could to crawl forward to search some of the dead for badly needed water, grenades, morphine, c-rations—anything that would help support the living. The smells I will never forget. How can you forget the smell of carbon burnt bodies?

We all knew we were six clicks (6 thousand meters) away from the Laos and Cambodia boarders and wondered if the NVA were getting reinforcements, but we kept alert and fought our hearts out. From my foxhole, I laid down a volume of fire where I knew was a NVA bunker. Minutes after, the NVA got a fix on my position and launched three mortar rounds very close to my foxhole, so I switched positions quickly. Most of the combat and fighting was to our north, the southeast, and to our rear. I was very fortunate to be on the west side of the hill, where we experienced light to heavy contact. Many of the wounded (my platoon's Sergeant Johnson was shot in the back) were being extracted as some of the dust-off helicopters made it on to our south. They dropped off several body bags and some water in those orange plastic tubes. At the end of the third day, an order was given for us to prepare to advance and take the hill the next morning. We were tired, feeling scared and empty and mad as hell. So we gathered what functioning weapons we could, grenades, M-72 Laws, and fixed our bayonets. Tomorrow morning was "do or die" in our minds.

The third day was hell. A company to my southeast was overrun by the NVA, using bayonets on the troopers. C Company reinforced A Company, driving back the NVA attack, but it took a lot of hard and long fighting. About an hour or so after the initial contact, it is important to point out—the north end of Hill 875 and the surrounding hills—helicopter gunships were firing rockets, artillery was pounding the hills when the gunships went to rearm and refuel. F-4 phantoms were dropping HEs and napalm—when we who were up front pulled back a little. I kept trying to locate the bunkers that were firing RPGs and automatic fire ahead of me. A resupply helicopter dropped our supplies (ammo, water, etc.) too far ahead of us on the NVA's position because of the heavy fire they were receiving. Behind us, south of the hill, another resupply helicopter was shot down. Amid all of the chaos and the artillery, and the jets pounding surrounding hills, there were a lot of wounded screaming for morphine and water. Lieutenant Weathers and Sergeant Shipman were to my right—Lieutenant Weathers had a bullet hole in his helmet but escaped injury somehow. Many of the dead and wounded were brought down to the south end of the hill in hopes of extraction. I tried crawling around to some of the dead bodies to search them for water and badly needed grenades. One guy, nicknamed Buckeye, from Ohio, was a combat engineer—I found blasting caps on his body. While the surrounding hills kept getting pounded by artillery and the firefight was still going on, resupply choppers were trying to drop orange plastic water bladders to us. The screaming wounded, crying for medics, morphine, and badly needed water, were deafening.[140]

Wednesday, 22 November 1967—The Fourth Day

Morning arrived, but there would be no attack on this day. Steve Vorthmann recalled:

At some point, probably Wednesday, 22 November, I was "volunteered" by my platoon sergeant to go to the CP and receive flamethrower training, despite my vigorous objections. Who wants to carry fifty pounds of highly volatile chemicals on his back when one little piece of shrapnel can turn him into a cinder?[141]

Stanley DeRuggiero, also from C/4/503rd, remembered the fourth day.

The next day was the same: continued mortar attacks with many casualties. I was told to go to an observation post with another man. We went about forty yards outside of the perimeter and picked what seemed to be a spot with a good vantage point: cover with good visibility for shooting. I told my comrade to nap for one hour and I would wake him up.

They started walking the mortar rounds across the hill, every round hitting someone on the crowded hill. As the rounds came closer and closer, I heard one shrieking through the air, and it landed next to me, a few feet away. It was a dud and woke my friend. He pointed at the mortar fins sticking out of the ground and said, "Let's get back inside our perimeter." Thinking that we might be assaulted after the bombing, we ran, and he veered off to my right. I saw six or seven men huddled in a hole, and I jumped in with them. The mortar rounds were coming in heavily. I didn't know that these men were from a different company. They were as terrified as I was. The mortar rounds just kept coming in on the hill. Something in my head told me to get out of the hole. Though it was safer in the hole, the voice again urgently said to get out of the hole, now. I jumped up and started running to the center of the perimeter. I got about ten feet and heard a mortar round screaming above in the air. It had landed behind me and exploded. I was on my knees and I turned and looked back. It had landed in the hole that I had been in, killing everyone. I could only see remnants of arms and a bloody mess. I continued on to my destination.

The bunkers that the enemy had were large and covered with six or more layers of dirt and logs, etc. They had ditches winding over the top of the hill connecting these bunkers. No air strike or artillery could penetrate this. Most of the mortar tubes were on a nearby hill. One brave sergeant (E-6) volunteered to crawl up and drop a satchel charge in a bunker. He was successful. The mortars continued to fire on us.[142]

The 173rd had no reinforcements to offer and continued frontal attacks would only increase the already heavy losses, so artillery and air pounded the top of Hill 875 all day. The 4ID quickly formed a task force to support the 173d. The 1/12th Infantry was lifted into the valley near Hill 875 in preparation for an attack on Thanksgiving Day. Meanwhile, contact continued on Hill 875. Dennis Hale, D/2/503rd, recalled that day.

Going into the fourth day, it's worth pointing out, a lot of us living stunk almost as badly as the dead. We hadn't showered or changed clothes in weeks. We reeked of blood, sweat, dirt, urine, and body odor. After the bombing on the CP, you rarely recognized the guy standing next to you. Some of the

Destroying enemy bunkers on the summit of Hill 875 (U.S. Government).

guys shouting orders or alerts were PFCs or Sgt.s from other platoons or companies. My RTO (Ronald Upsher) left me after the bombing to the south end of the hill, where medevacs were going on. There was some confusion among us, but most of us seemed to follow the orders from the PFCs or Sgt.s I just mentioned. The bombing and with A Company being overrun changed us, changed us a lot. After the artillery and air strikes that morning, there was a lot less hostility from the NVA, which made our advance forward only a little easier, but they were still there. There was a lot less mortar firing. A lot of us were so beat or tired on our feet, hungry and disoriented, we just fell where we were and held the ground we fell on. There was much less automatic and RPG firing. Those who tried taking up the lead giving orders got quiet all of a sudden. We were just beat and shellshocked. We didn't sleep much those four days; we just passed out and then came to. My pants were ripped out at the crotch and my shirt was ripped. But we seemed to gain some sort of reprieve and less fighting on the fourth day. Wednesday night (the fourth day) was much quieter than previous nights, and the artillery support was available on a moment's notice.[143]

Thanksgiving Day, Thursday, 23 November 1967—The Fifth Day

At 1100, the 4/503d moved forward to resume the attack, with Bravo Company on the left, Charlie on the right, and Alpha in reserve. Steve Vorthmann recalled:

Thursday, 23 November, Thanksgiving, was to be the day of the assault on the hill. Two of us were sent to the CP for what everyone thought was flamethrower duty. Instead we were assigned to a bunker to protect the flank as the assault took place. It had been quiet for a while, and nobody came to get us. We didn't want to leave the bunker if we were supposed to be there. Eventually we did leave the bunker and went the rest of the way up the hill to find our unit. Since they hadn't seen us, they thought we had been killed. I understand most of the enemy had left, leaving behind some snipers. That evening we dug fox holes (4' × 2' × 4' deep) with overhead cover. We fully expected a counterattack or at least incoming mortar rounds. The NVA did not attack, and I don't think we received mortar fire that night. However, we did receive a Thanksgiving turkey supper with all the trimmings. The press showed up at some point that afternoon. I believe we left Hill 875 the next day.[144]

At the same time, 1/12th Infantry, 4ID, moved out from the valley to attack Hill 875. Nasty things happened on the way up. SFC William Cates was carrying a satchel charge for use on bunkers when an incoming mortar round hit and exploded the charge. Cates and two others were killed. Other than a few mortar rounds, resistance was light, and at 1122 hours, the 4/503d secured Hill 875 and were joined by the 1/12th Infantry a few minutes later. The NVA had already withdrawn from Hill 875, using the tunnels that they had constructed. Losses had been heavy. The 4/503d lost over half of its strength: 130 were killed and 314 wounded. The 2/503rd and 4ID also had losses. Stanley DeRuggiero recalled:

The next day it was decided that we would assault the hill. Morning came, we linked up and started moving ahead. Some machine guns and AK-47s slowed us down, and we became a little disorganized. We had to stop and regroup. Just before we stopped to regroup, a combat journalist stepped to my left and took a photo of me. I thought, why is he here on this hill without a weapon. I hoped that I would live to see the photo. When I stopped, I was next to a fallen tree. It was huge, four or five feet in diameter. I was on my knees when a mortar round screamed down through the air. When it blew up, I went flying to my right and landed on a guy. I was stunned, and when I came to maybe five seconds later, I saw that the soldier had a large piece of shrapnel embedded in his jaw and neck. I could not hear and I realized that I had blood on me and a large piece of bone and flesh from the soldier I had landed on. With shaking hands, I removed it from me. My hearing returned, and I could hear terrible screaming from a man nearby who had been carrying a flamethrower. His legs had been blown off at the hips. The large arteries were pulsing out from his trousers. His flamethrower was full of holes. His agony was beyond my description and he was yelling for his mom. I thought that it was my responsibility to end his horrible misery, and I pointed my M-16 at his head, ten feet away. My finger was on the trigger and I was wondering if I was doing the right thing: would I want someone to do the same thing to me. As I anguished, everything seemed like slow motion, and after about fifteen seconds went by, he died. The mortar round had landed directly on a machine gunner. The bottom of his foot and boot sole were embedded on the side of a tree close by. The top of his head was in his helmet. The two men to his right were full of large holes, and they were dead.

I needed to stay on track, and I moved out. The hill was taken, and I was volunteered to move up further to try to knock out a couple of mortar tubes that were still hurting us. I was given M-72 LAWs to do this. I jumped into a crater and tried seven M-72s. They were all duds. I tried to recharge each one three times: shit equipment. A helicopter did the job.

Shortly after that, men from the 4th Infantry merged with us on the other side of the hill. There were body parts and blood all over the hill. It smelled like blood and urine. The triple canopy jungle was reduced to rubble stumps and trees with no branches. Everyone was exhausted and mourned our losses. We were bewildered. I was told that we had lost two hundred ten men and enemy losses were approximately 1,900. Choppers were finally able to land safely. Chopper after chopper of wounded and dead paratroopers was lifted out. Dud mortar rounds and bombs were all around. I think that it was Thanksgiving Day. They flew in turkey dinners for us. Large real turkeys and gravy: all we could eat; large pumpkin pies, blueberry, and apple; stuffing, cranberry, and whipped cream. Many could not eat and were still shaken and did not feel secure yet. Most of us still had blood on our hands, but we feasted. I felt that our generals cared, after all.[145]

The 4/503d was airlifted back to Dak To that night. Only 130 troops returned unscathed. Only twenty-two NVA dead were found on Hill 875, but undoubtedly there were many more that had been carried away. The NVA had plenty of time to recover and evacuate their dead between U.S. attacks. At one point, the 4/503d found a collection point for NVA bodies before they could be evacuated. Captured enemy documents in December 1967 revealed that the 174th NVA regiment had lost over half of its strength.[146] Dennis Hale recalled:

> Another order was shouted on the morning of the fifth day; "this is do or die"—we were determined to take Hill 875 at whatever the cost. Day five. It was probably 102 degrees; the air was heavy and still. There was some comfort in knowing the 4th Battalion was beginning its climb to the hill on the southeast side. Unknown to us at the time, an infantry company for the 4th Infantry Division was also ascending from the northeast. A couple of helicopter gunships just finished raking the surrounding hills with miniguns and rockets and were circling around us. Oddly, there was no enemy return fire. Somebody shouted out the order to "take the hill." After checking our equipment and weapons, we slowly advanced through the downed trees and branches blacked by all of the explosives. Not a shot was heard from atop the hill. We feared another ambush but kept moving. Suddenly, there was a massive clearing ahead from all of the artillery and air strikes. You could see for several yards; again, not a shot was fired, and again, we feared a possible ambush. We shouted warnings to each other.
>
> We were ordered to stop and take cover. Nothing happened as some of the guys provoked fire and evaluated the situation. All we could hear was the chatter going on—on the radio from the CP (what was left of the Command Post). We took up defensive positions waiting for the next command for several minutes. Then, word came, "We've got choppers coming in." I could not believe it. We took the fucking hill, but the worst was not over. Anyone who's been there will tell you, the hardest part of every battle is policing up after: the equipment and bodies. A couple of Hueys landed and (believe it or not!) news reporters got out with some brass from the battalion. By now the 4th battalion was helping with evacuations of dead and wounded to our rear, policing up some of the aftermath. A woman journalist walked up to me and started asking me questions. Then Major Kelly [XO of the 2/503rd], in clean, starched, pressed fatigues approached me and congratulated me and moved on to other guys. My fatigues were ripped open in front as I continued to not believe what was now happening.

American troops had won a major victory over a tough and aggressive foe, but that could not erase other, uglier memories. Hale continued:

> We finally got some C-rations, and that lifted my spirits a little. Shortly after, all of the journalists were rushed back into their choppers and took off. Then, pairs of other empty Hueys were landing in sequence, extracting the survivors. I stayed behind, helping with some of the cleanup. I saw the remains of the CP, which took a direct hit from the 500lb bomb. Medics and volunteers were policing body parts and putting them in sandbags, then tagging them. Maybe three or four hours passed after we finally took Hill 875. I was choppered out just before the final brass and survivors got out. From the door of the helicopter, I looked out and down at what was left of the hill. I felt like crying, hard, but swallowed hard and kept it in. We landed at an FSB. Incidentally, I have a small newspaper article that was published from the LA Times to the Buffalo Evening News—in November 1967 after Thanksgiving Day. It read:
>
> "JUST BEING ALIVE HOLIDAY for GI"
>
> Dak To, South Vietnam: "I thank God, I just thank God," said 19-year-old Dennis Hale of Buffalo, N.Y. an acting squad leader—as weary, grimy U.S. paratroopers sat down to a Thanksgiving dinner of cold C-rations Thursday on bloody Hill 875, captured after five days of some of the fiercest fighting of the year. Hale, who was in the lead unit in last Sunday's battle, added: "These have been the worst five days of my life. I didn't know it was Thanksgiving. But I heard about it this morning. You just can't understand how I feel. This is a holiday for me—just being alive after what we went through."
>
> I still have that article.[147]

1/503rd arrived at the end of the battle for Hill 875. Sa Won Chang recalled:

> I believe that on or about 22 November 1967, A/1/503rd moved in a southerly direction to Hill 875, to accomplish cleanup operations. When we reached Hill 875, I saw a CH-47 laying in its side on

a slope of hill. Remnants of combat gear, i.e. steel helmets, broken weapons, rucksacks, and other equipment, were already gathered up and loaded into many cargo nets to be carried out by CH-47s.

I believe that it was Thanksgiving Day, when mermite cans [food containers] full of Thanksgiving dinner were flown in. There was enough dinner for second helpings. Most of us received second helpings and couldn't eat it all, so we put a paper plate on top of our food plate and put it down by our bunker, thinking we would have a good breakfast. We found that the ants were having a feast instead of Sky Soldiers of A/1/503rd.[148]

One officer remembered: "We were there three days, couldn't get the helicopters in. The bodies were rotting in the sun. They got this cargo net. There must have been 30 bodies. As the cargo net swung back and forth, fluid and blood sprayed down from the sky. Arms and legs were falling out...." Peter Arnett of the Associated Press was on Hill 875 and recalled his departure.

The wounded were assembled in long lines, the most grievously hurt wrapped in ponchos and attended by medics. "It's a goddamn shame they haven't got us out of here," gasped a sergeant with tears in his eyes who had been lying on the hill for fifty hours with a serious groin wound. Others had ceased moaning; the blood had clotted on their bandages and their eyes were glazed. The evacuation helicopters began coming in even though the shell fire continued. We waited our turn to get out, squeezing into a small foxhole as the hours went by. I was praying to get off the hill, to get out of there with my story and my life intact—in that order—and eventually we got the call and dashed down to the landing zone where a chopper was hovering above us. The loadmaster yelled at us, "This is the last one of the day. We moved one hundred and forty wounded, ninety dead and three newsmen outta here," and I waved at him gratefully and scrambled aboard, lying on the floor as we lifted up and out, and I stayed that way for a while because I was crying. The helicopter dropped us off at the northwestern end of the Dak To airstrip and I looked thankfully at the familiar army tents and sandbagged walls of the headquarters barracks. Inside there would be sleeping cots and drinking water and food rations.[149]

The 173rd Airborne Brigade's survivors remembered their comrades with the traditional memorial service. It was celebrated in front of somber rows of boots in carefully dressed ranks, one pair for every dead trooper. The lines of dusty boots were terribly long that day.[150]

Back home, the press was reporting quite a different story. On Thanksgiving Day, the Washington, Iowa, *Evening Journal* reported the Hill 875 battle results with a note.

Col James Johnson whirled above the flaming, smoking peak and watched his battalion smash through the North Vietnamese bunkers to the front and crush hand grenade attacks from the rear. He ordered helicopters to fetch his conquering troops the turkey dinners cooks had kept warm far below the heights of Hill 875 [a separate column on the same page reported the menu].[151]

Also, on the same page, an article reported that Republican leader Gerald Ford told Congress that the Communists organized the recently completed antiwar protest march on the Pentagon.[152] While press reports at that time were riddled with errors, they show continued support for the war, something that would not continue.

On 22 November, The *New York Times* also reported the battle at Dak To with an account similar to that provided by the *Washington Evening Journal*, but the *Times* also correctly stated Giap's strategy.

American commanders believe that the surge of enemy offensive action around Dak To is designed to force the transfer of allied troops from the heavily populated coastal areas to the vastness of the Central Highlands. Such a shift which has in fact occurred is seen as a maneuver to allow the Viet Cong more freedom of action in resuming control over the civilian population.[153]

After the Battle

On Thanksgiving Day, General Westmoreland released a statement to the press about the battle around Dak To. "It was the beginning of a great defeat for the enemy." He added that the enemy had not been successful in destroying a U.S. battalion and that "at no time have U.S. or ARVN troops been considered trapped, cut off or surrounded in the area of Dak To."[154] General Westmoreland's statement was at odds with the facts. At the same time, the *New York Times* released General Westmoreland's forecast for the war to the National Press Club. His forecast was extremely optimistic. He started by reporting many encouraging things that had never happened in the war to date and then went on to outline expected future progress (his Phase IV, the final phase of the war).

> United States units can begin to phase down as the Vietnamese army is modernized and develops its capacity to the fullest; the military physical assets, bases and ports, will be progressively turned over to the Vietnamese. We know you want an honorable and early transition to the fourth and last phase. So do your sons and so do I. It lies within our grasp. The enemy's hopes are bankrupt. With your support we will give you a success that will impact not only on South Vietnam, but on every emerging nation in the world.[155]

Nobody said the obvious. The battle represented the conduct under extreme circumstances of America's best soldiers that always maintained incredible fighting spirit. After the battles in the Central Highlands, the 173d continued to serve in Vietnam.

Hill 530

While the 173rd fought to take Hill 875, the 4ID engaged the NVA east of Dak To near Tan Canh. The 1/8th Infantry began securing the area east of Tan Canh. Intelligence indicated that a rocket attack on Dak To would be initiated from that area. On 19 November, the 1/8 moved through the area near Hill 530. They made no contact; however, they did find recently constructed enemy protective and fighting positions. Subsequently, two companies continued the advance, and in the contact that followed, D/1/8 lost four KIA. NVA losses were ten KIA.[156]

While the 4ID engaged the NVA east of Dak To, ARVN airborne battalions were also moved to this area. On 18 November, the ARVN 3/42nd Infantry found the NVA 24th Regiment on Hill 1416. On 20 November, the Airborne battalions took Hill 1416. The 4ID Combat Operations After Action Report summarized the fighting.

> There was good information that the 24th NVA Regiment was in the mountains northeast of TAN CANH (BI1425). The 2d and 3d ARVN Airborne Battalions were north of the area and moved against the suspected location of the enemy regiment. The 3d Airborne Battalion came down Highway 14N, the 2d Airborne Battalion began sweeping southeast. The battalions had almost simultaneous contact, the 2d Airborne Battalion established contact with what they considered to be the headquarters of the group which had ambushed a convoy of the 3d Airborne Battalion. It was a strong contact and the 2d Airborne Battalion killed 72 of the enemy and lost five, the 3d Airborne Battalion killed 37 of the ambushing force and they lost five personnel.[157]

Hill 1338

As the 8th Infantry fought near Hill 530, the 3/12 Infantry of the 4ID was engaged in a fight as it advanced on Hill 1338. They drove off the NVA but lost four dead and seven wounded. Eighteen NVA bodies were counted. The after action report summarized:

3/12 Infantry on Hill 1338 (U.S. Army).

The 3rd Battalion, 12th Infantry continued the mission of clearing the heavily fortified Ngok Kon Kring Ridge (YB 9815-YB 9914) which overlooks Dak To Base from the south (see enclosure E). During the period 6–14 November the battalion fought continuously along the ridge; Hills 1124 YB 978171), 1089 (YB 967169) and 1021 (YB 948177), were all hard fought battles characterized by heavily fortified bunkers and trench complexes. Repeated attacks against enemy machine gun, B-40 rocket and 60mm mortar fires were required to neutralize each position. Often the fighting raged as close as five meters. On November 16, C Company engaged a heavily entrenched enemy force followed by A Company, it advanced on Hill 1338 (YB 9815). Under heavy enemy fire, including B-40 rockets and 60mm Mortar fire from an estimated battalion strength force, the company withdrew. Direct and general support artillery and accurately directed Air Force tactical fighters blasted the target throughout the night. At first light the next day, the companies advanced, with C Company leading, only to be met by intense enemy fire even heavier than the day before. Company A maneuvered southwest and established a base of fire as C Company fought its way uphill against the heavily fortified bunkers, trenches, and spider holes as it went forward. The battle weary companies secured the hill just at darkness, with time only to dig in and form a defensive perimeter; consequently, it was not until the following morning during a search of the area that they discovered that they had fought through six trench-lines studded with bunkers and open fighting positions. It was the most elaborate defense and most stubbornly defended complex faced by any unit of the brigade and had been secured only by an extraordinary gallant effort and exceptional team work.[158]

Lieutenant A. T. Lawrence, 2/8th Infantry, 4ID, summarized the Battle of Dak To.

The battle for Hill 875 was a perfect allegory of this war of attrition. It had cost the lives of more than a hundred American soldiers to take the hill, yet once they gained the summit, after the NVA had withdrawn, they promptly vacated the hill, which swiftly turned back into jungle and the domain once again of the NVA. At the end of the fighting, the Second of the 503rd (173rd Airborne) had suffered 113 KIA, the Third of the Eighth (Fourth Infantry Division) forty-six KIA, the Fourth of the 503rd (173rd Airborne) forty-five KIA, while the First of the 503rd (173rd Airborne) had twenty-four KIAs. The Third of the Twelfth (Fourth Infantry Division) also had twenty-four KIA, and this was the unit that relieved us just a couple days before the heavy combat began, and they were the first unit to be involved in a major engagement around Dak To. This battalion also suffered 155 wounded, in addition to their comrades that were killed in action, meaning that more than a third of their infantrymen had been either killed or wounded. If they hadn't replaced our battalion just before the fighting erupted, then we would have been in their place. Twelve other American units also suffered KIAs, though in lesser numbers.

Although the ferocious battle around the small village of Dak To was considered a tactical disaster by the NVA commanders in the field, it was viewed as a strategic success by the NVA high command, as their primary objective was to draw U.S. troops away from the populated areas in preparation for the Tet Offensive that was scheduled to commence two months later, on the thirtieth of January 1968—the first day of the Vietnamese (and Chinese) lunar New Year, ushering in the year of the Monkey; in this respect the NVA were quite successful.[159]

While people on both sides assessed the outcome of the battle, it was time to bury the dead and recognize those who paid. Below are the posthumous awards of the Medal of Honor.

John Andrew Barnes III

Rank and Organization: Private First Class, U.S. Army, Company C, 1st Battalion, 503d Infantry 173d Airborne Brigade

Place and Date: Dak To, Republic of Vietnam, 12 November 1967

Citation: For conspicuous gallantry and intrepidity in action at the risk of his life above and beyond the call of duty. Pfc. Barnes distinguished himself by exceptional heroism while engaged in combat against hostile forces. Pfc. Barnes was serving as a grenadier when his unit was attacked by a North Vietnamese force, estimated to be a battalion. Upon seeing the crew of a machine gun team killed, Pfc. Barnes, without hesitation, dashed through the bullet swept area, manned the machine gun, and killed 9 enemy soldiers as they assaulted his position. While pausing just long enough to retrieve more ammunition, Pfc. Barnes observed an enemy grenade thrown into the midst of some severely wounded personnel close to his position. Realizing that the grenade could further injure or kill the majority of the wounded personnel, he sacrificed his life by throwing himself directly onto the hand grenade as it exploded. Through his indomitable courage, complete disregard for his own safety, and profound concern for his fellow soldiers, he averted a probable loss of life and injury to the wounded members of his unit. Pfc. Barnes' extraordinary heroism, and intrepidity at the cost of his life, above and beyond the call of duty, are in the highest traditions of military service and reflect great credit upon himself, his unit, and the U.S. Army.[160]

Carlos James Lozada

Rank and Organization: Private First Class, U.S. Army, Company A, 2d Battalion, 503d Infantry, 173d Airborne Brigade

Place and Date: Dak To, Republic of Vietnam, 20 November 1967

Citation: For conspicuous gallantry and intrepidity in action at the risk of his life above and beyond the call of duty. Pfc. Lozada, U.S. Army, distinguished himself at the risk of his life above and beyond the call of duty in the battle of Dak To. While serving as a machine gunner with 1st platoon, Company A, Pfc. Lozada was part of a 4-man early warning outpost, located 35 meters from his company's lines. At 1400 hours a North Vietnamese Army company rapidly approached the outpost along a well-defined trail. Pfc. Lozada alerted his comrades and commenced firing at the enemy who were within 10 meters of the outpost. His heavy and accurate machine gun fire killed at least 20 North Vietnamese soldiers and completely disrupted their initial attack. Pfc. Lozada remained in an exposed position and continued to pour deadly fire upon the enemy despite the urgent pleas of his comrades to withdraw. The enemy continued their assault, attempting to envelop the outpost. At the same time enemy forces launched a heavy attack on the forward west flank of Company A with the intent to cut them off from their battalion. Company A was given the order to withdraw. Pfc. Lozada apparently realized that if he abandoned his position there would be nothing to hold back the surging North Vietnamese soldiers and that the entire company withdrawal would be jeopardized. He called for his comrades to move back and that he would stay and provide cover for them. He made this decision realizing that the enemy was converging on 3 sides of his position and only meters away, and a delay in withdrawal meant almost certain death. Pfc. Lozada continued to deliver a heavy, accurate volume of suppressive fire against the enemy until he was mortally wounded and had to be carried during the withdrawal. His heroic deed served as an example and an inspiration to his comrades throughout the ensuing 4-day battle. Pfc. Lozada's actions are in the highest traditions of the U.S. Army and reflect great credit upon himself, his unit, and the U.S. Army.[161]

Charles Joseph Watters

Rank and Organization: Chaplain (Maj.), U.S. Army, Company A, 173d Support Battalion, 173d Airborne Brigade

Place and Date: Near Dak To Province, Republic of Vietnam, 19 November 1967

Citation: For conspicuous gallantry and intrepidity in action at the risk of his life above and beyond the call of duty. Chaplain Watters distinguished himself during an assault in the vicinity of Dak To. Chaplain Watters was moving with one of the companies when it engaged a heavily armed enemy battalion. As the battle raged and the casualties mounted, Chaplain Watters, with complete disregard for his safety, rushed forward to the line of contact. Unarmed and completely exposed, he moved among, as well as in front of the advancing troops, giving aid to the wounded, assisting in their evacuation, giving words of encouragement, and administering the last rites to the dying. When a wounded paratrooper was standing in shock in front of the assaulting forces, Chaplain Watters ran forward, picked the man up on his shoulders and carried him to safety. As the troopers battled to the first enemy entrenchment, Chaplain Watters ran through the intense enemy fire to the front of the entrenchment to aid a fallen comrade. A short time later, the paratroopers pulled back in preparation for a second assault. Chaplain Watters exposed himself to both friendly and enemy fire between the 2 forces in order to recover 2 wounded soldiers. Later, when the battalion was forced to pull back into a perimeter, Chaplain Watters noticed that several wounded soldiers were lying outside the newly formed perimeter. Without hesitation and ignoring attempts to restrain him, Chaplain Watters left the perimeter three times in the face of small arms, automatic weapons, and mortar fire to carry and to assist the injured troopers to safety. Satisfied that all of the wounded were inside the perimeter, he began aiding the medics—applying field bandages to open wounds, obtaining and serving food and water, giving spiritual and mental strength and comfort. During his ministering, he moved out to the perimeter from position to position redistributing food and water, and tending to the needs of his men. Chaplain Watters was giving aid to the wounded when he himself was mortally wounded. Chaplain Watters' unyielding perseverance and selfless devotion to his comrades was in keeping with the highest traditions of the U.S. Army.[162]

> *By direction of the President of the United States of America, The Presidential Unit Citation (Army) for extraordinary Heroism is awarded to:*
>
> 173d AIRBORNE BRIGADE
>
> **THE PRESIDENTIAL UNIT CITATION (ARMY) FOR EXTRAORDINARY HEROISM**
>
> **TO THE**
>
> **173D AIRBORNE BRIGADE (SEPARATE)**
>
> **(LESS THE 3D BATTALION (AIRBORNE) 503D INFANTRY AND COMPANY D, 16TH ARMOR)**
>
> **AND TO THE FOLLOWING ASSIGNED AND ATTACHED UNITS: 39TH INFANTRY PLATOON (SCOUT DOG)**
>
> **75TH INFANTRY DETACHMENT (COMBAT TRACKER DOG)**
>
> **74TH INFANTRY DETACHMENT (LONG RANGE RECONNAISSANCE PATROL)**
>
> **AND THE**
>
> **335TH ASSAULT HELICOPTER COMPANY UNITED STATES ARMY**

The foregoing attached and assigned units of the 173d Airborne Brigade (Separate) distinguished themselves by extraordinary heroism in connection with military operations against an armed enemy during Operation MacArthur in Kontum Province, Republic of Vietnam from 6 November to 23 November 1967. The 173d Airborne Brigade (Separate) and assigned and attached units moved to Dak To in the central highlands during the period 1 to 6 November 1967 with the mission of initiating search-and-destroy operations in conjunction with elements of the United States 4th Infantry Division and allied forces. Opposed by the elite 24th, 32d, 66th and 174th North Vietnamese Infantry Regiments supported by the 40th Artillery Regiment of the 1st North Vietnamese Infantry Division, the 173rd Airborne Brigade (Separate) and its assigned and attached units displayed exceptional gallantry, determination, esprit de corps and professional skill in defeating a heavily armed, well-trained, well-disciplined and numerically superior enemy operating largely from well-prepared and heavily fortified positions. From the combat assault on Hill 823 on 6 November to the final victory on Hill 875 on Thanksgiving Day, the Battle of Dak To was characterized by countless displays of gallantry, relentless aggressiveness and quick reaction on the part of all United States Forces involved. During the establishment and defense of fire support bases and combat assaults into enemy strongholds, individual accounts of unhesitating courage and tenacity to achieve final victory were made a part of history. For 18 days of continuous combat at pointblank range, the friendly forces relentlessly pressed the attack against seemingly invulnerable fortified positions until they were reduced and the enemy destroyed. The separate and combined actions of the Brigade resulted in a hard-fought and unprecedented victory, rendering the 174th North Vietnamese Infantry Regiment combat-ineffective. The allied defeat of the 1st North Vietnamese Division frustrated a major enemy attempt to control the Dak To area and the surrounding highlands. The accomplishment of this mission by the officers and troopers of the 173d Airborne Brigade and assigned and attached units was in keeping with the highest tradition of the military service and reflects great credit upon their units and the United States Army.[163]

Other individual awards recognized the valor of those who served on Hill 875. On 13 August 2014 in Post Falls, Idaho, Representative Raul Labrador (R–ID) presented the Silver Star to Michael Atwell for his valor on Hill 875, forty-seven years after the event. The citation reads in part:

> Private First Class Michael A. Atwell distinguished himself by repeated acts of gallantry above and beyond the call of duty, while serving as the platoon's lead M-60 Machine Gunner during 19–21 November 1967, in conjunction with repeated ground combat assaults on Hill 875, Dak To, Vietnam. Even though wounded by gunfire to the face, PFC Atwell voluntarily continued his assault until darkness on 21 Nov 67.[164]

Michael Atwell's former company commander, Ron Leonard, and platoon leader, Larry Moore, were at the ceremony. They had helped get his long-delayed award. Larry Moore's comments at the ceremony recognized the significance of Atwell's contribution. "Atwell's enormous machine gun firepower rallied the other soldiers during the assault, and they followed him during the assault up the hill."[165]

Perhaps the longest-delayed award was given on 4 January 2016. Stanley S. DeRuggiero was recognized for his valor by the award of the Silver Star in a battle that followed Dak To.

The President of the United States of America, authorized by Act of Congress, 9 July 1918 (amended by act of 25, July 1963), has awarded the

SILVER STAR

to

Specialist Four Stanley S. De Ruggiero Jr. C Company, 4th Battalion, 503d Infantry

> **For Gallantry in Action:** On 17 June 1968, while serving as Fire Team Leader, 3d Squad, 3d Platoon, C Company, 4th Battalion, 503d Infantry, 173d Airborne Brigade is awarded the Silver Star for Personal Heroism during intense close combat near Bao Loc, Vietnam. Directed to withdraw after C Company violently assaulted a Viet Cong Main Force Battalion Basecamp, the wounded Fire Team Leader elected to collect, administer first aid, personally guard and evacuate three badly wounded paratroopers from No Man's Land between the lines of combat. With total disregard for his own life for more than five hours, Specialist Four De Ruggiero positioned himself in front of three wounded, fought off several Viet Cong flanking attacks with hand grenades and well-

aimed M-16 fire, provided care and assurance to these wounded, and then shielded another soldier who came out to help drag them to safety one by one. Specialist Four De Ruggiero maintained this guard position alone. Only when the third wounded paratrooper was safely inside the Platoon perimeter did Specialist Four De Ruggiero withdraw to safety. Specialist Four De Ruggiero's personal bravery and exceptional Gallantry in Action under intense enemy fire reflect great credit upon himself, his Airborne Unit, and the United States Army.[166]

4

Last of the Border Battles

While Border Battles had raged around Dak To since June 1967, Giap's Phase I Plan was also executed at other locations along the border, especially in the north, known as Military Region I (MR1), which included the northernmost province in South Vietnam, Quang Tri. From 1967 until the end of the war in 1975, 52 percent of U.S. troops who died in combat in Vietnam would die in MR1.[1] Con Thien was located close to the border with North Vietnam.

Captain James P. Coan served at Con Thien in the 3rd Tank Battalion, 3rd Marine Division. He wrote an excellent book about the battle of Con Thien and in it introduced the reader to the environment and the early days before the siege of Con Thien.

> This area of Vietnam experiences blowtorch hot days from May to August. Then almost overnight the weather changes into the fall/winter monsoon that blows in from the northeast, bringing typhoons that often produce flooding. Another facet of the monsoon is called the *crachin,* from the French word for "drizzle," and it consists of a light, steady, cold rain that lasts for two and three days at a time, accompanied by thick, blanketing fog. When not raining, the monsoon sky is often gloomily overcast. Even though temperatures rarely drop below forty-five degrees in the winter, the constantly damp chill in the air permeates one's very being. Northern I Corps is the rainiest place in Vietnam, averaging well over one hundred inches annually. Two dozen hamlets encircled the hill called Con Thien, but it was almost as if this high ground were off limits to the civilian inhabitants because the closest hamlet was a half-mile away. Connected by age-old cart trails and footpaths, this area of Gio Linh District was predominantly Catholic, as evidenced by the unusually large numbers of Catholic churches. Within two miles of Con Thien were six churches and cathedrals; some were elegant structures of concrete and brick and three stories tall.[2]

One of the goals of Hanoi's TCK/TKN general offensive was to seize the two northern provinces of South Vietnam, Quang Tri and Thua Thien, and to do that, it made sense to test the Allies stationed there.[3] A major attack would also give the NVA needed experience in carrying out a general offensive, something needed for the Tet Offensive in January 1968. MR1 was the responsibility of the U.S. Marines.

Fighting had been going on at Con Thien since February. It would reach new heights in September 1967 during the monsoon. Mud was everywhere, and foxholes filled with water as the marines tried to dig deeper.

Con Thien was a small outpost on the summit of a mountain near the Demilitarized Zone (DMZ) in Quang Tri province. It was famous for rats, mud, incoming artillery, and mines. The Vietnamese meaning of Con Thien is "Hill of the Angels." It was 158 meters

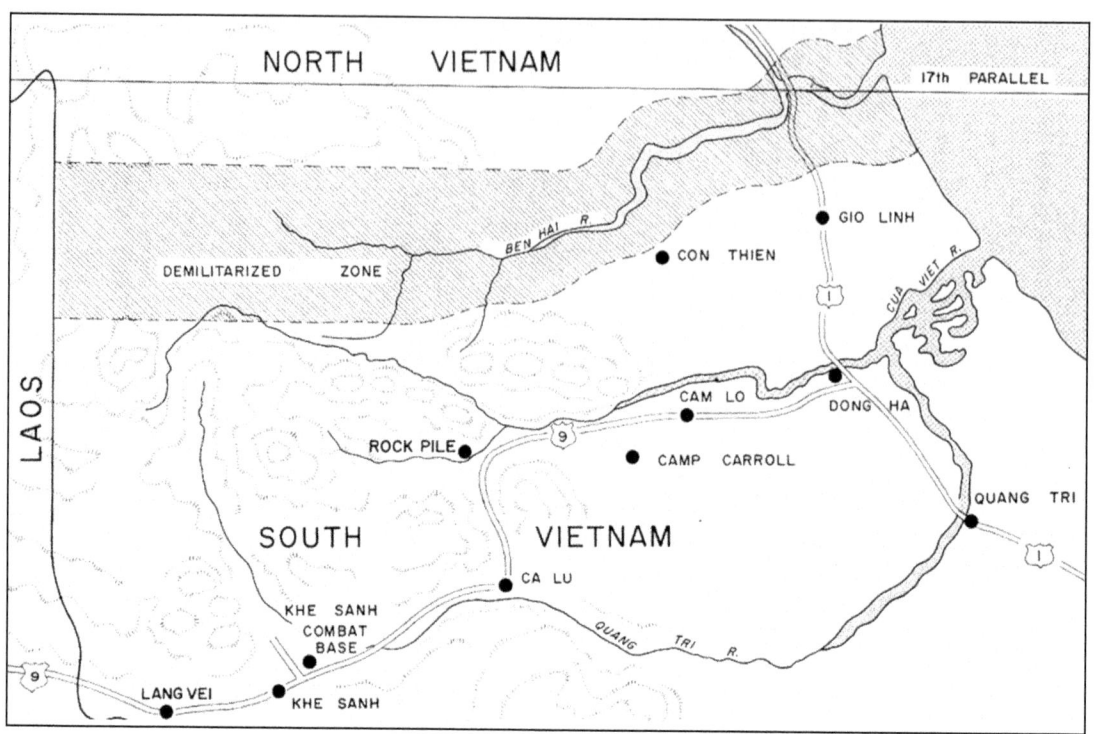
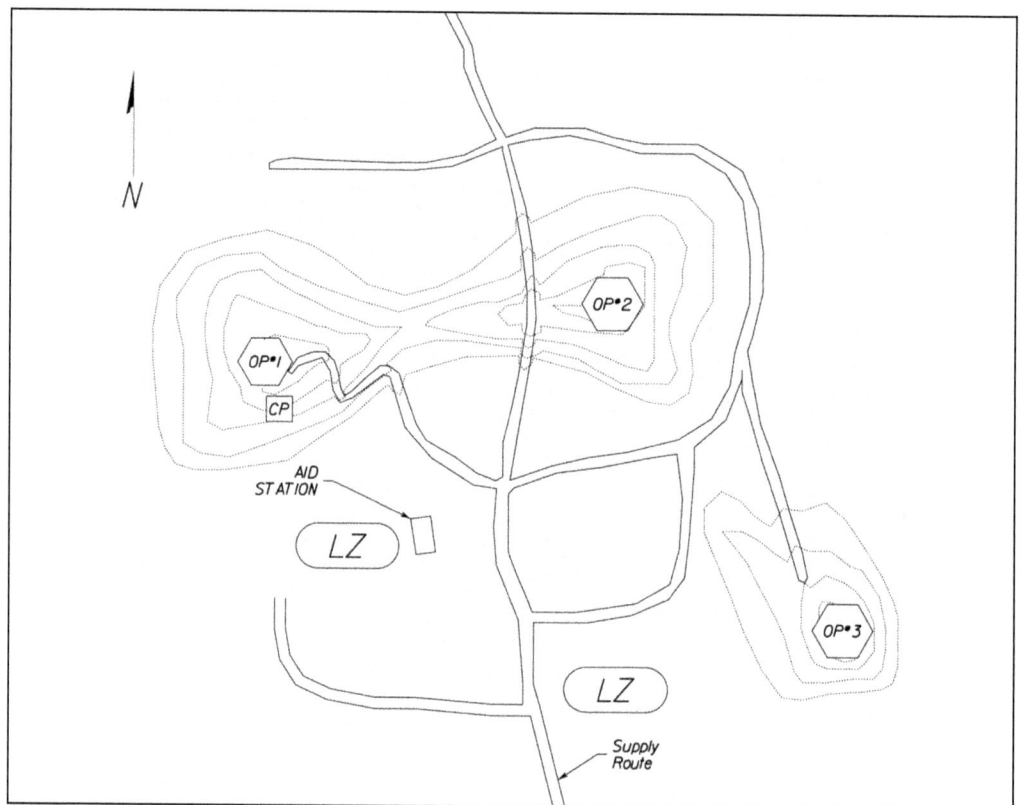

Top: Con Thien in Quang Tri Province (U.S. Government). *Bottom:* Con Thien, fall 1967 (courtesy Connor Eggleston).

high and was actually a cluster of three small hills.[4] The marines called it "The Meatgrinder" and "Our Turn in the Barrel" (marine battalions were rotated in and out of Con Thien every thirty days). With other bases, it enclosed an area known to the marines as Leatherneck Square. Con Thien was originally an Army Special Forces camp taken over by the marines in December 1966. It could accommodate a reinforced battalion-size unit and not much more within the perimeter, but additional units often patrolled outside the wire. Its value was that it offered unobstructed views to the coast, fifteen kilometers to the east, and into the DMZ only three kilometers away. The marines often called the DMZ the "Dead Marine Zone." The DMZ was established by the 1954 Geneva Agreements to divide Vietnam into the North and South along the 17th parallel. The DMZ followed the Ben Hai River and varied in width from 2.5 to ten kilometers. It was a combat-free area according to the Geneva Agreements, and the U.S. did not cross it, although the NVA did. After the DMZ was used by the NVA, U.S. operations in the southern half of the DMZ were authorized by Saigon.

The disadvantage was that the NVA could pound Con Thien with mortars, rockets, and howitzers located in North Vietnam and the DMZ. Counterbattery fire was largely ineffective. James Coan wrote:

> Mortars were the silent killers feared by everyone on The Hill. Preventing them was nearly impossible. A camouflaged mortar crew could sneak into position before dawn, wait until the time was right, drop several rounds down the tube rapid fire, and be gone with their tube and base plate before the first rounds impacted. Thus, counter-mortar fire with our 81s [mm mortars] and 4.2-inch mortars was, more often than not, only for morale purposes.[5]

Con Thien's purpose was to help prevent the NVA from crossing the DMZ into South Vietnam and was part of what was called "The McNamara Line." Named for the secretary of defense, the McNamara Line was a barrier plan that he ordered to prevent NVA infiltration across the DMZ. In March 1966, planning started when Robert McNamara asked the JCS to develop a plan to stop NVA infiltration. The result was a barrier plan that included barbed wire and mines that would stretch across the southern edge of the DMZ, a distance of more than 100 kilometers from the sea to the Laotian border. It would be 600 to 1000 meters wide and would include watch towers and electronic sensors. The cost was enormous, including fifty thousand miles of barbed wire and five million fenceposts, for a total of three to five billion dollars for the entire system. The barrier would be built and maintained by the U.S. Marines of III MAF, who were responsible for MR1. The marines strenuously objected, since it would divert resources from more important tasks such as pacification. Also, the marines favored a mobile defense, not fixed barriers such as World War II's French Maginot Line that was easily bypassed by the Nazis. General Westmoreland overruled marine objections and favored the plan, since he thought that it would reduce requirements to reinforce the marines in MR1. Also, he had a grand vision of what he called the "Grand Sea Pike." It would turn Highway 9 south of the line into an international highway, running from the South China Sea across Laos and into Cambodia. In April 1967, the marines started clearing a strip of land from Gio Linh to Con Thien for the McNamara Line. Author Eric Hamel summarized when he wrote, "The barrier is one of history's best examples of what can occur when too much logic, too much intellect and not enough experience are applied to the art of war." If the McNamara Line had not been devised, Con Thien would still be needed as a manned defensive position because of its field of observation. It was an artillery forward observer's paradise.[6]

The Siege of Con Thien—September 1967

On 27 February 1967, NVA mortars, rockets, and artillery started pounding Con Thien and nearby Gio Linh. This continued sporadically until 24 March, when 1/9th and 3/3rd Marines began Operation Prairie III. An NVA battalion was encountered, and a two-hour firefight ensued. Things got serious. A series of engagements followed, with search-and-destroy operations around Con Thien that continued into August.

The siege of Con Thien started with a whimper on 26 August with a noticeable increase in incoming rockets and artillery. After that, NVA activity escalated. There were many mines at Con Thien, some of which had been there for years. On 2 September, life at Con Thien started as usual with a mine sweep around the hill with engineers, grunts, and two tanks in the rear. "The usual" ended that morning, when the tanks came under attack from RPGs and the troops came under heavy fire. While the NVA ambush was quickly squelched, it was apparent that the NVA were making an attempt to cut the Main Supply Route (MSR) to Con Thien.[7] The marines withdrew with five wounded and one damaged tank.

Darryl Eigen, 2/9 Marines, described Con Thien in September 1967.

> Our assignment was to protect the artillery base at Con Thien. The artillery base was well dug in, with sandbagged bunkers reinforced with wooden shell boxes. We were to set up a perimeter around the base, outside the wire, with foxholes only. We were told they were expecting an invasion again and we were to be the first line of defense. We began to furiously dig in. The shelling started almost immediately and continued numerous times a day for the rest of my stay. Every day I dug my hole deeper. Some of the shelling was coming from the mountainsides, which were not good targets for our artillery or planes. They were too far for our mortars. The NVA bombarded 2/9 and the other two battalions (2/4 and 3/9) with savage artillery and mortar attacks for the next five days until the nineteenth of September. During the following period, September 19 to the twenty-seventh, more than three thousand mortar, artillery, and rocket rounds blanketed Con Thien.[8]

On 3 September, NVA artillery and mortar fire increased. Until then it was predictable, coming in early morning, noon, and late afternoon. Everyone knew to stay down at these times. Now it was coming in at all times. On 4 September, attempts to cut the MSR continued as efforts to breach the perimeter wire started in earnest. On 6 September, a wire-laying detail checking the wire found three gaps in the wire caused by Bangalore Torpedoes (explosive charges placed in tubes) slipped under the wire, probably by sappers.[9] The next day, four more breaches were found.[10] Meanwhile, attacks were occurring in Leatherneck Square at An Hoa and other locations. By 10 September, three regiments of the NVA 324B Division were poised to strike Con Thien, and another 20,000 troops were within a day's march. A little over 1,000 marines in the perimeter faced this threat.[11] These were supported by five tanks, mortars, and howitzers. On 12 September, over one hundred rounds impacted within the perimeter, and keeping the MSR open was becoming more difficult. A mine planted at the side of the road detonated, resulting in one KIA and three wounded. That night the enemy probed the perimeter, which kept the troops up all night, and the NVA attack was beaten back. Dawn revealed no enemy dead in front of the defenses, but numerous breaches in the wire were found. Apparently the NVA was testing the defenses, and more determined attacks could be expected. The next day, incoming rounds increased. The NVA had now set up fake guns made of logs and other materials to distract counter-battery fire from the real targets. While NVA artillery increased, U.S. artillery and air pounded the enemy artillery.

By 16 September, the monsoon flooding accomplished what the NVA had failed to do.

The MSR was cut by flooding. At one point, a raging creek ten feet deep and one hundred feet wide bisected the road.[12] Now, resupply could only be accomplished by air. *Life Magazine* was there. David Douglas Duncan of the magazine wrote:

> When rain lashes Con Thien, mud and mist enfold the Marines in a grip from which there is no escape. Almost all air support stops. Only lonely choppers hedgehop over the bleak misery of the front to bring in emergency supplies and evacuate the wounded.[13]

The marines were well entrenched with bunkers protected by sandbags and empty wooden artillery shell boxes filled with dirt. In some cases, Conex (large steel) containers were dug in and protected. The rain and flooding caused bunkers to collapse, trapping their occupants. John H. Edwards, in his essay "Trench Warfare," described the scene at Con Thien.

> The most noticeable first impression of Con Thien is mud, and a unique smell of mud, human waste, and decomposing flesh—not overwhelming, but there all the time.... One cannot go very far without seeing (and smelling) various small body parts.... We are really back in 1917 for all intents and purposes. There is no electricity; not only can the wheeled vehicles not move through the mud, there are no unpunctured tires or radiators left. We illuminate our bunkers with diesel lamps made from C-ration cans with wicks made from web belts—a smoky, but adequate solution.[14]

And James Coan wrote:

> An artilleryman was coming back from an errand to pick up a few cases of C-rations one day when he sank up to his crotch while crossing the main perimeter road. The more he struggled, the more stuck he became. While he was attempting to extricate himself from the muck, mortars started impacting on that portion of the perimeter. When the shelling ended, some grunts nearby heard loud cries for help. Expecting to find a wounded man somewhere, they saw instead a mud-covered creature with only his torso showing, frantically waving his arms. They laid out a path of wooden ammunition crates across the road and pulled the shaky man from the quagmire.[15]

The incessant rain helped the NVA because the reduced visibility hampered marine spotters. On 19 September, nearly five hundred rounds hit within the perimeter, killing three and wounding forty-three. Outside the wire, 132 rounds landed, killing one and wounding six.

It was policy that a marine wounded twice would be medevac'd, but that was not always possible. James Coan wrote:

> The North Vietnamese had kept up the pressure for more than three weeks. Casualties were mounting on both sides, with no end to the stalemate in sight. Con Thien had averaged fifty men wounded and two killed by incoming every day since the rains came September 16. Outside the wire, 2/9 was suffering almost as many casualties. Most of the shrapnel wounds caused by incoming were not serious enough to require being medevaced. Those less seriously wounded were treated at the battalion aid station (BAS) by the battalion surgeon, Navy Lieutenant Donald Shortridge, and his corpsmen, and then sent back to their units; otherwise, the battalion would have been incapable of continuing its mission by this time. It was not unusual to find men with three or four Purple Hearts on The Hill. By III MAF policy, anyone with two Hearts was supposed to be pulled out of harm's way and serve out the remainder of his tour "in the rear with the gear." The III MAF had to look the other way, though, as neither 2/9 nor 3/9 could afford to comply with that mandate.[16]

Daryl Eigen described his medical evacuation.

> Surprisingly I heard a helicopter coming in. I felt nothing. I was ready to be faked out again. When it landed, I went to the door. The pilot said he was only picking up a downed pilot, his friend. He wouldn't take anyone else. I heard myself saying, "Bullshit, you are taking me." I showed him my credentials: my medevac tag hanging on my jungle jacket, my orders, and my pistol, in that order. He started to take off, not willing to discuss it or stay a moment longer. As I had only one useful arm,

I holstered my .45 and grabbed the side of the chopper door and just jumped on board. I saved my own life.[17]

The constant pounding by incoming had its effect. Jack T. Hartzel recalled:

> I don't remember a day in which we didn't get hit with incoming rounds of some sort. We also suffered something that was almost unheard of elsewhere in South Vietnam. It was called "shell shock," and it was not unusual. The constant pounding every day could make you go nuts. You would sit there on edge, wondering if the next round that came in would have your name on it. We were in holes in the mud. Our holes would fill with water; we'd have to bail them out four or five times a day. We also had immersion foot[18] and your feet would bleed and hurt like hell. Then there was the damned mud! You walked in it, you sat in it, you slept in it and you even ate it. There was just no escaping it.[19]

And James Coan wrote:

> Another morning ritual was emptying the rat traps. Con Thien was overrun with the vile, loathsome creatures. As soon as all lights and movement ceased inside the bunkers after dark, they could be heard rustling through trash, squeaking their displeasure at rivals competing for the same bits of food. Occasionally, a sleeping Marine would be awakened by a rat bouncing across him.[20] Stories were told of some desperate Marines putting peanut butter or cheese on their toes and fingers at night, hoping a rat would chew on them. If it did happen, they would be evacuated to the rear and have to undergo a painful series of rabies shots. To their way of thinking, a few needles in the stomach were better than a rocket in their fighting hole.[21]

Some things never seem to change. Following is the account by Louis Linn, 5th Marine Regiment, from World War I.

> I froze. From right behind my head came that miserable each-each-each. In spite of the racket that night, my rat was coughing as usual. For a minute I saw red. I was more infuriated at that rat than at the whole German army.
>
> I reached my bayonet and softly rolled back my blankets. Then for a long time I remained with the bayonet poised, moving its point from hole to hole until I should be sure I was directly over that rat. Then I drove with fury.
>
> On the instant there issued from beneath my bed a scream of anguish, then squeal on squeal. I was startled myself and would have jerked the bayonet free, only it was embedded in some timber so far I could not release it. Then I realized what had happened. I had stuck the rat through a foot or some fold of skin, hurting but not killing him. Loosening the point very carefully, I tried to make another jab before he got away, but I missed and he was gone. In the silence, I became aware of a commotion at the end of the cellar. I heard Norton say, "Throw a hand grenade."[22]

The constant artillery fire at Con Thien also resembled World War I. Coan wrote:

> An artillery forward observer team was killed one night when a 152mm artillery shell scored a direct hit on their bunker, a sandbagged steel Conex box located on the saddle between OP#2 and the battalion CP behind OP#1. Replacements were brought in two days later by helicopter. The LZ was still too soggy for a landing, so the passengers had to jump off while the craft hovered a few feet over the LZ. Suddenly, the craft lifted up and banked sharply away to the south. Being new to Vietnam and never having set foot on Con Thien, one of the new lieutenants was still standing there, gawking at his surroundings, when the LZ was bracketed by incoming. He was killed instantly. All new arrivals to Con Thien were told that story to bring home the dangers of tarrying too long out in the open.[23]

To counter the growing mortar and howitzer attacks, General Westmoreland initiated Operation Neutralize on 11 September. This entailed close air support, long-range artillery, naval gunfire, and B-52 missions. Coan described the operation:

> In one nine-day period, Con Thien (including 2/9 and 2/4) was hit with more than three thousand rounds of mixed artillery, rockets, and mortars. Operation Neutralize responded with 790 B-52 Arc

Light missions "right in front of Con Thien" during September, dropping twenty-two thousand tons of bombs The III MAF artillery units fired 12,577 rounds at known or suspected enemy positions in the region; ships of the Seventh Fleet fired 6,148 rounds at the same area. Marine, Navy, and Air Force jets flew fifty-two hundred close air support missions in support of Con Thien.

A particularly awesome weapon was the giant B-52 Stratofortress. A typical payload carried by one of those behemoths was twenty-seven tons, or 108 mixed 500- and 750-pound bombs. One plane could easily wipe out a grid [one kilometer] square.[24]

Truong Nhu Tang was a member of the VC and lived most of his life during the war in the jungle. He described the B-52s.

During its involvement, the United States dropped on Vietnam more than three times the tonnage of explosives that were dropped during all of World War II in military theaters that spanned the world. Much of it came from the high-altitude B-52s, bombs of all sizes and types being disgorged by these invisible predators. The statistics convey some sense of the concentrated firepower that was unleashed at America's enemies in both North and South. From the perspective of those enemies, these figures translated into an experience of undiluted psychological terror, into which we were plunged, day in, day out for years on end.

From a kilometer away, the sonic roar of the B-52 explosions tore eardrums, leaving many of the jungle dwellers permanently deaf. From a kilometer, the shock waves knocked their victims senseless. Any hit within a half-kilometer would collapse the walls of an unreinforced bunker, burying alive the people cowering inside. Seen up close, the bomb craters were gigantic—thirty feet across and nearly as deep. In the rainy seasons, they would fill up with water and often saw service as duck or fishponds, playing their role in the guerrillas' never-ending quest to broaden their diet. But they were treacherous then too. For as the swamps and lowland areas flooded under half a foot of standing water, the craters would become invisible. Not infrequently, some surprised guerrilla, wading along what he had taken to be a familiar route, was suddenly swallowed up.[25]

This had an effect, and it appeared that a full-scale attack on Con Thien was unlikely, but casualties continued to mount. This was different from combat in other regions. Rather than search-and-destroy operations, the marines held on to a piece of terrain, rotating battalions in and out, which accounts for the nickname "Our Turn in the Barrel." There were occasional NVA ground attacks on Con Thien, such as on 13 September, but these were repulsed. The major threat to the marines was the constant incoming artillery. Daryl Eigen of the 2/9 Marines described the NVA artillery.

We were given a photograph, taken from a jet, of one of the facilities that was shelling us. It showed a line of trucks that were filled with racks of rockets. The trucks would drive up to two registering posts, fire their rockets a rack at a time until they were shortly exhausted, and then pull away, leaving room to let the next truck pull up. We became experts at hearing the incoming, never straying too far from our holes. We could do nothing but take the shelling.[26]

Roads washed out during the monsoon, and resupply by helicopter was difficult, since choppers were under fire as they tried to land. Very often, supplies were heaved out of the aircraft as it tried to land. Resupply was so difficult that marines were reduced to digging through trash in order to find things to eat. In one case, a wounded marine waiting for medical evacuation was killed when hit by a falling case of C-rations, confirming what many had thought: C-rations can kill you (but not quite in that way). Jack T. Hartzel of the 2/9 Marines recalled:

We caught more than our share of incoming, because every time a chopper or a truck arrived, they would shell the shit out of us. In the month of September 1967, from the 19th to the 27th, we received over 3,000 rounds of incoming. I will never forget September 25th, 1967. I thought the NVA were going to blow Con Thien off the map with artillery, rockets, and mortars. We took over 1200 rounds that day. I don't think there was hardly a spot on that hill not hit by an incoming round of some sort. To that point and time in the war, this was the most incoming rounds ever taken by a unit in Vietnam in one day. That's a lot of incoming rounds for such a small place! There was almost no place to hide! Every time a helicopter would arrive, incoming rounds would follow. That made it very hard for us to be resupplied. During that week in September, a helicopter didn't touch down at Con Thien except for a medevac; they just dropped the boxes of chow and mail out the doors without landing. The Marine Corps thought the choppers were too valuable to lose.[27]

The thing about September 25th that really sticks in my mind is a picture of a marine sitting in a puddle of blood and battle dressings on a poncho with his legs blown off from the waist down. He was numb from morphine and in shock from a loss of blood. He was smoking a cigarette very calmly as if nothing had even happened. He was waiting for a medevac. He probably died on the chopper ride back. Our platoon arrived at Con Thien with 45 men; when we left we had only 12. Now you know why we called it "The Meatgrinder."[28]

By 26 September, enemy pressure on Con Thien had started to diminish, and eventually it petered out. General Westmoreland said that Operation Neutralize was working, and perhaps it was. That is how the siege of Con Thien ended in September 1967. It started with a whimper and ended with one. Defense of Con Thien continued to be a struggle in the months that followed the siege. In his book *The Grunts*, Charles R. Anderson described an incident that occurred at Con Thien after the siege.

Everyone at Con Thien, including Roland Epps, knew there were minefields both around the outer perimeter and inside the wire in the fenced-in grassy areas. But those mines had been there over three years and probably didn't work anymore.... So, Roland Epps walked out into the grassy area behind his bunker with nothing more on his mind than finding the can of beans and franks he had thrown away two hours before.... Lance Corporal Epps's Bouncing Betty [land mine] picked him up and, while he flew through the air, ripped off his clothes, legs, hands, and all of his head but the lower jaw, then dumped him on his back-stumps of thighs and arms raised in supplication to a garish sun. The first man on the scene told a corpsman that he thought he saw a pink mist hanging over the corpse for a few seconds.... Roland Epps had won his plastic body bag with the big long zipper. About one hundred twenty of their son's one hundred seventy-two pounds were sent home to Mr. and Mrs. Epps.[29]

And Daryl Eigen recalled:

According to General Westmoreland, head of Military Assistance Command, Vietnam (MACV), "Con Thien had undergone the worse shelling in the history of warfare." He reportedly also said, "They tried to make Con Thien into a Dien Bien Phu, but we Dien Bien Phued them." Generals have been known to make nouns into verbs, but using a whole phrase as a verb was a new level of art. Dien Bien Phu was the French version of Custer's last stand. It was their last fateful battle the French fought, where the Viet Minh annihilated them. That battle finished the French tenure in Vietnam. I am glad I got to leave because there was one truth in Vietnam: it always got worse. Now there was a label for the worst that could happen to you: being Dien Bien Phued.... The marines, aided by U.S. air, naval, and artillery support, successfully defended the base (Con Thien), killing more than two thousand NVA soldiers. The battle served to distract U.S. forces' attention from South Vietnamese cities, which were about to be attacked in the surprise Tet Offensive. 2/9 was officially rotated out of Con Thien the day after I escaped. Their "turn in the barrel" was up.[30]

More than 1400 marines were killed and nearly 9300 were wounded during the fighting at Con Thien that lasted over a year. NVA losses were estimated at 7600 killed and 168 taken prisoner. During the war, B-52 strikes delivered thousands of tons of ordnance in and around the DMZ to counter the NVA. Tens of thousands of the NVA perished in these air strikes during the war. General Westmoreland provided his summary of the battle.

If comparable in any way to Dien Bien Phu, Con Thien was a Dien Bien Phu in reverse. The North Vietnamese lost well over 2,000 men killed, while Con Thien and Gio Linh continued to stand as barriers to enemy movement. Relinquish Con Thien, Gio Linh, and even Khe Sanh? Had we done that, the enemy would merely have moved his big guns forward, leading to other Con Thiens and Gio Linhs closer to the densely populated regions of the country.[31]

Song Be and Loc Ninh, October 1967

While the Border Battles continued in MR1 and MR2, enemy activity increased farther south along the Cambodian border. On 27 October 1967, a NVA regiment, the 88th, attacked

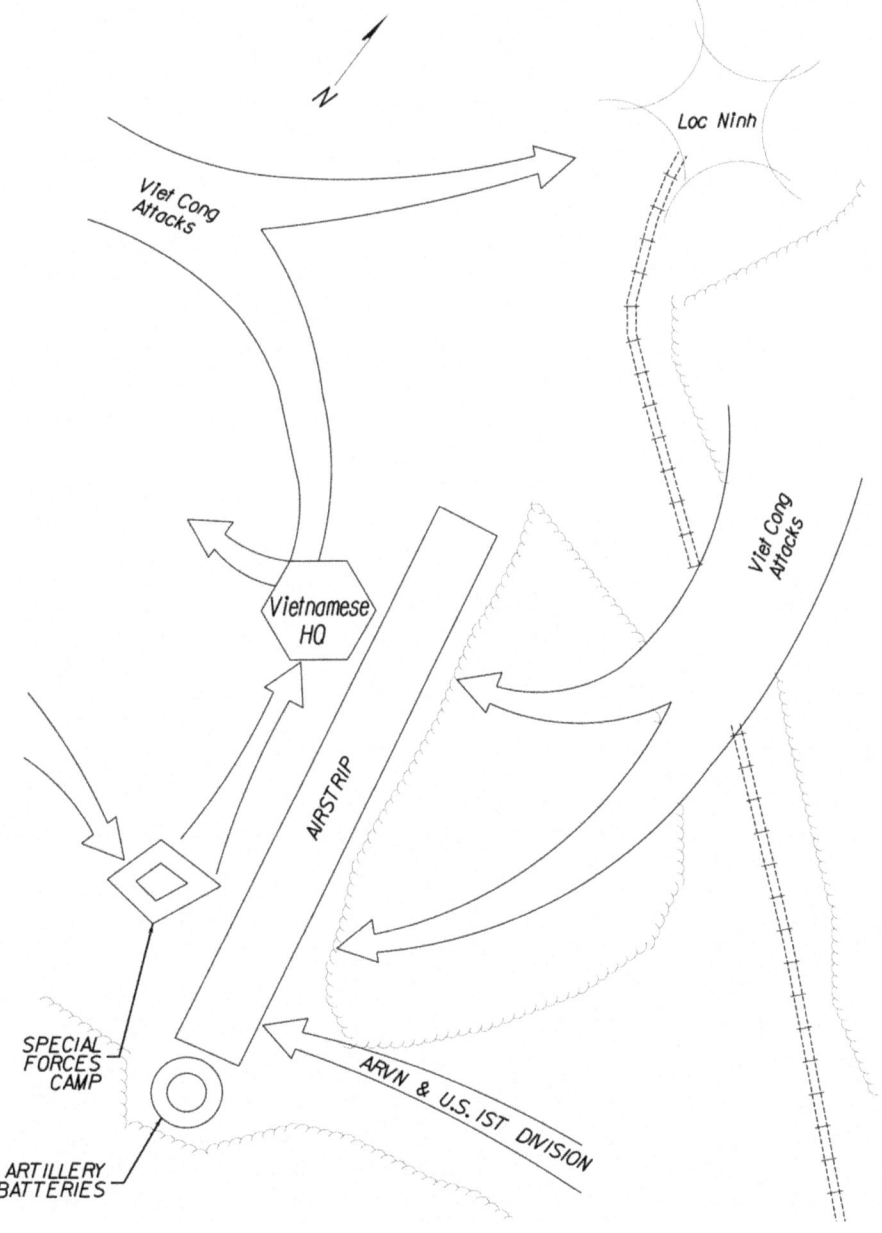

The Battle of Loc Ninh (courtesy Connor Eggleston).

an ARVN battalion at Song Be, the capital of Phuoc Long Province, near the Cambodian border in MR3. The outnumbered ARVN repulsed the attack and pursued the retreating NVA. The NVA lost 134 men killed, while ARVN losses were thirteen KIA.[32]

Two days later, the VC attacked nearby Loc Ninh in the adjacent province of Binh Long. Loc Ninh district town was located in MR3, eight miles from the Cambodian border in a VC-controlled area. Several battles were fought at Loc Ninh before and after this October 1967 fight, which was the most significant.

> Nestled in a gently rolling plain in rubber country—many of the 10,000 or so Vietnamese who lived in the district worked for the plantations—Loc Ninh had been little affected by the war. Some plantations had been abandoned, but the largest, the Societe des Caoutchoucs d'Extreme-Orient, fully met its schedules. The managers had their compound on a hill overlooking the town, complete with tile-roofed villas, flower beds, manicured lawns, a red-clay tennis court, and a nice-size swimming pool. Loc Ninh also featured a U.S. Special Forces camp, established the previous December to watch the border, held by Detachment A-331 of the 5th Special Forces, with three companies of Vietnamese, Nung, and Montagnard irregulars. The camp lay southwest of the plantation, at the edge of Loc Ninh's airstrip. At the other end stood the ARVN district headquarters, encompassing some old French buildings plus more recent bunkers, crowned by an observation tower and surrounded by concertina wire. The district chief, Captain Tran Minh Cong, held sway there, backed by two under-strength companies of ARVN Regional Forces, barely 100 men in all.[33]

The VC were less trained and poorly equipped compared to the NVA fighting in MR1 and MR2. In early October, the VC began preparation for an assault on Loc Ninh. Both the town and the camp would be seized. One of the motives for the attack was the inauguration of South Vietnam President Nguyen Van Thieu, which would occur at the end of October. The attack would occur at that time in an effort to embarrass the new president by seizing a district capital.

Author Gordon Rottman described the camp.

> The camp was unusually, but efficiently shaped. It was an elongated diamond shape oriented from southwest to northeast, but its four sides were indented with shallow "Vs," in effect giving it eight walls. The perimeter was a high berm topped with a zigzag trench and two-man fighting positions. These were constructed of sandbags with a speed pallet roof topped by one or two layers of sandbags. A firing port was provided in the front. The trench was unrevetted with a one-layer-thick sandbag parapet. Several coils of razor concertina wire fronted the berm. At the inner point of the indented "Vs" was a machine gun bunker with others on the corners. The southwest end was blunt and had two machine gun bunkers several yards apart.
>
> The entrance road ran from the airfield, which ran from southeast to northwest just outside the wire, curving through the wire barriers to enter the camp at the southeast wall's "V." Any attacker attempting to use the road would be exposed to short-range flanking fire from their right for the entire length of the wall. Above-ground Striker barracks were spotted at irregular intervals around the perimeter. A total of 530 Cambodians, Vietnamese, Montagnards, and Nungs manned four companies. One company was assigned to each of the four walls.[34]

The VC 272nd and 273rd Regiments of the 9th VC Division attacked Loc Ninh beginning at 0115 hours on 29 October. VC mortar rounds announced the start of the attack, and sappers penetrated the CIDG defenses at the camp but were driven off. The VC attack on the town was successful, but at dawn, two CIDG companies from the camp counterattacked and cleared the town. The U.S. advisor and the district chief, Captain Cong, who were holed up in the Tactical Operations Center (TOC), were rescued. Meanwhile, part of the 2nd Battalion, 28th Infantry of the 1st Infantry Division and two artillery batteries were brought into the airfield. John McCoy described events at the airfield.

> It was a LARGE python. I mean a really huge python. It took about eight or more men to pick it up. It was at least 12 feet long, maybe a lot longer. I have never seen a longer or bigger python before or since. We were out on patrol, headed back in to the NDP [Night Defensive Position] at the south end of the Loc Ninh airstrip, when Lt. Fortenberry walked up, holding the front of the snake, followed by several men from his platoon trying to hold the rest of this enormous constrictor. He informed me that we had all just walked over the snake. That didn't make me feel too comfortable. The snake apparently had eaten recently, as it had a bulge about the size of a small pig about three or four feet back from its head. We all speculated on what it had eaten. Lt. Fortenberry managed to find a large cardboard box, about the size of a refrigerator, and put the snake in that. They named the snake "Lurch." Either that night, or the next night, we came under attack again. I remember Fred Hill and I were heading for our bunker when the first mortar rounds started dropping in on the runway. Fred looked over at the box that had held Lurch, and realized the box had been tipped over somehow and Lurch was loose. When Fred brought this to my attention, I hesitated to jump in the bunker, as I figured Lurch just might be in there. The mortar rounds were moving down the runway, falling closer to our bunkers, so I opted to take my chances with the snake and jumped in the bunker. I may have let Fred go first. Lurch wasn't there, and we never saw him again. I hope he crawled out to the rubber trees and scared a few VC to death.[35]

Sporadic contact with the VC continued that day until 0055 hours on 31 October, when two battalions of the 272nd VC Regiment resumed the attack on the camp and the town. Devastating firepower met the attack from air, artillery, and direct ground fire by the defenders.

> This time an NLF [National Liberation Front—another name for the VC] battalion surged out of the rubber trees and hit the Green Berets from two directions. They never made it past the barbed wire. Captain Harry Downing's gun crews alone expended 575 shells before dawn, bore-sighting their 105mm howitzer [the tubes were set to the horizontal], trimming time fuses to the nub with nail clippers, and shooting so fast the paint on the barrels bubbled and burned from the heat. There were five separate assaults on the town too. Several hundred more bodies were added to the tally. Searchers counting the dead found brand-new Chinese AK-47 assault rifles. On November 2 came more attacks from both NLF regiments and from two more of the VPA [NVA]—the 141st and 165th. The Special Forces camp again bore the brunt. Almost 4,000 rounds of artillery, complemented by a B-52 Arc Light strike, flattened the enemy. Two full battalions of the U.S. 1st Division (joined later by a third), more of General Thuan's [ARVN] soldiers, some from the ARVN 18th Division, and the Green Berets swept the area over the succeeding days. South Vietnamese soldiers washed their uniforms in the swimming pool at the rubber plantation and helped themselves to its wine cellar. The last major contact occurred on November 7. U.S. troops began pulling out the next day. The battle was declared over. In all, defenders benefited from 452 air sorties, 8 Arc Light strikes, and 30,125 rounds of artillery fire. They claimed 900 enemy dead against 50 friendly killed and 234 wounded. *Time* magazine called Loc Ninh the enemy's biggest defeat since the spring, when the hill fights around Khe Sanh had yielded a body count of more than 1,200 adversaries.[36]

The major reason for the success of the defense was the close coordination and cooperation between U.S. Special Forces, LLDB (Vietnamese Special Forces), Vietnamese subsector, and U.S. Army units.

> Everyone got a little of what they wanted out of Loc Ninh. COSVN [NVA] had succeeded in coordinating attacks from two different divisions. According to Hanoi's war history, the campaign—which it considered active until December (including two division- and five regiment-size engagements, sixty in all)—"consolidated our offensive springboard north of Saigon and marked a new step forward in the capacity of COSVN's main force soldiers to fight a concentrated battle." MACV could claim a victory too, even though the 1st Division had given up a planned sweep of the Long Nguyen Secret Zone to fight at Loc Ninh. And Lyndon Johnson, who wanted publicity for the new, improved ARVN, could get Walt Rostow's Vietnam Information Group to give out details and induce MACV's public relations people to secure favorable press coverage.[37]

Siege of Khe Sanh Combat Base (KSCB)—April 1967–January 1968

"Attention to Colors." The order having been given, Captain William H. Dabney, a product of the Virginia Military Institute, snapped to attention, faced the jerry-rigged flag-pole, and saluted, as did every other man in Company I, 3d Battalion, 26th Marines. The ceremony might well have been at any one of a hundred military installations around the world except for a few glaring irregularities. The parade ground was a battle-scarred hilltop to the west of Khe Sanh and the men in the formation stood half submerged in trenches or foxholes. Instead of crisply starched uniforms, razor sharp creases, and gleaming brass, these Marines sported scraggly beards, ragged trousers, and rotted helmet liner straps. The only man in the company who could play a bugle, Second Lieutenant Owen S. Matthews, lifted the pock-marked instrument to his lips and spat out a choppy version of "To the Colors" while two enlisted men raced to the RC-292 radio antenna which served as the flag-pole and gingerly attached the Stars and Stripes. As the mast with its shredded banner came upright, the Marines could hear the ominous "thunk," "thunk," "thunk," to the southwest of their position which meant that North Vietnamese 120mm mortar rounds had left their tubes. They also knew that in 21 seconds those "thunks" would be replaced by much louder, closer sounds, but no one budged until Old Glory waved high over the hill.

When Lieutenant Matthews sharply cut off the last note of his piece, Company I disappeared; men

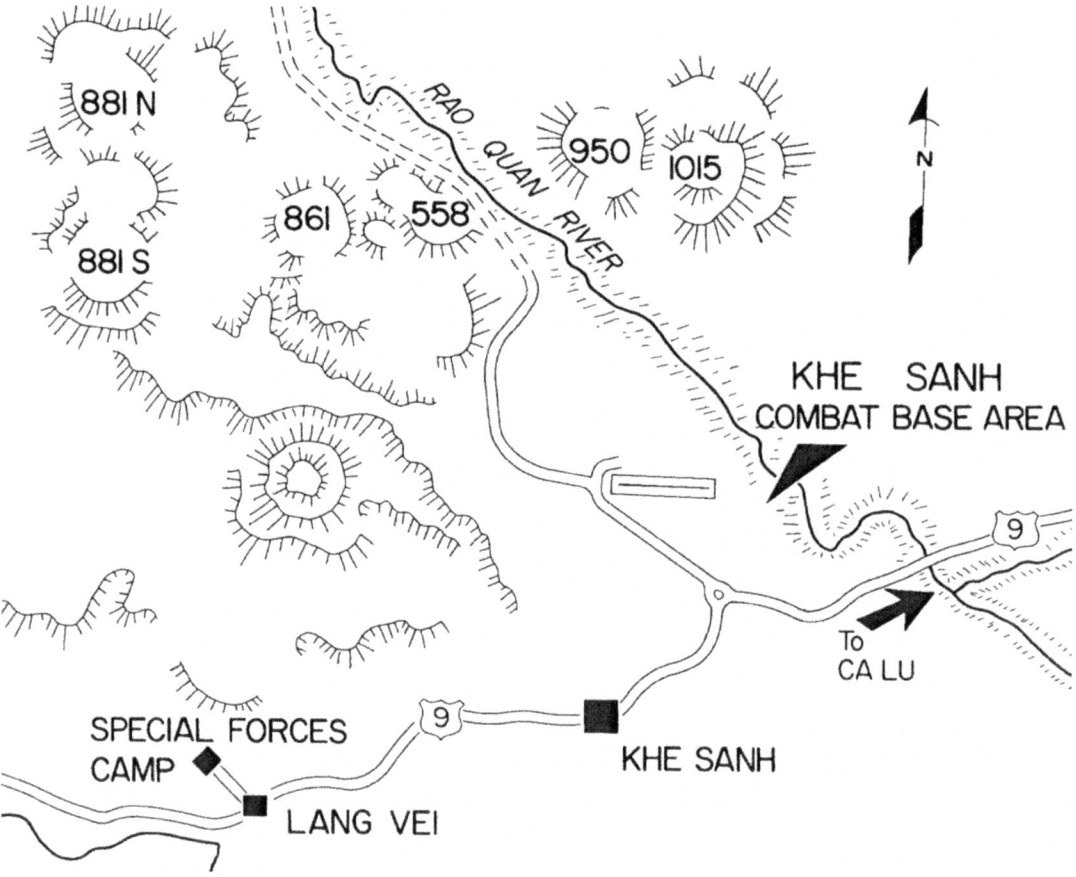

Khe Sanh Valley (from Moyers S. Shore, II, *The Battle of Khe Sanh* [Washington, D.C. History and Museums Division, Headquarters, U.S. Marine Corps, 1969]).

dropped into trenches, dived headlong into foxholes, or scrambled into bunkers. The area which moments before had been bristling with humanity was suddenly a ghost town. Seconds later explosions walked across the hilltop spewing black smoke, dirt, and debris into the air. Rocks, splinters, and spent shell fragments rained on the flattened Marines but, as usual, no one was hurt. As quickly as the attack came, it was over. While the smoke lazily drifted away, a much smaller banner rose from the Marines' positions. A pole adorned with a pair of red silk panties—Maggie's Drawers—was waved back and forth above one trench line to inform the enemy that he had missed again. A few men stood up and jeered or cursed at the distant gunners; others simply saluted with an appropriate obscene gesture. The daily flag raising ceremony on Hill 881 was over.[38]

On 9 July 1968, the NVA hoisted their liberation flag at KSCB long after the siege was over. Ho Chi Minh sent his congratulations to the troops. In the previous two years, many actions had occurred, and there was a great deal of controversy. President Johnson had ordered the KSCB held at all costs. General Westmoreland had held it for a time, believing that an attack on the KSCB would be part of an NVA invasion of South Vietnam. He also planned to use it as a base of operations to cross the Laotian border and cut the Ho Chi Minh Trail if he could get approval to do that. The marines wanted no part of it. In the end, the U.S. abandoned KSCB because it was no longer needed.

General Westmoreland did not believe the NVA's intention in attacking KSCB was to draw troops away from the populated regions in preparation for Tet. He even planned the use of nuclear weapons rather than lose KSCB.[39] The marines thought that Khe Sanh was a waste of time. North Vietnam's General Giap believed that the KSCB was held as the first step of a U.S. invasion of North Vietnam. He kept pressure on KSCB to draw the Allies away from the populated areas. The highest concentration of bombing during the war was accomplished around KSCB, and in the end KSCB was abandoned. The history of KSCB has been the subject of many books and articles. Following is what happened during the Border Battles, which is a short version of the long history of Khe Sanh.

In September 1966, Lieutenant General Lewis W. Walt commanded the III Marine Amphibious Force (MAF) that included the marines in Vietnam. He had a major disagreement with his boss, General Westmoreland. Walt fully supported the philosophy of the Commandant of the Marine Corps, General Wallace M. Greene, Jr.: "The real targets in Vietnam are not the Viet Cong or the North Vietnamese, but the Vietnamese people."[40] Author Edward Murphy summarized.

> So strongly did Walt believe in this strategy that he approved a number of innovative programs to rid the native villages of their insurgent infrastructure and make the South Vietnamese people feel safe in their homes. But this emphasis on pacification programs did not mean that Walt possessed an unwillingness to engage the enemy in full combat. Indeed, quite the contrary was true…. If anyone in the Marine Corps knew how to battle with an enemy, it was fifty-three-year-old Lewis William Walt. But he recognized that the civil war in South Vietnam would not be won by the Marines' historic method of wresting terrain objectives from the enemy's armies. In his view, if the Viet Cong and the North Vietnamese Army were to be vanquished, it would happen only if the people want it to happen. And the only way to get them to want that was to allow them to feel safe in their villages. General Westmoreland, however, had different plans for fighting this war. Although he acknowledged the benefits of pacification, … Westmoreland knew he could not protect the people and battle the enemy's main-force units. He had to make a choice. His 1966 battle plan revealed that choice. According to his master plan for conducting the war, American troops, better trained and with greater firepower than the Army of the Republic of Vietnam (ARVN), would conduct major "search-and-destroy" operations in the rural, unpopulated areas. Here the combat units could "find, fix and destroy" the enemy and his base areas. The ARVN would follow up with "clearing operations" designed to ferret out any surviving guerrilla forces. Then the local militia units, or Popular Forces, would move in to

provide a permanent defense for area villages. As far as Westmoreland was concerned, the Marines' preferred strategy for winning the war had been seriously downgraded.[41]

The village of Khe Sanh is west of Con Thien and about ten kilometers from the Laotian border. It is the seat of the Huong Hoa district government, in an area of coffee plantations and Montagnard villages. It was near a deteriorated road, Route 9, which ran east to west from the coast area and across the Laotian border. It was first occupied by the U.S. Special Forces in 1962. A runway was constructed at an old French fort near the village. The purpose was to monitor NVA infiltration along the border. U.S. Marines took over the plateau camp in 1966 and rebuilt the camp, extending the runway to twelve hundred meters.[42] Strength of the marines at Khe Sanh fluctuated to as low as a company by late January 1967.[43] If Giap's purpose was to draw the Allies away from the populated coastal regions, his plan was not working. Phase I of Hanoi's plan had included the positioning of two NVA divisions near Khe Sanh.[44] One U.S. Marine company tying up two divisions was a losing plan for the NVA. Before the siege of KSCB ended over a year later, NVA attacks would cause the marines to reinforce KSCB.[45] General Westmoreland summarized the situation.

> As the new year, 1967, began, evidence mounted of continued enemy build-up within the DMZ, including an influx of artillery pieces, which finally prompted the State Department to relax its restriction on firing into the DMZ. The upsurge of North Vietnamese activity in Quang Tri province apparently presaged an enemy attempt to overrun the province, then to close on Hue. Although the effort began with heavy shelling of Con Thien, Gio Linh, and the backup positions, the first attack by enemy ground troops was to be at Khe Sanh. Relative quiet having long prevailed at Khe Sanh, Lew Walt by April 1967 had substituted a company for the battalion that previously manned the combat base. From the base, located on a high plateau, the men of the company patrolled through elephant grass, bamboo thickets, and dense jungle covering nearby hills and mountains. On the morning of April 24, a platoon-size Marine patrol brushed against a seemingly small enemy force on one of the plateau slopes, but when another Marine patrol came to relieve the first, at least a company of North Vietnamese attacked. Outnumbered, the marines lost thirteen men killed, but the bulk of the two patrols got away. They had made contact, it turned out, with a regiment of the North Vietnamese 325 C Division that had occupied several of the heights in the vicinity and was bringing in artillery for an assault to take the Khe Sanh Combat Base. The patrol action triggered what became known as the "hill fights." Two battalions of the 3d Marine Regiment, flown in by helicopter and C-130 planes to the upgraded air strip, prepared to occupy three nearby peaks held by the enemy, Hills 861, 881S, and 881N.[46]

By April 1967, it became apparent that the NVA had moved major forces to attack KSCB, but the Marines also had other problems. The new combat rifle, the M-16, had been issued to replace the M-14.

> The M-16 used a smaller cartridge—5.56mm—than the standard NATO 7.62mm round fired by both the M-l4 and the M-60 machine gun. Thus, each Marine could carry more rounds. And they would need them. The M-16 fired at a higher rate than the M-14, meaning it would burn up rounds much faster. But that was the way it was supposed to be. The designers made the M-16 a weapon that sprayed out rounds in a wide pattern rather than the more selective, pinpoint accuracy of the M-l4.
> The situation at Khe Sanh meant Marines had only a limited time to practice with the new rifle. All they could do was sight their individual weapons on a makeshift twenty-five-meter range and fire off three or four magazines. Almost immediately the rifle displayed its tendency to jam. Often, after just a few rounds, a spent cartridge stuck in the breech. To remove it, a cleaning rod had to be shoved down the weapon's barrel, but only one cleaning rod was issued for every four men. So a Marine with a jammed rifle could either borrow the pieces of a cleaning rod or try to pry the jammed cartridge loose with the tip of a knife or bayonet. That took time and rarely worked.[47]

While few knew it, this was precisely the same situation that Custer faced at the Little Big Horn battle. His troops pried spent cartridges from their jammed Springfield rifles with knives as they were overrun by the Sioux. Not good then, nor was it any better a hundred years later. The M-16 problem would be solved, but not until months later.

On 20 April 1967, operational control of KSCB was passed to the 3rd Marine Regiment. On 24 April 1967, a Marine patrol engaged the NVA near Hill 861. This was the start of a twelve-day battle. This became known as the First Battle of Khe Sanh.[48]

> That portion of the enemy plan which pertained to Khe Sanh involved the isolation of the base by artillery attacks on the Marine fire support bases in the eastern DZ area (e.g., Camp Carroll, Con Thien, Gio Linh, etc.). These were closely coordinated with attacks by fire on the logistical and helicopter installations at Dong Ha and Phu Bai. Demolition teams cut Route 9 between Khe Sanh and Cam Lo to prevent overland reinforcement, and later, a secondary attack was launched against the camp at Lang Vei, which was manned by Vietnamese CIDG personnel and U.S. Army Special Forces advisors. Under cover of heavy fog and low overcast which shrouded Khe Sanh for several weeks, the North Vietnamese moved a regiment into the Hill 881/861 complex and constructed a maze of heavily reinforced bunkers and gun positions from which they intended to provide direct fire against the KSCB in support of their assault troops. All of these efforts were ancillary to the main thrust— a regimental-sized ground attack—from the 325C NVA Division which would sweep in from the west and seize the airfield.[49]

On the morning of 25 April, the K/3/3 Marines unit was brought in and immediately moved towards Hill 861 to support Company B, 1st and 3rd Platoons. Company K moved up Hill 861 on different approaches, and 1st Platoon was hit by fire from well-entrenched NVA 300 meters from the summit. Second Platoon was sent to reinforce 1st Platoon, and the fighting continued until nightfall, when the marines dug in. At 1800 hours, K Company, 9th Marines, was flown into KSCB to support the attack.

At 0500, 26 April, the 3rd Battalion command post and KSCB were hit by mortar and recoilless rifle fire. Company K continued its assault on Hill 861 and was joined by Company K, 9th Marines, around midday. The assault made little progress, and the marines withdrew, protected by fire from helicopter gunships. Company B was also heavily engaged throughout the morning, eventually breaking contact at 1200 and establishing a defensive perimeter on a knoll. Medevac helicopters were called in, but as they approached, they brought NVA mortar fire, and by 1445, the company commander reported that he was unable to move. Artillery hit around the company's position, forcing the NVA to fall back. A marine platoon was then sent to assist Company B as it fell back to the battalion command post.

On 27 April, the 3/3 Marines returned to KSCB. Marine artillery and aircraft were used to pound Hill 861 throughout the 27th and 28th, dropping 518,700 pounds of bombs and 1800 artillery rounds on the hill. Due to the dense foliage and overhead cover protecting many of the bunkers, aircraft dropped Snake Eye bombs to remove the foliage and expose the bunkers. Larger bombs (up to two thousand pounds) were used to destroy them. The marines' plan was for 2/3 Marines to take Hill 861, then 3/3 Marines would move west, securing the ground between Hill 861 and Hill 881S. The 2/3 Marines would then provide flank security for 3/3 Marines and take Hill 881N.[50]

On the afternoon of 28 April, 2/3 Marines moved up Hill 861 with little contact. The NVA had withdrawn from the hill. The marines found twenty-five bunkers and numerous fighting positions. They also reported an odor of dead bodies across the hilltop. On 29 April, the 2/3 Marines secured Hill 861, while the 3/3 Marines advanced from KSCB towards a hill 750m northeast of Hill 881S. This was to be used as an intermediate position for the

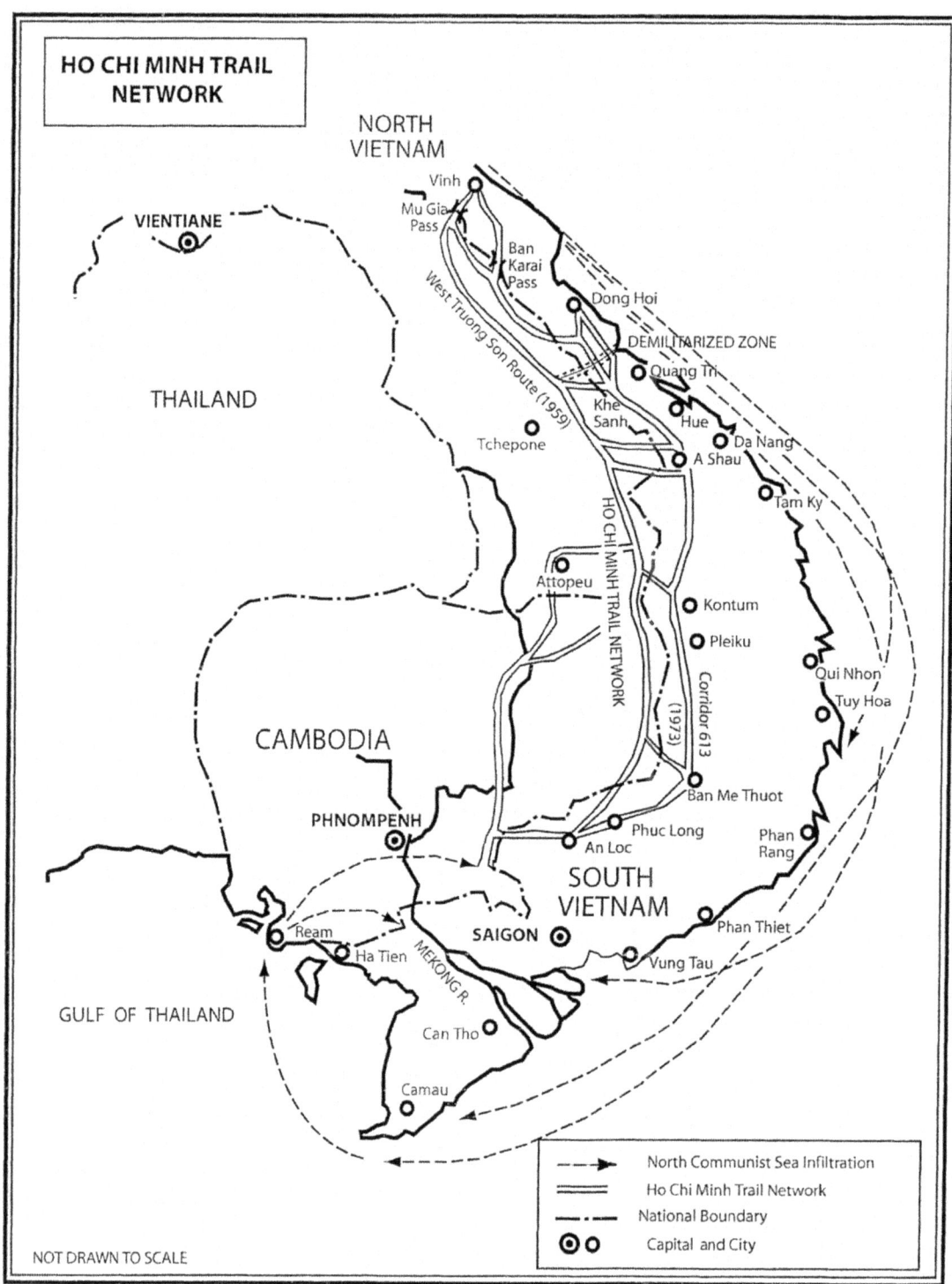

Ho Chi Minh trail network (courtesy Van Nguyen Duong).

attack on Hill 881N. Company M, 9th Marines, engaged an NVA platoon, while Company M, 3rd Marines, secured the intermediate position and dug in. On 30 April, 2/3 Marines moved from Hill 861 to support 3/3 Marines and walked into a NVA bunker complex, suffering nine killed and forty-three wounded. The marines backed off to let artillery and air support hit the bunkers and then overran them. Company M, 3rd Marines, and Company K, 9th Marines, began their assault on Hill 881S. Minimal resistance was encountered until 1025, when they were hit by mortar fire and then heavy fire from numerous NVA bunkers. The marines were pinned down and only able to disengage after several hours with gunship and air support. The marines suffered forty-three killed and 109 wounded in the engagement. NVA losses were 163 killed. As a result, Company M, 3rd Marines, was rendered combat-ineffective and was replaced by Company F, 2/3 Marines. Company E, 9th Marines, was also deployed to KSCB on the afternoon of 1 May. On 1 May, the marines withdrew from Hill 881S to allow for an intense air bombardment. One hundred sixty-six sorties were flown against Hills 881N and South and over 650,000 lbs. of bombs were dropped on them, resulting in over 140 NVA killed.

On 2 May, Companies K and M, 9th Marines, assaulted Hill 881S, capturing it with minimal resistance by 1420 hours. The marines discovered over 250 bunkers protected by two to eight layers of logs and then four to five feet of earth; only fifty bunkers remained intact after the bombing. At 1015 on 2 May, Companies E and G, 2/3 Marines, assaulted Hill 881N. Company G encountered an NVA position and pulled back to allow for artillery support. Company E almost reached the summit of the hill when it was hit by an intense rainstorm and the battalion was pulled back into night defensive positions.

At 0415 on 3 May, an NVA force attacked Company E's night defensive position. The attack broke through the east of the position and reoccupied some bunkers. A marine squad sent to drive out the NVA was hit by machine-gun fire. Air and artillery strikes were called in on the NVA. A flare ship arrived overhead, and the marines on Hill 881S could see approximately two hundred NVA forming up to attack Company E from the west. The marines fired over one hundred rounds of recoilless rifle fire to break up this fresh assault. At dawn, reinforcements were flown in to support Company E, while Company H, 2/3 Marines, attacked the NVA from the rear. The last bunker was cleared at 1500. Twenty-seven marines

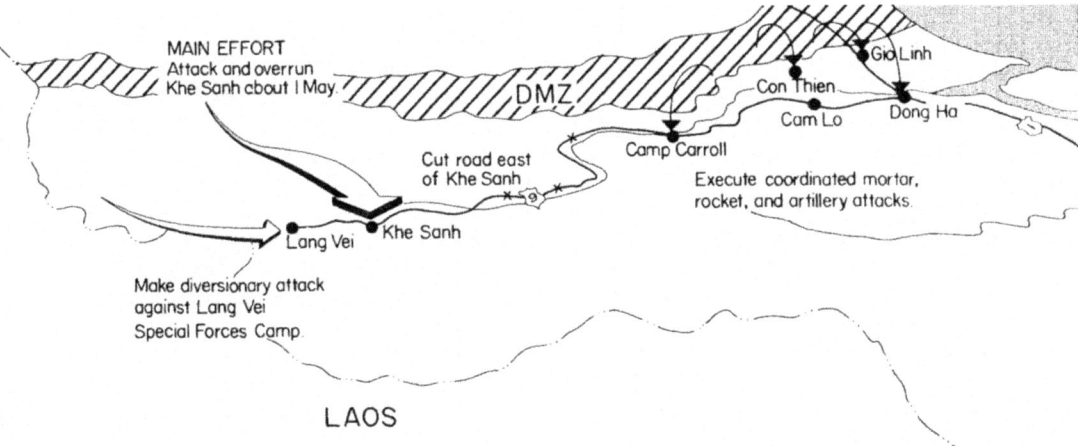

The NVA plan (from Moyers S. Shore, II, *The Battle of Khe Sanh* [Washington, D.C. History and Museums Division, Headquarters, U.S. Marine Corps, 1969]).

were killed and eighty-four wounded in the attack. The NVA lost 137 killed and three captured. Prisoner interrogations revealed plans for another attack on the marine positions that night, but this did not occur.

At 0850, 5 May, Companies E and F, 2/3 Marines, began their assault on Hill 881N. NVA fire increased as they neared the summit, and both companies pulled back to allow for air and artillery strikes. The assault resumed at 1300, and by 1445 the hilltop had been captured. After securing Hill 881N, the marines thoroughly searched the area around Hills 881N and 881S, and air and artillery strikes were called in on suspected NVA positions, but it appeared that the NVA had withdrawn north across the DMZ or west into Laos.

On 9 May, Company F, 2/3 Marines, encountered an NVA force three km northwest of Hill 881N. Artillery fire was called in, and Company E was deployed in support. The engagement resulted in twenty-four marines killed and nineteen wounded, while NVA losses were thirty-one killed. A total of 203 recent NVA graves were discovered in the area. At midnight on 9/10 May, the NVA attacked Reconnaissance Team Breaker of the 3rd Reconnaissance Battalion. The NVA easily could have overrun the marines, but instead targeted the marine helicopters attempting to extract them, severely damaging several. Marine losses were four Reconnaissance Team members and one helicopter pilot dead, while NVA losses were seven dead.

The Hill Fights ended on 10 May. Marine losses were 155 dead and 425 wounded, while NVA losses were 940 confirmed dead. Intelligence gathered after the battle found that the NVA plan was to build up stores and positions north of KSCB, isolate the base from resupply by attacks on marine bases in northern I Corps, and launch a diversionary attack on Lang Vei Special Forces Camp (which occurred as scheduled on 4 May), and then several regiments of the 325C Division would overrun KSCB. The encounter on 24 April had frustrated the NVA plan.

As a result, the marines occupied Hills 861, 881N, and 881S. This was necessary in order to prevent the NVA from having KSCB airfield and base under direct observation from these higher hills. The marines would hold these hills for the remainder of their stay at KSCB. Steven Johnson arrived after the Hill Fights and described the scene.

> The hills, numbered for their elevation in meters above sea level, were Hill 861 and Hill 881S. There was another 881, slightly to the north, so to avoid confusion, the two were always referred to as 881N and 881S. These hills overlooked the airstrip and provided excellent observation to their west. The only thing west of Khe Sanh was a tiny outpost of Army Green Berets at Lang Vei, and then there was Laos and the Ho Chi Minh trail. Small as the Khe Sanh area was, it was a very strategic location and a lot of marines died taking those hills from the NVA. That battle was to become known as the Hill Fights.
>
> The Marines now owned this real estate. A company of infantry was placed on 861 and 881S, and they began working like beavers to fortify them. Oddly, the NVA had barely threatened the main base, even though it was the source of supplies supporting the marines on the hills. Since most of the battalion that took the hills was now in residence on them, there were relatively few troops on the base. The brass must have felt that the location was going to become even more important, so the 26th Marines, currently in the Phu Bai tactical area of responsibility (TAOR), were being moved to Khe Sanh to reinforce. Since Bravo was the Recon company OpConned to 26th Marines, that meant we were moving with them. This move was supposed to take place in about a week, so there was much activity packing up the company office, supply, armory, and so on in preparation. Patrols were also suspended in order to allow teams already out in the bush to finish their patrols and get the company all back on base at the same time.[51]

For the balance of May and into June, the 1st Battalion, 26th Marine Regiment, continued to find traces of the NVA 325C Division near KSCB. On 6 June 1967, the NVA hit the

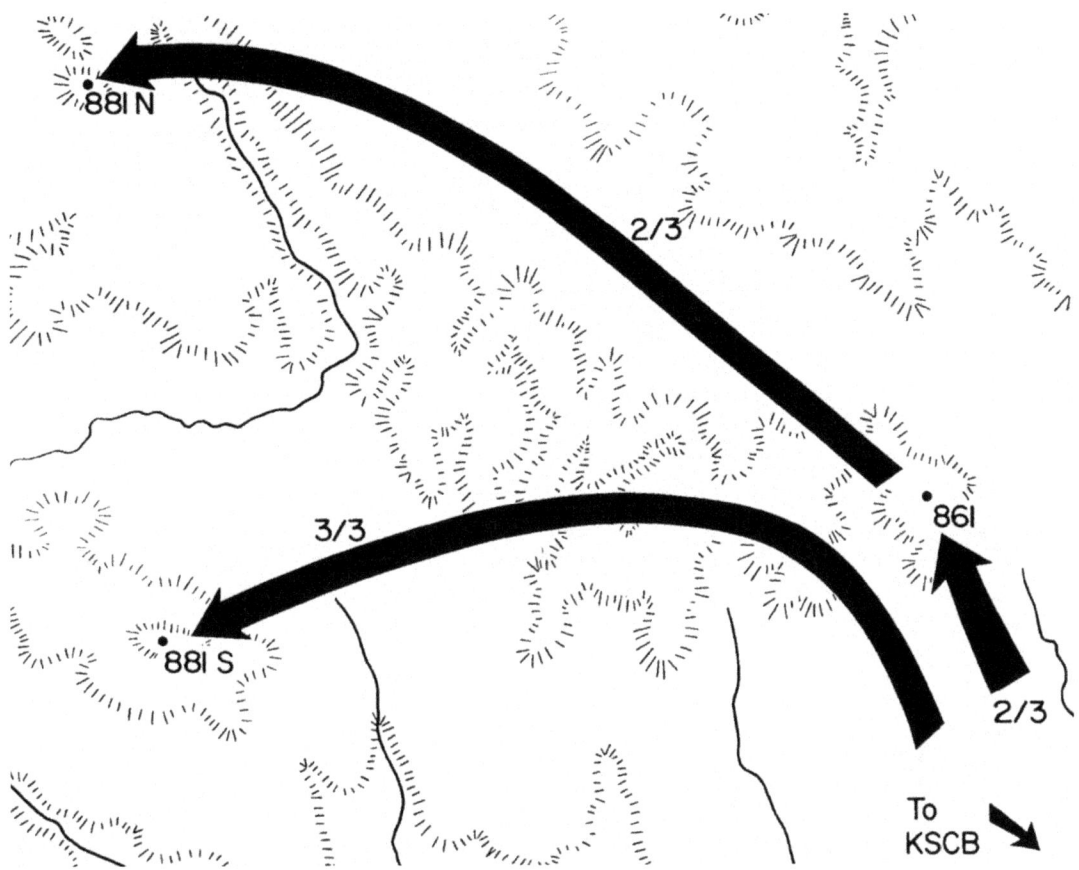

The marine plan for 28 April 1967 (from Moyers S. Shore, II, *The Battle of Khe Sanh* [Washington, D.C. History and Museums Division, Headquarters, U.S. Marine Corps, 1969]).

marines on Hill 950. Six marines were killed and nine wounded. The next day, a marine patrol from B/1/26 was hit near Hill 881S. In the ensuing fight, eighteen marines were killed and twenty-eight wounded. The NVA lost sixty-two dead. As a result, the 3/26th Marines were ordered to KSCB and arrived on 13 June. More contacts followed in June and July, but activity subsided as summer faded. Continuing patrols failed to locate any trace of the NVA.[52]

In August 1967, a supply convoy to Khe Sanh was ambushed on Route 9. This ended resupply by land. KSCB would be exclusively resupplied by air during the siege. As fall arrived, so did the monsoon and marine opposition to remaining at KSCB. As the assistant division commander of the 3rd Marine Division, General Lowell English, said, "When you're at Khe Sanh, you're not really anywhere. You could lose it and you really haven't lost a damn thing."[53] General Westmoreland disagreed, since he wanted a base to oppose an NVA invasion and to cut the Ho Chi Minh Trail. The marines would stay. While it was quiet at Khe Sanh in September 1967, the NVA had shifted its attention to Con Thien, a few kilometers northeast of Khe Sanh.

In November, intelligence reported that two NVA divisions were now located near KSCB, so the 3/26th was ordered back to reinforce KSCB. Operation Scotland kicked off on 14 December, but there were no major contacts. As 1968 arrived, so did more reinforcements to KSCB, since a major attack was expected.

As Tet approached in January 1968, Allied forces in and around KSCB included five infantry battalions, the 37th ARVN Ranger Battalion, and supporting artillery units.[54] On 19 January 1968, marine patrols from Hill 881S made heavy contact with the NVA on Hill 881N. For three weeks it had been quiet, but in the past few days, enemy presence was increasing. During the skirmish, the marines had lost a radio and code sheets. They needed to go back and search the area for these items. A platoon left for Hill 881N when an ambush struck and the platoon got pinned down. Air support and artillery were called in. The company commander, Captain Bill Dabney, ordered the platoon to break contact and fall back. The marines returned after losing one man, PFC Leonard Lee Newton, KIA.[55]

On Saturday morning, 20 January 1968, fog enshrouded Hill 881S. Captain Dabney led his men down Hill 881S to Hill 881N, less than 500 meters away. On the way down, they ran into the NVA and exchanged fire with the enemy. Medevac choppers were needed for a mounting number of wounded as the fight continued into the afternoon. As the wounded were evacuated, friendly artillery pounded Hill 881N. Captain Dabney had lost forty-two people, including seven dead or mortally wounded.[56] As the fight continued, Captain Dabney got a call on the radio from KSCB ordering him to return to his position on Hill 881S. The reason soon became apparent. On 20 January 1968, an NVA defector slipped into KSCB and warned the marines of an impending NVA attack. He provided the NVA attack plans against KSCB, including an attack that night against Hill 861.[57] Author John Prados tells the story of John Corbett.

> A recent arrival [21 January 1968] sent to Khe Sanh, Private Corbett was a gunner with the 81-millimeter mortar section that was a key fire support for the First Battalion, Twenty-sixth Marines on the eastern face of the combat base. John Corbett had just a few weeks in country when the siege began, with an early-morning bombardment by North Vietnamese mortars and rockets. By the standards of Con Thien, this shelling—a hundred mortars of roughly the same caliber (82 millimeter) as Corbett's own (81 millimeter), plus sixty rockets—was about a day's ration. But Khe Sanh Combat Base had not previously been targeted like this, and some facilities were not well protected against bombardment. This was true of the main ammunition dump, just a few dozen yards from Corbett's position, which sustained a direct hit. The first explosion started fires and destroyed some of the shells, while the heat and successive explosions ignited even more rounds. Private Corbett writes in the present tense.
>
> Even with our base's main dump exploding, with fires burning all around us, with our mortar's barrel still glowing and overheating, with an unexploded enemy mortar round sticking out of the dirt several feet away, the men in my squad are singing. Though I am undoubtedly the most scared Marine in Khe Sanh at that moment, I am also the proudest because of the song we are singing: the "Marine Corps Hymn." "From the halls of Montezuma to the shores of Tripoli, we will fight our country's battles on land or on the sea." I join in. This singing together, under these circumstances, keeps our courage up. I am very proud to be here with these Marines. [The ammo dump fire was a huge disaster at the very outset of the siege. The previous night Marine medium artillery (105 millimeter) had expended almost a third of its shells firing in support of a nearby position, Hill 861, which was under attack. Fortuitously, a few days earlier, some of the ammunition had been moved to another dump. Brave Marines rushed into the maelstrom of exploding shells to move—and save—the munitions. But the combination of expenditure and the fires deprived Khe Sanh of 80 percent of its 105-millimeter ammunition.] I am sure the explosions can be seen by the Marines on the hilltop(s). From our mortar emplacements we have the most spectacular view because Khe Sanh's ammunition dump is our neighbor. [The People's Army shifted target to Khe Sanh village, about three miles away, where VPA troops opened a ground assault. Marine commander Colonel Lownds, thinking it too dangerous to send reinforcements, restricted help to fire support. Corbett describes shelling on behalf of the defenders—one of those Marine combined action companies.] We fire for the Marines at Khe Sanh village with our mortar. We drop the bombs where they tell us. We use our remaining ammo in an attempt to help them. Hopefully, the Marines ... can hold. When we are out of mortar

rounds, an order is given from our fire direction center, via our radio headset: "Stand down. Take cover!" It's about time. Our mortars have been returning fire since the attack first started. I believe we are the last to leave our guns.[58]

When the siege started on 21 January with an NVA attack on Hill 861, the marines were ready. Four hundred members of the NVA 325C Division closed in on Hill 861 and were opposed by 150 marines of Kilo Company, 3/26. Enemy sappers (combat engineers) slipped up to the defenses in the darkness. The night was alive with sounds of the sappers as they closed in on the defenses of Hill 861. Clearly these were not the experienced, stealthy sappers seen in VC units. They were laughing and chatting as they approached the barbed wire in front of the marine trenches. At about 2100 hours, artillery was called in and pounded the hill in front of Kilo Company's positions, but the sappers were getting too close, less than thirty meters away, so the artillery did little good. By midnight, the wire was breached and the NVA reached the trench line. The marine outpost on Hill 881S was monitoring the fight. Most of the battalion staff had stayed on the hill after the previous day's engagement, and the following exchange occurred when a call came in from a rattled lieutenant on Hill 861.

> A frantic voice transmitting from 861 cut through the static. "We're being overrun! Command group is all down!" Major Matthew Caulfield, the battalion operations officer, took the handset. "A Marine unit doesn't get overrun," Caulfield coolly replied. "Now calm down and tell me what is really happening." The frantic voice belonged to Jasper's executive officer, First Lieutenant Jerry N. Saulsberry. The fear in Saulsberry's voice was palpable as he laid out the grim situation. "Get your gunny," Caulfield said. "Make sure you rely on him." "The gunny is dead," Saulsberry replied.
> "Get your first sergeant," Caulfield said, mindful of Ben Goddard's stellar reputation. "He's dying," came the response. (Goddard, in fact, would live.) Caulfield, a charming Irishman, summoned all his powers of inspiration to steel the overwhelmed lieutenant. "Now Jerry, I know you can do this," Caulfield exhorted. "I want you to take that ball and run with it!" There was silence on the other end. Finally, Saulsberry responded in a weak voice. "Run? Did you say *run*, sir?" "No, no, Jerry!" Caulfield shouted back into the handset. "You gotta stay right there!"[59]

Although the NVA broke through the perimeter, the attack was beaten off after hand-to-hand fighting.[60]

> The first hint of dawn found the men of Kilo Company shaken and bloodied, but still in control of the hill. During the night, the North Vietnamese assault commander had been overheard in a radio transmission, screaming for his reserves to join the attack. But the American response had been swift and decisive, from the riflemen and machine gunners on 861 to the artillery crews at 881S, Khe Sanh, and Camp Carroll, farther east along Route 9. Dead and dying North Vietnamese soldiers now littered the slopes of 861 and nearby terrain. The NVA attack had been broken.[61]

Meanwhile, the main base was being shelled with hundreds of rounds. The incoming ignited stored CS gas that blanketed KSCB, and a round touched off a large quantity of C-4 explosives. Two NVA divisions were now poised to attack KSCB, the 325th and 304th, a total of 20,000 men.[62] The base was reinforced by the 1/9 Marines and the 37th ARVN Ranger Battalion. In spite of the chaos caused by the shelling, it was not followed by an NVA ground attack on KSCB; however, the nearby village of Khe Sanh was attacked in the early hours of 21 January. The village was the home of one of Saigon's district headquarters and was defended by 175 Americans, South Vietnamese, and Montagnard Bru tribesmen. The NVA attack got under way at 0530 hours and was answered by artillery support from KSCB. After hours of fighting, the initial NVA attack failed and they withdrew. Jubilation at the district headquarters ended when the marine commander at KSCB, Colonel Lownds, called in and indicated that Khe Sanh village could no longer be provided with artillery support from KSCB. That made the village indefensible, and all troops would need to be withdrawn. As they withdrew to KSCB, a scene of shocking horror was observed by the troops from Khe Sanh village. Hundreds of NVA lay dead, the result of artillery support from KSCB. The fight at Khe Sanh village had cost the NVA 640 dead and wounded, while the Allies lost twelve ARVN and seven Bru killed and twenty-five wounded. No Americans had been killed. As night fell on 22 January, the NVA entered Khe Sanh village and claimed the district headquarters without firing a shot.[63]

As NVA reinforcements were rushed forward, U.S. air support was called in to hit suspected routes of advance and specific targets. At this point, General Westmoreland had decided that U.S. artillery and air would save Khe Sanh against a vastly superior force.[64] The massive air campaign was dubbed Operation Niagara. It was a wise move. General Giap had 20,000 troops surrounding Khe Sanh, with another 20,000 nearby. These presented many lucrative targets. The air campaign kicked off on 22 January, while a total of 6,000 marines defended Khe Sanh.[65]

Early on 22 January, the NVA probed the defenses of KSCB and pounded them with artillery. Something strange unfolded that morning.

> A frightened crowd of about 1,500 Vietnamese and ethnic Bru—young and old; men, women, and children—still huddled at the main gate. Hurried discussions between American and South Vietnamese officials produced an agreement to evacuate the Vietnamese, but not the Bru. The South Vietnamese I Corps commander, General Hoang Xuan Lam, insisted there was no place for the minority refugees, so they were told to return to their homes, now a no-man's-land between the combat base and the converging North Vietnamese troops. The virtual abandonment of the Bru people at Khe Sanh stands as a sordid chapter for the Americans and South Vietnamese, ultimately leading to the deaths of as many as several thousand men, women, and children caught in the escalating battle.[66]

The runway at KSCB was busy on 22 January. Incoming flights brought in ammunition and 1/9 Marines reinforcements, and shuttle flights lifted 1,100 noncombatants to safety during a 24-hour period. That night at 2200 hours, enemy probes were illuminated by flares and NVA scrambled back over their dead comrades after heavy fire cut down many. That morning, more supplies arrived, including a shipment of 4,000 body bags. It was large enough to be noticed and was not a morale builder. The NVA massed their artillery and presented their answer to Operation Niagara. Guns of all calibers as well as rockets and artillery rained down on KSCB and its outposts.

> As at Dien Bien Phu, the North Vietnamese forces set about weakening Khe Sanh and its outposts with artillery, mortar, and sniper fire. The bulk of the damage was inflicted by two NVA artillery regiments, the 45th and 675th, now scattered through the rugged countryside west of Khe Sanh. The North Vietnamese had targeted Khe Sanh with 212 heavy weapons, including eight 152-millimeter guns, sixteen 130-millimeter guns, thirty-six 122-millimeter guns, more than one hundred 122-millimeter rocket launchers, and a supporting cast of assorted smaller guns and howitzers. To protect the artillery from American air strikes, the North Vietnamese had forty-two 37-millimeter anti-aircraft guns, twelve 57-millimeter guns, and 130 anti-aircraft machine guns. Highly mobile mortar teams had completely surrounded the American outposts, and they unleashed deadly fire that was targeted and adjusted by artillery forward observers, who had established camouflaged positions around the combat base and forward posts.[67]

On 24 January, NVA howitzers pounded Hill 881S, Hill 861, and the main base. The troops hoped for a Tet truce scheduled from 29–31 January 1968, but on 30 January, KSCB was notified that the truce had been cancelled. People in Saigon and Washington were scurrying around considering General Westmoreland's warning that nuclear and chemical weapons would be needed if the situation deteriorated at KSCB, but use of these weapons was denied. What began then was considered by many to be "the most concentrated application of aerial firepower in the history of warfare."[68] The aerial firepower saved KSCB.

The Results of the Border Battles

On 30 January 1968, the battle of Tet started throughout South Vietnam, except at KSCB, where no ground attack occurred, but incoming artillery continued.[69] The Border Battles were over. As seen thus far, there were many results from the Border Battles. From the start it was Hanoi's plan to attract Allied forces from the highly populated coastal areas with their large cities to the border areas in preparation for the Tet attacks on the cities. It did not work. Many of the Border Battles were over long before Tet, and the U.S. forces with their superior mobility had been deployed from the border areas. The Border Battles did give the NVA experience in large-scale conventional attacks, which was one of General Giap's objectives. This would become important in the NVA Easter invasion of 1972 and the final invasion of South Vietnam in 1975. The Hanoi goal of destroying a major unit, such as was done in the French War, was nearly achieved on several occasions. In spite of General Peers's order that companies should remain within mutually supporting distance during operations in the jungle, this did not always happen. Some companies were isolated and badly mauled. The greatest losses were to the 173rd Airborne Brigade at Hills 1338, 830, and 875. The 173rd paid a high price for not heeding Colonel Adamson's warning that they would be fighting the highly professional NVA, not "those ragged-ass bastards" described by General Harkins years earlier. These losses caused some of the U.S. regiments to become combat-ineffective for a short time until replacements could be assigned and trained. On the other side, the 173rd and 4ID rendered several NVA regiments combat-ineffective due to the heavy casualties that they inflicted. This had very little effect on Tet '68 since it was fought (and lost) by the VC, not the NVA.

General Westmoreland's goal was to increase enemy body count, and the Border Battles did that far beyond his wildest expectations. Most of the NVA casualties were a result of air attacks and especially the B-52 missions. The problem was that the body count figures were inflated due to command pressure, as best seen by Colonel Schumacher's actions in the 173d battles. The sad thing was that the body count figures were irrelevant because Hanoi had no problem replacing massive losses. Students protesting the war were not found in North Vietnam. On the other side of the equation, many of the NVA dead were not counted because they were carried away by comrades or vaporized by explosives, especially B-52 bombs. One marine thought one could arrive at the correct body count by adding up all of the arms and legs and dividing by four. Killing and counting innocent civilians in the body count, such as was done at the My Lai massacre was, of course, immoral and did nothing but swell the ranks of the VC. General Westmoreland's tactics of search-and-destroy were very costly to U.S. units. Colonel (later general) William J. Livsey was one of the few senior officers who understood that it is less costly to find the enemy and use artillery and air to finish him. The final result of all of this is that the heavy U.S. casualties sustained in the Border Battles and the Tet campaign that followed eroded of support for the war on the home front. This led to our withdrawal from Vietnam. The U.S. won every major battle, but South Vietnam lost the war. By the time General Westmoreland was removed from command and sent home, it was too late to retrieve the situation.

5

Aftermath:
Tet '68: 31 January 1968

It will be straight, if slow, ploughing ahead with the light at the end of the tunnel growing brighter all the time.[1]—Henry Cabot Lodge, U.S. Ambassador

Hanoi gave final approval for what has become known as the Tet offensive in October [1967], later confirmed by a party resolution. Part of the scheme's genius lay in the realization that the groundwork could not be laid without Washington and Saigon becoming aware of it. The plan therefore included a deception, an alternative set of expectations the Americans could believe in. In each major war zone Hanoi would battle near the South Vietnamese border, giving the impression it intended to carry out a more conventional operation [away from the population centers].[2]

Tet, or the Vietnamese Lunar New Year, is the most important celebration in Vietnamese culture. The date usually falls in late January or early February, with celebrations lasting for three days. Vietnamese people usually return to their families during Tet to visit graves of their ancestors in their homeland or to worship at the family altar. In 1968, Tet was scheduled to start on 31 January. It was called in Vietnamese "Tet Mau Than": The Year of the Monkey.

General Westmoreland and his intelligence chief, General Davidson, thought that the enemy offensive would begin either before or after Tet, since all sides respected the Tet holiday. Hanoi intended the attack to coincide with Tet, starting on the first day of the holiday, but fate intervened to confuse the timing, to the advantage of the Allies. In Hanoi and the South's Central Highlands, the Lunar New Year started on 30 January, while in the remainder of South Vietnam it started on the 31st. When the error was discovered, there was a massive rush by the VC to move up their attacks in the South to 30 January. The mistimed VC moves and some early assaults alerted U.S. commanders that the attack would start at the beginning of Tet. General Weyand was II Force Commander responsible for MR3. At his headquarters, staff officers had established a betting pool on the start time, with fifteen-minute time blocks starting at dusk on the 30th. Most favored midnight to 0500 hours on 31 January.[3] The winner held the time of 0300 hours, when the VC attacked Saigon.

At Saigon, the VC penetrated Tan Son Nhut airbase and did damage there while attacks at Bien Hoa airbase at 0300 hours consisted of 122mm rockets and mortar attacks.[4] Other attacks included nearby Long Binh. Heavy fighting in the streets of Saigon proved that the VC had infiltrated thousands of troops into the capital for this offensive without being

5. Aftermath

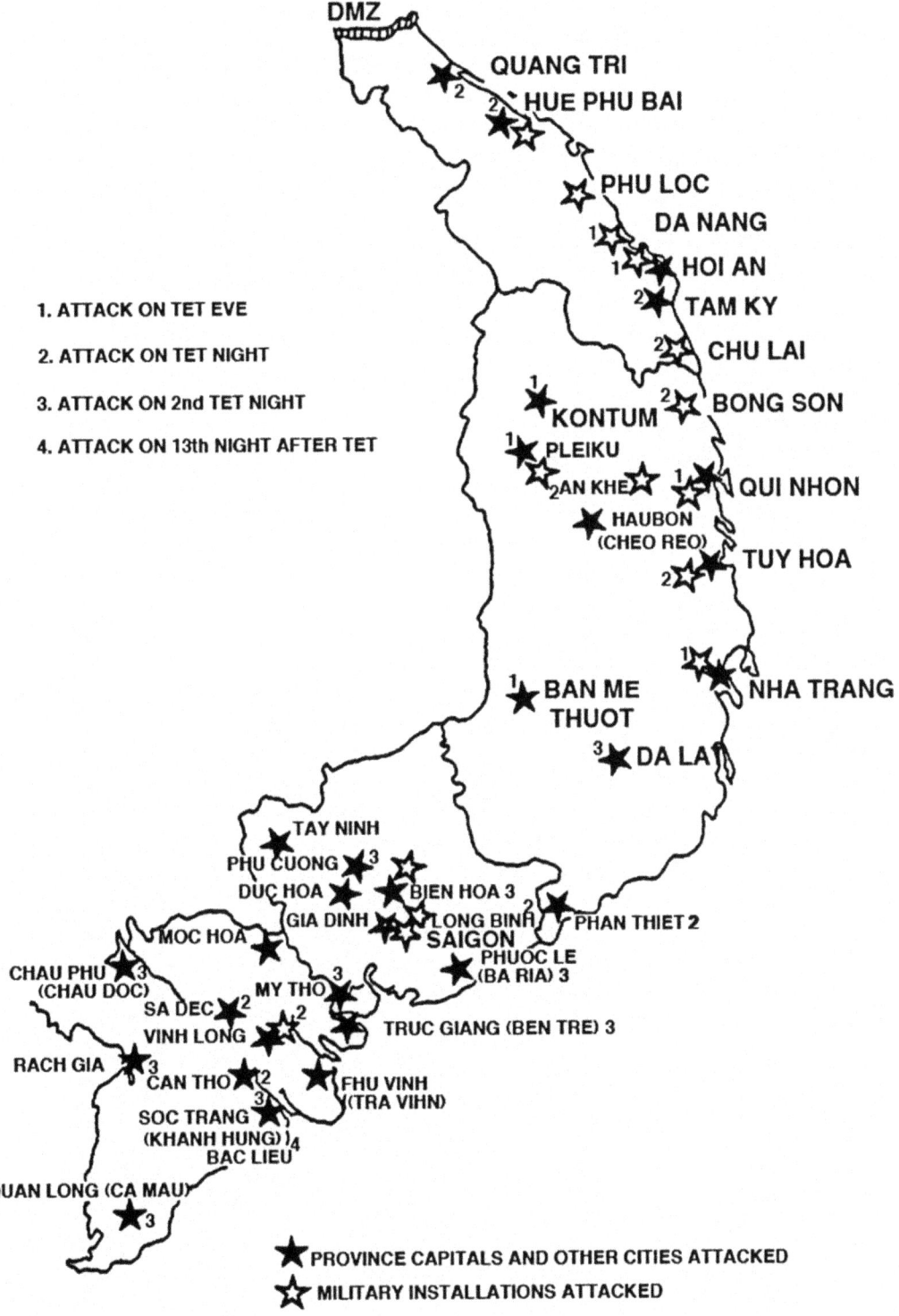

Tet Offensive of 1968 (from Ngoc Lung Hoang, *The General Offensives of 1968–1969* [Washington, D.C.: U.S. Center of Military History, 1981]).

detected. General Davidson, Westmoreland's chief intelligence officer, concluded years later that Hanoi had lost strategic surprise, but achieved tactical surprise at some locations.[5]

In South Vietnam, debates between the CIA and MACV continued over the strength of Communist forces in the South. The CIA estimated a total of 430,000 in the South, while MACV estimated no more than 300,000 were available. MACV realized that the higher number would indicate that Hanoi had the military strength to pursue a protracted war, something not acknowledged by General Westmoreland at this point in time.

U.S. public support for the war had declined. For this reason, the CIA estimate was suppressed. The number of troops available during Tet '68 were 325,000 to 595,000 Communists and nearly a million available to fight for the South. This number included 331,098 U.S. Army and 78,013 U.S. Marines.

It was a strange situation. All in the South realized that there would be a major offensive during Tet, but when and where were unknown.[6] In spite of the threat, business went on as usual. For example, South Vietnamese President Thieu insisted on sending many of his soldiers home on leave for Tet.[7]

General Westmoreland expected that the attack would consist of an NVA invasion of South Vietnam at Khe Sanh. He appears to be one of the few fooled by Hanoi's deception, but he made no major move of troops to the DMZ other than 15,000 that he sent to reinforce the marines.[8] He did not need to. The U.S. strategic mobility capability allowed the quick movement of troops to Khe Sanh if an invasion materialized. Similarly, the troops could be quickly moved back to the population centers, if needed.[9] He was prepared to use all means available to stop the invasion at Khe Sanh and recommended the use of nuclear weapons against what he perceived as a lucrative target of massed NVA troops. His request was denied. Most intelligence indicated an attack on Saigon. There were indicators in advance of the attack. For weeks, an unusually large number of funerals were seen in Saigon. Later it was realized that many of the coffins contained weapons smuggled into Saigon for the uprising. At Weyand's headquarters, a young intelligence officer noticed that the VC had realigned their zones of responsibility to converge on Saigon. This would facilitate an attack on the capital. In Hanoi, they likened it to a grapefruit with Saigon at the center.[10] Weyand responded quickly by doubling the number of U.S. battalions in Saigon between 11 January and Tet.[11] Weyand's actions may well have saved Saigon in the battle that followed.

As Saigon was attacked, thirty-five of South Vietnam's forty-four provincial capitals were also attacked as well as other government locations. The total number of VC targets was 166.[12] As the province capitals were attacked, Steve Vorthmann in the 173rd Airborne Brigade was at Tuy Hoa in MR2.

> C Company was involved in the defense of Tuy Hoa during the 31 January 1968 Tet Offensive. There were several KIAs from Charlie Company, including machine gunner Jack McKee, who was ten to twenty meters to my right and was killed as a result of a friendly air strike on the village. One night, six kilometers west of Tuy Hoa, our side of the company harbor site was attacked with grenades and small arms fire. All of my squad was wounded except for two of us. Our squad was disbanded, and we were assigned to another. I still have my grenade shrapnel imbedded in my canteen cup. C Company was also involved in a firefight at Ban Me Thout, where the attached ARVNs hid behind a little mound. The last month or two, I was in the rear at Tuy Hoa, where I was responsible for delivering supplies to the company in the field. Our company was in the field humping for twenty to thirty-five days at a time, getting resupplied every five days.[13]

General Davidson considered the broad conventional offensive spread across the country to be Hanoi's greatest blunder at Tet. The amount of coordination and synchronization needed to accomplish this seemed to be beyond Hanoi's capability, but, in fact, this had been practiced successfully during the Border Battles. Davidson believed that the offensive should have been centered on a few targets, but Hanoi's approach was entirely consistent with their plan to cause an uprising against the Saigon regime. By attacking across the entire country, they had the best chance for a general uprising. In Saigon, a diligent effort was made to seize the government radio station in order to announce the uprising, but it could not be held and was retaken by the government.[14] That did not matter, since the people were in no mood to listen to a broadcast to join an uprising against their government, and this was true throughout South Vietnam. Hanoi had failed. Throughout South Vietnam, at government locations, VC attacks were repulsed or towns were quickly retaken. It was only at Saigon and the Vietnamese traditional capital of Hue that fighting persisted. In Saigon, the fighting lasted two weeks before the VC were eliminated. In Hue, the VC took and held the city for twenty-five days. They entered the city with lists of names of government officials and others loyal to Saigon. Thousands of these were rounded up, executed, and buried in mass graves. In a twist of fate, one government official escaped with a list of names of local VC agents. When the South Vietnamese government returned, the suspects were rounded up and dealt with.[15]

By the end of January, it was over, and assessments were coming in. Eventually, it was concluded that Hanoi had suffered a total defeat on the battlefield, but the U.S. had sustained a political defeat at home from which it would not recover. Those in government blamed the media for turning a battlefield victory into a defeat, but it appears that the government did this with little help from the media.

General Bruce Palmer, the army vice chief of staff, said the Allies were surprised and likened the attack to Pearl Harbor.[16] As seen above, this was an unduly harsh judgment, given the planning to counter the enemy's attacks. One cannot conclude that it was a total surprise if staff officers had a betting pool for the hour of the attack. Yet many of the Allies behaved as if no attack were expected. Sending ARVN troops on leave on the eve of the attack is an example. General Westmoreland and his deputy, Creighton Abrams, were in their quarters when they were awakened by their aides and the gunfire.[17] The South Vietnamese president was enjoying the Tet holiday with his family in My Tho.[18]

> As for eyewitnesses, Ambassador Robert Komer would later reflect, "I knew in one day that whatever had happened out there, Tet had changed absolutely everything in Washington." Komer came to that insight instantly, before the media reporting had appeared. Ambassador Bui Diem comments, "The general feeling was consternation, and I was there during those days in Washington."[19]

The attacks provided two iconic images of the war: a VC officer executed in the street by a shot to the head and VC dead bodies strewn on the U.S. embassy grounds. Both had a negative impact on the U.S. public's support for the war.

The casualty numbers told the story. Hanoi had lost 40,000–72,000, mostly VC.[20] Enemy casualty numbers were always debatable, but this range of numbers seems correct. It was a devastating defeat for the enemy. Allied losses were much less: 11,500.[21] Senator Aiken of Vermont opined, "If this is a failure, I hope the Viet Cong never have a major success."[22]

Stanley Karnow reported a meeting in Ho Chi Minh City in 1981 with a prominent Communist figure, Dr. Duong Quinn Hoa:

> "We lost our best people," she said mournfully, recalling that Viet Cong units composed mostly of indigenous southerners had borne the brunt of the fighting and had suffered the heaviest casualties.

Over the next year, she went on, the southern Communist political organization was to be badly battered by the CIA's Phoenix program, a covert campaign to uproot the Viet Cong's rural structure.[23]

Although the real numbers of enemy dead were staggering, MACV and the Pentagon inflated the numbers, as they usually did, with interesting results. When General Westmoreland requested an increase in troop strength of 206,756, LBJ was stunned. This would require U.S. mobilization that he had always resisted, and in the current political climate, it was impossible.[24] When briefing at the State Department, General Depuy, from the Pentagon, claimed 80,000 enemy dead. When asked about enemy wounded, Depuy stated there were three wounded for every one dead, for a grand total of 320,000 enemy casualties. He should have seen where this was headed, but didn't. The next question was how many enemies faced the Allies during Tet. Depuy answered: 230,000. Arthur Goldberg, one of the president's Wise Men[25] replied "Who the Hell is there left for us to fight?" General Westmoreland's request for more troops was denied. The next day, the Wise Men recommended to President Johnson that it was time to "disengage,"[26] a polite term meaning get the hell out of Vietnam. After years of promising reports by General Westmoreland and others, it became obvious to the American public that we were not winning the war. A "credibility gap" was widening between the government and its citizens. As the Tet fighting concluded, Westmoreland stated, "We've got 'em on the run."[27] This was the same remark made by General Harkins years earlier, after the battle of Ap Bac.[28] It became obvious to the American public that if Hanoi could attack on the massive scale that they did, we were not winning the war.

Broadcaster Walter Cronkite made a hurried tour of Vietnam in late February 1968 and shortly thereafter on national television dolorously called Tet an American defeat, saying on 27 February that "the only rational way out will be to negotiate, not as victors but as an honorable people." President Johnson, watching this program, lamented to his press secretary, George Christian, "If I've lost Cronkite, I've lost middle America."[29]

For the U.S., some good came from Tet. McNamara was sacked, and Westmoreland would go home on 22 March 1968. McNamara would leave government to take over the World Bank, while Westmoreland took over the army as chief of staff. At Tet '68 and earlier, from the middle of 1967, Hanoi was losing the shooting war in Vietnam, but the U.S. was losing public support for the war among its own people.[30] Although there was support for the war during and immediately after Tet: "the rally around the flag and support our troops effect" had dwindled.[31] The Gallup Poll counted 53 percent support for the war in October 1967. In September 1968 it had dropped to 46 percent.

One of the most important results of Tet '68 was LBJ's decision to hand over the war to the South Vietnamese. Vietnamization was born.[32] The push for peace talks was also a key event. On 31 March 1968, President Johnson announced that he would not run for reelection and ordered a bombing halt in North Vietnam.[33] Since the 1950s, pundits in Washington had said that the last domino to fall would be the U.S. president, and it happened. The light at the end of the tunnel disappeared.

As an autopsy of Tet and the demise of Robert McNamara's career, author Deborah Shapley described McNamara's final performance in government.

The shock of the Tet offensive rippled instantly through the United States. Millions were appalled as television relayed images of spectacular defeat, contradicting official reports that the enemy was being defeated. McNamara was less shocked than many in the upper reaches of government. His mathematical mind had long since reckoned that the enemy was not being killed off at anything like the rates Westmoreland had claimed. "You couldn't reconcile the number" of enemy, "the level of infiltration, the body count and the resultant figures. It just didn't add up. I never did get the answer," McNamara said years later in a deposition for the Westmoreland-CBS lawsuit. In his posture statement released that January, he warned of a future enemy buildup in the South. McNamara had been struggling to stave off needless additional U.S. deaths for more than a year. But his power was running out daily, almost by the hour. McNamara's successor, Washington lawyer and superhawk Clark Clifford, would determine the choice with the president, not McNamara.[34]

Vietnamization

After the Border Battles, Vietnamization was our ticket out of Vietnam. The myth of Vietnamization started in March 1969. It was a fig leaf used to cover our bug-out from Vietnam. We had no choice. A disintegrating U.S. Army in Vietnam coupled with mounting opposition to the war at home and an incompetent U.S. bureaucracy meant that we needed to get out of Vietnam quickly. The nation was unable to cope with the war and the majority did not support the war. There were many other problems that forced our withdrawal as early as possible. The U.S., of course, did not have an unlimited budget, and paying for the war was at the expense of other things. Vietnam had already cost LBJ his program called the "Great Society."[35] Added to that was a recalcitrant, corrupt regime in Saigon under President Thieu that had not won the hearts and minds of its people. As the NVA took over Saigon in 1975, Thieu was seen running to an aircraft even though he had vowed to fight to the end. He had an entourage of assistants running after him with bags full of clanking gold bars to secure his comfortable exile.[36] As the South Vietnamese were disintegrating, the North Vietnamese with the help of their allies were becoming much stronger and more capable of overwhelming South Vietnam. Vietnamization was a foreign policy disaster. As Henry Kissinger was trying to negotiate a peace treaty for Vietnam, we gave away his biggest bargaining chip: U.S. Forces were withdrawing from Vietnam. Why would North Vietnam want to negotiate a treaty when the U.S. was leaving Vietnam and the South Vietnam regime was incapable of defending itself?

The Vietnamization concept was simple: turn the war over to the South Vietnamese. It started in 1969.

> Laird [the Secretary of Defense] coined the term *Vietnamization* as an improvement on *de–Americanization*, the more straightforward word for unilateral withdrawal then in use. Recognizing Laird's invention as a stroke of public-relations genius, Nixon immediately adopted the euphemism as official terminology.... Everyone present understood that Vietnamization was designed to mollify American critics of the war, not a policy for the effective defense of South Vietnam.[37]

The withdrawal would be conducted in three phases. First, the ground war would be turned over to the South Vietnamese. Second, the South Vietnamese would develop their own combat support capability, and finally, the U.S. presence would revert to an advisory role, where it had started over ten years earlier.

Vietnamization was to be done in about two years. It was an impossible schedule, and it would take longer. Some things were doable, such as training ARVN infantry troops and artillerymen who already had the weapons of their trade and had been using them for years. Training ARVN combat support troops was far more difficult. Combat support was the Achilles heel of the Vietnamization concept. It takes years to develop a training structure to produce troops capable of maintaining complex equipment such as a helicopter and establishing inventory control over weapons and spare parts.

Equipment

The U.S. was flooding the ARVN with large quantities of all sorts of equipment. Author Neil Sheehan identified hundreds of tanks, squadrons of jet fighter-bombers, and over 500 Hueys and Chinook helicopters.[38] How the South Vietnamese were expected to operate and maintain this extravagant flood of equipment is anyone's guess. Transferring signal equipment and aircraft was more complicated than other items that the ARVN already had in large quantities, such as rifles and artillery.

Horror stories started to appear. During the so-called Cambodian Incursion in May 1970, ARVN Major General Nguyen Viet Thanh was killed in an aircraft collision. Was it because the ARVN pilots had not had adequate training? No one can say. Lieutenant General Do Cao Tri was considered by many to be the best fighting general that the South Vietnamese had. He was killed when his helicopter crashed shortly after takeoff. The crash was attributed to mechanical failure. Since a *Newsweek* correspondent, François Sully, had also been killed in the crash, Ed Behr of *Newsweek* was sent to investigate the airworthiness of the now South Vietnamese helicopter fleet. Here is part of his report.

> At Bien Hoa, SFC John Keith had been a helicopter maintenance man for eight of his eighteen years in the U.S. Army. Keith showed him row after row of Hueys with serious maintenance deficiencies—oil and fuel leaks, engine filters and compressor blades caked with dirt, and missing rivets. Over U.S. objections, many of the helicopters had nevertheless been rated fit to fly by the Vietnamese maintenance men. One chopper, with a torque so low that the advisors called it a "potential crash just waiting to happen," had been rated unfit to fly early one day, but a Vietnamese technician later blithely gave the chopper a "positive checkout" and certified it as ready to fly. Taking the machine up, Sergeant Keith said, would be "tantamount to suicide."[39]

Training

As stated above for signal units, equipment training was extremely important because the ARVN had no experience with some of the items that would be transferred to them. The job was made more difficult because there were no operator or maintenance manuals written in Vietnamese. To provide for this need, a signal school was established to train South Vietnamese soldiers on complex equipment on 1 July 1970.[40] It was a bit late for that, given the U.S. withdrawal schedule. Nevertheless, most of the ARVN officers spoke some English, so the turnover was made to work.

There were exceptions. Some of the signal equipment was so huge and complex that there was no way training could be accomplished. For these sites, such as the communications complex at Pleiku, the army turned to the U.S. private sector to run these, and Federal Electric Corporation was hired.[41] The contractors were Americans for the most part, but Federal Electric tried to hire Vietnamese and would train the South Vietnamese to take over the Pleiku complex. Federal Electric was still in place long after the U.S. Army departed.

There were some training disasters. Toward the end of the war, most South Vietnamese aircraft were grounded due to the inability to locate needed parts. There were warehouses full of parts, but apparently no one trained the South Vietnamese on how to locate them in the warehouses. There was very little inventory control. Although the U.S. attempted to train some Vietnamese civilians, the ARVN officers had no interest in that.[42]

Return of the Border Battles—Lam Son 719

At the end of 1970, U.S. force levels had been reduced by 200,000, and more major reductions were scheduled for 1971.[43] Both President Richard M. Nixon and South Vietnamese President Thieu had elections coming up soon, and a military victory would fit nicely into their reelection plans. The Lam Son 719 operation into Laos in early 1971 was intended to demonstrate the success of Vietnamization, but it did not quite work out that way.

Henry Kissinger, President Nixon's national security advisor, summarized. "The operation, conceived in ambivalence and assailed by skepticism, proceeded in confusion. It soon became apparent that the plans on which we had been so eloquently and frequently briefed reflected staff exercises, not military reality."[44]

The name Lam Son was the place of an ancient Vietnamese victory over the Chinese. The number 719 was derived from the year, 1971, and the major axis of advance: Highway 9. Highway 9 ran along the south edge of the DMZ, past Khe Sanh and through Con Thien before reaching the Laotian border.

Early in the war, the Ho Chi Minh Trail was established to move men and materiel from North Vietnam to South Vietnam through Laos and Cambodia. Initially, it was footpaths used by porters and bicycles, but by 1971, it had expanded to a two-lane road. Fleets of trucks moved the materiel south in massive quantities. While there were efforts made to interdict the trail, they were largely ineffective. It was not just a single trail but a web that moved the materiel south. The total length of the web was 3,500 miles.[45] Incredibly, it included a fuel pipeline that ran south from North Vietnam to the Ashau Valley in the South.

On 31 January 1971, Hanoi's Van Tien Dung, deputy chairman of the Politburo's Central Military Party Committee and the chief of the general staff, visited the front to address the troops. He made Hanoi's objectives clear to the troops.

> The coming engagement will be a strategically decisive battle. We will fight not only to retain control of the strategic transportation corridor, but also to annihilate a number of units of the enemy's strategic reserve forces, to deal a significant defeat to a portion of the "Vietnamization plot," to advance our resistance effort to liberate South Vietnam and defend North Vietnam, to gloriously fulfill our international duty, and to hone our main force troops in the fires of combat. Our Army must certainly win this battle.[46]

To summarize Lam Son 719: Hanoi was committed to win with whatever resources were required. The U.S. would be on the sidelines watching the fight, since the Cooper-Church Amendment prohibited U.S. servicemen from entering Laos, but U.S. air support was not prohibited by the amendment. President Nixon was hopeful that Lam Son 719 would prove that Vietnamization was working and that this would help him secure his 1972 reelection. President Thieu wanted a victory and wanted to minimize casualties in order to secure his reelection.

Weather was a key factor in all of this. The dry season, from November to March, was prime time for the NVA to move supplies, stockpile, and prepare for an invasion of South Vietnam after the monsoons (rainy season) passed. The goal of the penetration into Laos was the town of Tchepone, forty-two kilometers inside the Laotian border. Tchepone was a valuable target since it was a crossroad for the Ho Chi Minh Trail but slightly west of it. Thieu, in a rare moment of candor, ordered Lieutenant General Lam, the MR1 commander and operation commander: "You go in there just long enough to take a piss and then leave quickly." Major General Nguyen Duy Hinh, an infantry division commander, put it more politely. "It was apparent that President Thieu had decided at the outset that once Tchepone had been entered by ARVN, the withdrawal should begin without delay."[47]

Lam Son 719 was planned as a six-week operation in February–March 1971 and was designed to disrupt the Ho Chi Minh Trail in Laos. With the monsoon approaching, it was thought that Hanoi would have great difficulty rebuilding supplies in the bad weather, and this would delay their invasion of South Vietnam scheduled for 1972.[48] Lam Son 719 would follow an unprecedented bombing campaign against the trail, ordered by Secretary of Defense Laird, that started in mid-October 1970.[49] The air force claimed that twenty-five thousand trucks were destroyed on the Ho Chi Minh Trail between October 1970 and May 1971, but Laird thought that the extensive bombing raid would not be enough to stop the NVA offensive in 1972.[50] Private First Class Clyde Baker wrote to Nixon. "In my opinion the Cambodian operation and this operation [Lam Son 719] are the 2 most intelligent moves we made since we have been in S. Vietnam. This operation may end the war and may save hundreds of lives in the long run, and everyone here is putting out 100%. I'm sorry for the lousy handwriting, but I'm writing this letter down inside a tank."[51]

On the first day, 8 February 1971, as the ARVN armored columns prepared to enter Laos, airlift was meeting unexpected resistance. "We are fighting a conventional war out there,"[52] said a U.S. helicopter pilot who came under heavy anti-aircraft fire. The NVA had carefully planned its air defenses, which consisted of various flak guns, surface-to-air missiles (probably the Soviet-made Strela), and the deadly 12.7mm machine guns. Some of the guns were radar-controlled. They were set up with interlocking fire, so that if a helicopter received fire and turned to avoid it, another anti-aircraft gun would engage. From the NVA

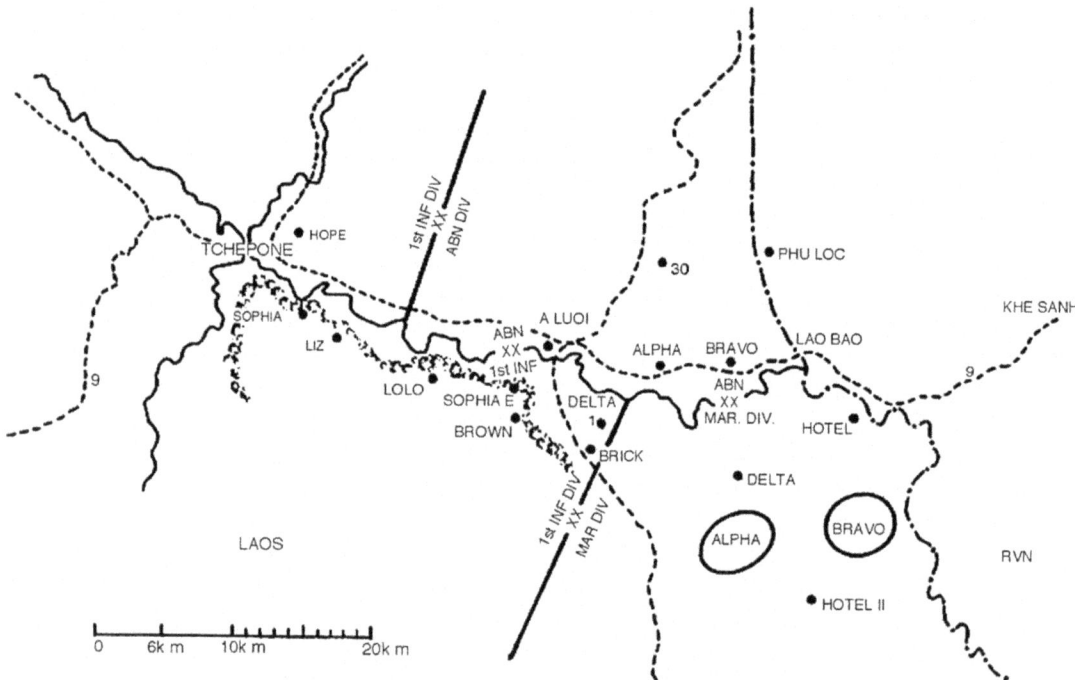

The move on Tchepone (from Ngoc Lung Hoang, *The General Offensives of 1968–1969* [Washington, D.C.: U.S. Center of Military History, 1981]).

point of view, it would be a "turkey shoot." This was a new phase of the war. Rather than fade away, the NVA would stand and fight, as it did during the Border Battles.

> A correspondent riding in the armored column reasoned the NVA patrols must surely be following and watching. But "with Cobra gunships firing rockets all around us," he wrote, "we advanced the next day 25 klicks into Laos. There was no return fire and I felt it was an NVA tactic to draw us in deeper."[53]

Inside Laos, progress slowed. On the first day in Laos, only nine kilometers were made by the ARVN troops. This was caused by bad roads and slow-down due to fear of ambush: nine kilometers; only thirty-three to go to get to Tchepone. On the second day, things got worse. The rains came, and everything bogged down. Route 9 turned into a quagmire.[54] On the third day, the ARVN had reached the half way point to Tchepone. As the campaign progressed, the NVA increased efforts to ambush convoys and attack rear bases.

By this time, the press smelled a disaster, and Laird held a news conference on 24 February. Lt. Gen Vogt, the director of the joint staff, explained the objectives of Lam Son 719 and showed a piece of pipe explaining that this was a part of the pipeline that carried fuel south to NVA forces. Vogt left the impression that this piece of pipe was fresh from the battlefield, which it was not. It had been collected months earlier during a Special Forces raid. Abrams called Laird, reminding him that bad information had been given to the press, and Laird held another press conference to correct the record. The press had a field day. Humorist Art Buchwald wrote an imaginative story that had Laird showing rifles from Custer's Last Stand, chickens from World War I, sandbags from Iwo Jima, etc.[55] The point of all of this was that the credibility of the U.S. government was never high and continued to decline. Laird was concerned that the press would turn a military victory into a defeat, as had been done after Tet in 1968, but at this point, no one knew the outcome of Lam Son 719 and Laird could not know that it would be a disastrous defeat. For weeks the ARVN move against Tchepone stagnated as casualties mounted.

Author David Fulghum described the "taking" of Tchepone.

> On March 6 an armada of 120 Huey helicopters, protected on all sides by Cobra gunships and fighter planes, lifted the 2d and 3d Battalions of the 2d Regiment from Khe Sanh to Tchepone—the largest, longest helicopter assault of the war. The NVA response to the assault on Tchepone was to increase fire against ARVN firebases, notably Lolo and A Luoi. On March 9 the battalions and the 2d Regiment command post set out on foot to climb the ridge to Firebase Sophia. Cautious about ambushes, the troops maintained radio silence so as not to disclose their location and moved their positions every two hours during the night. They arrived safely at the firebase the following day, and the ARVN "occupation" of Tchepone, a principal terrain objective of Operation Lam Son 719, was complete.[56]

ARVN General Hinh summarized best. "By this time, Tchepone was a worthless objective. It was a ruined town and [NVA] caches were stored in the forests and mountain tops."[57] On 9 March, Thieu ordered the ARVN out of Laos, and the ARVN withdrawal from Laos started while the NVA intensified its buildup. The NVA ability to reinforce, its use of tanks and anti-air to destroy ARVN troops and support, led to a rout. The NVA had every advantage: leadership, troop morale, firepower, terrain, weather, and numbers. It was a slaughter of the ARVN, which would be seen again in the fall of Vietnam in 1975. Some ARVN units were simply surrounded and annihilated. While U.S. helicopters tried to evacuate the ARVN from Laos, there were not enough, due to many helicopter losses earlier in the campaign. As the NVA overran ARVN bases in Laos, there were many accounts of ARVN valor. One ARVN survivor recalled what happened as ammunition ran out.

Ammunition began to run out, however, and the next day the NVA overran the base. They launched the assault from positions inside the marine perimeter, supported by ten flame throwing tanks. NVA infantrymen rushed over the bodies of their slain comrades to charge into the base. The marines knocked out four tanks, then fell back. Trying to break out, the three battalions ran into NVA ambushes. The troops scattered. One survivor recounted: The last attack came at about 8:00 P.M. They shelled us first and then came the tanks moving up into our positions. The whole brigade ran down the hill like ants. We jumped on each other to get out of that place. After each firing, there were fewer and fewer of us. A marine who escaped Delta described the agony of the Vietnamese leaving their wounded comrades. They lay there crying, knowing the B-52 bombs would fall on them. They asked buddies to shoot them, but none of us could bring himself to do that. So the wounded cried out for grenades, first one man, then another, then more. I could not bear it. We ran out at 8:00 P.M. and about midnight we heard the bombs explode behind us. No more bodies! They all became dust.[58]

U.S. helicopters suffered heavy losses getting the ARVN in, and after the failure of the operation, more helicopters were lost removing the South Vietnamese from Laos. In a pattern seen before and after, the ARVN panicked during the withdrawal. One pilot reported that it was so bad that the U.S. crews had to grease the skids of the helicopters to prevent ARVN soldiers from hanging on to the skids during takeoff and thus overloading the aircraft. South Vietnam announced 7,683 ARVN casualties (slightly less than half of their force engaged). U.S. losses were 215 killed and 1,187 wounded.[59]

It was very similar to the Ap Bac battle eight years earlier: the ARVN were slow and in many cases ran away when under fire, leaving their wounded behind. Lam Son 719 demonstrated that the Saigon regime had learned nothing in the eight years after Ap Bac.

By late March, panic had set in among the ARVN in Laos. While there were accounts of ARVN bravery (perhaps exaggerated for political reasons in the Saigon regime and the U.S.), the ARVN fled in panic. Images of healthy ARVN soldiers pushing their way through the wounded to invade waiting helicopters were the order of the day, as well as dozens of ARVNs hanging onto the helicopter skids in order to escape with their lives. President Nixon provided his view of the battle.

On February 8, the operation began. South Vietnamese troops fought bravely and effectively, but some problems soon developed. Communist forces put up stronger resistance than we had anticipated, and American military commanders in Saigon failed to respond with a corresponding increase in air cover. When South Vietnamese forces sustained large casualties about ten miles into Laos, they made the mistake of temporarily digging in, which gave the North Vietnamese a sitting target to hit. Thieu became overly cautious and ordered his commanders to stop their offensive as soon as casualties reached 3,000. By the middle of March, soon after the South Vietnamese reached Tchepone, their casualties hit Thieu's arbitrary ceiling and they began to retreat to the southeast along Route 914. American news media reports presented a distorted picture of the operation by focusing almost exclusively on the failings of the South Vietnamese troops. Because of inadequate air support during the withdrawal, a few units took such a severe pounding from enemy artillery that they panicked. It took only a few televised films of soldiers clinging to the skids of our evacuation helicopters to reinforce the widespread misconception that South Vietnam's armed forces were incompetent and cowardly.[60]

The disaster would not be repeated. Nixon noted that Lam Son 719 would be the last American-directed ground operation in Indochina.[61] Correspondents had their own opinions of Lam Son 719.

According to *Life* magazine "the NVA drove the invading forces out of Laos with their tails between their legs." *New York Times* reporter Gloria Emerson interviewed ARVN survivors at Khe Sanh and concluded that their morale was "shattered": Through an interpreter they spoke of how the North Vietnamese outnumbered them and advanced in wave after wave, running over the bodies of comrades and never stopping.... It was a test, and now most South Vietnamese forces admit frankly that their forces failed.... What has dramatically demoralized many of the South Vietnamese troops is the large number of their own wounded who were left behind, begging for their friends to shoot them or to leave hand grenades so they could commit suicide before the North Vietnamese or the B-52s killed them.... Some soldiers who had been in the drive into Cambodia said they had never dreamed that the Laos operation would not be as simple. Since there was no significant fighting in Cambodia, these South Vietnamese felt that the enemy was no longer a threat. They learned differently in Laos and they will not soon forget it. In American helicopters they came out of Laos this week without their combat packs, their rations or their steel helmets—and sometimes without their weapons. Nothing mattered, they said, except getting out."[62]

The whole debacle proved beyond any doubt that the ARVN command structure was flawed and could not fight. ARVN leadership was, at best, poor. This lesson was learned by Hanoi, and it was clear to Giap that the ARVN could be easily defeated once the U.S. departed. For Hanoi, it became a waiting game: wait for the U.S. to depart and then invade South Vietnam, which is exactly what happened in 1972 and later in 1975. President Thieu realized the incompetence of his commander in the North, General Lam, and ordered that he be replaced. Unfortunately, his replacement, one of ARVN's best generals, Do Cao Tri, was killed in a helicopter crash (apparently caused by bad ARVN maintenance: another example of the failure of Vietnamization), so Lam continued in charge of the debacle.

Thieu, Abrams, and Nixon were publically proclaiming that it was an ARVN victory and a proof that Vietnamization was working. The battle was supposed to set back the Hanoi plan to invade South Vietnam in 1972 but did not do that. Kissinger stated that it was hoped that the operation would delay the NVA invasion of 1972,[63] but the NVA moved forward into Vietnam on 30 March 1972.

In South Vietnam, the citizens wanted to know the truth. Thousands of ARVN soldiers had been killed. On 1 April 1971, Thieu announced in his press conference that Lam Son 719 was still under way.[64] This was a lie, matched by Nixon, who said that Lam Son 719 proved that Vietnamization was a success.

Kissinger was inclined to be lenient with the South Vietnamese for this failed operation. He blamed the lack of South Vietnamese planning and using only two divisions when four were needed. "On the whole, the South Vietnamese extracted themselves in tolerable fashion, except for unedifying and untypical television pictures of a few panicky soldiers clinging to the skids of helicopters."[65]

Historian Lewis Sorley, who transcribed tapes made by Abrams during this period, found that Abrams viewed the operation as a success. "I'm beginning to have a conviction about Lam Son 719 that it was really a death blow."[66] The question remains: Whose death blow? General Philip Davidson summarized.

> On 7 April, shortly after ARVN's forced withdrawal from Laos, President Nixon, in a television broadcast to the nation, proclaimed, "Tonight I can report that Vietnamization has succeeded"—an Orwellian untruth of boggling proportions. Lam Son 719 had demonstrated exactly the opposite, that Vietnamization had not succeeded.[67]

Author Jeffrey Kimball also quoted Davidson.

> Military analysts such as General Philip Davidson in his postwar history of the war not only agreed there were deficiencies but also viewed them as incurable. ARVN military leadership was politicized; Thieu was wanting in judgment and nerve; several commanders were inept [such as Lam], many officers, without American advisory support, lacked the professional skills necessary to coordinate ground, tank, artillery, and air operations; ARVN lacked offensive initiative and mobile fighting capability; and, like the Americans, the South Vietnamese relied too much on maneuver by helicopter

when walking would have been swifter. American blunders—hasty planning, poor judgment, inadequate coordination with the ARVN, and inter-service rivalry—had compounded the ARVN shortcomings.[68]

Press reporting of the disaster caused a national outrage. "In March 1971, a poll reported that public confidence in Nixon had dropped to 50 percent, the lowest rating since he had entered office. Support for his conduct of the war slid to 34 percent, another survey stated 51 percent of Americans were persuaded that the conflict was 'morally wrong.'"[69] Street protests resumed, followed by a 200,000-strong march on Washington.[70] Laird agreed to deliver a speech at the University of Wisconsin, which was clearly one of the most unfriendly environments and a hotbed of student unrest. Laird cancelled at the last minute and sent General "Chappie" James to give the address. James received a rather violent welcome, as would be expected at the University of Wisconsin during that period. Laird's biographer Dale Van Atta tells the story.

> General "Chappie" James went in his [Laird's] place and received an antiwar reprimand from the chancellor and a thirty-name petition protesting the war from the students serving the luncheon. Out in the cold were about two thousand antiwar protesters led by Rennie Davis, who had been convicted in the "Chicago Seven" trial of crossing state lines to incite a riot at the 1968 Democratic National Convention. He shouted to the demonstrators in Wisconsin, "If the government doesn't stop the war, we are going to stop the government." And he chided Laird for not showing up: "Laird is not all fool. If he would have come here today, we would have really kicked some ass!" On February 10, several hundred students at the University of Illinois in Champaign burned Laird in effigy.[71]

Bui Diem, South Vietnam's ambassador in Washington at this time, reported to Thieu.

> The view is of thousands of students carrying the VC flag in the streets of Washington, and of ten thousand troops. All these images coalesce on the TV screen every night. These things undoubtedly provoke reflections from the American people who ask the question, more than ever—when will the war end? These reflections will perhaps push the ordinary man into a situation where he thinks it is better to give up than continue. And this situation is like a mirror staring back at Richard Nixon when he looks at the future of the war.... In the meantime, the antiwar elements have tried their best to put forward the idea that it is past—time to think about such things as a schedule for withdrawing troops. Now it is simply—when will this war be ended? That is to say, the attitude is—we don't care about the consequences.[72]

For Hanoi it reaffirmed the opinion (perhaps shared by the world) that the South Vietnam bureaucracy was not capable of fighting a war without massive U.S. support. The ARVN soldiers were brave and fighting well, but their leadership was pathetic, and in many cases, politicians in uniform answering to Saigon were without regard for their troops. The NVA needed to restock its massive losses that occurred during Lam Son 719 due to air strikes, but this would not take long.

For the ARVN, any confidence in their fighting ability that had been built up over the past year was destroyed by Lam Son 719. While small units fought bravely against overwhelming odds, the senior ARVN leadership continued to be viewed as incompetent and corrupt.

The conclusion is that Lam Son 719 disrupted NVA operations in early 1971, but the NVA planned to invade South Vietnam in 1972, not 1971. The 1972 invasion went ahead as planned during the dry season in early 1972. Furthermore, it was a conventional attack across the DMZ, and supplies followed the NVA advance, as would be expected. Stockpiled supplies from the Ho Chi Minh trail were therefore less important, but the supply losses during Lam Son 719 may have affected the invasion. The worst impact was on the ARVN, whose morale had been building since the Cambodian Incursion the previous year. The NVA sustained devastating casualties, but these were quickly replaced, including those pulled in from other allies such as Laos. The 1972 invasion was thwarted in part by U.S. air power. U.S. air power would not be available as the NVA entered Thieu's palace in 1975.

Lam Son 719 was a disastrous defeat for the ARVN and the U.S. Both realized that South Vietnam was unlikely to survive long after the last U.S. combat troops were withdrawn.

The Home Front

Perhaps the greatest problem in the home front was that none of the administrations could adequately explain to the American people why we were in Vietnam and what was going on. It is very difficult for parents of a son just killed in action to understand how the domino theory explained why their son died. The American people watched the news every night, and it was fascinating getting daily video from the battlefield. When they saw the coverage of dead U.S. soldiers, could anyone blame them for asking "What in the hell are we doing there?" As their son's body was being shipped back to the states, they were told that we were fighting to defend our Cold War "credibility."[73] There is no evidence that Moscow or Beijing shared that view.[74] Media coverage of the war in Vietnam is the subject of many articles and books, but the point is that the U.S. government failed its people. Van Nguyen Duong, a South Vietnamese officer during the war, summarized the problem.

> On the first day Nixon arrived in the White House [20 January 1969] he heard the echoes of antiwar demonstrators from the Lincoln Memorial demanding peace. The president recognized the continued decline of American public support for the war in Vietnam rooted in the Johnson administration's deceitful war strategy for the intervention in South Vietnam by ground combat forces in the previous years. The anti-war movement was launched on college campuses by separate protest groups. At first it only expressed strong sentiment against the war and there was no structure or coordination among these groups. However, in March 1965, when President Johnson sent the first combat unit to Danang [Da Nang], some 25,000 people immediately demonstrated in Washington; the majority were students. Thereafter, anti-war sentiment congealed into a "movement" with the emergence of several anti-war organized groups on several campuses around the country. These groups were led by intellectuals, social and political activists, including several congressmen. Some of them were: David Dellinger, a journalist and founder of a pacifist newspaper, who first came to Hanoi and met Ho Chi Minh in 1966; Senator Eugene McCarthy, a Democratic Party liberal and presidential candidate, who had given the mass of young Americans the faith of "New Politics"; and Jerry Rubin, a newspaper reporter and socialist activist who led the "teach-in" speeches at Berkeley University and founded the Yippies, or Youth International Party. The anti-war movement largely opposed U.S. government on several crucial issues:
> - The war policy in Vietnam, attrition strategy, random air strikes and civilian massacre, U.S. troop casualties.
> - The draft of mostly poor black and white students for military services in Vietnam while favoring the sons of the rich and upper class by the so-called "deferment" system which allowed them to continue their studies in college.
> - Defense spending had cut into the domestic budget that pushed Congress to refuse to pass some civil rights measures. The cuts gravely affected the "Great Society."
> - The claim that Ho Chi Minh was a nationalist rather than a communist and the United States involvement in the war in Vietnam was illegitimate.[75]

Students were protesting because they did not want to be cannon fodder for the war, and in 1967, thirty thousand marched on the Pentagon.[76] Students also identified with the

Vietnamese people and their sacrifices.[77] Other extreme groups also protested and caused deaths. Bernardine Dohrn, a member of the Weathermen,[78] suggested that the protests would hasten the end of the war by raising its social cost.[79]

> The college and university campuses were in turmoil. Prior to 1967 the sons of the white middle class had largely avoided the war through the escape of the college deferment. By 1967 the needs of the Green Machine were such that the draft had taken significant numbers of them as they graduated. The threat of being conscripted for a war that was the object of wide-spread moral revulsion made marchers and shouters out of young men who might have been less concerned over the victimization of an Asian people and the turning into cannon fodder of farm boys and the sons of the working class and the minorities. The appeal of the cause aroused women students in equal number and with equal passion.[80]

Jim Long, recently returned from service in Vietnam, had a different view of the protests.

> One of the worst days of my life, Monday, 24 Aug 70, early morning after four anti-war extremists/cowards fertilizer-fuel-oil-bombed Sterling Hall [University of Wisconsin], housing the Army Mathematics Research Center, their purported target. As I came upon the scene and sat down on a grassy knoll next to the hall, and the remains of Robert Fassnacht, a physics research assistant, were being removed—my eyes welled.
>
> There was evil in my country, no different than the evil I experienced in South Vietnam. Anti-war groups stated he was a casualty of political necessity. Tell it to his widow and three orphaned children.[81]

President Nixon summarized the student protests. It was a statement of the unpopularity of the Vietnam War in the U.S. among students and others.

> Today, many Americans remember the demonstrations against the war as flocks of flower children marching in orderly candlelight processions. But what we saw from the White House at the time was quite different. Until 1968, antiwar demonstrators were basically peaceful, seldom doing more than holding "teach-ins" and symbolically burning their draft cards. But that had changed by 1969. Students shot at firemen and policemen, held college administrators hostage at knifepoint, stormed university buildings with shotguns in hand, burned buildings, smashed windows, trashed offices, and bombed classrooms. In the academic year 1969–70, there were 1,800 demonstrations, 7,500 arrests, 247 arsons, 462 injuries—two-thirds of them to police—and 8 deaths. The violence was not limited to college campuses; it was a national epidemic. From January 1969 through February 1970, there were over 40,000 bombings, attempted bombings, or bomb threats, most of which were war related. These caused $21 million of property damage, hundreds of injuries, and 43 deaths. Violence was becoming the rule, not the exception, in campus protests. Following the announcement of the incursions into Cambodia, a new wave of violent protest swept the country. At the University of Maryland, fifty people were injured when students ransacked the ROTC building and skirmished with police. In Kent, Ohio, a crowd of hundreds of demonstrators watched as two young men threw lighted flares into the army ROTC building on the campus of Kent State University and burned it to the ground. Ohio's governor called in the National Guard. A few days later, a large crowd of students began throwing rocks and chunks of concrete at the guardsmen, forcing them up a small hill. At the top, the soldiers turned, and someone started shooting. Four people—two protesters and two bystanders—were killed.[82]

Some veterans were unhappy because they did not get a parade when they got home, but most only wanted to be treated decently and not be attacked by crazy anti-war demonstrators. Below are a few accounts of veterans returning. One veteran related that he left for Vietnam at age nineteen and returned a year later. He met with his girlfriend and her mother. Her mother objected and told her that this man looked to be in his mid-thirties and could not be the same man that she had said farewell to a year earlier. She assured her mother that he was the same man and they married.

Philip Caputo summarized in his book, *A Rumor of War*.

Beyond adding a few more corpses to the weekly body count, none of these encounters achieved anything; none will ever appear in military histories or be studied by cadets at West Point. Still, they changed us and taught us, the men who fought in them; in those obscure skirmishes we learned the old lessons about fear, cowardice, courage, suffering, cruelty, and comradeship. Most of all, we learned about death at an age when it is common to think of oneself as immortal. Everyone loses that illusion eventually, but in civilian life it is lost in installments over the years. We lost it all at once and, in the span of months, passed from boyhood through manhood to a premature middle age. The knowledge of death, of the implacable limits placed on a man's existence, severed us from our youth as irrevocably as a surgeon's scissors had once severed us from the womb. And yet, few of us were past twenty-five.[83]

Phillip Hoffman shares his homecoming story:

Brothers Steve and Tom picked me up at the St. Louis airport, and we headed straight for the nearest airport bar to celebrate my return. It was there I had my first encounter with a civilian who showed bias against veterans in uniform. A surly waitress carded me and then refused to accept my military I.D. She insisted on a driver's license, which I didn't have. The conversation heated after my brothers got involved, and only when the bar manager stepped in did things quiet down. He apologized to me and made things right.[84]

This author, too, experienced a rocky homecoming:

On one occasion I had to talk to people about the war in Vietnam, so I was in uniform. This was common during the late 1960s. It was an attempt to educate the U.S. people about the war in Vietnam, something our leaders had failed to do. I had to stop for gas, and as the attendant topped up the tank and I got money out to pay him, a group of four people arrived behind me in an auto and saw my uniform. They started heckling and gave me the finger and that sort of thing. I got in my auto and they decided to pursue. I guess their objective was to stop my car and beat me up just because I was a U.S. soldier. I had the better car, and in my rearview mirror I watched them disappear. It occurred to me at that time that at least in Vietnam I had a rifle to defend myself when I was attacked. My thought was that many soldiers who returned from Vietnam observed the same thing. They were called "Baby Killers" and things like that by members of a self-focused society who only cared about their creature comforts. I suppose many soldiers reenlisted to return to Vietnam in order to escape this society. I also went back for a second tour, but it was not voluntary.[85]

U.S. Withdrawal

Because of Vietnamization, the U.S. could withdraw its forces. The very first U.S. troop withdrawal occurred as eight hundred men from the 9th Infantry Division were sent home. The phased troop withdrawal occurred in fourteen stages, starting in August 1969, through June 1972.[86] By the time the U.S. Army started its withdrawal in late 1969, it was obvious to everyone in the field that our army was disintegrating. A senior brigade officer spoke to the point when he said, behind the cloak of anonymity, "Nobody in the brigade gives a damn about this war any more, including me. We will be happy to get home, and when we do, the enemy will march down out of the hills and take over." That senior officer's bitter statement was widely shared among the departing American soldiers. The Vietnam experience had carried U.S. armed forces to the point of disintegration. Said army Captain Steve Adolph, a veteran of three tours, "When I came home, I didn't think the U.S. Army could whip the North Vietnamese Boy Scouts, and I wasn't sure about the Girl Scouts either." Brigadier General Theodore C. Mataxis, who had served as a MR2 advisor, brigade commander, and acting division commander, summed up the army's tortuous journey this way:

"It's been the opposite of Korea. There we went in with a bad army and came out with a good one. In Vietnam we went in with a good army and came out with a bad one."[87]

General Bruce Palmer, who had commanded II Field Force Vietnam (IIFFV) and later became the acting U.S. Army chief of staff, summarized:

> American direction and conduct of the war and the operational performance of our armed forces, particularly during the 1962–69 period, generally were professional and commendable. Performance continued to be of a high quality until the 1969–70 period, when dissent at home began to be reflected in troop attitudes and conduct in Vietnam. From 1969 until the last U.S. combat troops left in August, a decline in performance set in; the discovery of widespread drug use in Vietnam in the spring of 1970 signaled that more morale and disciplinary troubles lay ahead. The so-called "fraggings" of leaders that began in 1969–70 were literally murderous indicators of poor morale and became a matter of deep concern. Extremely adverse environmental conditions and very trying circumstances contributed to this decline in performance. Particularly galling to our forces in the field were the widely publicized statements of highly placed U.S. officials, including senators, against American involvement. Such statements were perceived to support the enemy and badly damaged the morale of our troops. The deteriorating climate at home also affected the conduct of American prisoners of war (mostly airmen) held in North Vietnamese POW camps; this was reflected in the increasing number of men who were accused of collaborating with the enemy in the 1969–71 period, as compared to the very few during the earlier years of the war.[88]

There are many other factors not mentioned by General Palmer in detail that also had an effect on the fighting ability of the U.S. Army in Vietnam. Historian Keith William Nolan summarized:

> Virtually no draftee wants to be fighting in Vietnam anyway, and in return for his reluctant participation he demands, and gets, personal freedoms that would have driven a MacArthur or a Patton apoplectic. It is an Army in which all questions—including "Why?"—are permissible. Alpha Company seethes with problems, and it has now fallen into chaos ... the company commander's continuing problem is to find an effective compromise between his own professional dedication and his draftees' frank disinterest in anything that might cost an American life.... Grunt logic argues that since the U.S. has decided not to go out and win the war, there's no sense in being the last one to die.[89]

Battles Lost and Search & Avoid

The Mary Ann affair[90] demonstrated that the U.S. Army had lost its fighting ability. Fire Support Base (FSB) Mary Ann was located in the westernmost part of the Americal Division's area of responsibility in Quang Tin Province, in the north of South Vietnam. It was scheduled to be handed over to the ARVN. At Mary Ann, security was lax, and the VC had been watching it for weeks. A carefully planned attack was launched against it by about one hundred sappers on the night of 28 March 1971. They cut the wire and swarmed over Mary Ann. The result was very heavy losses for the U.S. battalion there. Thirty were killed and eighty-two wounded. One medevac pilot described the scene. "It was the worst carnage I have ever seen.... Some [bodies were] burned to charcoal.... There were nine body bags full of bits and pieces of flesh."[91] An investigation followed, and the report concluded:

> The reduced level of combat activity and the increasing publicity by the news media focused upon ending of the war tend to create a great complacency among both the troops and their commanders. Coupled with this is the effect of anti–Vietnam and anti-military attitudes [in the United States] and the growth of permissiveness within the military establishment. All of these factors confront a commander in Vietnam today with a formidable task (challenge) of maintaining a high state of discipline and alertness among his troops.[92]

A part of the problem was the new Army Chief of Staff Westmoreland's policy to send people home who had served the longest in Vietnam rather than send units home.[93] Westmoreland overrode the objections of General Abrams, the commander in Vietnam, and others. It is difficult to understand what Westmoreland was thinking. If you send home your most experienced people and replace them with new people, it is disruptive to the effectiveness and discipline of the unit before the unit, itself, goes home.

As a result, as the war progressed, the U.S. forces in Vietnam were faced with multiple problems. The demonstrations at home against the war generated disrespect for authority, and this influenced the attitude of the troops. The system of rotation, especially the rotation of the officers within Vietnam to get their tickets punched, produced a less than competent force. Author Neil Sheehan summarized the problem.

> The American military system of the 1960s provided for the unlearning rather than the learning of lessons. The one-year tour that Westmoreland had decided to carry over from the advisory era because he thought it would help morale meant that all ranks from colonel to private first class left the country by the time they were beginning to acquire some experience and perspective. The turnover was twice as fast, every six months, at the operating levels of battalion and brigade (regiment was the equivalent of brigade in the Marine Corps), where experienced leadership was needed most. The officer spent the other six months of his tour in a staff job or as an executive officer at a higher level. There were few exceptions, and only rarely could a man hold a command longer than six months by volunteering to extend his tour. (Often the turnover was faster than six months because the officer became a casualty or got sick.)
>
> The Army personnel bureaucracy tended to view Vietnam as an educational exercise and rationalized the six-month rule as a way of seasoning more officers for the "big war" yet to come with the Soviets in Europe and for more of these "brushfire wars." The real reason, which held true for the Marine Corps too and which explained why the practice was derisively called "ticket-punching," was a mechanistic promotion process and the bureaucratic impetus this created. To win eagles, a lieutenant colonel had to punch a battalion command on his record. To gain a star, a colonel had to punch on command of a brigade or a regiment. To keep an officer in a battalion or brigade or regimental command longer than six months was regarded as unfair to his contemporaries. Much the same system of ticket-punching held true for the general officers, although they were on eighteen-month tours. A general was seldom permitted to hold a division or corps command for more than a year, because so many other generals were waiting in line to qualify for another star.... The Vietnamese could thus count on their American opponents to behave according to pattern.[94]

Ron Beckett, a veteran of three tours in Vietnam, echoed Neil Sheehan's assessment.

> The decision for a twelve-month tour was disastrous in U.S. units, and doubly so in the advisory effort. Although defended in terms of preventing "burn out," all it really did was cycle officers through command and other key combat assignments to punch their tickets and enhance their careers. About the time that an officer was starting to learn his job, he was moved to another position or his tour was over. We were constantly being led by the inexperienced, and the men serving under these officers paid the price. This practice led John Paul Vann to observe, "We didn't fight a ten-year war, we fought a one-year war ten times."
>
> For a district- or province-level advisor to be most effective, a minimum of a two-year tour would have been necessary to absorb all the knowledge that was essential, to establish rapport, and to build trust and confidence. Eighteen months should have been the minimum for those assigned as advisors to tactical units. The standard twelvemonth tour was simply an insufficient length of time.
>
> Compounding this problem was the army's decision, in the face of mounting criticism over repeated tours, to fill many advisory positions with officers below the required grade: lieutenants in captain positions, captains in major positions, and majors in lieutenant colonel positions. The net result was inexperienced junior officers frequently being assigned to advise experienced officers senior to them. The implicit message was that a young, inexperienced American officer was somehow more capable than an older, experienced, and more senior Vietnamese officer, and could therefore effectively advise

him—hardly the basis for the trust, respect, and rapport required. The enhancements in advisor training and the extension of the advisory tour to eighteen months in the latter part of the war were recognitions of this fact. While these were important improvements, they were too little, too late.[95]

Drugs, pills, and alcohol were plentiful and cheap. The unfairness of the draft system that sent young blacks to war while wealthy whites got student deferments was a national disgrace. Racial unrest in the United States caused by such events as the murder of Martin Luther King influenced the attitude of many black Americans toward authority. Senseless Westmoreland policies such as "body count" killed many innocent civilians by mistake did nothing but infuriate the Vietnamese and add to the ranks of the VC. All of these factors produced atrocities by those with no moral compass such as William Calley, and that led to the massacre at My Lai. War crimes by U.S. forces added to war protests at home and provided the enemy with propaganda that was used very effectively. In a strange twist of fate, General Westmoreland, while commanding forces in Vietnam, commended Calley's unit for the high body count at My Lai. Later as Army chief of staff, he moved to court-martial Calley and others for the murders at My Lai when it was discovered that the body count consisted of murdered civilians, not enemy bodies. By 1970, the U.S. Army in Vietnam was disintegrating.[96]

The result was that by 1970, all realized that the total effort should be in getting the troops home safely. For the infantry, it became an exercise of "search and avoid" rather than engaging the enemy.[97] All realized that this war was a lost cause. The corrupt regime in Saigon under President Thieu could never hope to win without U.S. forces, and the U.S. Army was disintegrating due to lack of discipline, drugs, racial problems, and opposition to the war on the home front. While there are many examples of valor by South Vietnamese units and their leaders, they were operating in a sea of incompetence that started in Saigon.

Napoleon is said to have remarked that a strategy of defense is deferred suicide, and this strategy was used during unit stand-downs. Firebase Ripcord is a good example. The 101st Airborne Division established the firebase in April 1970. The purpose of Ripcord is not clear, but the NVA moved in to attack the firebase in July 1970 and bombarded the firebase to the point that the army decided to withdraw the troops. Over a three-week period, while the 101st defended, it lost 61 killed and 345 wounded.[98] Another incident: Firebase Charlie 2 near the DMZ was attacked during meal time. The troops scattered to a nearby bunker, and a delayed-fuse round penetrated six feet of bunker protection, killing twenty-nine soldiers.[99]

The Easter Invasion

Nixon practiced the "Madman Theory" of foreign policy while in office. He explained it best during a discussion with his White House chief of staff, H.R. Haldeman, quoted below.

> I call it the Madman Theory, Bob. I want the North Vietnamese to believe I've reached the point where I might do anything to stop the war. We'll just slip the word to them that "For God's sake, you know Nixon is obsessed about Communism. We can't restrain him when he's angry—and he has his hand on the nuclear button" and Ho Chi Minh himself will be in Paris in two days begging for peace.[100]

There are problems with using the madman approach to foreign policy. If you use it on a nuclear power such as the Soviet Union, that power may launch a preemptive nuclear strike. During the Easter Invasion, Nixon proved that he was capable of anything. He threatened to mine Haiphong Harbor. This was risky business, since if a Soviet supply ship delivering supplies to North Vietnam hit a mine and Soviet citizens were killed, there could be major consequences and possibly confrontation between the U.S. and the Soviet Union. Nixon actually did order the mining in May 1972, but no Soviet citizens were injured. There is very little evidence that Nixon's madman approach achieved any positive result.

While Nixon was playing the madman in the Oval Office, Henry Kissinger was negotiating with the Soviets over the Strategic Arms Limitation Treaty and also with China. Vietnam was in the background, but Kissinger tried to connect treaties with Soviet support for a Vietnam peace treaty. The problem was that the Soviets had less leverage on the North Vietnamese than the U.S. did on the South Vietnamese.[101]

At the same time, the U.S. was trying to negotiate a peace settlement with Hanoi with South Vietnam as a reluctant participant. These secret peace talks were going on in Paris, and Kissinger, Nixon's national security advisor, represented the U.S. At the same time, Nixon was under fire from Congress and the American people over the Vietnam War. Since Lam Son 719 failed to delay the Hanoi invasion of South Vietnam, the NVA went forward as planned in March 1972. This invasion was called the Easter Invasion (the label "Spring

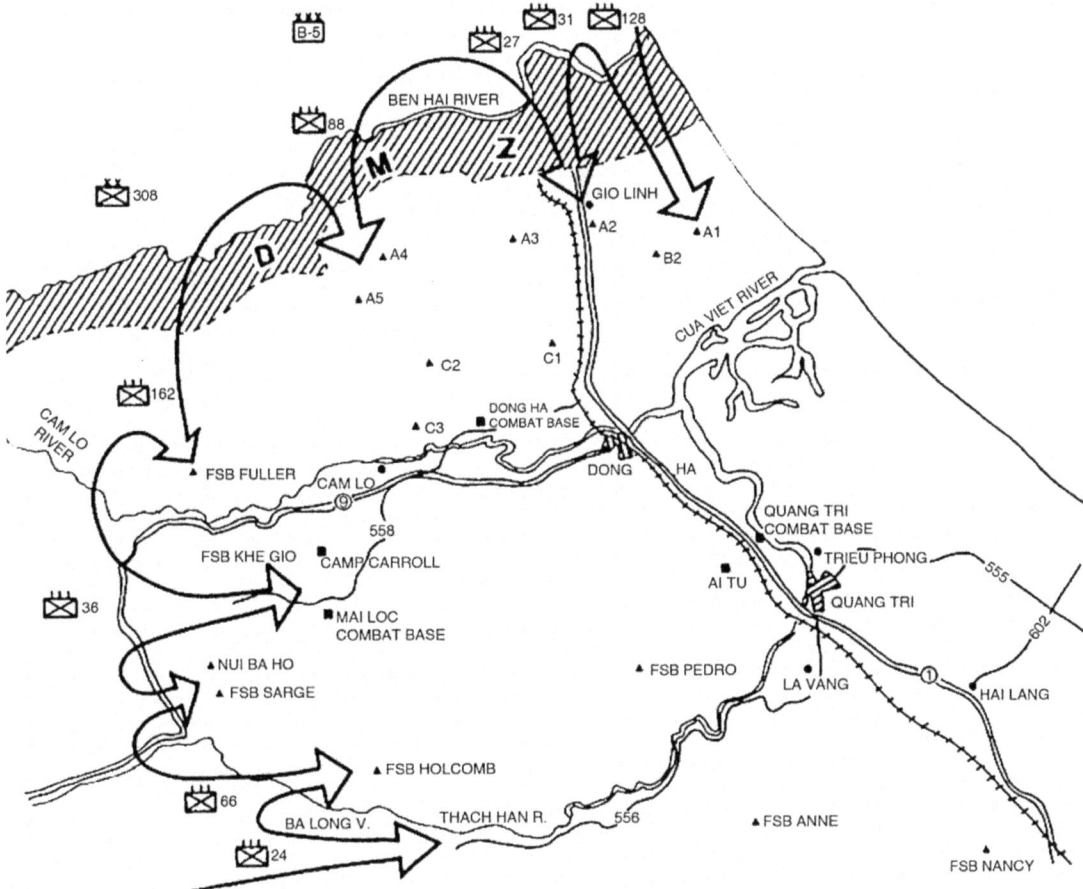

The NVA Easter Invasion, 1972 (from Ngo Quang Troung, *The Easter Offensive of 1972. IndoChina Monographs* [Fort McNair, Washington, D.C.: U.S. Army Center of Military History, 1980]).

Invasion" was also used). By this time, many U.S. troops had been withdrawn from Vietnam or were in stand-down mode, with about 6,000 combat troops of the 70,000 remaining, and the NVA invasion would be countered by ARVN units and U.S. air support.

> Figuring that domestic American pressures would prevent Nixon from reintroducing American forces in Vietnam, they [Hanoi] were also out to cripple the Vietnamization effort. Pham Van Dong publicly stated that it was necessary to prove the failure of Vietnamization to prove to Nixon that "he has everything to lose except the honorable exit we are determined to enable him to make." Nixon was privately glum. With the U.S. forces virtually out of action in Vietnam, America's position and prestige hinged on the Saigon regime: "the weak link in our whole chain," as he noted in his diary. "The real problem," he wrote, "is that the enemy is willing to sacrifice in order to win, while the South Vietnamese simply aren't willing to pay that much of a price in order to avoid losing."[102]

If the U.S. combat troops could not fight in this major NVA invasion, why were they not sent home in 1971? The answer was politics.

> As the New Year approached, Nixon considered making 1971 the last year of America's involvement in Vietnam. Just before Christmas, he had shared his thinking with Kissinger and Haldeman. In April 1971, Nixon said, he could go to South Vietnam, tour the country and reassure Thieu about the consequences of the impending final withdrawal. Then he would come home and announce that America's role in Vietnam was over. Kissinger strenuously protested Nixon's timetable. If U.S. combat troops came out by the end of 1971, he argued, the Communists could start trouble the following year. That meant the Nixon administration would pay the political price in the 1972 presidential election. Nixon should promise instead only that he would get American troops out by the end of 1972. That schedule would get him safely past his reelection. Nixon saw the wisdom in Kissinger's argument that guaranteeing his second term would require American soldiers to go on dying.[103]

The NVA had a good plan. It would strike across the DMZ in the north while other columns would attack east through the central highlands to the coast. In the south, the attack was launched above Saigon. Giap committed 120,000 NVA troops plus thousands of VC. This was not an attempt to conquer South Vietnam, but was intended to demonstrate to the U.S. that the ARVN would always lose. In this way Hanoi hoped to influence the peace talks going on at that time. The attacks were launched on 30 March 1972.

The ARVN numbers were impressive. South Vietnam had over one million men under arms and outnumbered the NVA by ten to one, but the ARVN was a hollow force. Nearly half of the force were local units tied to the ground. Thieu's maneuver battalions were spread across South Vietnam and had to counter three separate well-planned thrusts.

The NVA made good progress. In the MR2, one ARVN division fled as the NVA approached Kontum, the province capital. The Montagnards who watched them flee called them "the rabbit soldiers."[104] The ARVN province regional commander, General Nguyen Van Toan, was a crony of Thieu. For years he had reaped profits from the cinnamon trade. He was very smooth, a good talker, but could not fight. Thieu reached this conclusion and fired him during the Easter invasion.[105] To the north, in MR1, Thieu replaced the incompetent Lam, who had failed during Lam Son 719, with General Ngo Quang Truong. One of two of Troung's divisions was made up of recruits, and this division fled at the time the NVA approached.[106] The division that fled was the 3rd ARVN Division, two regiments of which were made up of convicts, deserters, and inept officers.[107]

This was de ja vu. In Ap Bac, 1963, and Lam Son 719 in 1971, the world had watched the bravery of some ARVN and the cowardice of many. It depended upon leadership. The U.S. was not in South Vietnam to see the same performance in 1975. General Abrams was well aware of the ARVN leadership problem and issued the following order. "Effective immediately, no Vietnamese commander will be air lifted out of a unit defensive position by U.S. fixed wing aircraft or helicopter unless such evacuation is directed personally by the ARVN corps commander. Inform your counterpart."[108] Some examples of what occurred in the Easter Offensive of 1972 are provided, below.

Cowardice and Deceit

The NVA invasion of South Vietnam in 1972 was met with bravery and competence by ARVN soldiers and small unit leaders, but the campaign was nearly lost by the corruption and cowardice of the ARVN leadership. Author David Fulghum provides an example when he tells the story of Camp Carroll, an ARVN position in MR1 that was under NVA attack.

> The sprawling firebase had endured three days of shelling, but as Easter Sunday dawned Camp Carroll, in Camper's [the U.S. Senior Advisor] opinion, remained strong enough to survive at least another week. At 2:30 P. M. on Easter Sunday, April 2, the ARVN officers held a meeting closed to the Americans, shortly after Dinh [the ARVN commander] came to Camper at his bunker and told him that a cabal of disaffected ARVN officers had forced him to negotiate a surrender of the camp complete with its artillery, ammunition, and American advisors. After being told by 3d Division headquarters that no reserves could be spared for Camp Carroll, Dinh said, in an interview aired on Communist radio after the fight, he believed "we would die if we remained in the base and we would also die in large numbers" if they tried to retreat. As a result, "The commanders of the various units reported to me that most of the soldiers did not want to resist the liberation forces anymore." The white flag was to go up in an hour. Col. Dinh offered to join Camper in a suicide pact to preserve their "honor." When the American declined, Dinh suggested that they mix in with the surrendering soldiers and escape into the high grass. Camper turned down that offer too.[109]

Camper organized a U.S. airlift out. There were a few ARVN soldiers who would refuse to surrender, and with his advisors, Camp got out while the cowards surrendered. Also in MR1, The NVA captured the province capital of Quang Tri on 1 May 1972.

At this point, Nixon stepped up the war and ordered the bombing of targets in North Vietnam. He increased B-52 bombing of the invading NVA forces. He threatened that he would mine the North Vietnamese port, Haiphong Harbor, to stop the flow of supplies to Hanoi. On 8 May 1972, Nixon addressed the nation.

> After describing the North Vietnamese invasion, I outlined our three options: an immediate withdrawal, a negotiated peace, or a decisive military action to end the war. I said that I had rejected the first option because it would be immoral to abandon our South Vietnamese allies to Communist tyranny and because it would encourage aggression throughout the world. I explained that while I preferred the second option, "it takes two to negotiate" and the North Vietnamese had proven to be unwilling partners. Therefore, I said, the United States really had no choice at all: "There is only one way to stop the killing. That is to keep the weapons of war out of the hands of the international outlaws of North Vietnam." In order to leave the door open for later negotiations, I concluded with a reiteration of our basic terms for a fair peace settlement.
>
> Antiwar critics and the news media competed with each other in denouncing our action. One senator remarked that the decision was "reckless and wrong." Another said that "the President must not have a free hand in Indochina any longer." One newspaper called the decision a "desperate gamble" and urged that Congress should cut off funds for the war to "save the President from himself and the nation from disaster." Another claimed that the President "has lost touch with the real world." One legislator topped them all when he breathlessly intoned that the President "has thrown down the gauntlet of nuclear war to a billion people in the Soviet Union and China.... Armageddon may be only hours away." There was nearly unanimous agreement that, as one network reporter put it, our action "practically kills prospects of a summit" with the Soviet leadership. Most of the members of Congress, my cabinet, and my staff shared the view that the summit would probably be off.[110]

The Invisible Army

While the ARVN soldiers were fighting for their lives to survive the NVA Easter Invasion, the remaining U.S. forces were in stand-down mode. U.S. Army forces would not be committed to counter the NVA invasion. Generally, the U.S. was out of Vietnam as a fighting force after 1973. Historian Lewis Sorley explained General Abrams's dilemma.

> Abrams noted the contribution of American support, and that it was only a contribution: "This invasion could not have been held at this point without U.S. air support; however, ten times the air power could not have done the job if the armed forces of South Vietnam had not stood and fought."
>
> And he concluded: "The South Vietnamese government, its armed forces and its people are holding together in this crisis. We can anticipate more heavy fighting and additional hardships for the people of South Vietnam in the coming weeks. The leaders of Hanoi are staking everything on military victory. The fabric of what the South Vietnamese have built here with our assistance has survived its severest test. The qualities demonstrated by the South Vietnamese people, in my judgment, assure that they will continue to hold."
>
> Because the drawdown had essentially stripped him of ground combat units, Abrams was, observed a contemporary account, "in a position almost unique in military history. Though a soldier all his life, General Abrams now finds himself fighting a war using massive American air and naval forces rather than ground-combat units."[111]

At the time of the Easter Invasion, John Paul Vann was the senior advisor to the ARVN general commanding MR2. He had the equivalent rank of a U.S. major general. By the Easter offensive, nearly all U.S. troops were out of MR2. He commanded no U.S. combat troops, but as senior advisor he controlled U.S. advisors that remained in MR2. Vann had a good ability to cajole and intimidate the ARVN generals, motivating them to fight: a badly needed gift.

One of the three NVA strikes into South Vietnam had as its objective the small provincial capital, Kontum, some miles north of Pleiku, the headquarters of MR2. If the NVA took Kontum, they could proceed south and seize Pleiku and then east to the sea, cutting South Vietnam in half. This was mountainous terrain near the tri-border area. In order to seize Kontum, the NVA took as its initial objective Tan Canh, near Dak To. If the NVA could seize Tan Canh or the nearby firebases along Rocket Ridge, they could overrun Kontum. Rocket Ridge was a string of fortified artillery positions that ran along Highway 14. These had been constructed by the U.S. Army and were passed on to the ARVN as a part of Vietnamization. They shielded the approaches to Kontum. Author Thomas McKenna explained the situation.

> The chain of FSBs along Rocket Ridge dominated the valleys and highways on either side of it. Those FSBs and the Border Ranger camps along the border were positioned to control the surrounding area with their own artillery fire and by tactical air strikes.
>
> Almost 50 kilometers north of Kontum City on Highway 14, there was a district town named Dak To. Five kilometers south of it was an airfield named Dak To I. Adjoining Dak To I on the south was a big ARVN base named Tan Canh, and four kilometers west of it was another airfield named Dak To II. Lieutenant General Dzu [the ARVN II Corps commander] was worried his forces in the Tan Canh/Dak To area would not be able to withstand an attack by the large enemy force headed his way. He proposed to reinforce his forward defenses by moving the two regiments of the 22nd ARVN Division in Binh Dinh Province on the coast to Kontum Province in the Highlands. Mr. Vann strongly opposed this move because it would leave Binh Dinh Province without any regular ARVN troops and defended by only its own province forces. Vann convinced Dzu to leave the two 22nd Division regiments in Binh Dinh and to free up 22nd Division forces to reinforce Tan Canh and Dak To by extending the 23rd Division's area of responsibility north to include part of Kontum. The II Corps

John Paul Vann in his Saigon headquarters (U.S. Government).

order of battle in the Highlands then included the 22nd Division's controlling its own 42nd and 47th Infantry Regiments and three Border Ranger battalions, plus scout companies, some armored cavalry, and province forces—all supported by 50 tubes of 105- and 155-mm artillery. The Airborne Division controlled six airborne battalions and one Border Ranger battalion and was supported by 16 tubes of 105-mm artillery. The forces in Kontum City were two Ranger battalions and the Kontum Province RF and PF units. The 14th and 19th Cavalry Regiments (actually battalion size) had 50 M-41 light tanks, but the tanks were spread out between Pleiku and Ben Het.[112]

The NVA assembled 35,000 troops to attack Kontum under one its best generals, Hoang Minh Thao, one of General Giap's favorite commanders.[113] The NVA force was methodical

Attack on Kontum (from Ngo Quang Troung, *The Easter Offensive of 1972. IndoChina Monographs* [Fort McNair, Washington, D.C.: U.S. Army Center of Military History, 1980]).

in its advance. First came the engineers with earth-moving equipment to build roads at night. Sound carries great distances in the mountains, and the defenders could hear the sounds of construction. Next came the NVA tanks, and the defenders could see the headlamps of the tanks from a very far distance as they moved toward them. This was a conventional war not seen in South Vietnam since the French war. It was terrifying for the ARVN.

NVA lack of experience in conventional warfare showed here. The NVA tanks (T-54s—

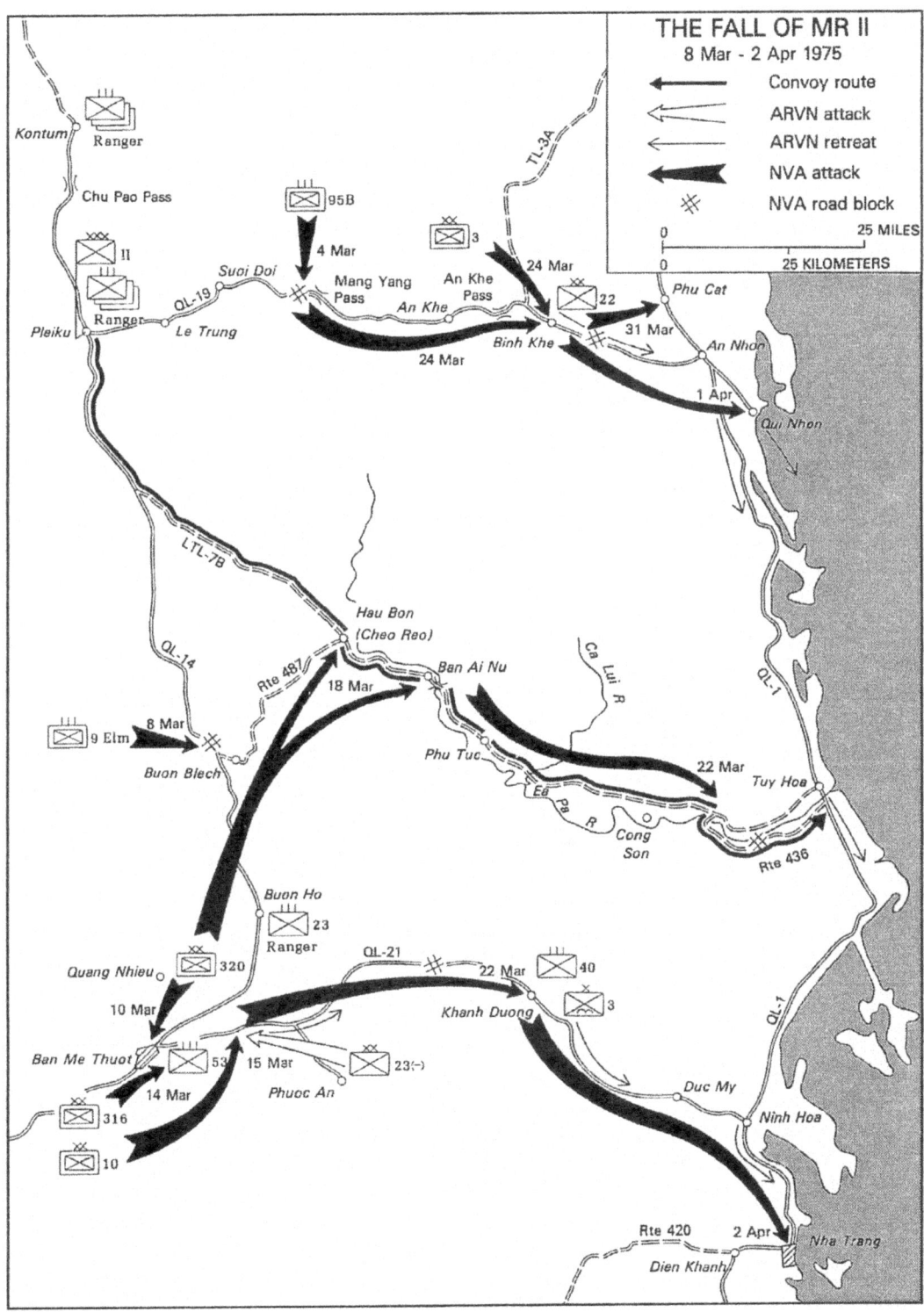

South Vietnam in 1975, showing the NVA attacks in MR2 (from J. Edward Lee and H.C. "Toby" Haynsworth, *Nixon, Ford and the Abandonment of South Vietnam* [McFarland: Jefferson, NC, 2002]).

late 1950s vintage) came on without supporting infantry, which made them vulnerable to anti-tank fire and ARVN infantry, especially at night. John Paul Vann had made sure that the ARVN division and Dak To had M-72 LAWs (light antitank weapons) available. While the M-72s were used effectively in other regions, there were problems at Dak To: the ARVN and PF militia ran away. Other approaches were tried. A C-130 aircraft was loaded with a 105mm howitzer and flew over the battlefield firing at tanks. The problem was that it only had high explosive (HE) ammunition and no anti-tank rounds. It did score hits on NVA tanks, but the HE rounds produced only a bad headache for crew members. The T-54s survived the hits.[114]

There were limited effective ARVN units in MR2 available to repel the NVA attack, but reinforcements were sent in. Vann coordinated air support and helped with resupply. He would fly through heavy fire to pinpoint targets, report results, adjust fire, and land in order to encourage ARVN commanders and provide supplies. His efforts were instrumental in stopping the NVA attack in western MR2.

Tan Canh did not hold long. The ARVN rabbit soldiers ran away quickly.[115] After taking Tan Canh, the NVA stopped to resupply and reinforce before attacking Kontum city. This was a three-week delay because the NVA was focused on the other two fronts in MR1 and MR3, which failed. While the NVA delayed the attack on Kontum city, U.S. B-52s devastated NVA troops with concentrated carpet bombing. Vann coordinated most of this battle. The NVA retreated.

In eastern MR2, Vann had a different problem. In Binh Dinh province on the coast, he was faced with ARVN leadership cowardice on an unimaginable scale, and Regional Forces-Popular Forces (RF/PF) troops were deserting by the thousands. The ARVN commander of the 40th Regiment, Colonel Tran Heiu Duc, refused to fight and did not fire a round. As the NVA approached, he withdrew his troops and fell back to higher ground; he kept falling back until he ran out of higher ground. Vann tried to intervene. On 19 April 1972, he arranged air support and a convoy of M-113s to allow Duc to withdraw in an orderly manner. At that point Duc fled, leaving all of his remaining troops and wounded behind. The Binh Dinh districts of Bong Son and Tam Quam easily fell before the NVA advance, and 200,000 people in Binh Dinh province were now under NVA control.[116]

There were worse examples of cowardice. ARVN medical helicopters landed to pick up the wounded. While the wounded lay ready for pickup, the ARVN Military Police (MPs) had concocted a scheme to extort money from the able-bodied ARVN troops for a place on the medevac helicopters. Half of the loot went to the ARVN helicopter crews. As the wounded were left dying at the medevac site, the ARVN MPs and helicopter crews counted their money.[117] The ARVN had lessons learned from Lam Son 719: allow the escape of able-bodied soldiers scrambling over the wounded, but also make a profit from it.

The distance between Pleiku, the ARVN MR2 headquarters, and the province headquarters at Kontum is 42 KM. On 9 June 1972, John Paul Vann loaded into his chopper at Pleiku. Even though it was night, he needed to go to Kontum. By this time, he was the senior U.S. person in MR2 and had a very busy schedule. He had always been a risk-taker and would rather take a helicopter and save time than go by road or air the next day. By his actions, he had secured a victory for the ARVN in MR2. After a celebration at Pleiku, he lifted off at 9 p.m. He said at the time, "I've been in Kontum every day since this thing got started."[118] En route, Vann's helicopter crashed before it reached Kontum. It was dark, and the aircraft went into the trees. There is no evidence to suggest that the crash was the result of enemy action. All aboard were killed. They were flying low. The Montagnards cut trees and burn foliage to plant their crops. Vann did not know or had forgotten that there was a spot between Pleiku and Kontum where the Montagnards preserved a small grove of trees to bury their ancestors. All other terrain was devoid of any trees on this route. On that night, the pilot went in at maximum speed to the grove of trees, and his helicopter exploded. ARVN Rangers saw the crash and wanted payment for finding John Paul Vann's body, which was untouched by the crash because he was thrown free of the aircraft, but he was killed instantly. The Rangers robbed Vann's body of his wristwatch, wallet, and his Rutgers ring before returning Vann's body.[119] This might be one of the best summaries of why the South Vietnamese lost the war. There was no ARVN leadership; no one in charge; every man for himself. The Easter Invasion proved that some units fought bravely, but many others fled, and most were only concerned about piling up money. They knew that the war was lost, and they needed money to escape Vietnam and find a new life. The leadership of the corrupt Saigon regime was doing the same thing. It all came down to a lack of ARVN professional leadership.

Neil Sheehan, Vann's biographer, was able to find the crash site several months after the crash. He found that there were few helicopter parts that could be identified except for a twisted tail boom. Sheehan provided this summary at the end of his book.

> The wreckage was scattered around the grove for fifty to sixty yards. I saw a small, low square of hewn logs planted upright in the ground nearby and asked the Montagnard lieutenant what it was. "Dead men here," he said. "Dead men here," he repeated, sweeping his hand about. The grove was the hamlet graveyard. The tribal people had left the trees in their natural state to guard the graves and to provide shade for their burial rites. Now I also knew what had happened on that night. John Vann had come skylarking up the road, mocking death again, unaware that these figures of death were waiting for him in this grove.[120]

By mid–September 1972, the NVA Easter Invasion had petered out, thanks to massive U.S. air support and determined ARVN resistance. The NVA had sustained as many as 100,000 casualties in this campaign, along with the loss of nearly half of its tanks, artillery, and other major implements of war.[121] In that year, 39,000 Saigon soldiers died.[122]

Nixon took advantage of this victory to push for a peace treaty. Kissinger negotiated a settlement with Hanoi, the VC, and with Thieu as a reluctant participant (he refused to recognize the VC as a legitimate government). On 27 January 1973, the Paris Peace Accords were signed. The agreement stipulated that all U.S. advisors and other troops (about 23,700 people) would withdraw within 60 days and our remaining bases would be dismantled. All U.S. prisoners of war would be released.

The U.S. embassy staff remained until the final defeat of the South Vietnam regime in 1975. There were many other U.S. people, such as aid workers, inspectors, and staff that were to coordinate the U.S. withdrawal.

The first POWs were repatriated in February 1973. North Vietnam pledged that it would not to try to reunify the country by force. An international control commission was set up to supervise the agreement. A sticking point throughout the negotiations was the status of remaining NVA in South Vietnam. Hanoi refused to withdraw these troops. In the end, Kissinger acquiesced and the U.S. signed with no guarantee that the NVA troops would be withdrawn. There was a vague reference that Hanoi would not resupply them. Kissinger said "A North Vietnam withdrawal had been unobtainable for ten years…. We could not make it a condition for a final settlement. We had long passed the threshold." In response to criticism, he said, "You don't understand. I want to meet their terms. I want to end this war before the election. What do you want us to do? Stay there forever?"[123] This

The fall of Saigon—refugee evacuation (U.S. Department of Defense).

left the South Vietnamese in a precarious position. With no U.S. forces to support them and a very dedicated force of NVA and VC within their border, it was only a matter of time before Hanoi would attack again. Nixon gave Thieu his personal assurances that if Hanoi attacked, the U.S. would come to South Vietnam's aid.[124] The problem was that Nixon would not be in the White House when Hanoi attacked. This set the stage for the last chapter in Vietnam.

The Last Chapter—1975

While Nixon was enjoying the start of his second term as president, the new Congress was busy at work to reduce his authority in Vietnam by reducing funding to that region. Congress was eventually successful. Meanwhile, Nixon became involved with the Watergate scandal, and he ultimately resigned on 9 August 1974. Previously, Nixon's vice president, Spiro Agnew, had been convicted of crimes and stepped down. Gerald Ford had been appointed vice president and then succeeded Nixon. If Thieu thought that he could count on Nixon's help in his coming conflict, that possibility was now gone.

Theiu's regime was in fairly good shape at the time of Paris Peace Accords. Thieu controlled about 75–85 percent of his population.[125] The Accords were signed in 1973, but some argued that they could have been signed in 1969, which would have saved 25,000 U.S. lives.[126] The U.S. had been pouring in an enormous amount of equipment during Vietnamization and beyond until Congress reduced aid in 1974. The totals provided to South Vietnam were staggering: artillery of all kinds, armored personnel carriers, hundreds of tanks, squadrons of jet fighter-bombers, and more than 500 helicopters.[127] Still, there had not been time to adequately train the ARVN to operate and maintain much of the equipment, as described earlier. It appeared that Thieu had sufficient troops to defend South Vietnam, but the enemy numbers were always a mystery. Hanoi had been secretly infiltrating troops into South Vietnam, and the exact number of these was not known. Most important, the ARVN leadership lacked the will to fight. Thieu's first mistake was to launch an attack into the Mekong Delta to purge it of NVA and VC troops. This was initially successful but stressed his resources. By late spring 1974, the area in the Mekong Delta had been recaptured by the NVA. Hanoi ordered its troops to attack only when they had clear superiority over the ARVN, and an enormous resupply campaign was initiated.

In the south, the economy was collapsing due to inflation, bribery, and corruption. "Quartermaster units often insisted on bribes in exchange for delivering rice and other supplies to the troops and even demanded cash to furnish fighting men with ammunition, gasoline and spare parts."[128]

"They won't come back even if we offered them candy."

Hanoi's target was Saigon. If the north could seize Saigon, it would end the war. They knew that Thieu would ultimately try to concentrate his forces to defend Saigon, the Capital Military Region. The initial NVA attack was against Pruco Long province in the southeast. It was a key junction on Route 14. The troops at the province capital of Pruco Binh were no match for the NVA and surrendered on 6 January 1975. There was no reaction from the U.S. The Saigon regime was stunned. The U.S. Congress had done a good job of limiting the power of the president to reenter the war. The possibility of the U.S. reentering the war was not a concern for Hanoi. In the words of the Hanoi diplomat Pham Van Dong, "They won't come back even if we offered them candy."[129] The initial success of the NVA at Pruco Binh encouraged Hanoi to mount a full-scale invasion of South Vietnam. This was years ahead of their plan to destroy the South Vietnam regime and reunite the country.

Kissinger tried to use diplomacy to prevent an NVA invasion. He met with the Soviet Union and the Chinese to obtain their intervention and offered better relations with the U.S. as an incentive, but he was not successful.[130]

Hanoi chose Ban Me Thuot in the central Highlands of South Vietnam as the target. Ban Me Thuot was a small village, originally the hunting lodge of Emperor Bao Dai. It is high in the mountains with a very pleasant climate. This was also the location where the first U.S. advisors were killed during the Eisenhower administration. General Vien Tien Dung would command the invasion of South Vietnam. He would later succeed Giap as Hanoi's Minister of Defense. Ban Me Thuot was a strange target for the invasion, and it surprised the South Vietnamese. A better target would have been Pleiku, which was a province capital, where the MR2 headquarters was located. Dung was faced by an incompetent ARVN regional commander, Phan Van Phu, who could assemble forces equal to those of Dung. Dung feinted an attack at Pleiku but concentrated his divisions far to the south.

It was a brilliant strategy, and it worked because it was unexpected. The NVA concentrated three divisions at Ban Me Thuot on 10 March 1975, and the South Vietnamese defenders fled. Thieu ordered Phu to retake Ban Me Thuot, but Phu had already abandoned his post in favor of safer places. He was with his family in Nha Trang.[131]

Corruption was not confined to the Saigon regime.

> Despite the alarm among many Americans, Thieu was getting no useful intelligence about the highlands from the CIA. Eighteen months earlier, its agent in Nha Trang had pocketed money earmarked for setting up a network of informants. Auditors discovered the embezzlement, and the man was sent home to Langley and early retirement. To avoid embarrassing the agency, he left with full pension and benefits. The incident helped to explain why Bill Colby had assured the White House earlier in the year that the CIA's latest National Intelligence Estimate foresaw no general offensive in 1975.[132]

At this point, Thieu lost his nerve and lost the war. He ordered the withdrawal of troops in MR2 south to retake Ban Me Thout. When that failed, it became a headlong flight to the coast. The best escape route appeared to be Highway 14 through Cheo Reo. It was a horror story. All of the ARVN officers and soldiers who had roots down in MR2 now had to pack quickly, load their families and belongings[133] acquired over perhaps as long as thirty years, and get on the road east to escape. The rich ARVN officers, such as Phan Van Phu, abandoned their troops and ordered or bribed helicopter pilots to fly them, their families, and gold to the coast.[134] That left behind about 200,000 soldiers and their families in MR2 that had been abandoned by their leadership.[135] As the ARVN officers and soldiers with their families fled east and south in panic, throwing away their uniforms and weapons, the NVA cut Highway 19 and other roads east and south. There is no accurate count of the Vietnamese who were killed in MR2 due to Thieu's bad decisions. Meanwhile, Thieu sat in his palace in Saigon, waiting for word about his army in MR2 and when it would arrive to help defend his Saigon regime. There was no longer an ARVN MR2 army. The army in MR2 was now NVA.

There was very little time, and at Dak To and Kontum, a mad rush to escape the NVA ensued. On 16 March, the ARVN 19th Armored Cavalry Regiment arrived at Pleiku from Kontum. It would be the lead element out of Pleiku toward Cheo Reo. Thieu had set a three-day deadline to complete the withdrawal from the Central Highlands. This was not possible since road repairs were needed for the heavy vehicles, and the entire operation was encumbered by tens of thousands of civilians fleeing in terror. The major obstacle was lack of time for planning.

> The other problem was controlling the civilians. Rolling behind the First Element was the ruin of whatever chance Phu's troops had to escape: a fleet of trucks, buses, motorcycles, and small cars, packed with frightened civilians, mostly the families of officers and enlisted men who had learned of the pullout. Phu later claimed that the Air Force had sabotaged the retreat by flying out their families ahead of time, thus alerting the town to the impending retreat. While partially right, he was mainly looking for a scapegoat. After the previous day's bedlam at the airfield, Pleiku was on edge.
>
> Although the VNAF flights certainly tipped off the civilians, it was only a matter of time before a mass exodus began. Pleiku was swollen with people from Kontum and outlying areas who had fled to the city when the North Vietnamese first cut the roads. After BBC radio broadcasts announcing their deployment of the II Corps headquarters to Nha Trang, the commencement of the destruction of supplies was the final signal. Thousands of civilians soon fled. Panic-stricken, few thought to bring food, fuel, or water, a tragic mistake that was compounded by vast overcrowding of wildly driven vehicles. It was this unruly mob of civilians that finally caught the Communists' attention. By mid-afternoon on 16 March, approximately nine hundred vehicles had crowded into Cheo Reo. Because of the steep grades at the Tu Na Pass, a major traffic jam soon clogged the road south of town. Yet by the early evening of 16 March, a large number of these vehicles had crossed the existing bridge

over the river. The bulk of Phu's troops, however, including all the tanks and artillery, still remained in Pleiku.

As night fell on 16 March, thousands of hungry civilians and soldiers began searching Cheo Reo for food and shelter. The town quickly descended into anarchy when Vietnamese civilians fled their homes, while some Jarai RF troops fought gun battles with the rioters to protect their families. Tu [an influential correspondent for the *Chinh Luan*] noted that in the early hours of 16 March, with the beginning of the destruction of supplies, citizens flooded out into the streets. People "hastily and fearfully loaded goods, furniture, and personal belongings onto every type of vehicle imaginable—trucks, jeeps, garbage trucks, motorcycles, tractors, and even fire trucks.... The saddest part, however, was the thousands of people who were walking. Tu, fifty-six years old, was walking along with these forlorn refugees. He was especially worried about the "young and old, babies and toddlers carried by their parents, and pregnant women. They walk along," he wrote, "each carrying a few bamboo sleeping mats and bundles of clothing. Sad and worried, family after family walks along in a long line on one side of the road to avoid being run over. The headlights of the vehicles illuminate the bent backs of adults carrying heavy burdens and the smaller shadows of little children desperately holding onto the shirttails of their mothers or fathers." All night the column proceeded toward Cheo Reo. At 5:00 p.m. on 18 March, the 1st and 2nd Battalions, 48th [NVA] Regiment, launched their attacks on Cheo Reo. The 2nd Battalion assaulted the province headquarters, while the 1st Battalion swept down from the north to take the main RF camp. Despite resistance by small groups of desperate Rangers, by midnight the PAVN forces held complete control of Cheo Reo. Only the remainder of Dong's armor and some Rangers and support troops south of town remained free.

By 1:00 p.m. on 19 March, the 64th Regiment had eliminated all remaining ARVN forces in the Cheo Reo valley. For the next two days, VNAF air strikes attempted to destroy the abandoned vehicles and equipment. Although Colonel Dong managed to get away, he was captured on 26 March in Phu Yen province. He spent twelve years in prison. The 320th Division claims that after three days of fighting, it had killed 755 ARVN soldiers, while capturing 5,590, including 512 officers. Another 7,225 soldiers "turned themselves in voluntarily to our forces" for a total of 13,570. According to Dang Vu Hiep, the B-3 Front political officer, some 20,000 civilians remaining in the Cheo Reo valley were fed and then sent back to Pleiku and Kontum. Given the large numbers of civilians that were later reported at Cung Son, this would indicate that the vast majority of South Vietnamese civilians escaped the carnage at Cheo Reo, but that the bulk of II Corps soldiers did not. Only a third of Dong's vehicles escaped the pocket and made it to Cong Son, mainly after the 7th Rangers broke through. The defeat, therefore, was staggering. The 4th, 22nd, 23rd, and 25th Ranger Groups were destroyed, the 2nd Armor Brigade and II Corps artillery were rendered combat ineffective, and the II Corps support and maintenance units were decimated. It was the worst defeat of the war inflicted on ARVN up to this point.[136]

By late March 1975, Da Nang, South Vietnam's second largest city, on the Northern coast in MR1, was a South Vietnamese stronghold and nearly a million refugees were streaming into it for safety. It did not work. On 29 March 1975, the NVA entered the city as the ARVN threw away their uniforms and weapons and fled. There are some remarkable videos taken at that time. While thousands of women and children waited to be airlifted out of Da Nang or by boat to safety, Pan Am sent a jet to Da Nang to evacuate people. ARVN soldiers pushed aside women and children and rushed the aircraft and quickly overloaded it. As the aircraft took off, the many ARVN soldiers outside the aircraft hung on to the cargo hatch and other parts of the aircraft. As the aircraft gained altitude, they fell to their deaths.

At the port of Da Nang, things were much worse. Thousands of women and children crowded the docks to escape on fishing boats or other craft. ARVN soldiers shot women and children in order to make room for themselves.[137]

By this time the Hanoi strategy had shifted. Based upon the collapse of the ARVN seen so far, Hanoi decided to accelerate and destroy the Saigon regime, now rather than later. Dung received orders to liberate the south quickly before the rains started in May.

On 7 April 1975, Dung had planning under way. The offensive against Saigon would be launched no later than the last week in April.[138] At that time, there were six thousand Americans remaining in South Vietnam. The U.S. ambassador, Graham Martin, delayed evacuation because he believed that Saigon could be held. It was a fatal error for many South Vietnamese who should have been evacuated but were not because time ran out.

After a desperate fight at Xuan Loc, thirty-five miles northeast of Saigon, the NVA broke through. This was the only battle where ARVN soldiers put up a good fight. Thieu deserted his country on 25 April and flew to Taiwan with his gold. He was eventually replaced by General Duong Van "Big" Minh, the man who had replaced Diem twelve years earlier.[139]

At this time, General Nguyen Cao Ky flew over the battlefield and concluded that the NVA would win. He then flew his helicopter to land on a U.S. carrier.[140] He died in the U.S. on 23 July 2011.

As the NVA approached Saigon, the evacuation of U.S. citizens and some South Vietnamese was in full swing. It was a tight schedule to get people out to carriers and other ships standing by. Many strange things happened as the South Vietnamese regime collapsed. South Vietnamese IBM employees were told to stay at their jobs because they were needed to process payrolls for the ARVN. This was de ja vu. In the last days of Hitler in April 1945, as he prepared to commit suicide and the Soviet army was overwhelming Berlin, German army clerks were writing out requisitions for paper clips and other admin supplies that would be needed in 1946.

On 30 April 1975, many South Vietnamese were evacuated by helicopters landing on U.S. carriers that were standing by.

General Minh, the last Saigon regime head of state, prepared to meet the NVA representatives.

> Colonel Bui Tin, deputy editor of *Quan Doi Nhan Dan,* the North Vietnamese army newspaper, was covering the campaign as a correspondent. But as the ranking officer with the unit, his first duty was to take the surrender. "I have been waiting since early this morning to transfer power to you," announced General Minh as Bui Tin entered the room. "There is no question of your transferring power," replied Bui Tin. "Your power has crumbled. You cannot give up what you do not have…. The war for our country is over."[141]

It was evident that the NVA did not want to interfere with the U.S. departure from Vietnam. A greater concern was renegade South Vietnam soldiers who would turn their guns on Americans trying to depart, but this did not occur. The final chapter captured by many cameras was U.S. helicopters landing and shuttling people out to the fleet. As far as is known, all U.S. personnel were evacuated, but many South Vietnamese key officials and intelligence people were left behind. By delaying the evacuation, Ambassador Martin caused the deaths of many South Vietnamese who were later executed by the NVA, but the total will never be known. Ambassador and Mrs. Martin were among the last to be taken out, clutching the U.S. flag. He looked like a corpse. Martin's stepson was among the 58,000 U.S. service men and women killed in Vietnam. This was a very sad ending to a tragic war.

Summary

Throughout this conflict, public opinion and policy shifted a great deal from the early days in the Eisenhower administration, when we were preventing dominoes from falling,

5. Aftermath

to the Kennedy years, when the press and the public realized that this was a bad war, to the LBJ years when there were massive demonstrations against the war. By the time of Nixon's administration, the view was to get out at all cost. Since then there have been a spate of histories describing how we betrayed South Vietnam. These seem to forget that we lost over 58,000 of our people and a large part of our national treasure because of a corrupt Saigon regime. I would let the reader decide who betrayed whom. South Vietnam lost the war, and there was nothing that we could do to prevent it.

Author A.J. Langguth summarized. "South Vietnam's leaders deserved to lose. The American leaders for thirty years failed ... the people of the South and the people of the United States."[142]

Perhaps the most important part of this book is the oral history of the U.S. enlisted soldiers and junior officers who fought there. Many contributed to this book, and their oral histories and mine are included. One thing we learned is that you cannot dwell on this or any part of it. Move on, but do not forget. When I circulated the draft manuscript to veterans and posted it on my website, I got a surprisingly large response from Vietnam veterans, U.S. enlisted soldiers, and junior officers. They said that at last there was someone who would tell their story and put it together in a book that also included the official history. This helped them understand better why we were in Vietnam. I did my best.

Biographical Sketches

This section provides the history of the lives of the key participants mentioned in this book.

Creighton Williams Abrams, Jr., was born in Springfield, Massachusetts, on 15 September 1914. Abrams graduated from the U.S. Military Academy with the class of 1936. He was commissioned in the armor branch and served during World War II. He was an aggressive and successful armored commander, receiving two Distinguished Service Crosses for bravery. He served in the Korean War and was promoted to general in 1964. He was assigned as General Westmoreland's deputy in Vietnam and succeeded him on 10 June 1968. Abrams stressed pacification rather than Westmoreland's policy of search and destroy. Abrams returned to the U.S. and was appointed U.S. Army chief of staff in June 1972. He died of cancer in September 1974. He was the only army chief of staff to die in office.

Dean Gooderham Acheson was born on 11 April 1893 in Middletown, Connecticut. He attended Yale and served in the National Guard during World War I. He served in the State Department during World War II. He was appointed secretary of state on 21 January 1949. He served four years in this position. He was accused of responsibility for the loss of China after Mao defeated the Nationalists in 1949. Acheson returned to private life in 1953 and died of a stroke in Sandy Spring, Maryland, on 12 October 1971.

Bao Dai was the last emperor of Vietnam. He was born in Hue, Vietnam, on 22 October 1913. His reign as emperor was from 8 January 1926 to 25 August 1945. He collaborated with the Japanese during World War II, but was retained by Ho Chi Minh as his "supreme advisor" to add legitimacy to Ho's regime. From 13 June 1949 to 25 August 1955, he was chief of state. He was ousted by Ngo Dinh Diem in 1955 and moved to France, where he died in Paris on 30 July 1997.

William Laws Calley was a U.S. Army officer and was convicted as a war criminal for the murders that he committed at My Lai, South Vietnam. Calley was born in Miami, Florida, on 8 June 1943. He dropped out of college due to failing grades and then held jobs such as bellhop and dishwasher before entering the army, where he graduated from OCS and was commissioned a second lieutenant in the infantry in 1967. He was deployed to South Vietnam as a platoon leader. He was not well liked by his troops, who described him as lacking in common sense. At My Lai he murdered unarmed civilians and was convicted of the murders and sentenced to life in prison. President Nixon later issued Calley a conditional pardon, reducing the sentence to time served but upholding Calley's dishonorable discharge. After his release, he resided in Atlanta, Georgia.

Christian de Castries was the French commander at the Battle of Dien Bien Phu in 1954. de Castries was born in Paris on 11 August 1902. He served in World War II and was assigned as the French commander at Dien Bien Phu in December 1953. After the defeat of the French, he was repatriated and retired from the French army in 1959. de Castries died in Paris on 29 July 1991.

Sa Won Chang of the 173rd Airborne Brigade was wounded and medevac'd to Fitzsimmons General Hospital in Denver, Colorado, in March 1968. He retired from the army after twenty-six years of active duty service and now resides in Kenmore, Washington, with his wife, Kyu Sung.

Ngo Dinh Diem was born on 3 January 1901 in Quang Binh, Vietnam. Following the 1954 Geneva Accords and the departure of the French from Vietnam, Diem became president of the Republic of Vietnam (South Vietnam). Diem was a Catholic and adopted oppressive polices toward the Montagnard natives and the Buddhist majority. His lack of popular support and his losing policies in the war led the U.S. to support a coup to replace Diem. Diem was assassinated along with his brother Ngo Dinh Nhu on 2 November 1963 in Saigon.

Mike Eggleston, the author, returned home from his second Vietnam tour of duty in 1971 and continued his career in the U.S. Army, retiring in 1986. In the twenty years that followed, he worked in industry before retiring a second time and now writes history. While he did not serve at Dak To, he learned of the incredible valor and fighting spirit of the people who served there while they worked with him on this book. As he approached his eightieth birthday, he reflected on what might have been if the young soldiers who died there had survived to enjoy a full life as he did.

Bernard B. Fall was a war correspondent and historian who covered the Vietnam War from its earliest days. Fall was born in Austria on 19 November 1926. He moved to France, and after the fall of France during World War II, he fought with the Resistance against the Nazis. After the war, he moved to the U.S. and studied at Syracuse and Johns Hopkins University. Fall visited Vietnam several times, writing several books, including *The Street Without Joy*, which may have been his best. He predicted the defeat of the French and the U.S. because of their failure to understand the Vietnamese society and adopt tactics such as pacification. On 21 February 1967 while accompanying a U.S. unit in Vietnam, Fall stepped on a land mine and was killed.

Vo Nguyen Giap was born in Quang Binh Province, Vietnam, on 25 August 1911. He commanded NVA forces during the French war and the Vietnam War that ended in 1975. Giap graduated from the University of Hanoi with bachelor's degree in politics, economics, and law. He fought with the resistance against the Japanese during World War II. During the French war, he defeated the French in the battle of Dien Bien Phu in 1954. He continued in command of NVA forces in the war against the U.S. that ended with the surrender of the Saigon regime in 1975. Since his retirement after the war, he has written books and is active in political affairs in Vietnam. At this writing he is over one hundred years old.

Alexander Meigs Haig, Jr., was born in Philadelphia, Pennsylvania, on 2 December 1924. He studied for two years at the University of Notre Dame before entering the U.S. Military Academy, where he graduated in 1947. He served in the Korean War and commanded a battalion in Vietnam before returning to the U.S., where he was assigned to the U.S. Military Academy in 1967. In 1969 he was appointed an assistant to national security advisor Henry Kissinger. In that position, he helped negotiate the Vietnam ceasefire talks in 1972. When H.R. Haldeman resigned as Nixon's chief of staff due to the Watergate scandal, Haig was assigned to that position until 1974, when he became NATO supreme commander. He retired from the army in 1979. After retirement, he held various civilian positions in industry. When Ronald Reagan was elected president, he appointed Haig secretary of state. When Reagan was wounded in an assassination attempt on 30 March 1981, Haig committed what could be considered the most publicized gaffe in U.S. history. Haig implied that he was in charge of the government until the vice president arrived in Washington from a trip. To the press, he said, "Constitutionally, gentlemen, you have the president, the vice president, and the secretary of state in that order.... I am in control here, in the White House pending the return of the vice president." Apparently, Haig had forgotten about the 25th Amendment to the Constitution, which places two people between the secretary of state and the vice president. The media had a field day. After that, Haig continued as secretary of state, resigning on 5 July 1982. He died on 20 February 2010. He is respectfully remembered by all who served with him, including this author and Henry Kissinger, who gave Haig's eulogy at the Basilica of the National Shrine of the Immaculate Conception on 2 March 2010.

Paul D. Harkins was born in Boston, Massachusetts, on 15 May 1904. He graduated from the U.S. Military Academy with the class of 1929. He advanced in rank to command U.S. forces in Vietnam (1962–1964). He was known by his staff as "General Blimp" because he inflated the success of the RVNAF. He was removed from command in Vietnam and retired in 1964. Harkins died in Dallas, Texas, on 21 August 1984.

Colonel Oran Henderson was court-martialed for his effort to cover up the My Lai massacre. Henderson was born in Indianapolis, Indiana, on 25 August 1920. At the time of the massacre, Henderson had twenty-five years of service, including World War II and the Korean War, and commanded a brigade in the American Division that was responsible for the My Lai massacre. Henderson was found not guilty. He died of pancreatic cancer in 1998.

Ho Chi Minh was born Nguyen Sinh Cung in Nghe An Province, Vietnam, on 19 May 1890. He used a number of aliases throughout his life in order to avoid arrest but is known today as Ho Chi Minh. Ho Chi Minh was educated in Hue and traveled extensively, visiting France, the U.S., Russia, China, and the United Kingdom. In 1941, he returned to Vietnam to lead the Viet Minh independence movement. He led the Viet Minh against the French and the Japanese, receiving support from the U.S. At the end of World War II, Ho declared the independence of Vietnam under the title of the Democratic Republic of Vietnam. A war with France ensued that ended with the 1954 Geneva Accords, which divided the country with Ho as leader in the North. The war with the South and the U.S. that followed ended in 1975. Ho Chi Minh died of a heart attack at his home in Hanoi on 2 September 1969.

Harold K. Johnson was born in Bowesmont, North Dakota, on 22 February 1912. He attended the U.S. Military Academy, graduating with the class of 1933. He was commissioned in the infantry, and his assignments included the 57th Infantry (Philippine Scouts). With the fall of Bataan, Johnson became a prisoner of war of the Japanese. After World War II, he served in the Korean War and in Vietnam. He was appointed the U.S. Army chief of staff in 1964. Johnson retired from the army in 1967 and died of cancer in Washington, D.C., on 24 September 1983.

Henry Alfred Kissinger was born in Furth, Germany, on 27 May 1923. He and his family fled Germany in 1938 to escape persecution by the Nazis. They settled in New York City, where Kissinger attended high school and started community college. He was drafted into the army in 1943 and served in the 84th Division in Europe. Following the war, he earned his bachelor's degree, followed by his master's and Ph.D. at Harvard in 1954. He advanced in the academic community and was the director of the Harvard Defense Studies Program between 1958 and 1971. Nixon chose Kissinger to be his national security advisor in 1968, and Kissinger later served as secretary of state under Nixon and Gerald Ford. He helped achieve a settlement to the war in Vietnam and also worked to achieve detente with the Soviet Union and the opening of China. Since retiring, he has authored several books and resides today in Kent, Connecticut, and New York City.

Samuel W. Koster was the commander of the U.S. Army Americal Division, which tried to cover up the My Lai massacre of 1968. Koster was born in West Liberty, Iowa, on 29 December 1919 and graduated from the U.S. Military Academy with the class of 1942. Koster was investigated for his efforts to cover up the massacre, but charges were dropped due to lack of evidence. Subsequent investigations led to his demotion, and he retired in disgrace after he was stripped of his Distinguished Service Medal in 1973. Koster died in Annapolis, Maryland, on 23 January 1986.

Nguyen Cao Ky was born in Hanoi, Vietnam, on 8 September 1930. Ky started as an infantry officer but was sent for pilot training by the

French before Vietnam was partitioned. Ky moved to South Vietnam and joined the air force. He rose through the ranks and eventually became the commander of South Vietnam's air force. In November 1963, Ky participated in the coup that resulted in the assassination of Ngo Dinh Diem. In the succession of generals who followed Diem, Ky eventually sided with Nguyen Van Thieu, and the two ran for office in 1967, Thieu for president and Ky as his running mate. In the 1971 election, Ky was sidelined, and Thieu won the presidency. When the NVA defeated the South in 1975, Ky fled to the U.S. and settled in Westminster, California, where he ran a liquor store. Ky died in Kuala Lumpur, Malaysia, on 23 July 2011.

Melvin R. Laird was born in Omaha, Nebraska, on 1 September 1922. Laird graduated from Carleton College in Minnesota and served in the navy during World War II. After the war, he succeeded his deceased father in the Wisconsin State Senate and became secretary of defense under President Nixon in 1969. Laird became the architect of Vietnamization, the policy that allowed the U.S. to exit the war in Vietnam. He left office in 1973 and has written many articles since then.

Curtis LeMay was born in Columbus, Ohio, on 15 November 1906. LeMay worked his way through college, graduating from Ohio State University with a bachelor's degree in civil engineering. He received a reserve commission in the United States Air Force in 1929 and a regular commission in 1930. He served in World War II and directed a campaign of massive bombing of Japan that caused hundreds of thousands of Japanese casualties. He was appointed chief of staff of the U.S. Air Force in 1961. During the war in Vietnam, he continued to urge the use of massive air power to defeat Hanoi, and this may have caused Hanoi to return to the conference table in 1972. He retired in 1965 and died at March Air Force Base, California, on 1 March 1990.

Marshal Lon Nol was born in Prey Veng, Cambodia, on 13 November 1913. He served as prime minister and defense minister of Cambodia. In 1970, he mounted a successful coup against Prince Norodom Sihanouk, the Cambodian head of state. Lon Nol proclaimed himself to be the president of the Khmer Republic. He then gave Hanoi and the VC twenty-four hours to leave Cambodia, and he closed the port Sihanoukville, a source of supply for them. Lon Nol suffered a stroke in 1971, and his effectiveness started to decline. He had relied on U.S. aid, but by 1975, he was only able to hold the capital, Phnom Penh, against the Khmer Rouge. On 1 April 1975, he resigned and fled the country to Indonesia and then to the U.S. while the Khmer Rouge took over. Lon Nol died in Fullerton, California, on 17 November 1985.

Robert S. McNamara was selected by President John F. Kennedy to be his secretary of defense shortly after Kennedy took office. McNamara was born on 9 June 1916. He remained in office, serving Lyndon B. Johnson, after Kennedy was assassinated. McNamara is the longest-serving secretary of defense, 1961–1968. He resigned to head the World Bank and departed his position as secretary of defense during the Tet Offensive of 1968. Toward the end of his life he admitted that the Vietnam War was wrong and regretted his involvement. He died on 6 July 2009.

Doung Van Minh "Big Minh" was born in My Tho province, Vietnam, on 16 February 1916. Minh joined the French army at the start of World War II. He became a South Vietnamese general and politician who helped Ngo Dinh Diem consolidate power after Vietnam was partitioned in 1955. Later he led the coup that resulted in the death of Diem, for which he was blamed. Minh lasted only three months as president after Diem's death. He was replaced by General Khanh in a bloodless coup that occurred in January 1964. Khanh allowed Minh to remain in South Vietnam, but Minh was ultimately exiled. In 1975, as South Vietnam collapsed during the North Vietnamese invasion, Minh took over as president and surrendered to the NVA on 30 April 1975. Minh was allowed to leave the country, and he died in Pasadena, California, on 6 August 2001.

Thomas Hinman Moorer was born in Mount Willing, Alabama, on 9 February 1912. He graduated from the U.S. Naval Academy with the class of 1933 and served as a pilot during World War II. Moorer served as chief of naval operations between 1967 and 1970. He became chairman of the Joint Chiefs in 1970 and retired in 1974. Moorer died in the U.S. Naval Hospital in Bethesda, Maryland, on 5 February 2004.

Irvin (Bugs) Moran returned from Vietnam in April of 1968 and was honorably discharged after three years of military service. He utilized the G.I. bill to obtain a degree in criminal justice and had a thirty-year career as a special agent with the U.S. Justice Department's Bureau of Alcohol, Tobacco & Firearms (ATF). He is retired and resides on a farm in rural Virginia with his wife, Becky. Not a day goes by when he doesn't think about the absolutely fearless and highly intelligent men he served with in the 173rd LRRP during the trying times in Dak To.

Nguyen Van Thieu was born in Phan Rang, Vietnam, on 5 April 1923. Initially, Thieu joined the Viet Minh communists but quit after a year and joined the South Vietnamese army, rising in rank to command a division by 1960. Thieu participated in the coup against Diem in November 1963 and became a member of the military junta after Diem's death. He became head of state in 1965 and then president until the fall of Saigon in 1975. His regime was noted for corruption and the appointment of commanders based upon their politics and loyalty to him rather than their competence. He fled the country shortly before the communists overran South Vietnam in 1975. Thieu died in Boston, Massachusetts, on 29 September 2001.

Madame Nhu was born of a wealthy family in Hanoi, Vietnam, on 22 August 1924. She married Ngo Dinh Nhu in 1943. He was the brother of Ngo Dinh Diem, who would become the president of South Vietnam. At the time of her marriage, she converted from Buddhism to her husband's religion, Catholicism. Since Diem was a lifelong bachelor, Madame Nhu became the First Lady of South Vietnam. She was considered by many to be a schemer like her husband and was prone to making candid public statements, sometimes critical of the United States. When Diem and Ngo Dinh Nhu were assassinated in a coup d'état on 2 November 1963, Madame Nhu was traveling in the U.S. She moved to Rome in exile and later moved to France. Her property in Vietnam was confiscated by the new government. In her last years she returned to Rome, where she died on 24 April 2011.

Ngo Dinh Nhu was born in Phu Cam, Vietnam, on 7 October 1910. He was the younger brother of the first president of South Vietnam, Ngo Dinh Diem. Nhu received his bachelor's degree in literature in Paris. He pursued academic interests until the end of World War II, when he became politically active and helped in mobilizing support for his brother Diem. In 1963, the Buddhist majority rose up against the pro-Catholic regime of Diem. Both Nhu and his brother were assassinated on 2 November 1963.

Bruce Palmer, Jr., was born in Austin, Texas, on 13 April 1913. He graduated from the U.S. Military Academy with the class of 1936. He served in World War II and commanded the XVIII Airborne Corps, 1965–1967. In Vietnam he commanded II Field Force and became acting chief of staff of the U.S. Army in 1972. Palmer retired from the army in 1974 and died on 10 October 2000.

William R. Peers was born in Stuart, Iowa, on 14 June 1914. He graduated from the University of California with a degree in education in 1937 and served during World War II, the Korean War, and Vietnam. In Vietnam he commanded the IFFV and the 4ID before being assigned to investigate the My Lai massacre in 1969. His report assigned blame and led to courts-martial. General Peers died in San Francisco, California, on 6 April 1984.

Ed Placencia, one of thirteen children, was born and raised in Indiana. His father was a naturalized citizen from Mexico, arriving in Indiana as a migrant worker. As a child he recalls the words of his parents stating that this was the greatest country in the world, you can become anything you desire with hard work and determination. He enlisted in the U.S. Army in November 1965. He volunteered for duty in Vietnam and was assigned to the 2nd Battalion, 173rd Airborne Brigade. After his tour in Vietnam, Placencia finished his stint in the military with the 82nd Airborne Division. Placencia was awarded a Purple Heart, Bronze Star with "V" device, and the Silver Star. Placencia retired as a painter/paper hanger after fifty years. Placencia was blessed with three children, two sons and one daughter, who all served in the army and had a tour of duty in Iraq. He also has three granddaughters and one grandson. Enjoying retirement, he has been commander of American Legion Post 178 in Garrett, Indiana, for the last eight years. He works with kids as head coach of the DeKalb County Boxing Club.

Pol Pot was born in Kampong Thom Province, Cambodia, on 19 May 1925. He joined a communist cell in 1951. He gained control of the Khmer Rouge movement in Cambodia and took Phnom Penh on 17 April 1975. With the Khmer Rouge in control of the country, a bloodbath started that caused the deaths of an estimated 1.7 million people, or 21 percent of the population, due to executions and starvation. In 1976, Vietnam took control of Cambodia and ended most of the deaths. Pol Pot died on 16 April 1998.

John R. Robinson was born in Montreal, Canada, on 26 July 1940 and moved to the United States, with his family, in 1957. He joined the U.S. Army in 1960 and attended Infantry OCS in 1966. He reported to the 173rd in June 1967. On 1 Nov 1967, he took over the 1st Platoon, A/1/503, and remained in the field until March 1968, when General Schweiter sent the brigade chaplain aboard a CH-47 (the only aircraft available) to take him out of the field. The general had a standing order that any 173rd trooper, regardless of rank or time in the field, was to spend the remainder of his tour in the rear area upon receiving three Purple Hearts. Robinson had four. Once in the rear area, he learned that his younger brother (still a Canadian) was a medic in country with the 101st Airborne Division. A transfer was effected, and PFC Norman G. Robinson joined his older brother. When they got together, which wasn't often, they would joke about how they were a couple of Canadian replacements for the "chicken-shit draft dodgers" that were going north. Norman died 22 May 1971, the indirect result of wounds received during his tour with the 101st. This happened while his older brother was once again in Vietnam, this time with the 1st Cavalry Division. as an aviator. He remained in the army, retiring as a lieutenant colonel in 1986, and he now resides with his wife in Florida. Among his awards are the DSC, SS, BS w/V w/2OLC, and PH w/3OLC.

Prince Norodom Sihanouk was born in Phnom Penh, Cambodia, on 31 October 1922. He attended cavalry school in France and was selected as King of Cambodia in 1941. During World War II, the Japanese took control of Cambodia. At the end the war, Sihanouk proclaimed Cambodia's independence and held a series of appointments as prime minister until 1960, when he was elected head of state. Sihanouk worked to maintain Cambodia's neutrality during the Vietnam War but allowed North Vietnam and China to maintain bases in eastern Cambodia. He was deposed by Lon Nol in 1970 and fled to Beijing, China. Lon Nol was deposed by the Khmer Rouge in April 1975, and Vietnam invaded Cambodia and ousted the Khmer Rouge in 1978. Sihanouk returned to Cambodia and in 1993 became the King of Cambodia. He departed on a self-imposed exile in January 2004, first to North Korea and then to China, where he died on 15 October 2012.

Rayburn C. "Cliff" Stovall began his career in the 82d Airborne Division on June 6, 1960, as a second lieutenant, ROTC Distinguished Military Graduate, in the U.S. Army. He had graduated from Presbyterian College in South Carolina. He served in the 82nd Airborne Division Artillery for two years and then commanded the 82d Parachute Rigger Company. He went to Japan with a Rigger company. His company supported SE Asia and the 173d with heavy drop support. Years later, as a lieutenant colonel, he commanded a direct support field artillery battalion in the 3d Armored Division (2/6 FA, 155) stationed in Hanau, Germany. After that he attended the War College in Carlisle, Pennsylvania. Cliff Stovall served for twenty-seven years on active duty, retiring in 1987.

Mercer "Nick" Vandenburg graduated from Westminster College, Fulton, Missouri, with a BA in 1966. He was a Distinguished Military Graduate from the ROTC program and was commissioned in the U.S. Army. Nick arrived in Vietnam in June 1967 and was assigned to A Company, 4th Battalion, 503rd Regiment. He was badly wounded at Dak To on Hill 875 in November 1967. He was stabilized and started getting blood. He waited sixteen hours before he was loaded on a plane for Quin Nhon and the

67th Evacuation Hospital. He recalled that on the plane ride he began to feel awful and very light-headed. He sensed that the medic panicked when he checked on him. "Oh hell, now things go wrong," was the thought in his mind. He was the first off of the plane after landing, and the wait to go into surgery for debriding the wounds was not long, but long enough for a chaplain to come by and ask if Vandenburg wanted a prayer. He said yes, but it sounded a lot like the last rites and he wanted to say, "Is this absolutely necessary?" His road to recovery was just beginning, and it would be a long struggle. He spent a week in Vietnam, a month at Camp Zama in Japan, and more than a year at Walter Reed, with so many surgeries that he lost count. He was retired from the army in August 1969 for physical disability and attended the graduate program in Healthcare Administration at the University of Missouri. Nick was subsequently employed by the McDonnell Douglas Health Information Company. He is retired and working with retired race horses as a volunteer in Kentucky. He stays in touch with some of the former members of his platoon. He has not forgotten the mountains around Dak To. Some of the names and faces have faded, but not the feel of rain, the weight of the rucksacks, nor the smell of death. Those images are very much alive.

John Paul Vann was born in Norfolk, Virginia, on 2 July 1924. Vann enlisted during World War II and remained in the service after the war. He also served in the Korean War and Vietnam. He was an outspoken critic of the RVNAF at the battle of Ap Bac and retired from the army in 1963. Vann returned to Vietnam as a U.S. civilian employee in 1965 and became senior advisor in MR2. His greatest contribution may have been during the NVA Easter Invasion of South Vietnam, when he coordinated air support and was instrumental in the defeat of the NVA. Vann was killed in a helicopter crash near Kontum on 9 June 1972. He was posthumously awarded the Presidential Medal of Freedom and the Distinguished Service Cross for his actions from 23–24 April 1972.

Steve Vorthmann left his mother, dad, brother, and fiancé behind after enlisting in the army for three years on 21 October 1966. He had graduated from high school in May. He survived basic training at Fort Leonard Wood, Missouri, Airborne Advanced Individual Training (AIT) at Fort Gordon, Georgia, and Airborne School at Fort Benning, Georgia. Vorthmann volunteered for Airborne and Vietnam "to see what I was made of." He left Vietnam on 25 September 1968. He was disappointed to spend the last year of his enlistment in a non-airborne unit at Fort Ord, California, where he spent most weeks to the south in the desert on Hunter-Liggett Military Reservation, repairing range targets, ninety miles from his new wife and their apartment. Vorthmann ended his enlistment on 20 October 1969 as a Sergeant E5 with five training jumps plus four jumps in the 82nd. He has not had nightmares or flashbacks, which he attributes to faith and family.

Gary F. Walls was honorably discharged from the U.S. Army as a staff sergeant at Ft. Lewis, Washington, in January 1970 at the end of a three-year enlistment. He worked in manufacturing in the San Diego area for some years and is still employed today, in retail. He draws, paints, and is an amateur writer and historian and a fair musician. He's a life member of the 173rd Airborne Brigade Society and of the Disabled American Veterans and rarely misses the Memorial Day services at Fort Rosecrans National Cemetery. The experience at Dak To remains an indelible memory, as does the memory of so many courageous and selfless young American paratroopers who fought and sometimes died for liberty in a faraway, beautiful land.

William Childs Westmoreland was born in Saxon, South Carolina, on 26 March 1914. He attended the U.S. Military Academy, graduating with the class of 1936. He served in World War II and the Korean War and commanded U.S. forces in Vietnam. He has been criticized for his focus on search-and-destroy operations when most agree that pacification should have been our primary policy. The NVA Tet Offensive of 1968 was a military victory for the U.S. and its allies but was a political disaster in the U.S. and caused an increasing percentage of the population to turn against the war. Westmoreland was replaced by General Creighton Abrams in 1968 and then became U.S. Army chief of staff. Westmoreland retired from the army in 1972 and spent a good deal of the rest his life defending his reputation. Mike Wallace interviewed Westmoreland for a CBS special. Wallace implied that Westmoreland had lied about enemy strength prior to Tet '68 for political reasons. Westmoreland sued, and a lengthy trial ensued. Westmoreland settled for an apology from CBS. Westmoreland died in Charleston, South Carolina, on 18 July 2005.

Appendix A: Names, Acronyms and Terms

I Corps or I Corps Tactical Zone (CTZ)—RVNAF military command controlling forces in Military Region 1, which includes South Vietnam's five northernmost provinces.

II Corps or II Corps Tactical Zone (CTZ)—RVNAF military command controlling forces in Military Region 2, the central highlands and adjoining coastal lowlands.

III Corps or III Corps Tactical Zone (CTZ)—RVNAF military command controlling forces in Military Region 3, the area from the northern Mekong Delta to the southern highlands.

IV Corps or IV Corps Tactical Zone (CTZ)—RVNAF military command controlling forces in Military Region 4, the area of the Mekong Delta.

IFFV—I Field Force, Vietnam, located in Nha Trang, exercised control over U.S. forces located in II CTZ.

IIFFV—II Field Force, Vietnam, located in Bien Hoa province, exercised control over U.S. forces located in III and IV CTZ.

4ID—U.S. 4th Infantry Division.

Advisors—Term applied to U.S. service personnel who provided advice and assistance to South Vietnamese units.

AK-47—An assault rifle used by Soviet Bloc, Chinese, and North Vietnamese forces.

AO—Area of Operations.

APC—Armored personnel carrier.

ARCOM—Army Commendation Medal. When awarded for valor, a "V" device is added.

ARVN—Army of the Republic of South Vietnam.

AWOL—Absent without leave.

B-52—U.S. heavy bombers that composed the U.S. strategic response.

Baby Boomer—A person born in the U.S. between the end of World War II and 1964.

Back-Channel—Informal flag officer correspondence.

Base Area—Communist base camp. Usually containing fortifications, supply depots, hospitals, and training facilities.

Black Panthers—A far left group founded in 1966 and active until 1982. Its doctrine called primarily for the protection of black neighborhoods from police brutality, but it also espoused Marxism-Leninism doctrine.

Bouncing Betty—A land mine that when triggered launches an anti-personnel mine about a meter into the air before it explodes.

BS—Bronze star medal. When awarded for valor, a "V" device is added.

C-130—Four-engine turboprop military cargo aircraft used extensively in Vietnam.

C-rations/C-rats—Individual canned rations used in the field.

Cambodian Liberation Army—also called Khmer Liberation Army. Communist armed forces of National United Front of Kampuchea (FUNK).

Central Highlands—A highland area of the western part of MR2 stretching roughly from Ban Me Thout in Darlac Province north to Kontum Province and the southern border of MR1.

Cherries—Newly assigned troops.

CHICOM—Chinese communist.

Chinook—CH-47 cargo/troop carrying helicopter.

CIA—Central Intelligence Agency.

CIDG—Civilian Irregular Defense Group was a program established by the CIA in 1961 to counter Viet Cong influence in the rural areas. Local people were trained by U.S. Special Forces to defend their villages. Later, the CIDG unit activity was expanded to include conventional operations against the VC and NVA.

CINCPAC—Commander-In-Chief, Pacific: Commands all U.S. forces in the Pacific.

Click—A kilometer.

Cloverleaf Pattern—A patrolling pattern.

Cobra-Bell AH-IG Huey Cobra—Fast attack helicopter armed with machine guns, grenade launchers, and rockets.

COMUSMACV—Commander, United States Military Assistance Command, Vietnam.

Conex—A large steel storage container.

Cooper-Church Amendment—Enacted on 5 January 1971. It ended funding for U.S. ground troops and military advisors in Cambodia and Laos after 30 June 1970. It barred air operations in Cambodian airspace in direct support of Cambodian forces without congressional approval, and it ended American support for Republic of Vietnam forces outside territorial South Vietnam.

CORDS—The Civil Operations and Revolutionary Development Support was established under MACV in 1967. CORDS organized U.S. civilian agencies in Vietnam within the military chain of command.

Corps—Two or more divisions, responsible for the defense of a Military Region.

Cosmoline—A rust preventative, brown-colored, grease-like paste applied to weapons after they are manufactured in order to protect them from weather while they are shipped to the users.

COSVN—Central Office for South Vietnam. Communist military and political headquarters for southern South Vietnam.

CP—Command post.

CTZ—Corps Tactical Zone. Identifies the four military regions that composed South Vietnam. The CTZs are the same as Military Regions (MRs).

D-Day—A day set for launching a military operation.

DEROS—Date eligible for return from overseas. The date a soldier's tour of duty was to end.

Div.—Division.

DMZ—Demilitarized zone. Established by the 1954 Geneva accords, provisionally dividing North Vietnam from South Vietnam along the seventeenth parallel.

Dog Tags—Metal tags that soldiers carried that identified their name and other information.

Domino Theory—President Eisenhower defined the Domino Theory that expressed the belief that if a country fell to the Communists, others would follow like dominos.

Draw-down—Reduction in force.

DRV—Democratic Republic of Vietnam (North Vietnam).

DSC—Distinguished Service Cross. The nation's second highest medal of valor. The equivalent for valor in flight is the DFC or Distinguished Flying Cross.

DZ—Drop zone. Preplanned landing area for parachutists and/or parachuted equipment.

Elephant Soldiers—Name used by the NVA to describe U.S. troops. It depicted the enormous amount of equipment carried by each soldier.

FAC—Forward air controller. Pilot or observer who directs strike aircraft and artillery.

Fast Mover—A military jet aircraft.

Flak—Anti-aircraft fire.

FNG—Fucking new guy.

Fragging—Killing or attempting to kill a fellow soldier or officer, usually with a fragmentation grenade.

Freedom Bird—Term applied to all aircraft that carried U.S. service members back to the U.S. after serving in Vietnam.

Friendly Fire—Fire impacting on friendly troops by mistake.

FSB—Fire support base. Semi-fixed artillery base established to increase indirect fire coverage of an area and to provide security for the firing unit.

FULRO—The autonomous movement of Montagnards in Vietnam to separate themselves from the South Vietnamese regime.

Great Society—The LBJ policy with a set of domestic programs whose aims were elimination of poverty and racial injustice. Anti-war Democrats complained that spending on the Vietnam War choked off the Great Society.

Grunt—Slang word for an infantry soldier or marine.

Guerrilla Warfare—Guerrilla warfare is a form of irregular warfare using military tactics including ambushes, sabotage, raids, hit-and-run tactics, and mobility to fight a larger traditional military force.

Hamlet Program—The rural peasants would be provided security, being physically isolated from Communist insurgents, and support services in defended hamlets, thereby strengthening ties with the central South Vietnamese government It was hoped this would lead to increased loyalty by the peasantry towards the government. In the end, the program led to a decrease in support for Diem's regime and an increase in sympathy for Communist efforts.

Harbor Site—A location used to set up camp for the night.

HE—High Explosive.

Hooch—A small living quarter or hut.

Huey—Helicopters that were used to move troops and provide fire support and medevac.

Hump or Humping—A term meaning a foot soldier's march across terrain.

Immersion Foot—A skin condition of the feet that results after exposure to warm, wet conditions for long periods of time. Large watery blisters appear, which are painful and begin to peel away from the foot itself. It is also called trench foot.

Indirect Fire—Bombardment by mortars or artillery in which shells travel on an indirect trajectory to an unseen target.

Indochina—A term used to describe the French colony in Southeast Asia that included Cambodia, Laos, and Vietnam.

JCS—Joint Chiefs of Staff. Consisting of chairman, U.S. Army chief of staff, U.S. Navy chief of naval operations, U.S. Air Force chief of staff, and the U.S. Marine Corps commandant. Advises the president, the National Security Council, and the secretary of defense.

JGS—Joint General Staff, the South Vietnamese military organization that directed the activities of the RVNAF.

KIA—Killed in action.

Klicks—Distance measurement in kilometers.

Laager—A fortified camp site.

LAW—M72 light anti-tank weapon. A shoulder-fired rocket with a one-time, disposable launcher.

LLDB—South Vietnamese Special Forces.

LRRP—Long-range reconnaissance platoon.

LZ—Landing zone (for helicopters).

M72—Light anti-tank weapon (LAW) is a shoulder-fired, 66mm, unguided missile used by U.S. troops and Allies against tanks, bunkers, and other targets.

M79—A U.S. single-shot, shoulder-fired grenade launcher that fires a 40x60mm grenade.

M113—Armored personnel carriers used by both ARVN and U.S. forces.

MACV—Military Assistance Command, Vietnam: U.S. command for all U.S. military activities in Vietnam.

Mad Minute—Concentrated fire by all weapons at maximum rate. Usually used to demonstrate fire power.

Maggie's Drawers—A red flag waved across the face of a target, indicating a miss.

MARS—Military auxiliary radio system. Sponsored by the Department of Defense, this system, manned by volunteers, allowed service members to contact their families in the U.S. via radio from Vietnam.

Me Generation—Also called America's "worst generation;" "baby boomers" who were totally self-focused and did not wish to provide any service to their country.

Medevac—Medical evacuation by helicopter.

Mermite Can—A food container.

Minigun—A weapons system composed of a series of Gatling-style rotating barrels that rotate and fire at a high rate, powered by an electric motor.

Monsoon—A seasonal reversing wind, accompanied by corresponding changes in precipitation: heavy rain for weeks that blocks roads.

Montagnard/Yards—minority mountain people who live in simple societies in the Central Highlands.

MP—Military Police.

MPC—Military payment certificate. A form of currency used to pay U.S. military personnel in Vietnam and other overseas countries. This prevented the circulation of U.S. greenbacks that could be used for illegal purposes.

MR—Military Region. Term that replaced Corps Tactical Zone. One of four geographic zones (MR1, MR2, MR3, and MR4) into which South Vietnam was divided for purposes of military and civil administration.

MSR—Main supply route.

Napalm—Jellied gasoline that explodes when dropped and produces intense heat.

NCO—Noncommissioned officer (noncom): enlisted ranks including corporal and sergeant, up to and including command sergeant major.

NDP—Night defensive position.

NLF—National Liberation Front, officially the National Front for the Liberation of the South. Formed on December 20, 1960, its aim was to overthrow South Vietnam's government and reunite the North and the South. NLF included Communists and non–Communists.

Nungs—A Vietnamese minority group of ethnic Chinese descent.

NVA—North Vietnamese Army.

OCS—Officer Candidate School; provided a way for enlisted soldiers to obtain commissions after they entered active duty.

OER—Officer efficiency report, an officer evaluation used to determine promotions and assignments.

Pacification—A process of countering a counterinsurgency by controlling the terrain to provide security for the population.

Palace Guard—In Vietnam, these were units that could be called in to protect the South Vietnamese president against coup attempts.

PAVN—People's Army of Vietnam (the NVA).

Pearls—During the French war in Vietnam, captured French soldiers were held for ransom by the Viet Minh until cash was paid for their release. For this reason, they were called pearls.

Percs—Benefits available to service members.

PF—Popular Forces. South Vietnamese village defense units.

Phoenix Program *(Phung Hoang)*—An intelligence-gathering program designed to neutralize the Vietcong infrastructure through identification and arrest of key party cadres. It was also perverted by locals to settle old scores.

Point—Lead soldier/marine on a patrol.

Politburo—Policy-making and executive committee of the Communist party.

POW—Prisoner of war.

Punji Stake—A sharpened bamboo stake placed in the bottom of a pit.

RC-292—Combat net radio antenna.

REMF—Rear-echelon motherfucker. An expression to describe soldiers in rear areas who performed administrative duties and were not assigned to combat units. The term overlooks the fact that in a guerrilla war, those in rear areas frequently find themselves in the front lines of combat.

RF—Regional Forces. South Vietnamese provincial defense units.

ROTC—Reserve Officer Training Corps: a college-based program for training commissioned officers of the United States armed forces.

RPD—Ruchnoy Pulemyot Degtyaryova (RPD) is a light machine gun developed by the Soviet Union and used by NVA, VC, and other countries.

RPG—Rocket-propelled grenade used by enemy forces.

RVNAF—Republic of Vietnam Armed Forces, including ARVN, PFs, RFs, VNAF, VNMC, and VNN.

S-1—A unit personnel/admin officer.

S-2—A unit intelligence officer.

S-3—A unit operations officer.

S-4—A unit supply officer.

SAM—Surface-to-air missile.

Sapper—NVA/VC sappers were commando raiders adept at penetrating allied defenses.

Satchel Charges—Explosive packs small enough to be easily carried and placed on targets.

Slicks—Helicopters used to lift troops or cargo with only protective armaments systems.

Snake Eye—A low-level bomb with pop out fins.

SOG—Studies and Operations Group—conducted covert unconventional warfare operations.

Spider Hole—Is typically a shoulder-deep, protective round hole, not as deep as a foxhole, and often covered by a camouflaged lid. In a spider hole, a soldier can stand and fire a weapon.

SS—Silver star: a valor award.

Starlight Scope—An optical instrument that allows images to be produced in levels of light approaching total darkness.

Strela—A series of Russian-manufactured anti-aircraft missiles.

TAOR—Tactical area of responsibility.

Tet—Vietnamese lunar New Year holiday period.

TOW—Tube-launched optically-tracked wire-guided anti-tank missile.

Tracers—An ammunition round that has a small pyrotechnic charge in its base. When fired, it makes the trajectory of the round visible and allows the firer to track the flight of the bullet and adjust his aim.

Tropospheric Scatter or Tropo—A method of transmitting and receiving microwave communications signals over long distances.

USMA—United States Military Academy, located at West Point, New York.

Viet Cong or VC—Guerilla soldiers in South Vietnam.

Viet Minh—Term used in the French war to describe the communist army under Ho Chi Minh.

Ville—A small village.

VNAF—South Vietnamese Air Force.

VNMC—South Vietnamese Marine Corps.

VNN—South Vietnamese Navy.

VPA—Vietnam Peoples' Army (see also PAVN).

Appendix B: Vietnam Chronology

1930

Ho Chi Minh organizes the Indochinese Communist Party to oppose French colonial rule.[1]

1932

March 9: Bao Dai, a puppet leader of the French, proclaims himself emperor of Vietnam.

1941

May: Ho Chi Minh forms the Viet Minh Forces to fight the French and Japanese.

1945

July: At the Potsdam Conference, Vietnam is divided in two along the seventeenth parallel by a demilitarized zone.

September 2: Ho Chi Minh declares Vietnam's independence from the French by establishing the Democratic Republic of Vietnam in Hanoi.

September 26: The first American advisor is killed in Vietnam. Lieutenant Colonel A. Peter Dewey, of the Office of Strategic Security (the precursor to the Central Intelligence Agency), is mistaken for a French officer and shot by Communist Viet Minh soldiers.

1946

December 19: The Vietnam War begins when Ho's Viet Minh forces attack French forces in Hanoi.

1949

July: Bao Dai proclaims the establishment of the State of Vietnam.

1950

January 18: China recognizes the Democratic Republic of Vietnam.

February 7: The United States recognizes Bao Dai's government.

June 27: President Harry S Truman sends military aid to French forces in Vietnam.

December 30: The United States, France, Vietnam, Cambodia, and Laos sign a Mutual Defense Assistance Agreement.

1954

May 7: The Viet Minh defeat the French at Dien Bien Phu.

July 20–21: The French sign a ceasefire agreement. Vietnam is divided along the seventeenth parallel. Ho Chi Minh controls North Vietnam; Bao Dai rules South Vietnam.

1955

February 12: U.S. military advisors start to train South Vietnamese army officers.

October 26: Ngo Dinh Diem defeats Bao Dai in a referendum and declares himself president of South Vietnam.

1959

July 8: Two Americans are killed during an attack at Bien Hoa. Major Dale Buis and Master Sergeant Chester Ovnard are the first Americans to die in combat in Vietnam.

1960

December 20: The National Liberation Front (NLF)—the Viet Cong—is formed to overthrow the government in South Vietnam.

1961

May: President John F. Kennedy announces that the United States may have to send troops to Vietnam.

December 8: A "white paper" published by the U.S. State Department claims that South Vietnam is threatened by Communist aggression from North Vietnam.

1962

December 31: The number of military advisors in Vietnam reaches 11,300.

1963

May 1: Buddhists gather in Hue to protest against the Diem government. Riots ensue for several months.
August 24: The U.S. embassy in Saigon receives a cable from Washington that recommends removing Diem from office.
November 1: A military coup overthrows President Diem, who is later executed. Diem is replaced by Vice President Nguyen Ngoc Tho and General Duong Van Minh.
November 22: President Kennedy is assassinated.

1964

January 30: General Minh is overthrown in another military coup.
August 2: The U.S. destroyer *Maddox* is attacked by North Vietnamese torpedo boats in the Gulf of Tonkin.
August 4: The Maddox receives signals indicating it is under attack, but it was determined that this attack did not occur.
August 5: Everett Alvarez, Jr., is shot down near the North Vietnamese coast and becomes the first American prisoner of war in Vietnam.
August 7: Congress approves the Gulf of Tonkin Resolution, which gives President Lyndon B. Johnson the authority to use "all necessary steps, including the use of armed force," to protect any member of the Southeast Asia Treaty Organization (the United States, France, Britain, Australia, New Zealand, Pakistan, Thailand, and the Philippines).

1965

March 8: The first American combat troops–3,500 Marines—land at Da Nang.
April 17: The Students for a Democratic Society hold the first major antiwar rally in Washington, D.C.
December 31: United States military strength in Vietnam reaches 184,300. The number of U.S. dead this year is 1,928. The cumulative number of U.S. dead since the start of our involvement is 2,344.

1966

April 12: American B-52s bomb North Vietnam for the first time in retaliation for a Viet Cong attack on U.S. troops.
July 6: American POWs are marched through the streets of Hanoi and attacked by an angry mob.
December 31: The official number of U.S. military personnel in Vietnam reaches 385,300. The number of U.S. dead this year is 6,350. The cumulative number of U.S. dead since the start of our involvement is 8,694.

1967

January 1: 4th Infantry Division launches Operation Sam Houston in the Central Highlands.
April 6: 4th Infantry Division Operation Francis Marion starts in the Central Highlands.
April 24: The First Battle of Khe Sanh (The Hill Fights) starts.
June 17: Operation Greeley (4th Infantry Division and 173rd Airborne Brigade) launched at Dak To followed by Operation MacArthur on 3 November.
August 26: The Battle of Con Thien starts.
September: General Nguyen Van Thieu is elected president of South Vietnam.
October 27: The Battle of Song Be starts.
October 29: The Border Battle of Loc Ninh starts.
December 1: The Border Battle of Dak To ends.
December 31: The number of American military personnel in Vietnam is now 485,000. The number of U.S. dead this year is 11,363. The cumulative number of U.S. dead since the start of our involvement is 20,057.

1968

January 21: The siege of Khe Sanh by the North Vietnamese begins.
January 31: The North Vietnamese begin the Tet Offensive, a massive surprise attack against South Vietnam.
March 16: Lieutenant William L. Calley and men in his platoon massacre between 400 and 600 Vietnamese civilians in the small village of My Lai.
March 31: President Johnson announces he will not run for reelection.
May 10: Peace talks between U.S. and Vietnamese officials begin in Paris.
October 31: President Johnson halts the bombing of North Vietnam.
December 31: U.S. military personnel in Vietnam officially number 536,600. The number of U.S. dead this year is 16,899. The cumulative number of U.S. dead since the start of our involvement is 36,956.

1969

March 18: President Richard M. Nixon approves the secret bombing of Viet Cong bases in Cambodia. The bombings continue through April 1970.

June: U.S. troop strength peaks at 543,400. President Nixon announces that 25,000 U.S. troops will be withdrawn from Vietnam, the beginning of "Vietnamization."

September 3: Ho Chi Minh dies.

December 31: The number of U.S. troops in Vietnam declines to 475,000. The number of U.S. dead this year is 11,780. The cumulative number of U.S. dead since the start of our involvement is 48,736.

1970

February 20: Henry Kissinger, President Nixon's advisor on national security, meets secretly with North Vietnamese officials in Paris to negotiate a peace treaty.

April 30: The U.S. and South Vietnamese armies invade Cambodia to attack North Vietnamese and Viet Cong bases.

June 24: The U.S. Senate repeals the Gulf of Tonkin Resolution.

December 31: U.S. forces in Vietnam fall to 334,600. The number of U.S. dead this year is 6,173. The cumulative number of U.S. dead since the start of our involvement is 54,909.

1971

February: South Vietnamese troops, in a test of Vietnamization policy, invade Cambodia. They are decisively beaten.

March 29: Lieutenant Calley is the only U.S. service member convicted of the My Lai massacre.

June 13: The *New York Times* begins publishing excerpts from the Pentagon Papers, a massive study by the Pentagon on the military policy in Vietnam.

October 3: President Thieu is unopposed and reelected as president of South Vietnam.

November 7: President Nixon is reelected in a landslide victory.

December 31: Almost 200,000 troops have been withdrawn from Vietnam. The official figures of U.S. troops still in Vietnam fall to 156,800. The number of U.S. dead this year is 2,414. The cumulative number of U.S. dead since the start of our involvement is 57,323.

1972

March 30: The North Vietnamese launch a massive attack on three fronts in South Vietnam called the Spring Offensive.

April: U.S. troops left in Vietnam number 69,000.

May 8: U.S. forces begin mining Haiphong and other ports in North Vietnam.

October 21: The United States and North Vietnam reach a ceasefire agreement.

December 18: The "Christmas Bombing Raids" on Hanoi and North Vietnam begin; they go on for eleven days.

December 31: U.S. forces in Vietnam number 24,000. The number of U.S. dead this year is 759. The cumulative number of U.S. dead since the start of our involvement is 58,082.

1973

January 27: The United States, South Vietnam, and North Vietnam sign the Paris Peace Accords, ending the U.S. war in Vietnam.

February–March: North Vietnam returns 591 American prisoners of war.

March 29: The last remaining U.S. combat troops leave Vietnam.

August 14: American military operations in Vietnam end.

December 31: Only 50 U.S. troops are left in Vietnam. The number of U.S. dead this year is 68. The cumulative number of U.S. dead since the start of our involvement is 58,150.

1974

January 4: The war in South Vietnam resumes.

1975

Spring: The North Vietnamese Army launches its final offensive against South Vietnam.

April 21: President Thieu resigns.

April 30: The North Vietnamese Army enters Saigon, the capital of South Vietnam. The remaining Americans and some South Vietnamese in Saigon are evacuated by helicopter from the embassy's roof. The war in Vietnam ends. The cumulative number of U.S. dead since the start of our involvement is 58,220 including those who died of wounds after 1975.

1977

January 21: President Jimmy Carter pardons most Vietnam War draft dodgers.

Appendix C: Unit Organization

This appendix describes the organization units in Vietnam and identifies those engaged in the Border Battles.[1]

The squad, which usually fielded five to ten soldiers in Vietnam and was led by a sergeant, was the basic building block of the military infantry machine. Squad weapons ordinarily consisted of M-16 rifles, pistols, and M79 grenade launchers. Weapons squads contained machine guns or heavier weapons, such as recoilless rifles.

Ideally, there were four squads in each platoon (one of them a weapons squad), which was led by a lieutenant. Three rifle platoons and a weapons platoon composed the infantry company, which was commanded by a captain or a lieutenant. Army rifle companies in Vietnam were authorized [for] 164 men, but most operated at half this strength. Battalions were commanded by lieutenant colonels and were authorized [for] a total of 920 men. Most of the time they were lucky to have an assigned strength of five hundred, and not all of these would be present in the field.

Army battalions were grouped into brigades, commanded by colonels. Brigades had from three to four battalions under them.

Three Marine regiments or three Army brigades composed a division, although there were several separate brigades, independent in their own right, which were commanded by brigadier generals.

The division was commanded by a major general. It had nine or ten battalions of infantry, four battalions of artillery, a reconnaissance cavalry squadron, a combat engineer battalion, and division support aviation. Divisions in Vietnam varied in size from fifteen to twenty-two thousand personnel, but most had around seventeen thousand soldiers.

The two Army field forces, III Marine Amphibious Command and XXIV Corps, were the higher headquarters that controlled these tactical formations in their respective regions of South Vietnam. They were commanded by lieutenant generals, and had large artillery and support assets under them.[2]

Dak To (February 1967–December 1967)

173rd Airborne Brigade
503rd Infantry Regiment
1st Battalion
2nd Battalion
4th Battalion
3/319th Airborne Field Artillery Regiment
335th Assault Helicopter Company (The Cowboys)
E Company, 17th Cavalry

4th Infantry Division
1st Battalion, 8th Infantry Regiment
2nd Battalion, 8th Infantry Regiment
3rd Battalion, 8th Infantry Regiment
1st Battalion, 12th Infantry Regiment
3rd Battalion, 12th Infantry Regiment
6th Battalion, 29th Artillery

Appendix C: Unit Organization

25th Infantry Division
1st Battalion, 35th Infantry Regiment
2nd Battalion, 35th Infantry Regiment

1st Air Cavalry Division
2nd Battalion, 8th Cavalry Regiment
1st Battalion, 12th Cavalry Regiment
52nd Combat Aviation Battalion

ARVN
3rd Battalion, 42d Infantry Regiment
1st Airborne Task Force (the 5th and 8th Battalions)
2nd and 3rd ARVN Airborne Battalions
23rd and 26th Mike Force Companies

Con Thien (26 August–26 September 1967)

2nd Battalion, 9th Marine Regiment
3rd Battalion, 9th Marine Regiment
3rd Battalion, 4th Marine Regiment
3rd Battalion, 26th Marine Regiment
2nd Battalion, 12th Marine Regiment
11th Engineers

Song Be (27 October 1967)

ARVN

Loc Ninh (29 October–2 November 1967)

1st Infantry Division
1st Battalion, 28th Infantry Regiment
2nd Battalion, 28th Infantry Regiment
1st Battalion, 18th Infantry Regiment
1st Battalion, 26th Infantry Regiment
CIDG

Siege of Khe Sanh (April 1967–January 1968)

1st Battalion, 3rd Marine Regiment
2nd Battalion, 3rd Marine Regiment
3rd Battalion, 3rd Marine Regiment
1st Battalion, 9th Marine Regiment
1st Battalion, 26th Marine Regiment
2nd Battalion, 26th Marine Regiment
3rd Battalion, 26th Marine Regiment
1st Battalion 13th Marine Artillery
37th ARVN Ranger Battalion

Appendix D: The Wall

U.S. personnel who were killed in the Dak To fight are identified, below, by unit. These records are compiled from the National Archives and the Vietnam Veterans Memorial.

173rd Airborne Brigade (HQ)

Thursday, June 22, 1967
Erling A. Anderson, PFC, Age 22, Eau Claire, WI
Willie C. Warren, SP4, Age 20, Crockett, TX

Tuesday, August 22, 1967
Lindsay D. Baldoni, SP4, Age 21, Detroit, MI

Saturday, November 11, 1967
Robert M. Staton, Jr., SP4, Age 19, Jamesville, NC

Monday, November 13, 1967
Richard V. Myers, SP4, Age 20, Glenmoore, PA
Edward A. Scully, SP4, Age 22, West Point, NY

Saturday, November 18, 1967
Harry C. Wilson, II, SP4, Age 20, Richboro, PA

Sunday, November 19, 1967
Gary R. Cooper, SP4, Age 21, Bosworth, MO
Charles J. Watters, MAJ, Age 40, Berkeley Heights, NJ—*Awarded the Medal of Honor*

Monday, November 20, 1967
Bruce W. Cunningham, SP4, Age 19, Denver, CO

Thursday, November 23, 1967
Alan J. Impelithere, PFC, Age 20, Liverpool, NY

3/319th Airborne Field Artillery Regiment

Monday, July 10, 1967
Kenneth L. Brown, SGT, Age 23, Sheridan, WY
Michael S. Mitchell, PFC, Age 20, Richmond, CA
Arthur C. Retzlaff, 1LT, Age 24, Westfield, NJ

Saturday, November 11, 1967
Gary F. Shaw, PFC, Age 19, Toledo, OH

Saturday, November 18, 1967
Douglas G. Magruder, 1LT, Age 24, Coral Gables, FL

Monday, November 20, 1967
Richard T. Busenlehner, 1LT, Age 21, Rowena, TX

Troy A. Galyan, SP4, Age 20, Concord, NC
Jesse Sanchez, SP4, Age 24, Union City, CA
Jerome C. Shomaker, 1LT, Age 25, Newport Beach, CA

Saturday, November 25, 1967
Carl R. Barnhart, PFC, Age 18, East Peoria, IL

Wednesday, December 13, 1967
Donald R. Burgess, PFC, Age 20, Tulsa, OK
Paul G. Hamilton, Jr., PFC, Age 21, Des Moines, IA
Michael R. McCord, SP4, Age 18, Carmi, IL

The Vietnam Veterans Memorial, Washington, D.C. (Angela B. Pan Photography).

335th Assault Helicopter Company

Saturday, November 25, 1967
Dewey A. Midgett, PVT, Age 19, Chesapeake, VA

17th Cavalry

Wednesday, June 21, 1967
Clifford W. Leathers, Jr., SP4, Age 19, Wright City, OK

Monday, August 14, 1967
Harry J. Moser IV, SGT, Age 18, Birdsboro, PA

Friday, August 18, 1967
Charles J. Holland, SFC, Age 28, Elizabeth, NJ

Tuesday, September 19, 1967
Eduard A. Auer, SSG, Age 29, Mansfield, OH

503rd Airborne Infantry Regiment

Friday, June 16, 1967
Charles R. Mears, SP4, Age 21, Patterson, CA

Wednesday, June 21, 1967
Jimmy L. Cook, PVT, Age 18, Phoenix, AZ

Thursday, June 22, 1967
Terry L. Allen, PFC, Age 19, Kansas City, MO
James Arnold, PFC, Age 22, Greenville, SC
William J. Boehm, PFC, Age 19, Silver Spring, MD
Ervin L. Burns, 1LT, Age 28, Providence, KY
Albert Butler, Jr., PFC, Age 24, Tyler, TX
Darrell W. Butts, PFC, Age 19, Wichita, KS
Carlin M. Campbell, Jr., PFC, Age 19, San Diego, CA
Ronald C. Clark, SP4, Age 19, Gainesville, GA
Thorne M. Clark, III, PFC, Age 19, Lompoc, CA
Jack L. Cripe, SP4, Age 18, Onondaga, MI

Lloyd D. De Loach, SP4, Age 22, Dallas, TX
Lester M. De Riso, PFC, Age 19, Warren, RI
Charles O. Deedrick, Jr., SP4, Age 22, Winona, MN
Thomas A. Deschenes, SP4, Age 20, Fitchburg, MA
Thomas B. Duffy, Jr., PFC, Age 22, Glen Ellyn, IL
Timothy J. Egan, PFC, Age 19, Chicago, IL
James R. Emmert, SGT, Age 31, Huntington, WV
Russel W. Engle, SP4, Age 20, Madison, NJ
Bobby L. Finney, SP4, Age 21, Boston, MA
Burrell Gibson, SP4, Age 23, Dayton, OH
Kenneth L. Greene, PFC, Age 20, Somerville, MA
David J. Heller, PFC, Age 20, South Boone, CO
Alvin G. Hill, SGT, Age 21, Bartow, FL
Doyle Holcomb, PFC, Age 23, Johnson City, TN
Richard E. Hood, Jr., 1LT, Age 22, Winter Haven, FL
Vins R. Hooper, SP4, Age 20, Somerset, NJ
David E. Johnson, SGT, Age 22, Natchez, MS
Harry J. Johnson, SGT, Age 22, Tarrant City, AL
Richard B. Johnston, SP4, Age 21, Candia, NH
Richard J. Johnston, SP4, Age 19, Sacramento, CA
Donald R. Judd, 1LT, Age 24, Alexander, NY
Stephen A. Kelly, SGT, Age 19, Atlanta, GA
Kenneth K. Lima, SSG, Age 33, Honolulu, HI
Frederick H. Liminga, PFC, Age 19, Pontiac, MI
Robert R. Litwin, PSGT, Age 25, Willimansett, MA
Jimmy C. Lowry, SP4, Age 20, Nocatee, FL
Gary A. Luttrell, SP4, Age 18, Sterling, IL
Walter C. Mayer, PFC, Age 19, San Antonio, TX
William S. McBroom, PFC, Age 20, Russell, NY
Frank McCray, Jr., SP4, Age 20, Miami, FL
John H. McEachin, Jr., SP4, Age 21, New York, NY
Stephen A. Mika, PFC, Age 22, Willowick, OH
Donald M. Munden, PFC, Age 18, Quail Valley, CA
William A. Munn, PFC, Age 18, Detroit, MI
Timothy J. Murphy, PFC, Age 19, Avenel, NJ
Daniel L. Negro, PFC, Age 20, Wakefield, MI
Jerry L. Noe, PFC, Age 18, Knoxville, TN
Michael D. O'Connor, SP4, Age 20, Mount Pleasant, IA
George Patton, PFC, Age 19, New York, NY
John P. Patton, SGT, Age 26, Oakland, CA
Leonard B. Poore, SP4, Age 20, Beaumont, TX
George A. Poor, Jr., PFC, Age 19, Hillsdale, NJ
Robert L. Preddy, SP4, Age 19, San Bernardino, CA
Floyd E. Quarles, PFC, Age 20, New York, NY
Ralph J. Rizzi, SP4, Age 20, Canandaigua, NY
Trine Romero, Jr., PFC, Age 20, Roswell, NM
Hector M. Saenz, PFC, Age 20, Roswell, NM
James W. Sanford, PFC, Age 20, Orangeburg, SC
Warren H. Schrobilgen, Jr., PFC, Age 19, Pacoima, CA
Jeffrey R. Sexton, 2LT, Age 22, Maricopa, AZ

John Sharber, Jr., SP4, Age 20, Jackson, MS
Lloyd E. Smith, SP4, Age 21, Portales, NM
Charles H. Snow, PFC, Age 19, Medford, OR
Johnson A. Steidler, PFC, Age 19, Gibbstown, NJ
David A. Stephens, SGT, Age 20, Largo, FL
David R. Stephenson, PFC, Age 18, Sand Springs, OK
Robert L. Stevens, Jr., PFC, Age 18, Kalamazoo, MI
Fa'asaviliga V. Tafao, PFC, Age 21, San Diego, CA
Larry B. Turner, SP4, Age 21, Oakboro, NC
Daniel V. Valdez, PFC, Age 20, Antioch, CA
Charlie L. Walker, PFC, Age 20, Munford, AL
Michael J. Waterman, PFC, Age 20, Westminster, MA
Edwin J. Williams, PFC, Age 20, Detroit, MI
Alexander C. Zsigo, Jr., SP4, Age 21, Durand, MI

Friday, June 23, 1967
Ellis A. McBride, Jr., 1LT, Age 23, Lithia, FL

Tuesday, June 27, 1967
Michael Parker, PFC, Age 20, New York, NY

Thursday, June 29, 1967
Gene F. Colvin, SGT, Age 20, Fort Edward, NY
James R. Lester, PSGT, Age 34, Stockton, CA

Sunday, July 9, 1967
Clifford G. Burch, PFC, Age 19, Langley Park, MD
Szolton S. Klein, PFC, Age 19, Arnold, PA
Wesley R. Sexton, PFC, Age 21, Cornelia, GA

Monday, July 10, 1967
Myron S. Beach, Jr., SFC, Age 29, Elmira, NY
John C. Borowski, PFC, Age 20, Chicago, IL
Roger W. Clark, SP4, Age 20, Pittsfield, VT
David P. Crozier, SGT, Age 23, Baltimore, MD
Jimmy E. Darby, PFC, Age 18, Opp, AL
William J. Deuerling, SGT, Age 23, New Smyrna Beach, FL
Larry A. Doring, SP4, Age 21, Mankato, MN
Arthur A. Erwin, SP4, Age 19, Eugene, OR
James Fabrizio, PFC, Age 21, Norwalk, CT
Frazier D. Huggins, CPL, Age 19, Seffner, FL
David H. Johnson, PFC, Age 18, Jonesboro, AR
Daniel W. Jordan, 1LT, Age 24, Griffith, IN
Siegfried Kofler, SGT, Age 29, Ventura, CA
Peter G. Lechnir, SP4, Age 24, Milwaukee, WI
Oris L. Poole, SP4, Age 19, Screven, GA
Joel M. Sabel, CPL, Age 23, West Covina, CA
Walter A. Samans, Jr., SP4, Age 21, Richmond, VA
William A. Scott, SFC, Age 38, Magnolia, NJ
Franklin S. Shepherd, SP4, Age 20, North Wilkesboro, NC
Malton G. Shores, PFC, Age 19, Clarksville, AR
Harry D. Spier, PFC, Age 19, Tyler, TX

Jesus M. Torres, SGT, Age 19, New York, NY
Walter D. Williams, MAJ, Age 33, Glyndon, MD

Saturday, July 15, 1967
Gerald E. Davis, PFC, Age 19, Bethlehem, PA
Ronald R. Jones, PFC, Age 20, New York, NY

Thursday, July 20, 1967
Ronald B. Hamblin, PFC, Age 21, Phoenix, AZ
Bobby H. Sorrells, SSG, Age 31, East Point, GA
Ralph M. Stacey, Jr., PFC, Age 19, Pinole, CA

Sunday, July 23, 1967
Donald M. Sower, PFC, Age 20, Camp Red Cliff, UT

Tuesday, July 25, 1967
Edward Barden, CPL, Age 19, Whiteville, NC

Sunday, August 27, 1967
James C. Banks, PFC, Age 18, Flint, MI

Thursday, September 28, 1967
John R. Bamvakais, Jr., SGT, Age 20, Jefferson City, MO

Tuesday, October 3, 1967
Terry L. Martin, SP4, Age 19, Minneapolis, MN
Daniel R. Meador, SP4, Age 20, Vinton, VA

Saturday, October 14, 1967
Willie Franklin, SSG, Age 29, Detroit, MI

Wednesday, October 18, 1967
Nathaniel Harris, SP4, Age 20, Bessemer, AL

Thursday, October 19, 1967
Robert L. Fleck, CPL, Age 19, Costa, WV

Saturday, October 21, 1967
Rodney B. Cline, PFC, Age 20, Garden City, MI

Sunday, October 22, 1967
Frank B. Dunford III, SSG, Age 19, Covington, KY

Wednesday, October 25, 1967
Elec McCoy, SGT, Age 20, Oswego, SC
Lavern L. Salzman, SGT, Age 21, Montclair, CA

Monday, October 30, 1967
Larry F. Coggins, CPL, Age 22, Troy, NC

Monday, November 6, 1967
Robert J. Bickel, PFC, Age 19, Rochester, NY
Charles G. Bowersmith, PFC, Age 19, Marysville, OH

David F. Burney, PFC, Age 19, Palatka, FL
Joaquin P. Cabrera, SSG, Age 35, Piqua Merizo, GU
Linwood C. Corbett, SP4, Age 22, Hollis, NY
Robert H. Darling, 1LT, Age 27, Pittsburgh, PA
Rufus J. Dowdy, PFC, Age 19, Suffolk, VA
Dewain V. Dubb, PFC, Age 20, Bellingham, WA
James L. Ellis, Jr., SP4, Age 20, Jesup, GA
Sherman L. Jones, PFC, Age 20, Jacksonville, FL
Emory L. Jorgensen, SP4, Age 20, Salt Lake City, UT
Richard F. Laird, PFC, Age 20, Alexander, NY
Clarence A. Miller, Jr., PFC, Age 26, Steger, IL
Louis C. Miller, SP4, Age 18, Watsonville, CA
James D. Shafer, SGT, Age 25, Lima, OH
Edrick K. Stevens, PFC, Age 19, Simi, CA
Richard A. Stone, SGT, Age 23, Palo Alto, CA
Willie A. Wright, CPL, Age 29, Chicago, IL

Wednesday, November 8, 1967
John M. Kapeluck, SP4, Age 21, Cresskill, NJ

Friday, November 10, 1967
Luis Barreto, Jr., PFC, Age 20, New Orleans, LA

Saturday, November 11, 1967
George B. Gunn, PFC, Age 18, Schenectady, NY
Glenn D. Kerns, PFC, Age 19, Lumberton, NC
Edwin J. Martinez-Mercado, PFC, Age 20, New York, NY
Larry Martin, SGT, Age 19, Chicago, IL
Ronald A. Parsons, PFC, Age 23, York, ME
Charles F. Riley, PFC, Age 25, St Joseph, MO
John S. Stuckey, Jr., PFC, Age 21, Cloverdale, IN

Sunday, November 12, 1967
Dan S. Allen III, SGT, Age 20, Memphis, TN
John A. Barnes III, PFC, Age 22, Dedham, MA—*Awarded the Medal of Honor*
John H. Barnes, PFC, Age 20, St Louis, MO
Harold E. Couch, SGT, Age 20, Durham, NC
Hubert Croom, PFC, Age 24, Winona, MS
Aldon J. Dedeaux, PFC, Age 19, De Lisle, MS
Armando L. Escareno, PFC, Age 19, Muskegon Heights, MI
Charles Favroth, SGT, Age 24, New York, NY
Daniel W. Foster, SP4, Age 20, Ansonia, CT
Wiley Guerrero, PFC, Age 19, Austin, TX
Abraham L. Hardy, CPT, Age 25, Houston, TX
James E. Jenkins, PFC, Age 20, High Point, NC
Jerry C. Kelley, SP4, Age 21, Englewood, CO
Charles H. Morris, Jr., PFC, Age 20, Algoma, WV
Leonard A. Thomas, PFC, Age 20, New York, NY

Monday, November 13, 1967
James C. Berry, PFC, Age 19, Royal Oak, MI
David E. Bunker, SP4, Age 21, Kingston, NH

Nathaniel Chatman, PFC, Age 22, Pittsburgh, PA
Horace W. Cowdrick, Jr., PFC, Age 19, College Point, NY
Gregory L. Dunn, PFC, Age 18, Santa Rosa, CA
Lamont G. Epps, PFC, Age 23, Baltimore, MD
Robert S. Ferrulla, PFC, Age 24, Lynwood, CA
La Francis Hardiman, PFC, Age 19, Wyandanch, NY
Zan Hess, SP4, Age 19, Wichita Falls, TX
Vanester L. Hester, SP5, Age 22, Fort Pierce, FL
Milford Jones, PFC, Age 21, St Petersburg, FL
Ray M. Jones, SP4, Age 20, Jonesboro, TN
Francis L. Maples, SP4, Age 20, La Feria, TX
William O. McKoy, PFC, Age 22, Wilmington, NC
Vernon Means, SGT, Age 22, Cordele, GA
Wayne P. Murray, PFC, Age 20, Potsdam, NY
James E. Raffensperger, Jr., SP4, Age 20, Des Moines, IA
Robert L. Ross, PFC, Age 20, Waterproof, LA
Leroy A. Rost, PFC, Age 19, Moline, IL
Richard A. Scheiber, SP4, Age 25, Huntington, IN
Willie J. Simmons, SGT, Age 19, Detroit, MI
Vernon P. Sprinkle, PFC, Age 19, Portland, OR
Larry K. Williams, PFC, Age 20, Torrance, CA

Saturday, November 18, 1967

Douglas B. Baum, SGT, Age 20, La Mesa, CA
Samuel L. Carmichael, PFC, Age 19, Chicago, IL
William A. Collins, SFC, Age 38, Pembroke, NC
Michael A. Crabtree, CPT, Age 28, Portland, OR
Joseph F. Dyer, Jr., PFC, Age 20, Pittsburgh, PA
Raymond Garcia, Jr., PFC, Age 21, San Diego, CA
Richard D. McGhee, CPL, Age 20, Yawkey, WV
Thomas J. Riley, SP4, Age 19, Columbia Heights, MN
Charles H. Robinson, CPL, Age 20, Elkhart, IN
Ignacio Torres, Jr., SGT, Age 22, Laredo, TX
Leonard B. Washington, Jr., PFC, Age 20, Chicago, IL

Sunday, November 19, 1967

Michael E. Adams, SGT, Age 19, Granite City, IL
Roy J. Blackwell, Jr., SP4, Age 20, Clinton, SC
Mario A. Cisneros, PFC, Age 18, Riverbank, CA
Jack L. Croxdale II, SP4, Age 18, Lake Charles, LA
Benjamin D. De Herrera, PFC, Age 19, Colorado Springs, CO
Michael L. Ellis, SP4, Age 21, Valinda, CA
James W. Flynt III, SP4, Age 21, Pittsboro, NC
James C. Frederick, SFC, Age 26, Margate, FL
Gerald L. George, Jr., SP4, Age 18, Colorado Springs, CO
Prelow Grissette, PFC, Age 21, Shallotte, NC
Mark R. Hering, SP4, Age 20, North Tonawanda, NY
Thomas P. Huddleston, SP4, Age 21, Newnan, GA
Donald Iandoli, SGT, Age 21, Paterson, NJ
Jeffrey W. Koonce, SGT, Age 20, Union, NJ
Roger A. Kros, PVT, Age 18, Lake Village, IN
Robert C. Lavallee, Jr., PFC, Age 20, Middletown, RI
Witold J. Leszczynski, PFC, Age 19, New York, NY
Andrew J. Orosz, SP4, Age 21, New York, NY
William A. Ross, PFC, Age 21, Columbus, GA
Robert J. Sanders, SP4, Age 19, Philadelphia, PA
Jack H. Shoop, Jr., SP4, Age 19, Rural Ridge, PA
Donald E. Smith, 1LT, Age 27, Columbus, GA
Lewis B. Smith, SP4, Age 20, Camden, NY
James R. Speller, PFC, Age 18, Windsor, NC
Harry E. Stephens, SP4, Age 22, Richmond, VA
Richard W. Thompson, 1LT, Age 26, Atchison, KS
Richard Walker, Jr., PFC, Age 19, Chicago, IL
Rudolph N. Ward, PFC, Age 22, Portsmouth, VA
Remer G. Williams, SSG, Age 31, Raleigh, NC

Monday, November 20, 1967

Louis G. Arnold, PFC, Age 19, Detroit, MI
Gregory C. Bauer, PVT, Age 19, Central Bridge, NY
Bruce M. Benzing, PFC, Age 24, Miami Springs, FL
Neal I. Best, PFC, Age 19, Myrtle Beach, SC
David B. Betchel, SP4, Age 20, Los Angeles, CA
Robert T. Bly, SP4, Age 20, Toledo, OH
Harvey L. Brown III, SP4, Age 21, St Louis, MO
Manfred F. Camarote, SGT, Age 21, Philadelphia, PA
Ernesto S. Cantu, SP4, Age 20, Encino, TX
Thomas L. Corbett, SP4, Age 21, Hampton, VA
Claude L. Crawford, PVT, Age 18, Los Angeles, CA
Charles R. Crews, PFC, Age 19, Starke, FL
John D'agostino, PFC, Age 21, New York, NY
Larry A. D'entremont, PFC, Age 19, Kittery Point, ME
Robert P. Degen, PFC, Age 19, Vancouver, WA
Casimiro Dianda, PFC, Age 20, Yuma, AZ
John M. Dunbar, SP4, Age 18, Villa Park, IL
James C. Farley, PFC, Age 19, Cookeville, TN
Michael W. Ference, PFC, Age 19, Chicago, IL
Angel R. Flores-Jimenez, PFC, Age 20, New York, NY
Juan M. Garcia, PFC, Age 18, Mammoth, AZ
Michael J. Gladden, SP4, Age 20, Odessa, TX
Herbert H. Gray, PFC, Age 21, Gray, GA
Dennis Greenwald, PFC, Age 18, Southfield, MI
William T. Hagerty, SP4, Age 21, Vineyard Haven, MA
Clarence Hall, SP4, Age 19, Newport, KY
Bobby G. Hastings, PSGT, Age 34, Trumann, AR
William A. Hawthorne, PFC, Age 20, Eureka, KS
William D. Herst, Jr., SP4, Age 24, El Paso, TX

Appendix D: The Wall

Aaron K. Hervas, SP5, Age 22, Mobile, AL
Kenneth J. Jacobson, SP4, Age 20, Winslow, WA
Harold J. Kaufman, CPT, Age 26, Spring Valley, NY
Michael J. Kiley, CPT, Age 26, Long Beach, CA
Weston J. Langley, SP4, Age 19, Houlton, ME
Carlos J. Lozada, PFC, Age 21, New York, NY—
Awarded the Medal of Honor
Roger D. Mabe, PFC, Age 19, Haymarket, VA
George M. Mattingly, PFC, Age 19, Oxon Hill, MD
Tracy H. Murrey, 1LT, Age 25, Miles City, MT
Josh C. Noah, SGT, Age 23, Hugo, OK
James W. Nothern, Jr., SP4, Age 20, Clarendon, AR
Wallace L. Ogea, SGT, Age 22, Bossier City, LA
John M. Ortiz, PFC, Age 21, Chicago, IL
Robert E. Paciorek, SP4, Age 20, Ravenna, OH
Joseph Pannell, PFC, Age 20, East St Louis, IL
James R. Patterson, PFC, Age 19, Orlando, FL
Roy C. Payne, Jr., SP4, Age 20, Saginaw, MI
Arnold Pinn, Jr., PFC, Age 23, Jamaica, NY
Steven R. Powell, PFC, Age 20, Danville, VA
Walter D. Ray, SP4, Age 20, Belmont, MA
Leonard J. Richards, PFC, Age 24, Mount Vernon, IL
John W. Smith, PFC, Age 21, Celina, OH
Ervin Spain, SP4, Age 32, Chicago, IL
Harry H. Spencer, PFC, Age 19, Cleveland, OH
Frank E. Stokes, PFC, Age 20, Monticello, NY
Robert T. Szymanski, SGT, Age 23, Milwaukee, WI
Ernest R. Taylor, Jr., SP5, Age 21, Loveland, OH
Nathaniel Thompson, PFC, Age 19, St Louis, MO
Arthur Turner, Jr., SGT, Age 20, Mount Pleasant, SC
Lester Tyler, PFC, Age 23, New York, NY
Ernesto Villarreal, PVT, Age 19, Detroit, MI
Thomas J. Wade, PFC, Age 24, Antlers, OK
Earl K. Webb, SP4, Age 27, New Orleans, LA
Merrel P. Whittington, SP4, Age 31, Toppenish, WA
Lemuel T. Williams, SP4, Age 20, St Louis, MO
John R. Wolf, PFC, Age 22, Renton, WA
John W. Wooten, SSG, Age 24, Garten, WV
Ronald W. Young, SP4, Age 26, Tulsa, OK

Tuesday, November 21, 1967

William C. Hinkle, PFC, Age 20, Granite City, IL
Gerald Klossek, PFC, Age 21, Newark, NJ
Roy R. Lee, SP4, Age 20, Dunn, NC
Robert W. Lindgren, SP4, Age 20, Minneapolis, MN
Roland W. Manuel, SSG, Age 26, Asbury Park, NJ
Thomas C. Mays, SGT, Age 20, Hamtramck, MI
Raymond W. Michalopoulos, SP4, Age 21, Pawtucket, RI

David R. Reynolds, PFC, Age 18, Buffalo, NY
Olis R. Rigby, SP4, Age 19, Hays, KS
Jesse E. Smith, PFC, Age 23, Augusta, GA

Wednesday, November 22, 1967

Billy R. Cubit, PFC, Age 18, Chicago, IL
Kenneth G. Owens, PFC, Age 18, Orlando, FL
John L. Ponting, SFC, Age 31, Emporia, KS
Valdez Sharp, PFC, Age 20, McLean, TX
Charles E. Willbanks, PFC, Age 20, Mountain View, GA

Thursday, November 23, 1967

William L. Cates, MSG, Age 34, Stanfield, AZ
Le Roy E. Fladry, SGT, Age 21, Union City, PA
Richard N. Kimball, Jr., PFC, Age 24, Granite City, IL
Peter J. Lantz, 1LT, Age 24, Orlando, FL
Richard F. Mason, PFC, Age 19, Erwin, NC
Gary D. Roerink, PFC, Age 20, Pontiac, MI
John D. Willingham, SP4, Age 31, Salisbury, MD
James R. Worrell, PFC, Age 20, Fort Lauderdale, FL

Monday, November 20, 1967

Ronald Gilmore, SGT, Age 19, Dozier, AL

Thursday, November 30, 1967

John W. Hartman, SP4, Age 20, Long Beach, CA
Wilmer Watson, PFC, Age 24, Seaside, CA

Saturday, December 2, 1967

Robert L. Morris, SGT, Age 19, Columbus, OH

Friday, December 8, 1967

Mark J. Cullen, PFC, Age 19, Niagara Falls, NY

Sunday, December 10, 1967

Ivan D. Miller, Jr., PFC, Age 19, Fort Wayne, IN

Monday, December 25, 1967

Francis E. Sanders, PFC, Age 19, Augusta, MI

Wednesday, December 27, 1967

Clarence M. Adams, SSG, Age 25, Detroit, MI
John R. Arrington, PFC, Age 19, Columbus, IN
Richard N. Eddy, SP4, Age 20, Buffalo, NY
Michael D. Fuller, PVT, Age 19, Des Moines, IA
Francis D. Greenwood, PFC, Age 19, Oxford, IN
Bruce Hall, SP4, Age 19, Midland, TX
Darrel W. Heeren, SGT, Age 20, Maywood, CA
Moses Hegler, Jr., PFC, Age 19, Magazine Point, AL
Ted D. Holliman, Jr., CPL, Age 19, Greensboro, NC
Dan T. Klindt, PFC, Age 19, Astoria, OR

Irville J. Knox, PFC, Age 21, Sturgis, MI
Michael J. Minor, CPL, Age 18, Columbus, OH

Benny R. Owens, SGT, Age 20, Indianapolis, IN
Gary R. Schwellenbach, CPL, Age 19, Chico, CA

4th Infantry Division

Friday, June 2, 1967
Ronald J. Bonert, SGT, Age 21, Chicago, IL
Daniel L. Harmon, SP4, Age 21, Kodiak, AK

Thursday, August 24, 1967
Richard J. Schell, MAJ, Age 32, Minneiska, MN

Friday, September 8, 1967
Russell G. Garrison, SP4, Age 21, Elmer, NJ
Gaylord L. Westbay, Wo, Age 29, Hanford, CA

Thursday, November 2, 1967
Richard E. Smith, SP4, Age 21, Pontiac, MI

Tuesday, November 21, 1967
Thomas G. Brady, SGT, Age 20, Fremont, CA
Harold Burton, PFC, Age 21, Rural Hall, NC

Monday, December 4, 1967
Thomas P. Ciecura, SP4, Age 20, Detroit, MI

8th Infantry Regiment, 4th Infantry Division

Thursday, February 16, 1967
Richard L. Adams, SP4, Age 20, Cincinnati, OH
Carlton Amerson, SP4, Age 21, Darien, GA
William L. Andrews, SP4, Age 21, Center, TX
Michael O. Batson, PFC, Age 21, La Marque, TX
Jeffrey L. Beaty, SP4, Age 20, Blair, WI
Robert W. Coffey, SSG, Age 29, Coatesville, IN
George E. Dickerson, SP4, Age 20, Grayson, KY
Chester W. Eden, SP4, Age 22, Carter, KY
James L. Elliott, PFC, Age 22, Fayetteville, NC
Joseph P. Foran, SP4, Age 21, Milwaukee, WI
Thomas V. Ford Jr., SP4, Age 22, Lowell, MI
Frank F. Gagliano, CPL, Age 21, Mount Prospect, IL
Giuseppe Giannelli, SGT, Age 21, Oakland, CA
Robert E. Holcomb, PFC, Age 19, Minneapolis, MN
William D. Holden, SGT, Age 26, Somerville, MA
Jesse W. Ivy Jr., CPL, Age 21, Chicago, IL
Lemen E. Jones, CPL, Age 20, Tatum, TX
Richard L. Kollmann, SP4, Age 21, Stonington, IL
J. L. Lyles, CPL, Age 21, Rockford, IL
Maurice J. Marier, SP4, Age 18, Montreal, PQ
Lionell Powell, PFC, Age 20, Patterson, LA
John E. Quam, PFC, Age 20, Mason City, IA
Elmelindo R. Smith, PSGT, Age 31, Wahiawa, HI—
  Awarded the Medal of Honor
William A. Thomas, SSG, Age 27, Brantville, WV

Tuesday, February 21, 1967
Robert C. Allen, SGT, Age 23, Pineville, LA
Robert E. Gelonek, Jr., PFC, Age 21, Taylorville, IL
William A. Gilmore, SP4, Age 22, Oklahoma City, OK
James D. Hunter, 1LT, Age 24, Arlington, VA

Wilbert G. Pennell, SP4, Age 21, Dearborn, MI
James T. Seymour, SP4, Age 18, Commack, NY
Troy F. Tomblin, PFC, Age 19, Harts, WV
Wayne T. Woodruff, PFC, Age 20, Malvern, OH

Wednesday, March 1, 1967
Joseph J. Grande, Jr., SP4, Age 21, New York, NY

Tuesday, March 14, 1967
Steven R. Withers, PFC, Age 20, Kansas City, MO

Wednesday, March 22, 1967
Floyd Barker, Jr., PFC, Age 19, Winchester, KY
James A. Cunningham, PFC, Age 21, College Grove, TN
Blair E. Dennis, PFC, Age 22, Sacramento, CA
Ralph Gray, PFC, Age 18, Medford, NY
Charles F. Harrison, PFC, Age 18, New York, NY
Jacob A. Horn, PFC, Age 25, Inez, KY
Robert D. Jenkins, PFC, Age 22, Clarksville, TN
Richard D. Kaminski, PFC, Age 21, Lincoln Park, MI
William T. Kauffer, SP4, Age 21, Milton, WV
Gary M. Ladd, PFC, Age 20, Cottage Grove, OR
Raul Montes, SP4, Age 22, Los Angeles, CA
John A. Mott, SP4, Age 23, Iola, KS
Timothy X. Murphy, SGT, Age 21, Sacramento, CA
William J. O'Brien, PFC, Age 21, South Connellsville, PA
Joseph R. Piambino, PFC, Age 21, Bellmore, NY
Dennis A. Prentice, SP4, Age 21, San Pablo, CA
William D. Sands, III, CPT, Age 27, Daisy, GA
Calvin E. Schwartz, SP4, Age 20, New York, NY
Richard S Sedies, SP4, Age 23, Seattle, WA
Daniel M. Taylor, PFC, Age 22, Chicago, IL

David Vasquez, SP4, Age 21, San Juan Bautista, CA
Ralph M. Wentzel, PFC, Age 19, Reading, PA
Junior Wilkerson, PFC, Age 25, Waterbury, CT
Billy J. Witzkoski, PFC, Age 19, Houston, TX
John Zupan, PFC, Age 24, Hempstead, NY

Saturday, April 1, 1967
Manuel B. Valle, PFC, Age 22, Tucson, AZ

Wednesday, April 5, 1967
Eddie L. Marshall, SSG, Age 26, New York, NY

Monday, April 17, 1967
John F. Bense, Jr., SGT, Age 21, Philadelphia, PA
Richard H. Bridges, SP4, Age 21, Easley, SC
Earl L. Derby, SGT, Age 24, Pequot Lakes, MN
Francisco Garza, PFC, Age 20, Corpus Christi, TX
Johnny W. Gould, SSG, Age 25, Crestview, FL
Graham R. Hicklen, PFC, Age 24, Tyler, TX
Julio Masso-Perez, PFC, Age 20, Guayama, PR
David A. Richardson, PFC, Age 20, Long Beach, CA
Emory L. Taylor, PFC, Age 18, Huntington, WV

Wednesday, April 26, 1967
Emmanuel S. Fenech, SP4, Age 21, Detroit, MI
Jerry B. Formey, SP4, Age 22, Washington, DC
Edward S. Towe, PSGT, Age 35, New York, NY

Friday, April 28, 1967
Daniel C. Fowler, PSGT, Age 29, Citrus Heights, CA

Sunday, April 30, 1967
David H. Bass, PFC, Age 20, Durham, NC
Barry J. Short, PSGT, Age 25, Milwaukee, WI

Monday, May 1, 1967
Kenneth A. Varney, PFC, Age 21, Tonawanda, NY

Thursday, May 4, 1967
Robert B. Beeson, SGT, Age 20, Elgin, NE
Richard A. Cassin, SGT, Age 23, Torrington, CT
Marvin C. Ellerbrock, PFC, Age 20, Ottawa, OH
Alexander Fore, PFC, Age 19, Trenton, NJ
Anthony E. Kunz, SGT, Age 21, Kerrville, TX
Marshall K. Morris, PFC, Age 20, Des Moines, IA

Monday, May 8, 1967
James Mays, Jr., SP4, Age 21, Memphis, TN
Robert D. Sells, Jr., PFC, Age 20, Central City, IA

Thursday, May 18, 1967
Charles E. Aronhalt, Jr., 1LT, Age 24, Cumberland, MD

Christopher W. Beavers, PFC, Age 20, Naperville, IL
William A. Blackwell, PFC, Age 19, Bluefield, WV
James E. Burch, SGT, Age 21, Freedom, IN
James T. Burns, PFC, Age 18, New York, NY
Joseph Calhoun, SP4, Age 21, Detroit, MI
Steve J. Churchill, PVT, Age 20, Elmhurst, IL
Louis W. Coleman, Jr., PFC, Age 19, McComb, MS
Esteban Colon-Motas, SSG, Age 29, Benning Park, GA
Joe L. Delong, SSG, Age 20, McMinnville, TN
Duaine K. Fisher, SP4, Age 21, York, PA
Patrick J. Flavin, PFC, Age 20, East Syracuse, NY
James L. Foreman, SGT, Age 21, Warsaw, IN
Horace R. Gore, SGT, Age 19, Ocean Drive Beach, SC
Wesley I. Goswick, SP5, Age 23, Gainesville, FL
Bruce A. Grandstaff, PSGT, Age 32, Spokane, WA—*Awarded the Medal of Honor*
Edward C. Hultquist, PFC, Age 20, Norway, MI
Clifford A. Johnson, PSGT, Age 32, Pittsburgh, PA
Danny E. King, SP4, Age 20, Loudon, TN
Joe P. Larsen, PFC, Age 20, Everett, WA
Charles E. Ranallo, Jr., SP4, Age 21, Allison Park, PA
Charles O. Reed, PFC, Age 20, Powell, TN
Alfred W. Robinson, SGT, Age 22, Bedford, VA
Robert B. Sanzone, SGT, Age 21, Levittown, NY
Michael Sessa, Jr., PFC, Age 19, New York, NY
Melvin L. Shields, PFC, Age 21, Detroit, MI
Charles B. Watson, Jr., PFC, Age 23, Seneca, SC
William Wells, PFC, Age 20, Brentwood, NY
James A. Workman, SP4, Age 21, Bloomington, IN

Friday, May 19, 1967
Joseph A. Mancuso, SP4, Age 21, North Bellmore, NY

Saturday, May 20, 1967
Robert D. Alexander, PFC, Age 25, Claymont, DE
John Atkins, SP4, Age 21, Elmer, NJ
Leslie A. Bellrichard, PFC, Age 25, San Jose, CA— *Awarded the Medal of Honor*
Raymond J. Borowski, SGT, Age 32, Dearborn, MI
Lee B. Buan, PFC, Age 19, Duluth, MN
Frederick A. Buza, 1LT, Age 22, Barnesboro, PA
Mario O. De Leon, SP4, Age 18, San Antonio, TX
Gary L. James, PFC, Age 23, Santa Anna, TX
Vernon L. Leino, PFC, Age 22, Hibbing, MN
Frankie Z. Molnar, SSG, Age 24, New Brunswick, NJ—*Awarded the Medal of Honor*
Ronald J. Moore, SP4, Age 21, Columbus, OH
Eugene F. Poeling, PFC, Age 21, Worden, IL
Gary W. Ritchey, PFC, Age 22, Newark, OH

Allen T. Rogers, Jr., 2LT, Age 24, Johnson City, TN
Eliseo E. Tarin, PFC, Age 23, San Antonio, TX
Leon A. Wangerin, SP4, Age 20, Milwaukee, WI

Monday, May 22, 1967
Michael W. Ramsey, SP4, Age 21, Port Chicago, CA

Wednesday, May 24, 1967
Michael S. Lyle, PVT, Age 21, Denver, CO

Friday, May 26, 1967
Lawrence R. Dodd, SP4, Age 21, Aromas, CA
Terence P. Fitzgerald, SP4, Age 27, San Francisco, CA
Phillip R. Gaines, PFC, Age 20, East St Louis, IL
Clayton W. Johnson, 1LT, Age 21, Evanston, IL
Donald E. Mesarosh, SP4, Age 20, Louisville, KY
Ramon J. Morales, PFC, Age 21, Alton, IL
James C. Powers, CPT, Age 27, Dubuque, IA
Michael C. Roell, PFC, Age 20, Hillsdale, NJ
Bruce Townsend, SGT, Age 27, Miami, FL
Richard E. Wilkins, SP4, Age 20, Mountlake Terrace, WA
Paul M. Wooldridge, Jr., PFC, Age 21, Metropolis, IL

Sunday, June 18, 1967
Phillip R. Venekamp, SGT, Age 23, Valparaiso, IN

Monday, July 10, 1967
Revelry L. Kerwin, SGT, Age 21, Chicago, IL

Thursday, July 20, 1967
Michael J. Menchise, Jr., PFC, Age 19, Cambria Heights, NY

Friday, July 21, 1967
Paul L. Domke, SGT, Age 21, Detroit, MI

Sunday, July 23, 1967
Charles A. Barrett II, 1LT, Age 24, Glenville, WV
Dean M. Beranek, SGT, Age 21, Rice Lake, WI
Ronald P. Blaese, PFC, Age 20, Combined Locks, WI
Stanley W. Dix, SP4, Age 20, New Orleans, LA
James R. Fischer, SGT, Age 21, Oshkosh, WI
Roger D. Goldsmith, SP4, Age 20, Black River Falls, WI
Jose A. Irizarry, PFC, Age 20, New York, NY
Lemoyndue Jarrett, SP4, Age 20, Alton, IL
Samuel A. Johnson, SP4, Age 24, Peebles, OH
Stephen Lebitz, Jr., SP4, Age 22, Forest Hills, NY
Gary O. Mooer, SP4, Age 22, Rosebud, MT
Robert A. Nelson, SGT, Age 20, Alton, IL
Charles E. Oliver, PFC, Age 23, Seminole, OK
Eugenio Rodrigues, SP4, Age 22, Santa Fe Springs, CA
James J. Saltmarsh, PFC, Age 20, Ausable Forks, NY
Richard D. Stinnett, SGT, Age 20, Roseburg, OR
Larry I. Sutton, SP4, Age 21, Danbury, WI
Daniel Tramell, PFC, Age 19, Bakersfield, CA
Dante Volpone, PFC, Age 20, Newark, NJ
Bobby G. Wells, PFC, Age 20, Flowery Branch, GA

Saturday, July 29, 1967
Bobby R. Tabron, PFC, Age 21, Spring Hope, NC

Saturday, August 12, 1967
George C. Alvarez, SGT, Age 21, Monterey Park, CA
Leonard R. Ludwig, SP4, Age 19, Oxnard, CA
Edward D. Randazzo, PFC, Age 20, New York, NY

Thursday, August 24, 1967
Kenneth B. Goff, Jr., MAJ, Age 35, Warwick, RI

Saturday, September 2, 1967
Gail F. Wilson, LTC, Age 39, Roswell, TX

Wednesday, September 13, 1967
Johnny Williams, Jr., SP5, Age 22, Montgomery, AL

Sunday, September 24, 1967
O'Neal Dunmore, SP4, Age 24, Columbia, SC

Wednesday, September 27, 1967
Arthur R. Ewing, PFC, Age 21, Roosevelt, NY

Sunday, October 8, 1967
Jose C. Santiago-Lugo, Jr., PFC, Age 20, New York, NY

Sunday, October 29, 1967
Walter L. Clark, SGT, Age 20, Roseville, MI

Saturday, November 4, 1967
C. G. Nuckles, 1LT, Age 25, Rockport, TX
John V. Taylor, Jr., CPT, Age 27, Berkeley, MO

Sunday, November 5, 1967
George R. Greenwood, SSG, Age 27, Oahu, HI

Tuesday, November 7, 1967
Donald R. Campbell, SP4, Age 21, Reno, NV
Gregory W. McFadden, PFC, Age 19, Jersey City, NJ
Henry H. McGee, SSG, Age 29, Hollis, NY
Dennis E. Moore, PFC, Age 19, Riverside, CA
Jesse J. Pearson, PFC, Age 23, Davis Station, SC

Krag B. Roydes, PFC, Age 19, Norwalk, OH
Secundino G. Sosa, Jr., PFC, Age 22, Dallas, TX
James O. Thomas, SP4, Age 20, Fieldon, IL

Wednesday, November 8, 1967
Alpha L. Buford, PFC, Age 26, El Reno, OK
Charles Doty, PFC, Age 21, Natchitoches, LA
David A. Hayes, PFC, Age 23, Bell Gardens, CA
Marion F. Henderson, SP4, Age 21, Oklahoma City, OK
William L. Juett, PFC, Age 26, Owenton, KY
Earl D. Lawrence, PFC, Age 19, Palestine, TX
Richard A. Mehne, PFC, Age 20, Oshkosh, WI
Gary W. Schmitt, PFC, Age 24, Denver, CO
Douglas E. Solomon, SP4, Age 20, West Point, AR
Todd Tate III, 1LT, Age 21, Chicago, IL
Kenneth W. Tingle, SP4, Age 21, Mira Loma, CA

Thursday, November 9, 1967
Larry D Sharp, PFC, Age 20, San Lorenzo, CA
James C Whitmore, PFC, Age 21, Elyria, OH

Saturday, November 11, 1967
Ralph H. Barlett, Jr., PFC, Age 21, Mount Carmel, IL
John L. Barnhart, PFC, Age 20, Greenville, SC
Thomas J. Carter, SP4, Age 21, Sacramento, CA
John J. Collins, SP4, Age 21, Vandergrift, PA
Gregory J. Dellamandola, PFC, Age 21, Stockton, CA
Harold Dickerson, PSGT, Age 36, Poland, IN
John P. Falcone, Jr., CPT, Age 28, Hampton, NH
Calvin C. Hudson, SP4, Age 21, Abbeville, GA
Jesse Johnson, PFC, Age 25, Benton, LA
Vernon J. Johnson, SP4, Age 24, Del City, OK
James H. McCrae, PFC, Age 24, Miami, FL
Dennis C. McPherson, PFC, Age 20, Gregory, SD
Weldon J. Miles, PFC, Age 19, Cinnaminson, NJ
William G. Muir, PFC, Age 22, Eugene, OR
Jimmie D. Rogers, SSG, Age 29, Mesquite, TX
Gerald K. Taylor, SP4, Age 21, Cocoa, FL
Jerome Thompson, SP4, Age 20, Washington, DC
Nathaniel A. Thompson, PFC, Age 24, Tulsa, OK
Edward Urbaniak, SP4, Age 21, Chicago, IL
Larry R. Wade, 1LT, Age 27, Pottstown, PA
Bruce A. Wagner, PFC, Age 23, Lansing, MI
Charles J. Williams, PFC, Age 25, Oakland, CA

Monday, November 13, 1967
Joseph L. Hyatt, SP4, Age 19, Fayetteville, GA

Sunday, November 19, 1967
Joseph G. Gregg, PFC, Age 20, London, OH
Joe L. Lyons, SSG, Age 32, Terrell, TX
Pedro R. Montanez, PFC, Age 23, Lovell, WY
Lesley W. Reed, SSG, Age 21, Buckhannon, WV

Monday, November 20, 1967
Ambrose J. Cerene, SP5, Age 26, Olyphant, PA

Tuesday, November 21, 1967
Charles R. Acheson, PFC, Age 20, Palco, KS

Friday, November 24, 1967
Allen H. Marinsic, SP4, Age 22, Chehalis, WA

Thursday, November 30, 1967
William E. Groves, SGT, Age 21, Seattle, WA
Whyley E. Josh, SGT, Age 20, Spencer, WV
Norman F. Loeffler, Jr., 1LT, Age 26, Oklahoma City, OK

Sunday, December 3, 1967
Christopher Andrews, PFC, Age 23, Sanford, FL
Lawrence E. Leiba, PFC, Age 19, New York, NY

Monday, December 4, 1967
Albert W. Frazier, PFC, Age 22, St Louis, MO
William Y. Hadley, SGT, Age 23, Thomasville, GA

Wednesday, December 13, 1967
Lloyd L. Hitchins, 2LT, Age 21, Champaign, IL

Thursday, December 14, 1967
Gregory P. Curtis, PFC, Age 19, Longview, WA

Friday, December 15, 1967
Kenneth R. Dau, SP4, Age 19, Warren, MN

Saturday, December 16, 1967
James C. Groover, PFC, Age 19, Jackson, MS
Fathies Kelly, Jr., PFC, Age 20, New York, NY

Wednesday, December 20, 1967
Glen D. Belnap, LTC, Age 44, Red Bluff, CA
Herbert Roberts, Jr., SMAJ, Age 46, Sunbright, TN

Thursday, December 21, 1967
Richard J. Janski, PFC, Age 24, Minneapolis, MN

Friday, December 22, 1967
William E. Bridges, Jr., PFC, Age 24, Lenoir City, TN

12th Infantry Regiment, 4th Infantry Division

Sunday, February 12, 1967
Ronald W. Hutson, SP4, Age 23, Sapulpa, OK
Patrick H. Pettway, II, SP4, Age 25, Tyler, TX
Jerry P. Setzer, PFC, Age 23, Baltimore, MD
Pedro A. Smith, CPL, Age 19, Sturgis, MI

Tuesday, February 14, 1967
James E. Berard, SP4, Age 20, Saratoga, CA

Wednesday, February 15, 1967
Harvey M. Carkin, SGT, Age 22, Vienna, VA
Richard A. Carver, PSGT, Age 39, Escondido, CA
Johnie N. Daniels, SP4, Age 21, Redfield, AR
Ronald C. Gehler, SP4, Age 23, Sioux Falls, SD
James L. Kramer, SP4, Age 20, Las Vegas, NV
Van Dyke W. Manners, PFC, Age 21, Ringoes, NJ
John J. Raymond, SSG, Age 49, Taunton, MA
Michael P. Reilly, SP4, Age 21, La Grange, IL
Eric B. Speak, CPL, Age 19, Costa Mesa, CA
Louis E. Willett, PFC, Age 21, Richmond Hill, NY

Thursday, February 16, 1967
Wayne N. Card, CPL, Age 19, Whittier, CA
Lawrence R. Kusilek, SP4, Age 21, St Paul, MN
William D. Wessells, SSG, Age 22, Accomac, VA

Friday, February 17, 1967
John D. Volner, PFC, Age 20, Lexington, TN

Tuesday, February 21, 1967
Ray M. Harmon, SP4, Age 21, Flemingsburg, KY
Walter L. Howard, SSG, Age 21, College Station, TX

Friday, February 24, 1967
Raymond D. Kesling, SSG, Age 27, Buckhannon, WV
Harold W. Maddox, CPL, Age 24, Steger, IL

Saturday, February 25, 1967
Harvey R. Chambers, PFC, Age 20, Leitchfield, KY
William A. Coggeshall, SP4, Age 20, Marshfield, MA
Leon D. Eckhart, SP4, Age 21, Lehighton, PA
Heriberto Romero-Oyola, SP4, Age 25, Trujillo Alto, PR

Sunday, February 26, 1967
John K. Davis, SSG, Age 23, Fort Jackson, SC
Edward J. Ginter, SP4, Age 20, Greensburg, PA
Robert J. Gold, SP4, Age 20, Sidney, OH
Warren F. Muhr, PFC, Age 21, Chicago, IL
Donald L. Pender, SGT, Age 25, Tacoma, WA

Tuesday, February 28, 1967
Michael J. Molina, SP4, Age 21, Los Angeles, CA
Donald S. Vaughan, SP4, Age 21, Pittsburgh, PA

Thursday, March 2, 1967
George M. Sloan, PFC, Age 20, New Castle, IN
Richard H. Tissier, PFC, Age 20, New York, NY

Friday, March 3, 1967
John P. Taillon, SGT, Age 19, Jamaica Plain, MA

Tuesday, March 7, 1967
Cecil D. McCann, SP4, Age 21, Melvindale, MI
John A. Sickel, III, SP4, Age 22, Longmeadow, MA

Thursday, March 16, 1967
Elbert F. Blackburn, PFC, Age 22, Norwalk, CA
Clark A. Miller, SP4, Age 21, Somerville, MA
Michael J. Monahan, SP4, Age 21, San Francisco, CA

Friday, March 17, 1967
Jerry M. Chunges, SP4, Age 24, Alvin, IL
Julio Kaneko, SSG, Age 31, Lemon Grove, CA
Otto D. Tucker, PFC, Age 20, Fort Worth, TX

Sunday, March 19, 1967
James A. Blanchard, PFC, Age 20, Pascoag, RI

Tuesday, March 21, 1967
Larry D. Barton, SP4, Age 21, Millersburg, OH

Wednesday, March 22, 1967
Galen L. Moore, SP4, Age 21, Newport Beach, CA

Wednesday, March 29, 1967
John Coyle, SP4, Age 21, Hackensack, NJ

Sunday, April 9, 1967
Michael R. Nelson, SP4, Age 19, Garden Grove, CA

Sunday, April 23, 1967
George R. Harrison, CPL, Age 20, Clearmont, WY

Sunday, April 30, 1967
Jose I. Garcia-Maldonado, SP4, Age 20, Naguabo, PR

Monday, May 1, 1967
James B. Bell Jr., SSG, Age 23, Tampa, FL
Willie J. Myrick, PFC, Age 20, Cleveland, OH
Alfonza Watson, SP4, Age 22, Los Angeles, CA

Wednesday, May 3, 1967
Clarence Blanks, SP4, Age 25, Tupelo, MS
Robert H. Carr, PFC, Age 21, Philadelphia, PA

Saturday, May 6, 1967
Gary W. Price, PFC, Age 19, Dorchester, IL

Sunday, May 7, 1967
John J. Hermanowicz, SP4, Age 21, Chicago, IL
John W. McCoy, SP4, Age 21, Milford, OH

Saturday, May 13, 1967
Dennis L. Hubbard, PFC, Age 20, Gary, IN
Paul E. Manske, PFC, Age 20, Oshkosh, WI

Appendix D: The Wall

Thursday, May 18, 1967
Bobby G. McElhaney, PFC, Age 20, Huntsville, AR

Friday, May 19, 1967
James M. Mosgrove, Jr., SSG, Age 25, Baltimore, MD
Ronald T. Waldrop, PVT, Age 22, Santee, CA

Saturday, May 20, 1967
Eugene A. Ward, PFC, Age 20, Oelwein, IA

Sunday, May 21, 1967
Thomas G. Modisette, SGT, Age 19, Irving, TX

Monday, May 22, 1967
Randal R. Aylworth, PFC, Age 19, Jenison, MI
Thomas J. Burke, 1LT, Age 25, Gloucester, MA
Wallace S. Dworaczyk, SP4, Age 20, Yorktown, TX
Harold A. Ford, 2LT, Age 23, Pittsburgh, PA
Antonio G. Garza, Jr., PVT, Age 20, Jourdanton, TX
Julius E. Jenkins, SP4, Age 21, Aliquippa, PA
Clarence L. Morris, SP4, Age 21, Spencer, NC
Carl W. Scallions, SP4, Age 21, Ripley, TN
Mack D. Simmons, III, SP4, Age 21, Rocky Mount, NC
Terry G. Straub, SP4, Age 20, Lykens, PA

Tuesday, May 23, 1967
James W. Cartwright, SGT, Age 22, Eugene, OR

Wednesday, May 24, 1967
Bernard L. Franke, SGT, Age 20, Mount Olive, IL
James L. Kachline, SP4, Age 20, Tatamy, PA
Gary Murray, SP4, Age 20, Elizabethton, TN
Gerald J. Pysher, SP5, Age 24, Ackermanville, PA

Thursday, May 25, 1967
Kurney J. White, Jr., PFC, Age 21, Berwick, LA

Sunday, May 28, 1967
John J. Finnegan, PFC, Age 20, New Hyde Park, NY
Michael N. Harley, SP4, Age 20, Buffalo, NY
Charles E. Johnson, PFC, Age 22, Chicago, IL

Tuesday, May 30, 1967
Alfred Ellis, SP4, Age 21, Chicago, IL
Jimmie L. Jones, CPL, Age 21, Zellwood, FL

Thursday, June 1, 1967
Paul J. Petersen, SP4, Age 21, Taylor, MI

Saturday, June 3, 1967
Daniel W. White, PFC, Age 23, Herndon, VA

Tuesday, June 20, 1967
James E. Fields, SP4, Age 21, New York, NY

Monday, June 26, 1967
James E. Delrie, PFC, Age 20, Homer, LA
Reynaldo B. Florez, PFC, Age 20, Visalia, CA

Tuesday, June 27, 1967
Jimmy E. Carter, PFC, Age 19, Smithfield, NC

Saturday, July 1, 1967
Wayne M. Rockenbaugh, PFC, Age 23, Baltimore, MD

Sunday, July 2, 1967
Edward C. Miller, PFC, Age 23, Indianapolis, IN

Tuesday, July 4, 1967
Edward K. Ferguson, PFC, Age 23, San Lorenzo, CA
James E. Turner, PFC, Age 19, Franklin, VA

Wednesday, July 12, 1967
Pernell R. Claud, SP4, Age 20, Newport News, VA
Gary T. Coleman, PFC, Age 22, Alameda, CA
Tyrone Combs, SP5, Age 21, Dayton, OH
Ronald E. Crain, SP4, Age 21, Jonesboro, AR
Robert E. Echols, PFC, Age 19, Bowman, GA
Gerald L. Fox, PFC, Age 20, New York, NY
Willie K. Fullilove, PFC, Age 26, Chicago, IL
Eddie C. Gibson, PFC, Age 19, Cleves, OH
Stephen J. Groth, SP4, Age 22, Enderlin, ND
John A. Harlan, PFC, Age 20, Johnson City, TN
Wandle L. Hickman, PFC, Age 26, Columbus, OH
David M. Horn, PFC, Age 19, Dayton, OH
Jerry L. Hughes, SGT, Age 20, Center, TX
Rockwell G. Jamison, SGT, Age 22, Los Angeles, CA
Charles M. Judge, Jr., SP4, Age 20, Short Hills, NJ
Ronald R. King, PFC, Age 22, Coatesville, PA
Jerry D. Lanier, SP4, Age 21, Siloam Springs, AR
Milford G. McKee, PFC, Age 25, Sloans Valley, KY
Joseph L. Miller, PFC, Age 20, Hopkinsville, KY
Owen R. Montgomery, SGT, Age 24, Lost Creek, KY
Floyd R. Noe, PFC, Age 19, Huntington, IN
Gaylord E. Nootz, 2LT, Age 22, Rialto, CA
Salvatore F. Polizzi, PFC, Age 20, Wantagh, NY
Brian W. Rushton, CPT, Age 26, Memphis, TN
James F. Schiele, SSG, Age 31, Granger, UT
Troy L. Sexton, PFC, Age 20, Seattle, WA
Robert A. Strange, PFC, Age 20, Northville, MI
James L. Van Bendegom, SSG, Age 18, Kenosha, WI
Gary L. Waguespack, PFC, Age 20, New Orleans, LA
Floyd C. Williams, PFC, Age 22, Hornbeck, LA
Moses Williams, SGT, Age 26, Columbus, GA

Friday, November 17, 1967
Jackie R. Combs, PFC, Age 21, Okanogan, WA
Robert W. Deyo, Jr., PFC, Age 20, Waterloo, IA
Terry M. Enriquez, PFC, Age 22, Burbank, CA
Robert J. Farley Sr., SP4, Age 26, Houston, TX
Leroy J. Kling, PFC, Age 20, Baton Rouge, LA
Hubert J. Payne, PFC, Age 26, Vermilion, OH
John W. Terrell, 1LT, Age 22, Akron, OH
Larry P. Thurman, SGT, Age 19, Dumas, TX
Darrell D. Venenga, PFC, Age 20, Sioux Falls, SD

Sunday, November 19, 1967
James A. Belveal, PFC, Age 22, Sacramento, CA
Ronald D. King, PFC, Age 20, Vaughn, WA
Tyrone C. Marsden, SP4, Age 20, New York, NY
Walter R. Riddle, PFC, Age 21, Anadarko, OK

Monday, November 20, 1967
Gregory S. Fennimore, PFC, Age 19, Elwood, IN
Kenneth A. Peterson, PFC, Age 20, Roanoke, TX

Sunday, November 26, 1967
Dale P. Berthoux, SP4, Age 31, Jerseyville, IL
James W. Hickey, PFC, Age 24, New York, NY
Edward C. Higgins, III, PFC, Age 20, New York, NY
Charles R. Pitts, 1LT, Age 23, Lakeland, FL
Richard G. Stamper, Jr., SGT, Age 21, Cincinnati, OH

Tuesday, November 28, 1967
William T. Poston, SSG, Age 23, Dallas, TX

Saturday, December 2, 1967
Thomas L. Herring, PFC, Age 19, Richmond, VA
Donald W. Thompson, CPL, Age 22, Montezuma, IA

Tuesday, December 5, 1967
Richard R. Weise, PFC, Age 20, St Peter, MN

Wednesday, December 6, 1967
Robert O. Buckner, Jr., PFC, Age 25, Irving, TX
John C. Filippi, PFC, Age 18, Seven Hills, OH
Gary G. Hahn, SGT, Age 24, San Gabriel, CA
Durward A. Limbacher, PFC, Age 20, Farragut, IA
David M. Midcap, PFC, Age 21, Fort Morgan, CO
William H. Pruitt, Jr., SGT, Age 21, Pedro, OH

Joseph L. Reynolds, PFC, Age 20, Bellevue, WA
Terrence L. Sund, SP4, Age 20, Menomonee Falls, WI
Teddy G. Whitton, SP5, Age 20, Paragould, AR
Eugene Zeigler, SP4, Age 23, Montgomery, AL

Sunday, December 10, 1967
Robert C. Campbell, PFC, Age 20, Independence, MO
Robert J. Larson, SP4, Age 19, Minneapolis, MN
John Nishimura, PFC, Age 21, Morgan Hill, CA
Ronald L. Sandmann, SGT, Age 20, Sleepy Eye, MN

Thursday, December 14, 1967
Lloyd Slack, SP4, Age 23, Grand Rapids, MI

Tuesday, December 19, 1967
John D. Barnett, Jr., PFC, Age 19, Reading, PA
Junius C. Collier, SP4, Age 21, Memphis, TN
Junior E. Lott, CPL, Age 24, Athens, AL
Anthony R. Mantouvales, SP4, Age 27, Boston, MA
Winfield A. Spoehr, Jr., CPL, Age 26, New London, WI
Raymond L. Zimmerman, PFC, Age 23, Compton, CA

Saturday, December 23, 1967
John R. Phillips, PFC, Age 20, Bowen, IL

Sunday, December 24, 1967
William D. Dickson, 2LT, Age 25, Oxnard, CA
Larry W. Pierce, PFC, Age 21, Baden, PA
Vernie H. Powers, PFC, Age 20, Baltimore, MD

Tuesday, December 26, 1967
Sammy Buffington, SP4, Age 22, Barnesville, GA
Daniel C. Faulks, Jr., SP4, Age 21, Eureka, CA
Timothy J. Kennedy, SP4, Age 23, Burlington, WI
Renny D. Schoel, PFC, Age 20, Marysville, CA

Wednesday, December 27, 1967
Gordon T. Dalton, PFC, Age 23, Hamilton, OH
Guillermo Estrada, CPL, Age 24, Gary, IN
Guy D. Kistner, PFC, Age 20, Burlingame, CA
James E. Loudermilk, SP4, Age 20, Vero Beach, FL
Thomas W. Malloy, SP4, Age 19, Dunmore, PA
Richard J. Solczyk, 1LT, Age 23, Chicago, IL

22nd Infantry Regiment, 4th Infantry Division

Thursday, February 16, 1967
Channing Allen, Jr., PFC, Age 24, Albertson, NY
Lee R. Bays, SGT, Age 31, Olivehurst, CA

Anastacio H Beltran, SP4, Age 20, Elgin, TX
William M. Berenwick, PFC, Age 21, Hillside, NJ
Lanny R. Bolding, PFC, Age 24, Bells, TN

Douglas R. Colbert, PFC, Age 21, Norwood, NY
Donald R. Dorman, SGT, Age 22, West Hyattsville, MD
Curtis L. Duck, PFC, Age 19, National City, CA
Larry S. Fetherolf, PFC, Age 19, Lilburn, GA
Edward E. Fortenberry, SP4, Age 21, Foxworth, MS
Walter W. Haring, SSG, Age 35, Easton, PA
Clemente D. Hernandez, PFC, Age 22, San Bernardino, CA
Elmer F. Kepsel, PFC, Age 20, Mount Clemens, MI
Kenneth L. Koster, SP4, Age 21, Atlanta, GA
Richard A. Lawrence, CPL, Age 21, Detroit, MI
Lee Lewis, SP4, Age 20, Pickens, SC
Marlow M. Loecker, SP4, Age 21, Crofton, NE
Colin D. MacManus, CPT, Age 25, Newark, NJ
Ronald G. Mottishaw, SGT, Age 21, Pocatello, ID
John E. Oocumma, PFC, Age 25, Cherokee, NC
Donald L. Schnee, CPL, Age 21, Cincinnati, OH
Richard Tarkington, Jr., SP4, Age 21, Okmulgee, OK
Alton J. Zerangue, Jr., SSG, Age 30, Arnaudville, LA

Saturday, February 18, 1967
Daniel P. Donnellan, PFC, Age 20, Ferndale, WA

Sunday, February 19, 1967
Dale W. Moore, SP4, Age 20, Princeton, IL

Tuesday, February 21, 1967
Dennis M. Thompson, CPL, Age 20, Aberdeen, WA

Thursday, February 23, 1967
William R. Sanders, PFC, Age 21, Chicago, IL

Monday, February 27, 1967
James R. Hubbard, SP4, Age 21, Memphis, TN
Teddy W. Steelman, SP4, Age 21, Roodhouse, IL

Thursday, March 2, 1967
Terry A. Patterson, PFC, Age 22, Waukegan, IL

Friday, March 3, 1967
Edwin Jones, PFC, Age 18, Jacksonville, FL

Saturday, March 11, 1967
Edward M. Howell, SFC, Age 29, Cleveland, OH

Tuesday, March 14, 1967
Leslie P. Bernstein, SP4, Age 21, Mastic, NY
Marshall E. Clements, SP4, Age 21, Chicago, IL
James A. Cran, PFC, Age 26, Hayfield, MN
James B. Cummings, Jr., SGT, Age 28, Long Beach, CA
Anibal De Jesus-Sanchez, PFC, Age 21, Guayama, PR
Fred N. Hanshew, Jr., SSG, Age 24, Camby, IN
Matthew Higgins, PFC, Age 21, Philadelphia, PA
Robert W. Hill, SGT, Age 28, Chicago, IL
Edwin N. Holloway, III, PFC, Age 20, Flourtown, PA
Roger S. Kohut, PFC, Age 19, Detroit, MI
William Kuhne, PFC, Age 20, New York, NY
Melvin Lipscomb, SP4, Age 21, College Park, GA
Larry R. Lumpkins, PFC, Age 19, Phoenix, AZ
William C. Pearce, VI, PFC, Age 19, Detroit, MI
Clarence E. Rollen, PFC, Age 20, Winnsboro, LA
Charles P. Terhune, PFC, Age 19, Indianapolis, IN

Thursday, March 16, 1967
Ronald B. Price, SGT, Age 22, Swainsboro, GA
James E. Santos, SP4, Age 20, Dededo, GU

25th Infantry Division
35th Infantry Regiment, 25th Infantry Division[1]

Saturday, March 11, 1967
Francis B. Concannon, PFC, Age 19, Forestville, MD

Sunday, March 12, 1967
Charles W. Barrett, SP4, Age 20, San Francisco, CA
Stephen F. Burlingame, SP4, Age 24, Glendale, CA
Andrew T. Castelda, SP4, Age 19, Arlington, VA
Boyd G. Garner, PFC, Age 23, St. Paul, MN
Lamar Horne, PFC, Age 19, McRae, GA
Richard J. Hutchinson, PFC, Age 19, Cincinnati, OH
Stephen E. Karopczyc, 1LT, Age 23, Bethpage, NY—*Awarded the Medal of Honor*
La Marre A. Major, PFC, Age 20, Benton Harbor, MI
Filiberto G. Miranda, SP4, Age 20, El Paso, TX
Daniel F. Perez, SP4, Age 22, Mathis, TX
James P. Perrone, SP4, Age 19, Wanaque, NJ
Danny D. Rhoads, SP4, Age 20, Lemoore, CA
Victor J. Ruggero, PFC, Age 20, Freeport, NY
Douglas W Stegall, PFC, Age 20, Graham, TX

Tuesday, March 21, 1967
Carl T. Anthony, SP4, Age 19, Springfield, LA

Juan P. Aviles-Aviles, SP4, Age 20, Lajas, PR
Scott C. Bowcutt, PFC, Age 21, Tremonton, UT
Joseph M. Champion, SP4, Age 20, Decatur, GA
Timothy Easley, PFC, Age 22, New York, NY
James H. Hopson, PFC, Age 21, Muskegon, MI
Robert L. Kaster, CPL, Age 23, Kirksville, MO
William E. Lund, PFC, Age 20, Philadelphia, PA
Henry R. Matthews, SP4, Age 21, Cameron, NC
Johnnie M Mayo, PFC, Age 19, Beaufort, NC
David E. McLemore, SGT, Age 20, Fort Worth, TX
Lewis E. Milam, CPL, Age 20, Gadsden, AL
Thomas F. Minogue, PFC, Age 20, New York, NY
Daniel J. Newman, CPL, Age 22, Niagara Falls, NY
John W. Odierno, SP4, Age 20, Farmingdale, NY
Percie E. Owens, SP4, Age 20, New York, NY
Robert H. Reinke, CPL, Age 20, Appleton, WI
Dennis B. Stockwell, CPL, Age 22, Parker, SD
Michael G. Sudborough, 1LT, Age 24, Ashland, OR
Hayzell C. Turner, SP4, Age 20, Batesville, MS

Wednesday, March 22, 1967

Roy W. Chamberlain, PFC, Age 24, Wayland, MI

1st Air Cavalry Division

Wednesday, August 10, 1966

Ernest P. Gulledge, Jr., CPT, Age 27, Yazoo City, MS

Tuesday, October 4, 1966

Johnnie L. Daniel, CPT, Age 35, Johnston, SC
Richard M. Prociv, SSG, Age 32, Salt Lake City, UT

Tuesday, October 18, 1966

Bobbie J. Dennis, WO, Age 36, Fayetteville, NC

Thursday, October 20, 1966

Christopher J. Miller, Jr., CPT, Age 34, Westminster, MD

Sunday, December 4, 1966

Richard H. Grunberg, SP4, Age 22, Hollis, NY

Saturday, March 18, 1967

Myron T. Goddard, WO, Age 26, Windsor, IL

Sunday, March 19, 1967

Alfred J. Moody, BG, Age 49, Hamden, CT

Sunday, April 2, 1967

Charles W. McKinnie, Jr., SGT, Age 21, Immokalee, FL

Saturday, April 8, 1967

James N. Katrenics, CPL, Age 20, Gary, IN
John E. Tarantowicz, 1LT, Age 24, Dickson City, PA

Tuesday, April 18, 1967

Robert J. Crabbe, 1LT, Age 25, Ann Arbor, MI

Thursday, June 15, 1967

Wilhelm L. Keglewitsch, CPL, Age 23, Chicago, IL

Friday, June 23, 1967

Edwin W. Martin, Jr., MAJ, Age 33, Polacca, AZ

Tuesday, July 25, 1967

Jerry W. Campbell, SGT, Age 20, Statesville, NC

Sunday, July 30, 1967

William V. Hearns, PFC, Age 20, Chicago, IL
Terry L. Winters, SP4, Age 20, Geneva, OH

Sunday, August 13, 1967

Lonnie J. Ducote, Jr., CPL, Age 22, Corpus Christi, TX

Saturday, August 26, 1967

Charles Green, Jr., CPL, Age 19, Chicago, IL

Wednesday, August 30, 1967

Alan J. Smith, SGT, Age 22, Springfield, MA

Wednesday, September 6, 1967

J. D. Singleton, SP4, Age 20, Bokchito, OK

Friday, September 8, 1967

Dalton T. Goff, SP4, Age 22, New Castle, PA

Thursday, September 28, 1967

Tracy H. Riffey, SP4, Age 21, Downingtown, PA

Thursday, November 2, 1967

Keith J. Andres, SP4, Age 20, Carpentersville, IL
Kenneth J. Arent, SGT, Age 23, Sacramento, CA

Sunday, November 12, 1967

Jack M. Smith, 2LT, Age 21, Bartlesville, OK

Wednesday, December 6, 1967

Lewis E. McDermott, MSG, Age 35, Fulton, MO

Thursday, December 7, 1967
George F. Eubanks, SGT, Age 21, Barboursville, WV

Sunday, December 10, 1967
Randy E. Dillinder, CPL, Age 19, Dearborn, MI

8th Cavalry Regiment, 1st Air Cavalry Division

Thursday, June 1, 1967
Lonney L. Ehlers, CPL, Age 19, Rhodes, MI

Monday, June 5, 1967
James P. Burns, PFC, Age 21, Poughkeepsie, NY

Tuesday, June 13, 1967
Clyde R. Houser, Jr., PFC, Age 21, Trexlertown, PA

Friday, June 23, 1967
Oddie C. Hailey, SGT, Age 29, Texarkana, TX

Saturday, June 24, 1967
Gerrit J. Schouwburg, SP5, Age 22, Kalamazoo, MI

Sunday, July 2, 1967
William E. Allison, PFC, Age 19, Decatur, IN
Dennis D. Aschenbrenner, 1LT, Age 25, Lead, SD
Edward L. Brown, SP4, Age 19, New York, NY
David J. De Rue, PFC, Age 20, Marion, NY
Luther M. Jones, SP4, Age 24, Statesboro, GA
David B. Kline, PFC, Age 18, Hurdsfield, ND
William D. Lewis, SGT, Age 22, Detroit, MI
Jimmy McBroon, PFC, Age 20, Emery, UT
Nick Panella, Jr., PFC, Age 21, Aliquippa, PA
Franklin H. Penn, PFC, Age 19, Aiken, SC
John D. Salmieri, SP4, Age 20, New York, NY
Frank W. Sawyer, Jr., CPL, Age 31, Louisville, KY
Malcolm F. Tassey, 1LT, Age 24, Rutherford, NJ
Robert Vargo, CPL, Age 21, Cadiz, OH

Tuesday, July 4, 1967
Samuel E. Witcher, SGT, Age 21, Martinsville, VA
Robert A. Woodrow, SP4, Age 20, Ocean City, NJ

Wednesday, July 5, 1967
James E. Hoeweler, SP4, Age 20, Cincinnati, OH
Norman E. Treest, SP4, Age 20, Marseilles, IL

Wednesday, August 9, 1967
Andrew C. Conrad, Jr., SP5, Age 35, Millington, MI
Joel D. Fendley, CPL, Age 21, Richmond, TX
Joseph Harrison, CPL, Age 19, Thomasville, GA
Michael J. Hotchkiss, SP4, Age 20, Anaheim, CA
Prentice D. Le Clair, SP4, Age 25, Tulsa, OK
Robert J. Maxwell, SGT, Age 18, Fresno, CA

Monday, August 21, 1967
Roger D. Root, SP4, Age 20, Jenison, MI

Saturday, August 26, 1967
John P. Carey, CPL, Age 19, Pittsburgh, PA

Sunday, August 27, 1967
Gennaro J. De Carlo, CPL, Age 20, Kankakee, IL

Monday, August 28, 1967
Julian Mendez, SP4, Age 21, Wharton, TX

Thursday, August 31, 1967
Marvin L. Franklin, Jr., SGT, Age 22, Oklahoma City, OK
Lawrence G. Grass, SP4, Age 22, Belleville, IL
Gerald J. Roberts, Jr., CPL, Age 21, Torrington, CT

Sunday, September 3, 1967
Bob J. Goodwin, CPL, Age 19, Wichita, KS

Tuesday, September 5, 1967
Earl W. Fernandez, SSG, Age 24, Westminster, CA

Wednesday, September 6, 1967
Michael P. Santoroski, PFC, Age 20, Kingston, NY

Friday, September 8, 1967
Robert L. Righter, Jr., SP4, Age 18, Reynoldsburg, OH
Wilbert A. Tynes, Jr., SSG, Age 27, Hampton, VA
Frank L. Zigalo, SFC, Age 39, Bartlett, TX

Sunday, September 10, 1967
Ronald B. Kerner, PFC, Age 20, Parma, OH

Monday, September 11, 1967
Charles A. Johnson, CPL, Age 22, Racine, WI

Tuesday, September 12, 1967
Jerry L. Rogers, SP4, Age 20, Struthers, OH

Saturday, September 16, 1967
Ernest N. Kroll, PFC, Age 24, Portland, OR

Saturday, September 23, 1967
James A. Swancy, CPL, Age 20, Mesquite, TX

Monday, September 25, 1967
Joseph M. Archuleta, SP4, Age 23, Las Vegas, NM
Richard M. Yelland, SGT, Age 24, Ely, NV

Friday, October 6, 1967
Peter B. Cook, Jr., CPL, Age 19, Yazoo City, MS

Sunday, October 15, 1967
David J. Spinali, SP4, Age 22, San Mateo, CA

Wednesday, October 18, 1967
Nathan Johnson, Jr., CPL, Age 20, Lancaster, VA
Owen C. Kelley, SP4, Age 24, St Louis, MO
James S. Kell, SGT, Age 19, Montebello, CA
Louie Ochoa, PFC, Age 23, Hanford, CA

Friday, October 27, 1967
Robert P. Cook, SP4, Age 19, El Monte, CA
Johnnie Walker, CPL, Age 20, Washington, DC

Wednesday, November 1, 1967
Michael E. Bennett, 2LT, Age 21, Brentwood, NH
Walter E. Bentley, CPL, Age 19, New Britain, CT
Moses Mickle, PSGT, Age 34, Columbia, SC

Thursday, November 2, 1967
Melvin E. Foad, PFC, Age 18, Chicago, IL

Saturday, November 4, 1967
Robert A. Albertson, PFC, Age 20, Ypsilanti, MI
Jimmy R. Baggarly, PFC, Age 19, Stanley, KY
David M. Herendon, PFC, Age 24, Cherrylog, GA

Friday, November 17, 1967
Maurice Brooks, SGT, Age 22, Mexia, TX

Sunday, November 19, 1967
David J. Decker, CPT, Age 30, Yardley, PA
William H. Fowler, III, SP4, Age 21, San Jose, CA
Thomas Olearnick, SP4, Age 20, Mount Carmel, PA
Ronald N. Rodreick, 2LT, Age 21, Fresno, CA

Wednesday, November 22, 1967
James P. Saurini, SP4, Age 21, Dallas, TX

Thursday, November 30, 1967
Edward O. Bilsie, SSG, Age 26, Olympia, WA

Wednesday, December 6, 1967
Walter R. Boettcher, Jr., 2LT, Age 23, Concord, CA
Frank Brackett, CPL, Age 21, Decatur, IL

Thursday, December 7, 1967
Donald L. Cummings, Jr., SGT, Age 21, Glendora, CA
Jimmy C. Elrod, PFC, Age 20, Pinson, AL
Thomas M. Flatley, CPT, Age 29, Chicago, IL
Tom Gonzales, Jr., SGT, Age 20, Midvale, UT
Thomas A. McDermott, CPL, Age 20, West New York, NJ
Richard G. Sherwood, SGT, Age 20, Jackson, MI
Robert W. Tewksbury, CPL, Age 20, South Portland, ME
Larry A. Winslow, SP4, Age 24, Plainwell, MI

Friday, December 8, 1967
Thomas Grant, PSGT, Age 37, Plainfield, NJ
Larry J. Martin, PFC, Age 20, Arvin, CA

Monday, December 11, 1967
Allan E. Follett, SP4, Age 23, Independence, MO
John P. Paulson, Jr., SP4, Age 20, Neenah, WI

Friday, December 15, 1967
Anthony N. La Pardo, SGT, Age 25, New York, NY
Edward M. Looney, SGT, Age 19, New York, NY
Joe Pena, Jr., SGT, Age 23, Plainview, TX

Tuesday, December 26, 1967
Michael E. Berdy, CPT, Age 23, New York, NY
Allen D. Ford, SSG, Age 20, Pueblo, CO
James L. Russ, Jr., CPL, Age 22, Youngstown, OH
Thomas M. Van Zandt, 1LT, Age 28, Austin, TX
Stephen M. Vuga, SGT, Age 20, Pittsburgh, PA

12th Cavalry Regiment, 1st Air Cavalry Division

Sunday, April 9, 1967
Rodney C. Edwards, PFC, Age 19, Columbiaville, MI
Cario Fuller, CPL, Age 20, Benton, AR
Glenn J. Hlavacek, CPL, Age 20, Chicago, IL
James F. Madden, CPL, Age 20, Brewton, AL
William C. Madison, PFC, Age 25, Memphis, TN
Dale E. Milam, SGT, Age 24, Prosperity, WV

Charles A. Stoken, CPL, Age 23, Grand Rapids, MI
Ronald M. Thomas, II, PFC, Age 23, Lewiston, ME
Joseph A. Tomko, CPT, Age 31, Aliquippa, PA

Wednesday, April 19, 1967
Le Roy Young, Jr., PFC, Age 21, Wabash, AR

Appendix D: The Wall

Wednesday, May 3, 1967
Earlie M. Rand, SGT, Age 25, Prichard, AL

Thursday, May 4, 1967
Scott S. McCloskey, PFC, Age 21, Hollywood, FL

Thursday, May 11, 1967
Bradford B. Greene, SP4, Age 18, Dunedin, FL

Saturday, May 13, 1967
Caballero F. Figueroa, PFC, Age 19, Caguas, PR
Gary L. Stevens, PFC, Age 19, East Gary, IN

Sunday, May 14, 1967
Henry G. Hampton, PFC, Age 24, Van Nuys, CA

Tuesday, May 16, 1967
Dennis R. Hooks, PFC, Age 20, New Douglas, IL
Freddie L. Robinson, SP4, Age 20, Orangeburg, SC

Saturday, May 20, 1967
Gary C. Bannon, PFC, Age 21, Leon, KS

Wednesday, May 24, 1967
Mark A. Anderson, PFC, Age 19, Pennington, MN
Ronald R. Joseph, PFC, Age 20, Gary, IN
Rodney D. Pickett, PFC, Age 19, Coeburn, VA

Sunday, May 28, 1967
Frederic C. Styer, SP4, Age 21, Menomonie, WI

Tuesday, May 30, 1967
Clark E. Sapp, CPL, Age 20, Littlerock, CA

Wednesday, May 31, 1967
Hervey H. Allen, PFC, Age 18, Richmond, VA
Teddy R. Dunn, SGT, Age 22, Wichita Falls, TX
William W. Money, SGT, Age 20, Millbrook, NY
Dennie Neace, SGT, Age 19, Bonnyman, KY
Jerald A. Vokish, PFC, Age 20, Natrona, PA

Friday, June 9, 1967
Samuel R. Durham, SP4, Age 22, Lomita, CA
James L. Johnson, PFC, Age 20, Gilmer, TX
Rufus Ray, PFC, Age 24, Odessa, TX

Sunday, June 11, 1967
Jose H. Velasquez, PFC, Age 20, Alamosa, CO

Monday, June 12, 1967
Danny O. Kennell, PFC, Age 19, Portland, MI

Wednesday, June 28, 1967
Roger L. Blake, PFC, Age 23, Baltimore, MD
Thomas E. Broome, PFC, Age 18, Sun Prairie, WI
Rodger T. Gross, SP4, Age 20, Godfrey, IL
Dennis L. Hall, PFC, Age 19, Burlington, NC
Geoffrey L. Ham, 1LT, Age 24, Ivyland, PA
Bob R. Layne, PFC, Age 19, Lewiston, UT
Walter N. Locher, PFC, Age 21, Lame Deer, MT
Graham N. Lowdon, Jr., CPT, Age 28, Wilmington, DE
Walter Przybylowicz, Jr., PFC, Age 19, Detroit, MI
Kenneth M. Wright, PFC, Age 20, Alton, IL

Tuesday, July 11, 1967
Dave R. Kingsbury, MAJ, Age 35, Sunset Lake, OK

Monday, July 17, 1967
Gerald R. Brines, PFC, Age 20, Shullsburg, WI

Thursday, July 27, 1967
Myron D. Lucas, SGT, Age 20, Bakersfield, CA
Phillip M. Myles, PFC, Age 20, Minden, LA
Richard Smith, Jr., PFC, Age 19, Stuart, FL

Tuesday, August 1, 1967
Robert J. D'amico, PFC, Age 20, New York, NY

Saturday, August 5, 1967
Harry B. McFadden, PSGT, Age 33, Charleston, SC

Tuesday, August 15, 1967
Jerry E. Butts, PFC, Age 20, Long Beach, CA
James E. Milligan, PFC, Age 19, Pleasure Ridge Park, KY
Valentine D. Uncapher, PFC, Age 19, Hartford City, IN

Wednesday, August 16, 1967
Leland W. Hyslop, CPL, Age 20, Warner, OK

Thursday, August 17, 1967
Robert W. Bates, SP4, Age 20, Independence, MO
Steve D. Campbell, PFC, Age 19, Phoenix, AZ
Louis A. Cobarrubio, PFC, Age 19, Philadelphia, PA

Monday, August 21, 1967
Jerry L. Allen, SP4, Age 20, Norfolk, NE
Raymond E. Allen, SP4, Age 20, Independence, MO
Clarence L. Chase, SP4, Age 19, Camden, ME
Leroy L. Gerber, SGT, Age 21, Dalton, OH
Archie W. Morris, SGT, Age 23, Seattle, WA
Frederick H. Tims, SGT, Age 21, St Louis, MO

Tuesday, August 22, 1967
Eddie J. Allen, SFC, Age 34, Richmond, IN
Richard J. Balthazor, CPL, Age 19, Eland, WI
Leonard R. Johnson, SGT, Age 21, Oakland, CA

Maurice J. Nile, PVT, Age 20, North New Portland, ME
James E. Schlottman, SP4, Age 20, Carmichael, CA

Wednesday, September 6, 1967
Jessie L. Barlow, SSG, Age 36, Columbus, GA

Tuesday, September 19, 1967
Gabriel Betancourt, PFC, Age 21, Hollister, CA

Friday, September 29, 1967
William M. Skovran, PFC, Age 19, Warren, OH

Tuesday, October 3, 1967
Theodore Howard, SP4, Age 20, Prichard, AL

Thursday, October 12, 1967
William T. Edgerton, Jr., SGT, Age 19, Asheville, NC
Edward C. Jarvis, PFC, Age 20, Pittsfield, MA
Ronald S. Penman, SP4, Age 20, Los Angeles, CA

Saturday, October 14, 1967
Woody J. Frost, CPL, Age 18, Maud, TX
William R. Henry, CPL, Age 21, Sunnyvale, CA
Kurt B. Pearson, CPL, Age 20, Deming, NM
Robert A. Van Ballegooyen, PFC, Age 23, Ireton, IA
John D. Williams, SP4, Age 20, Butler, IL

Wednesday, October 18, 1967
Robert B. Petersen, CPL, Age 22, Puyallup, WA

Thursday, October 26, 1967
Melvin C. Lapp, CPL, Age 20, Sacramento, CA
Stanley W. Tunall, SGT, Age 22, El Monte, CA

Saturday, October 28, 1967
David Baker, PFC, Age 19, Morganton, NC
Thomas G. Naile, PFC, Age 22, Charleston, MO

Wednesday, November 1, 1967
John D. Michaelis, SFC, Age 22, Portland, OR

Monday, November 6, 1967
Ralph L. Avery, 2LT, Age 22, Flint, MI
Robert L. Carter, CPL, Age 23, Columbus, OH
William A. Michael, SP4, Age 19, Blue Springs, MO
Martin F. Sterud, PFC, Age 20, Oakley, CA

Thursday, November 9, 1967
Larry R. Arwood, SGT, Age 20, Sweetwater, TN
Barry J. Baker, CPL, Age 20, Oakland, CA
Edwin M. Gray, CPL, Age 20, Chicago, IL

Saturday, November 11, 1967
Chester A. Winchell, Jr., SSG, Age 23, Fort Gay, WV

Tuesday, November 14, 1967
Richard Kovalcsik, CPL, Age 19, Linden, MI

Thursday, November 16, 1967
W. C. Johnson, SP4, Age 27, Tyler, TX

Wednesday, November 22, 1967
George Osborne, Jr., SP4, Age 19, Gary, IN
Stephen N. Thomas, PFC, Age 21, Raleigh, NC

Sunday, November 26, 1967
Albert H. Horton, CPL, Age 21, Oakland, CA

Thursday, November 30, 1967
Peter N. Anderson, SGT, Age 26, Uniondale, NY

Friday, December 8, 1967
Larry H. Bowers, SP4, Age 21, Columbus, OH

Sunday, December 10, 1967
Billy A. Kelsall, SP4, Age 21, Savannah, GA

Monday, December 11, 1967
Daniel J. Maguire, SP4, Age 20, New York, NY

Friday, December 15, 1967
Richard J. Boeshart, SGT, Age 20, Sioux City, IA
Richard A. Choppa, CPL, Age 22, Hubbard, OH
Ramon Cortes-Rosa, SP4, Age 24, Hialeah, FL
Robert L. Flores, SGT, Age 20, Parker, AZ
Willie French, Jr., SP4, Age 22, Pittsboro, NC
Charles W. Hicks, SP4, Age 20, Butner, NC
David P. Jewell, SSG, Age 20, Owensboro, KY
Ronald L. Klausing, SP4, Age 19, San Diego, CA
James J. Koprivnikar, PFC, Age 21, Cheswick, PA
Omar Lebron-Domenech, SP4, Age 20, San Sebastian, PR
Robert Levine, SFC, Age 27, Jamaica, NY
James E. Lynn, SFC, Age 28, Kenosha, WI
Steven Matarazzo, CPL, Age 18, Montgomery, NY
Riley C. O'Neil, Jr., CPL, Age 20, Kansas City, KS
Juan S. Ozuna, SGT, Age 21, Wapato, WA
Richard M. Proscia, PFC, Age 21, New Hyde Park, NY
John D. Roche, SFC, Age 34, Bay City, MI
Wayne D. Ryza, SP4, Age 20, Houston, TX
Michael D. Sander, CPL, Age 21, Oakland, CA
Roy E. Southerland, 1LT, Age 22, Morristown, TN
James Tierno, CPL, Age 22, Jackson Heights, NY

Friday, December 22, 1967
Dennis P. Wood, SP4, Age 20, Cleveland, OH

Wednesday, December 27, 1967
Robert M. Thompson, PFC, Age 19, Tacoma, WA

Chapter Notes

Preface

1. Edward F. Murphy, *Dak To: America's Sky Soldiers in South Vietnam's Central Highlands* (New York: Ballantine Books, 2007).

Introduction

1. William C. Westmoreland, *A Soldier Reports* (New York: Doubleday and Company, Inc., 1976), 287.
2. Nguyen Duy Hinh, *Indochina Monographs, Lam Son 719* (Fort McNair: U.S. Army Center of Military History, 1979).
3. Stanley Karnow, *Vietnam, A History, The First Complete Account of Vietnam at War* (New York: The Viking Press, 1983).
4. Neil Sheehan, *A Bright Shining Lie: John Paul Vann and America in Vietnam* (New York: Random House, 1988).
5. Shelby L. Stanton, *The Rise and Fall of an American Army, U.S. Ground Forces in Vietnam, 1965–1975* (New York: Ballantine Books, 2003), xviii.
6. Tom Marshall, *The Price of Exit* (New York: Ballantine Books, 1998), 180.

Chapter 1

1. Indochina included Vietnam, Laos, and Cambodia. Hereafter, references to Indochina are omitted since the focus is on Vietnam.
2. Karnow, 135.
3. Karnow, 85.
4. Ho was known by several names over the years, but in this history I refer to him by the last name that he used: Ho Chi Minh.
5. Karnow, 121.
6. Alan Axelrod, *The Real History of the Vietnam War, A New Look at the Past* (New York: Sterling Publishing, 2013), 55.
7. Karnow, 140.
8. Karnow, 144.
9. Karnow, 145.
10. Not really; the Japanese were allowed to retain their emperor; Hirohito who was not tried as a war criminal as some say he should have been.
11. Karnow, 147.
12. Karnow, 135.
13. Karnow, 149–150.
14. Philippe Devillers, *Historia du Vietnam de 1940 a 1952* (Paris: Editions du Seuil, 1953).
15. Karnow, 178.
16. Karnow, 188.
17. Dean Acheson, *Present at the Creation, My Years in the State Department* (New York: W. W. Norton, 1969), 677.
18. Acheson, 691.
19. McCarthy was called "Tail-Gunner Joe" because he claimed that he was a tail-gunner in a U.S. aircraft in the Pacific during World War II: he flew one mission. He started a witch hunt looking for communists in the U.S. that at times violated the rights of citizens.
20. Karnow, 169.
21. Bernard B. Fall, *Street Without Joy: The French Debacle in Indochina.* (Mechanicsburg: Stackpole Books, 1994), 190.
22. Karnow, 189. In some ways this battle was similar to Lam Son 719, fought nearly twenty years later.
23. Karnow, 196.
24. Karnow, 191.
25. The U.S. had decided to shore up its ally, France, by providing a small amount of air support, but it did not come close to what was needed at Dien Bien Phu.
26. Karnow, 195.
27. Karnow, 196.
28. McGovern and Buford are not listed on the Vietnam Veterans Memorial wall, nor are several other people killed before the earliest casualties on the wall. Criteria needed to be established when the people who invented the wall got started, and Jan Scruggs, who founded the memorial, and others

chose 1959 as the start of casualties on the wall. On the other end were the criteria established for those who died after the war. Suicides and those who died of Agent Orange and other diseases were not added. A famous example is Lewis Burwell Puller, Jr. Puller was a marine like his father, the famous "Chesty" Puller, and was badly wounded in Vietnam. He survived but lost both legs and was the subject of at least one book. He finally killed himself years later. Puller's name is not on the wall.

29. Fall, 211.
30. Stanton, *The Rise and Fall of an American Army*, 3–4.
31. Karnow, 204.
32. Karnow, 238.
33. Karnow, 214.
34. Michael Lind, *Vietnam, The Necessary War* (New York: Simon and Schuster, 1999), 35.
35. Lind, 35. Subsequent history proved the domino theory wrong. Thailand, Malaysia, and other countries did not fall after North Vietnam's victory in 1975.

Chapter 2

1. Axelrod, 96–97.
2. Martin J. Dockery, *Lost in Translation: Vietnam, A Combat Advisor's Story* (New York: Ballantine Books, 2003), 25.
3. John C. Loving, *Combat Advisor: How America Won the War and Lost the Peace* (New York: Universe, Inc., 2006), 28.
4. Michael A. Eggleston, *Exiting Vietnam: The Era of Vietnamization and American Withdrawal Revealed in First-Person Accounts* (Jefferson: McFarland & Company, Inc., Publishers), 199.
5. Maurice Isserman and Michael Kazan, *American Divided: The Civil War in the 1960s* (Oxford: Oxford University Press, 2008), 88.
6. A.J. Langguth, *Our Vietnam: The War 1954–1975* (New York: Simon & Schuster, 2000), 202. Ap Bac was considered to be the first major victory of the Viet Cong since Dien Bien Phu.
7. Isserman, 87.
8. Langguth, 204–205; Neil Sheehan, 263–265.
9. George C. Herring, *America's Longest War: The United States and Vietnam, 1950–1975* (Boston: McGraw-Hill, 2002), 113.
10. Langguth, 208; Arthur M. Schlesinger, Jr., *A Thousand Days: John F. Kennedy in the White House* (New York: Houghton Mifflin Company, 2002), 985.
11. Deborah Shapley, *Promise and Power: The Life and Times of Robert McNamara* (Boston: Little, Brown, and Company, 1993), 250. Diem would be killed later in 1963. The point is that Diem's views and actions in 1963 were precisely the same as South Vietnamese President Thieu's in 1971 during and after Lam Son 719. It seems that the South Vietnamese would never change their way of doing business.

12. Karnow, x.
13. This conclusion by Karnow is hard to support. It would appear that most historians provide evidence to prove that Ho was a communist and not a nationalist, but it all depends upon the time frame. When as a young man he appeared in Geneva in 1919, where World War I peace accords were being discussed, he was apparently a nationalist.
14. Karnow, 11.
15. Karnow, 262.
16. Karnow, 262.
17. Sheehan, 313.
18. Karnow, 323–324.
19. Sheehan, 316. Vann shared the same dry sense of humor as Sheehan. It made life livable.
20. Sully would return after Diem's death. He was later killed when his aircraft crashed.
21. Sheehan, 283.
22. Sheehan, 270–272
23. Langguth, 204.
24. Karnow, 265.
25. Langguth, 216.
26. Karnow, 277.
27. Karnow, 310–311.
28. Karnow, 324.
29. Karnow, 325.
30. Karnow, 326.
31. Karnow, 367–374.
32. CBS was sued by General Westmoreland because a CBS broadcast alleged that General Westmoreland deliberately underestimated enemy strength before the Tet offense in order to show progress in Vietnam. The case was settled out of court.
33. Shapley, 600–601.
34. Shapley, 606.
35. Lt. General Harold G. Moore (Ret.) and Joseph L. Galloway, *We Were Soldiers Once...and Young: Ia Drang, the Battle That Changed the War in Vietnam* (New York: Random House, Inc., 1992).
36. Karnow, 436–437.
37. Stanton, *The Rise and Fall of an American Army*, 21–22.
38. Langguth, 427.
39. Axelrod, 167. Infiltration increased to 6,000 per month in 1967.
40. Axelrod, 169.

Chapter 3

1. Phillip B. Davidson, *Vietnam at War, The History 1946–1975* (New York: The Oxford Press, 1988), 468.
2. The Europeans viewed the war as a dangerous conflict that could explode into wider conflict, involving China and perhaps even the Soviet Union. Further, the war was eroding U.S. support to the Allies.
3. Davidson, 441.
4. Davidson, 441.
5. James P. Coan, *Con Thien: The Hill of Angels*

(Tuscaloosa: The University of Alabama Press, 2004), 24.

6. Davidson, 466.
7. Davidson, 442.
8. This was unlikely to succeed, because in addition to dog tags, the dead soldier had to be identified by someone who knew him. If it did succeed, it would have a devastating effect on next of kin and would get media attention. Another nasty reminder of the war.
9. Stanton, *The Rise and Fall of an American Army*, p270.
10. Murphy, *Dak To: America's Sky Soldiers in South Vietnam's Central Highlands*, 172.
11. CIDG troops were known by various names such as Mike Force or Mike Mikes.
12. Davidson, 468–469.
13. Stanton, *The Rise and Fall of an American Army*, 168.
14. SOG carried out covert operations against the North Vietnamese.
15. 4ID Combat Operations After Action Report, 16 May 1967, 1.
16. "Army Officer Describes Fierce Gunfight in Vietnam," NBC News, New York, NY: NBC Universal, 02/28/1967.
17. Combat Operations Report—Francis Marion, 1–3.
18. John Prados, *In Country: Remembering the Vietnam War* (New York: Ivan R. Dee, Publisher, 2011), 40–41.
19. "The Battle of the Slopes," 2/503d Vietnam Newsletter, Issue 29 (June 22, 2011): 6.
20. Murphy, *Dak To: America's Sky Soldiers in South Vietnam's Central Highlands*, 43.
21. Clifton F. Clifton, Jr., *The Illustrated History of Sky Soldiers: The Vietnam War* (New York: Bantam Books, 1987), 91.
22. Murphy, *Dak To: America's Sky Soldiers in South Vietnam's Central Highlands*, 42–43.
23. Gary Walls, unpublished memoir.
24. Coan, 34.
25. Coan, 34–36.
26. The CIDG was an indigenous local defense unit very often composed, in the central highlands, of Montagnard tribesmen.
27. Stanton, *The Rise and Fall of an American Army*, p. 168.
28. Sa Won Chang, unpublished memoir.
29. A persistent form of tear gas that lies on the ground until disturbed.
30. "Battle of the Slopes," *Sky Soldier Magazine*, Autumn 2015, Volume 31, Number 4, 11.
31. Jimmy Lee Cook, C/2/503rd, died on 21 June 1967. His name is found in Appendix D, The Wall. He is listed on Panel 22E, Line 29 of the Vietnam Veterans Memorial.
32. Murphy, *Dak To: America's Sky Soldiers in South Vietnam's Central Highlands*, 64.
33. Murphy, *Dak To: America's Sky Soldiers in South Vietnam's Central Highlands*, 65.

34. Lawrence D. Okendo, *Sky Soldier, 173rd Airborne Infantry Brigade Separate, Battles of Dak To Vietnam* (Lawrence D. Okendo, 1988), 44–45.
35. John Leppelman, *Blood on the Risers: An Airborne Soldier's Thirty-Five Months in Vietnam* (New York: Ballantine Books, 1991), 170–171.
36. A better method was to establish teams that specialized in clearing LZs before the troop transports arrived. These were called LZ commandos, named and employed by Lieutenant Colonel Jackley, 4/503rd (see Murphy, 83). There was nothing new about this approach. Soldiers called "Pathfinders" were employed for this in other wars and locations, including Vietnam.
37. Paul Donahue, unpublished memoir.
38. Leppelman, 171–173.
39. Appendix D provides a listing of names. All of the 2/503rd dead on 22 June were from Alpha Company. Apparently Captain Leonard's caution paid off. He lost no one killed in the battle. Later, Captain Milton blamed Leonard for the high number of Alpha Company people killed. Lieutenant Ellis A. McBride, B/2/503rd, died on 23 June 1967. His name is found in Appendix D, The Wall. He is listed on Panel 22E, Line 55 of the Vietnam Veterans Memorial.
40. Leppelman, 175. DEROS stood for Date Eligible for Return from Overseas, the date a soldier's tour of duty was to end.
41. Murphy, *Dak To: America's Sky Soldiers in South Vietnam's Central Highlands*, 79.
42. Okendo, 47. In his memoir, Sergeant Okendo quoted 513, from the MACV press release that had inflated the NVA casualties.
43. Murphy, *Dak To: America's Sky Soldiers in South Vietnam's Central Highlands*, 79.
44. Murphy, *Dak To: America's Sky Soldiers in South Vietnam's Central Highlands*, 80.
45. Leppelman, 174–175.
46. "The Battle of the Slopes," 2/503d Vietnam Newsletter, Issue 29 (June 22, 2011), 16.
47. Murphy, *Dak To: America's Sky Soldiers in South Vietnam's Central Highlands*, 78.
48. Search-and-destroy operations were designed to insert a unit into enemy territory, make contact with the enemy unit, and destroy it. It was a battle of attrition.
49. Murphy, *Dak To: America's Sky Soldiers in South Vietnam's Central Highlands*, 82.
50. Mercer Vandenburg, unpublished memoir.
51. Murphy, *Dak To: America's Sky Soldiers in South Vietnam's Central Highlands*, 95.
52. Okendo, 55.
53. The 335th Assault Helicopter Company known as the "Cowboys" provided support to the 173rd.
54. Okendo, 56.
55. Murphy, *Dak To: America's Sky Soldiers in South Vietnam's Central Highlands*, 103.
56. Murphy, *Dak To: America's Sky Soldiers in South Vietnam's Central Highlands*, 104. This was

common in Vietnam. Rather than punish the guilty, offenses were frequently covered up in order to avoid bad media coverage.

57. Murphy, *Dak To: America's Sky Soldiers in South Vietnam's Central Highlands*, 105.
58. "The Battle of Dak To," https://en.wikipedia.org/wiki/Battle_of_Dak_To#Hill_875.
59. Albright, 85.
60. Paul Donahue, unpublished memoir.
61. Murphy, *Dak To: America's Sky Soldiers in South Vietnam's Central Highlands*, 109.
62. Murphy, *Dak To: America's Sky Soldiers in South Vietnam's Central Highlands*, 127.
63. A.T. Lawrence, *Crucible Vietnam: Memoir of an Infantry Lieutenant* (Jefferson: McFarland & Company, Inc., Publishers, 2009), 98.
64. Gallup Poll, http://www.shmoop.com/vietnam-war/statistics.html (accessed 5 March 2016).
65. Okendo, 24.
66. Murphy, *Dak To: America's Sky Soldiers in South Vietnam's Central Highlands*, 133.
67. An account of the battle on Hill 724 was presented in a video entitled "The Battle of Dak To, The Lost Film," 2014.
68. Juan Alex Quintanar, unpublished memoir.
69. Juan Alex Quintanar, unpublished memoir.
70. Okendo, 63.
71. Albright, 92–93.
72. Albright, 93–94.
73. Murphy, *Dak To: America's Sky Soldiers in South Vietnam's Central Highlands*, 145.
74. Murphy, *Dak To: America's Sky Soldiers in South Vietnam's Central Highlands*, 149.
75. Murphy, *Dak To: America's Sky Soldiers in South Vietnam's Central Highlands*, 151.
76. Murphy, *Dak To: America's Sky Soldiers in South Vietnam's Central Highlands*, 157.
77. Albright, CMH, 98–99.
78. Courtesy of John Albright, CMH, 100–101.
79. Murphy, *Dak To: America's Sky Soldiers in South Vietnam's Central Highlands*, 166–167.
80. Albright, 108.
81. Murphy, *Dak To: America's Sky Soldiers in South Vietnam's Central Highlands*, 178.
82. Murphy, *Dak To: America's Sky Soldiers in South Vietnam's Central Highlands*, 176.
83. Murphy, *Dak To: America's Sky Soldiers in South Vietnam's Central Highlands*, 181.
84. Sa Won Chang, unpublished memoir.
85. Gary Walls, unpublished memoir.
86. Steven C. Vorthmann, unpublished memoir.
87. Gary Walls, unpublished memoir.
88. Murphy, *Dak To: America's Sky Soldiers in South Vietnam's Central Highlands*, 206.
89. Gary Walls, unpublished memoir.
90. Gary Walls, unpublished memoir.
91. Murphy, *Dak To: America's Sky Soldiers in South Vietnam's Central Highlands*, 205.
92. The McGuire Rig was suspended from a helicopter and used to extract soldiers from areas without a suitable pick-up zone. It was simple, inexpensive, and effective. It was fashioned from a long nylon cargo tie-down strap, two inches wide, with a quick-fit buckle on one end.
93. Bugs Moran, unpublished memoir.
94. Murphy, *Dak To: America's Sky Soldiers in South Vietnam's Central Highlands*, 211. The nickname meant that you would not return home alive and came from the Battle of Hill 1338 when Alpha Company was nearly wiped out. FNGs meant Fucking New Guys.
95. Gary Luoma, unpublished memoir.
96. Murphy, *Dak To: America's Sky Soldiers in South Vietnam's Central Highlands*, 229.
97. Murphy, *Dak To: America's Sky Soldiers in South Vietnam's Central Highlands*, 229.
98. Murphy, *Dak To: America's Sky Soldiers in South Vietnam's Central Highlands*, 231.
99. John R. Robinson, unpublished memoir.
100. Gene Boedeker recalled that he and other members of his squad dug the gun out of the ground and discovered that it was still packed in Cosmoline, a thick preservative used to prevent rust. They also uncovered a lot of ammunition for the gun.
101. Sa Won Chang, unpublished memoir.
102. Tom Means, unpublished memoir.
103. John R. Robinson, unpublished memoir.
104. Murphy, *Dak To: America's Sky Soldiers in South Vietnam's Central Highlands*, 236.
105. Murphy, *Dak To: America's Sky Soldiers in South Vietnam's Central Highlands*, 238.
106. Gene Boedeker recalled that one reporter was still holding a camera. Gene told him to put it down and get a rifle. When the reporter said he wasn't supposed to fight. Gene told him that the NVA didn't know that.
107. Murphy, *Dak To: America's Sky Soldiers in South Vietnam's Central Highlands*, 243.
108. Sa Won Chang, unpublished memoir.
109. John R. Robinson, unpublished memoir.
110. Sa Won Chang, unpublished memoir.
111. PFC Raymond Garcia, Jr., A/1/503rd died on 18 November 1967, and his name is found in Appendix D, The Wall. He is listed on Panel 30E, Line 15 of the Vietnam Veterans Memorial.
112. Sp4 Thomas J. Riley, A/1/503rd, died on 18 November and was awarded the Bronze Star for valor. His name is found in Appendix D, The Wall. He is listed on Panel 30E, Line 18 of the Vietnam Veterans Memorial.
113. Gene Boedeker, unpublished memoir.
114. Gene Boedeker, unpublished memoir.
115. John R. Robinson, unpublished memoir.
116. Rick Atkinson, *The Long Gray Line, The American Journey of West Point's Class of 1966* (New York: Henry Holt and Company, 1989), 243.
117. Atkinson, 243.
118. Leonard B. Scott, LTC, *The Battle for Hill 875: Dak To, Vietnam, 1967* (Carlisle Barracks: U.S. Army War College, 1988), 2–3.
119. Okendo, 98.
120. Cliff Stovall, unpublished memoir.

121. Scott, 9.
122. Scott, 9.
123. Kenneth Jacobson, 2/503rd, died on 20 November 1967. His name is found in Appendix D, The Wall. He is listed on Panel 30E, Line 44 of the Vietnam Veterans Memorial.
124. Atkinson, 244.
125. Ed Placencia, unpublished memoir.
126. Atkinson, 244.
127. Ed Placencia, unpublished memoir.
128. Scott, 22–23.
129. Ed Placencia, unpublished memoir.
130. Atkinson, 245.
131. Ed Placencia, unpublished memoir.
132. Dennis Hale, unpublished memoir. Casualty numbers from the blast vary, but the best estimate (Scott's) is forty-two killed and another forty-five wounded. Appendix D lists all of the dead, but it is difficult to determine if they were killed before the blast or died afterward.
133. Steven C. Vorthmann, unpublished memoir.
134. Peter Arnett, *Live from the Battlefield* (New York: Simon & Schuster, 1994), 232.
135. Stanton, *The Rise and Fall of an American Army*, 269.
136. Steven C. Vorthmann, unpublished memoir.
137. Stanley J. DeRuggiero, unpublished memoir.
138. Sergeant Thomas C. Mays died on 21 November. He is listed on Panel 30E, Line 87 of the Vietnam Veterans Memorial.
139. Mercer Vandenburg, unpublished memoir.
140. Dennis Hale, unpublished memoir.
141. Steven C. Vorthmann, unpublished memoir.
142. Stanley J. DeRuggiero, unpublished memoir.
143. Dennis Hale, unpublished memoir.
144. Steven C. Vorthmann, unpublished memoir.
145. Stanley J. DeRuggiero, unpublished memoir.
146. Scott, 35.
147. Dennis Hale, unpublished memoir.
148. Sa Won Chang, unpublished memoir.
149. Arnett, 234.
150. "Ten Great Battles of Vietnam," *Vietnam Magazine*, 2012, 25.
151. "Win Bitter Viet Battle," *Washington Evening Journal*, Washington, Iowa, 23 November 1967, 1.
152. "Win Bitter Viet Battle," *Washington Evening Journal*, Washington, Iowa, 23 November 1967, 1.
153. "U.S. Troops Take Top of Hill 875; Defy Fierce Fire," *New York Times*, 22 November 1967, 3.
154. Scott, 35.
155. "Excerpts From Talk by Westmoreland," *New York Times*, 22 November 1967, 1.
156. "Battle for Dak To," 4ID *Combat Operations After Action Report*, 12.
157. "Battle for Dak To," 4ID *Combat Operations After Action Report*, 15.
158. "Battle for Dak To," 4ID *Combat Operations After Action Report*, 12.
159. A. T. Lawrence, 100–101.
160. http://www.cmohs.org/recipient-archive.php.
161. http://www.cmohs.org/recipient-archive.php.
162. http://www.cmohs.org/recipient-archive.php.
163. http://armypubs.army.mil/epubs/pdf/go6942.pdf.
164. "Ten Great Battles of Vietnam," *Vietnam Magazine*, 2012, 25.
165. "Ten Great Battles of Vietnam," *Vietnam Magazine*, 2012, 25.
166. Courtesy of Stanley De Ruggiero.

Chapter 4

1. Sheehan, 651.
2. Coan, 14.
3. Coan, 167.
4. Jack T. Hartzel, *Reflections of My Past!* (Middletown: Great Published, 2015), 59.
5. Coan, 220.
6. Coan, 25–29.
7. Coan, 173.
8. Daryl J. Eigen, *A Hellish Place of Angels, Con Thien: One Man's Journey*. (Bloomington: iUniverse, 2012), 251.
9. Enemy engineers who could slide under the barbed wire to set up explosives or attack troops.
10. Coan, 178.
11. Coan, 216.
12. Coan, 225.
13. "Inside the Cone of Fire at Con Thien," *Life Magazine*, 27 October 1967, 37.
14. John H. Edwards, "Trench Warfare," Unpublished Essay, 2003, 4.
15. Coan, 229.
16. Coan, 245.
17. Eigen, 159.
18. Warm-water immersion foot is a skin condition of the feet that results after exposure to warm, wet conditions for long periods of time. It is characterized by wrinkling of the soles, padding of toes (especially the big toe) and padding of the sides of the feet. Large watery blisters appear, which are painful and begin to peel away from the foot itself.
19. Hartzel, 60.
20. Some things never change. Following is an account from the trenches of World War I.
21. Coan, 246.
22. Michael A. Eggleston, *The 5th Marine Regiment Devil Dogs in World War I, A History and Roster* (Jefferson: McFarland & Company, Inc., Publishers), *43*.
23. Coan, 244.
24. Coan, 240.
25. Troung Nhu Tang, *A Viet Cong Memoir: An Inside Account of the Vietnam War and Its Aftermath* (New York: Vintage Books, 1986), *167–168*.
26. Eigen, 151.
27. Hartzel, 60–61.
28. Hartzel, 66–67.

29. Charles R. Anderson, *The Grunts* (New York: Berkley Books, 1985), 65.
30. Eigen, 160.
31. Westmoreland, 247.
32. Davidson, *Vietnam War*, 468.
33. John Prados, *Vietnam: The History of an Unwinnable War, 1945-1975* (Lawrence: University Press of Kansas, 2009), 224-225.
34. Gordon L. Rottman, *Special Forces Camps in Vietnam, 1961-1970* (New York: Osprey Publishing, 2005), 52-53.
35. John McCoy, unpublished memoir.
36. Stanton, *The Rise and Fall of an American Army*, 10-11.
37. Prados, *Vietnam*, 226.
38. Shore, 1-2.
39. Aside from many political reasons why this would never happen, the fact was that nuclear weapons delivered in that area would be largely ineffective because of the terrain.
40. Edward F. Murphy, *The Hill Fights: The First Battle of Khe Sanh* (New York: Ballantine Books, 2003), 4.
41. Murphy, *The Hill Fights*, 4-6.
42. Murphy, *The Hill Fights*, 17.
43. Murphy, *The Hill Fights*, 23.
44. Davidson, 443.
45. Numbers of troops on both sides at Khe Sanh fluctuated at different times. Most sources indicate that two NVA divisions, or about 20,000 people, were in place at the time the siege started on 20 January 1968. They were opposed by two marine battalions with supporting units, or about 2,000 people. Both sides could quickly reinforce, if required, and did.
46. Westmoreland, 244-245.
47. Murphy, *The Hill Fights*, 56.
48. Shore, 10.
49. Shore, 11.
50. Shore, 13.
51. Steven A. Johnson, *Cammie Up! Memoir of a Recon Marine in Vietnam 1967-1968* (Jefferson: McFarland & Company, Inc., Publishers, 2012), 49.
52. Murphy, *The Hill Fights*, 279-281.
53. Clark Dougan and Stephen Weiss, *The American Experience in Vietnam* (Boston: Boston Publishing Company, 1988), 42.
54. Murphy, *The Hill Fights*, 281.
55. Greg Jones, *Last Stand at Khe Sanh: The U.S. Marines Finest Hour in Vietnam.* (Boston: De Capo Press, 2014), 9.
56. Jones, 20.
57. Murphy, *The Hill Fights*, 283.
58. Prados, *In Country*, 215-216.
59. Jones, 33.
60. Jones, 25-27.
61. Jones, 34.
62. Jones, 1.
63. Jones, 61.
64. Jones, 61.
65. Jones, 62.
66. Jones, 68-69.
67. Jones, 76.
68. John Morocco, *Thunder from Above: Air War, 1941-1968* (Boston: Boston Publishing Company, 1984), 52.
69. Jones, 89.

Chapter 5

1. General Westmoreland used similar words in late 1967, but later denied that he had used them.
2. Prados, *Vietnam*, 224.
3. Sheehan, 708.
4. Sheehan, 712-713,
5. Davidson, 478.
6. Prados, *Vietnam*, 232.
7. Prados, *Vietnam*, 232.
8. Edward Doyle and Samuel Lipsman, *The Vietnam Experience: America Takes Over 1965-1967* (Boston: Boston Publishing Company, 1982), 183.
9. Davidson, *Vietnam at War*, 446.
10. Prados, *Vietnam*, 231.
11. Prados, *Vietnam*, 231.
12. Prados, *Vietnam*, 239.
13. Steven C. Vorthmann, "Hill 875, Dak To, Vietnam," 2016.
14. Prados, *Vietnam*, 236.
15. Prados, *Vietnam*, 241.
16. Davidson, 477.
17. Westmoreland later claimed that he gave the appearance of being unaware because he did not want Hanoi to know that he knew of their impending attack.
18. Prados, *Vietnam*, 233.
19. Prados, *Vietnam*, 242.
20. James H. Willbanks, *The Tet Offensive: A Concise History* (New York: Columbia University Press, 2007), 81.
21. Prados, *Vietnam*, 243.
22. Prados, *Vietnam*, 233.
23. Karnow, 534.
24. Sheehan, 720.
25. The Wise Men were a group of prestigious leaders such as Dean Acheson and Averell Harriman that LBJ convened to offer him advice.
26. Prados, *Vietnam*, 249.
27. Langguth, 474.
28. Langguth, 474.
29. Davidson, *Vietnam at War*, 486.
30. Davidson, 450.
31. Prados, *Vietnam*, 242.
32. Prados, *Vietnam*, 249.
33. Prados, *Vietnam*,249.
34. Shapley, 442-444. Years later, when McNamara participated in the documentary *"Fog of War,"* he was asked if he had been fired or just resigned. His immediate answer was he didn't know. Then, in a rare moment of honesty, he said that he had asked his long-time friend from the *Washington Post*, Martha Graham. Her reply: "Bob, you were fired.

Everyone knows that." McNamara lived on to die at age ninety-three.

35. The Great Society was a set of domestic programs such as the Job Corps and Head Start launched by President Johnson in 1964–1965. Many of the programs were choked off by a lack of funding due to the Vietnam War.

36. Morley Safer, *Flashbacks: On Returning to Vietnam* (New York: Random House, 1990), 203.

37. Alexander M. Haig, Jr., *Inner Circles: How America Changed the World, A Memoir* (New York: Warner Books, 1992), 226.

38. Neil Sheehan, *A Bright Shining Lie: John Paul Vann and America in Vietnam* (New York: Random House, 1988), 739.

39. David Fulghum and Terrence Maitland, *The Vietnam Experience: South Vietnam on Trial, Mid-1970 to 1972* (Boston: Boston Publishing Company, 1984), 61–64.

40. General Thomas Matthew Rienzi, *Communications-Electronics, 1962–1970 (Vietnam Studies)* (Washington: U.S. Government Printing Office, 1972), 144.

41. Rienzi, 145–146.

42. Eggleston, *Exiting Vietnam*, 123.

43. Lewis Sorley, *Thunderbolt: General Creighton Abrams and the Army of His Times* (Bloomington: Indiana University Press, 2008), 305.

44. Henry Kissinger, *Ending the Vietnam War* (New York: Simon and Schuster, 2003), 198.

45. David Fulghum and Terrence Maitland, 64–65.

46. Historical Division Joint Secretariat, *History of the Joint Chiefs of Staff and the War in Vietnam 1971–1973* (Washington: Department of Defense, 1970), 7.

47. Lewis Sorley, *A Better War: The Unexamined Victories and Final Tragedy of America's Last Years in Vietnam* (New York: Harcourt, 1999), 255.

48. Sorley, *Thunderbolt*, 307.

49. Van Atta, 345.

50. Van Atta, 345.

51. Sorley, *A Better War*, 270–271.

52. David Fulghum and Terrence Maitland, 88.

53. David Fulghum and Terrence Maitland, 70.

54. David Fulghum and Terrence Maitland, 75.

55. Van Atta, 348.

56. David Fulghum and Terrence Maitland, 85–86.

57. Nguyen Duy Hinh, *Lam Son 719* (Fort McNair: U.S. Army Center of Military History, 1979), 90.

58. David Fulghum and Terrence Maitland, 87.

59. Eggleston, *Exiting Vietnam*, 152.

60. Richard Nixon, *No More Vietnams* (New York: Arbor House, 1985), 137.

61. Jeffrey Kimball, *Nixon's Vietnam War* (Lawrence: The University Press of Kansas, 1998), 246; Langguth, 579.

62. Historical Division Joint Secretariat, 15.

63. Kissinger, *Ending the Vietnam War*, 188.

64. Eggleston, *Exiting Vietnam*, 154.

65. Kissinger, *Ending the Vietnam War*, 204.

66. Van Atta, 350.

67. Davidson, 660.

68. Kimball, 247.

69. Karnow, 632.

70. Karnow, 632.

71. Van Atta, 351.

72. Bui Diem, *In the Jaws of History* (Bloomington: Indiana University Press, 1999), 287.

73. Isserman, 67–68.

74. Isserman, 78.

75. Van Nguyen Duong, 126.

76. David Reynolds, *One World Divisible: A Global History Since 1945* (New York: W. W. Norton & Company, 2000), 283.

77. Jeremy Varon, *Bringing the War Home: The Weather Underground, the Red Army Faction, and Revolutionary Violence in the Sixties and Seventies* (Berkeley: University of California Press, 2004), 123.

78. An American radical left-wing organization.

79. Varon, 157.

80. Sheehan, 717.

81. Eggleston, *Exiting Vietnam*, 87. Three of the murderers were apprehended, tried and convicted. The fourth fled to Canada and as of 2014 was still at large.

82. Nixon, *No More Vietnams*, 126.

83. Philip Caputo, *A Rumor of War* (New York: Henry Holt and Company, 1977), xv.

84. Philip Duncan Hoffman, *Humping Heavy: A Vietnam Memoir*, 2011, 195.

85. Eggleston, *Exiting Vietnam*, 88.

86. Fulghum and Maitland, 23.

87. Fulghum and Maitland, 25.

88. General Bruce Palmer, Jr., *The 25 Year War: America's Military Role in Vietnam* (Lexington: The University Press of Kentucky, 1984), 155.

89. Keith William Nolan, *Into Laos: The Story of Dewey Canyon II/Lam Son 719, 1971* (Novato: Presidio Press, 1986), 23.

90. Fulghum and Maitland, 9.

91. Fulghum and Maitland, 8.

92. Fulghum and Maitland, 9.

93. Sorley, *A Better War*, 129.

94. Sheehan, 650–651.

95. Ronald L. Beckett, *Jack of All Trades: An American Advisor's War in Vietnam, 1969–70* (Mechanicsburg: Stackpole Books, 2016), 228–229.

96. Fulghum and Maitland, 37.

97. Fulghum and Maitland, 16.

98. Fulghum and Maitland, 20.

99. Fulghum and Maitland, 22.

100. H. R. Haldeman, *The Ends of Power* (New York: Time Books, 1978), 122.

101. Karnow, 644.

102. Karnow, 642.

103. Langguth, 576.

104. Sheehan, 775.

105. Karnow, 641.

106. Karnow, 639–641.

107. Langguth, 598.
108. Sorley, *Thunderbolt*, 322–323.
109. Fulghum and Maitland, 140.
110. Nixon, *No More Vietnams*, 146.
111. Sorley, *Thunderbolt*, 320.
112. Thomas P. McKenna, *Kontum: The Battle to Save South Vietnam* (Lexington: The University Press of Kentucky, 2011), 84.
113. Sheehan, 755.
114. Sheehan, 770.
115. Sheehan, 775.
116. Sheehan, 760–763.
117. Sheehan, 763.
118. Sheehan, 785.
119. Sheehan, 786.
120. Sheehan, 789.
121. Sorley, *Thunderbolt*, 328.
122. Sheehan, 785.
123. Karnow, 648.
124. Kissinger, *Ending the Vietnam War*, 462.
125. Karnow, 657.
126. J. Edward Lee and H. C. Haynsworth, *Nixon, Ford and the Abandonment of South Vietnam* (Jefferson: McFarland & Company, Inc., Publishers, 2002), 154.
127. Sheehan, 739.
128. Karnow, 661.
129. Karnow, 664.
130. Karnow, 664.
131. Langguth, 647.
132. Langguth, 647.
133. In Saigon one could visit what could today be called a mall. There were many vendors selling gold in all forms at the prevailing rates. The convenient thing was that aside from gold bars (bulky and heavy), one could purchase gold-leaf sheets. These were small and light, the sort of thing that you could split up among your family members if you were fleeing for your lives.
134. Phu killed himself as the NVA entered Saigon.
135. Karnow, 665.
136. George J. Veith, *Black April, the Fall of South Vietnam 1973-1975* (New York: Encounter Books, 2012), 209–217.
137. Karnow, 666.
138. Karnow, 666.
139. Karnow, 290–291.
140. Langguth, 658.
141. Karnow, 669.
142. Langguth, 668.

Appendix B

1. Tamara Roleff, *The Vietnam War* (San Diego: Greenhaven Press, 2002), 208–214 and the author.

Appendix C

1. Units listed below included support such as artillery.
2. Stanton, *The Rise and Fall of an American Army*, 383–384.

Appendix D

1. Attached to 4ID.

Bibliography

Books

Abu-Lughod, Janet L. *Race, Space, and Riots in Chicago, New York, and Los Angeles*. Oxford: Oxford University Press, 2007.

Acheson, Dean. *Present at the Creation: My Years in the State Department*. New York: W. W. Norton, 1969.

Adler, Bill. *Letters from Vietnam*. New York: Ballantine Books, 2003.

Albright, John, John H. Cash, and Allan W. Sandstrum. *Seven Firefights in Vietnam*. Washington: Office of the Chief of Military History, United States Army, 1970.

Allen, Michael J. *Until the Last Man Comes Home: POWs, MIAs and the Unending Vietnam War*. Chapel Hill: The University of North Carolina Press, 2009.

Anderson, Charles R. *The Grunts*. New York: Berkley Books, 1985.

Anderson, Louis E. *John F. Kennedy*. Stamford: Brompton Books Corporation, 1992.

Andreas, Peter and Kelly M. Greenhill. *Sex, Drugs and Body Counts: The Politics of Numbers in Global Crime and Conflict*. Ithaca: Cornell University Press, 2010.

Apply, Christian G. *Patriots: The Vietnam War Remembered from All Studies*. New York: Penguin Books, 2003.

_____. *Working Class War: American Combat Soldiers in Vietnam*. Chapel Hill: University of North Carolina Press, 1993.

Archer, Michael. *A Patch of Ground: Khe Sanh Remembered*. Ashland: Hellgate Press, 2004.

Arnett, Peter. *Live from the Battlefield*. New York: Simon & Schuster, 1994.

Arthurs, Ted G. *Land with No Sun: A year in Vietnam with the 173rd Airborne*. Mechanicsburg: Stackpole Books, 2006.

Association of Graduates, United States Military Academy. *The Register of Graduates and Former Cadets of the United States Military, 2010*. West Point: Association of Graduates, 2010.

Atkinson, Rick. *The Long Gray Line: The American Journey of West Point's Class of 1966*. New York: Henry Holt and Company, 1989.

Axelrod, Alan. *The Real History of the Vietnam War: A New Look at the Past*. New York: Sterling Publishing, 2013.

Bacn Research. *Vietnam War Photography*.

Baker, Mark. *Nam*. New York: William Morrow and Company, 1982.

Ball, Phil. *Ghosts and Shadows: A Marine in Vietnam 1968–1969*. Jefferson: McFarland, 1998.

Beckett, Ronald L. *Jack of All Trades: An American Advisor's War in Vietnam, 1969–70*. Mechanicsburg: Stackpole Books, 2016.

Berman, Larry. *No Peace, No Honor: Nixon, Kissinger, and Betrayal in Vietnam*. New York: The Free Press, 2001.

Berman, Paul. *A Tale of Two Utopias: The Political Journey of the Generation of 1986*. New York: W. W. Norton & Company, 1996.

Bernstein, Jonathan. *U.S. Army AH-1 Cobra Units in Vietnam*. Oxford: Osprey Publishing, 2003.

Berry, F. Clifton, Jr. *The Illustrated History of Sky Soldiers—The Vietnam War*. New York: Bantam Books, 1987.

Blakeley, H. W. *Famous Fourth: The Story of the 4th Infantry Division*. Whitefish: Kessinger Publishing, 2013.

Blehm, Eric. *Legend*. New York: Crown Publishers, 2015.

Bradley, Mark Phillip. *Imagining Vietnam and America: The Making of Postcolonial Vietnam, 1919–1950*. Chapel Hill: The University of North Carolina Press, 2000.

Braestrup, Peter. *The Big Story*. Novato: Presidio Press, 1994.

Burns, Richard R. *Pathfinder: First In, Last Out*. New York: Ballantine Books, 2002.

Califano, Joseph A. *The Triumph & Tragedy of Lyndon Johnson: The White House Years*. New York: Touchstone, 1991.

Caputo, Philip. *A Rumor of War*. New York: Henry Holt and Company, 1977.

_____. *10,000 Days of Thunder: A History of the*

Vietnam War. New York: Byrun Priess Visual Publications, Inc., 2005.
Carey, Elaine. *Plaza of Sacrifices: Gender, Power, and Terror in 1968 Mexico*. Albuquerque: University of New Mexico Press, 2005.
Carnes, Mark C., and John A. Garraty. *American Destiny: Narrative of a Nation, Volume II, Since 1865*. New York: Penguin Academics, 2006.
Carter, James M. *Inventing Vietnam: The United States and State Building 1954–1968*. New York: Cambridge University Press, 2008.
Casey, Michael, Clark Dougan, Denis Kennedy, and Shelby Stanton. *The Vietnam Experience: The Army at War*. Boston: Boston Publishing Company, 1987.
Central Intelligence Agency, Office of Current Intelligence. *Lam Son Summary*. 1973.
Chafe, William H. *Civilities and Civil Rights: Greensboro, North Carolina and the Black Struggle for Freedom*. Oxford: Oxford University Press, 1980.
_____. *The Unfinished Journey: America Since World War II*. New York: Oxford University Press, 2007.
Chapla, John D. *The Men of Alpha Company: Combat with the 173rd Airborne Brigade, Vietnam 1969–1970*, 2012.
Childs, Leo, Major. *The First Infantry Division in Vietnam*. Vietnam: 121st Signal Battalion, 1969.
Clancy, Tom, and General Carl Stiner. *Shadow Warriors: Inside the Special Forces*. New York: P. G. Putnam's Sons, 202.
Clodfelter, Michael. *Mad Minutes and Vietnam Months: A Soldier's Memoir*. Jefferson: McFarland, 1988.
Coan, James P. *Con Thien: The Hill of Angels*. Tuscaloosa: The University of Alabama Press, 2004.
Coleman, J. D. *Air Cav: History of the 1st Air Cavalry Division in Vietnam 1965–1969*. New York: Turner Publishing Company, 2011.
_____. *Incursion*. New York: St. Martin's Paperbacks, 1991.
_____. *Pleiku: The Dawn of Helicopter Warfare in Vietnam*. New York: St. Martin's Press, 1988.
Collier, Peter. *Medal of Honor: Portraits of Valor Beyond the Call of Duty*. New York: Artisan, 2003.
Colodny, Len. *Silent Coup*. New York: St. Martin's Press, 1991.
Daddis, Gregory A. *Westmoreland's War: Reassessing American Strategy in Vietnam*. New York: Oxford University Press, 2014.
Daugherty, Kevin, and Jason Stewart. *The Timeline of the Vietnam War*. San Diego: Thunder Bay Press, 2008.
Daugherty, Leo, and Gregory Louis Mattson. *Nam: A Photographic History*. Singapore: Michael Friedman Publishing Group, 2001.
Davidson, Phillip B. *Vietnam at War: The History 1946–1975*. New York: Oxford University Press, 1988.
_____. *Secrets of the Vietnam War*. Novato: Presidio Press, 1990.
Denny, Warren M. *The Long Journey Home from Dak To: The Story of an American Infantry Officer Fighting in the Central Highlands Republic of Vietnam 1967–1968*. New York: iUniverse, Inc., 2003.
Devillers, Philippe. *Historia du Vietnam de 1940 a 1952*. Paris: Editions du Seuil, 1953.
Diem, Bui. *In the Jaws of History*. Bloomington: Indiana University Press, 1999.
Dockery, Martin J. *Lost in Translation, Vietnam: A Combat Advisor's Story*. New York: The Random House Publishing Group, 2003.
Dooley, George E. *Battle for the Central Highlands: A Special Forces Story*. New York: Ballantine Books, 2003.
Doubek, Robert W. *Creating the Vietnam Veterans Memorial: The Inside Story*. Jefferson: McFarland, 2015.
Dougan, Clark, and Stephen Weiss. *The American Experience in Vietnam*. Boston: Boston Publishing Company, 1988.
_____, and _____. *Nineteen Sixty-Eight*. Boston: Boston Publishing Company, 1983.
Doyle, Edward, and Samuel Lipsman. *The Vietnam Experience: America Takes Over 1965–1967*. Boston: Boston Publishing Company, 1982.
Dudziak, Mary L. *Cold War Civil Rights: Race and the Image of American Democracy*. Princeton: Princeton University Press, 2000.
Dunstan, Simon. *1st Air Cavalry in Vietnam, "The First Team."* Hersham: Allan Publishing Limited, 2004.
Duong, Van Nguyen. *Tragedy of the Vietnam War: A South Vietnamese Officer's Analysis*. Jefferson: McFarland, 2008.
Edelman, Bernard. *Dear American: Letters Home from Vietnam*. New York: W. W. Norton & Company, 1985.
Eggleston, Michael A. *Exiting Vietnam: The Era of Vietnamization and American Withdrawal Revealed in First-Person Accounts*. Jefferson: McFarland, 2014.
_____. *The 5th Marine Regiment Devil Dogs in World War I*. Jefferson: McFarland, 2016.
Eigen, Daryl J. *A Hellish Place of Angels: Con Thien, One Man's Journey*. Bloomington: iUniverse, 2012.
Ellsberg, Daniel. *Secrets: A Memoir of Vietnam and the Pentagon Papers*. New York: Penguin Group, 2002.
Epp, Karen Ross. *A Soldier's Letters from Vietnam to the World*. Bloomington: Author House, 2007.
Fall, Bernard B. *Street Without Joy: The French Debacle in Indochina*. Mechanicsburg: Stackpole Books, 1994.
Fitzgerald, Frances. *Fire in the Lake: The Vietnamese and the Americans in Vietnam*. New York: Back Bay Books, 1972.
Flamm, Michael W. *Law and Order: Civil Unrest, and the crisis of Liberalism in the 1960s*. New York: Columbia University Press, 2005.
Flood, Charles Bracelen. *The War of the Innocents*. New York: Bantam Books, 1970.
Foley, Michael S. *Confronting the War Machine: Draft*

Resistance During the Vietnam War. Chapel Hill: University of North Carolina Press, 2003.

Foster, Randy E. M. *Vietnam Firebases 1965–1973, American and Australian Forces*. Long Island City: Osprey Publishing, 1987.

Frost, David. *Frost/Nixon: Behind the Scenes of the Nixon Interviews*. New York: Harper Perennial, 2007.

Fulghum, David, Terrance Maitland, and the editors of Boston Publishing Company, *The Vietnam Experience: South Vietnam on Trial: The Test of Vietnamization, 1970–1972*. Boston: Boston Publishing Company, 1984.

Gettleman, Marvin E., Jane Franklin, Marilyn B. Young, and H. Bruce Franklin. *Vietnam and America: The Most Documented History of the Vietnam War*. New York: Grove Press, 1995.

Giap, Vo Nguyen. *How We Won the War*. Philadelphia: Recon Publications, 1976.

Goldman, Peter, and Tony Fuller. *Charlie Company: What Vietnam Did to Us*. New York: William Morrow and Company, 1983.

Goldstein, Joseph, Burke Marshall, and Jack Schwartz. *The My Lai Massacre and Its Cover-up: Beyond the Reach of the Law? The Peers Report with a Supplement and Introductory Essay on the Limits of Law*. New York: The Free Press, 1976.

Goodwin, Doris Kearns. *Lyndon Johnson and the American Dream: The Most Revealing Portrait of a President and Presidential Power Ever Written*. New York: St. Martin's Griffin, 1976.

Green, Anna, and Kathleen Troup. *The House of History: A Critical Reader in Twentieth-Century History and Theory*. New York: New York University Press, 1999.

Gross, Chuck. *Rattler One—Seven: A Vietnam Helicopter Pilot's War Story*. Denton: University of North Texas Press, 2004.

Haig, Alexander M., Jr. *Inner Circles: How America Changed the World, A Memoir*. New York: Warner Books, 1992.

Hair, Joseph E. *Contact Charlie Company & "The Headhunter Platoon."* Middletown: Self-Published, 2015.

Halberstam, David. *The Fifties*. New York: Random House Publishing Group, 1993.

_____. *The Making of a Quagmire*. New York: Ballantine Books, 1964.

Haldeman, H. R. *The Ends of Power*. New York: Time Books, 1978.

Hallin, Daniel C. *The Uncensored War: The Media and Vietnam*. Berkeley: University of California Press, 1986.

Hammond, William M. *Reporting Vietnam: Media & Military at War*. Lawrence: University of Kansas Press, 1998.

Hartzel, Jack T. *Reflections of My Past!* Middletown: Great Published, 2015.

Hay, John J., Jr. LTG. *Vietnam Studies: Tactical and Material Innovations*. Washington, D.C.: U.S. Printing Office, 1989.

Herman, Edward S. and Noam Chomsky. *Manufacturing Consent: The Political Economy of the Mass Media*. New York: Pantheon Books, 1988.

Herring, George C. *America's Longest War: The United States and Vietnam, 1950–1975*. Boston: McGraw-Hill, 2002.

_____. *LBJ and Vietnam (Administrative History of the Johnson Presidency)*. Austin: University of Texas Press, 1994.

_____. *The Pentagon Papers*. New York: McGraw-Hill, Inc., 1993.

Hinh, Nguyen Duy. *Lam Son 719*. Fort McNair: U.S. Army Center of Military History, 1979.

Historical Division Joint Secretariat. *History of the Joint Chiefs of Staff and the War in Vietnam 1971–1973*. Washington: Department of Defense, 1970.

Hoang, Ngoc Lung. *The General Offensives of 1968–1969*. Washington, D.C.: U.S. Center of Military History, 1981.

Hoffman, Philip Duncan. *Humping Heavy: A Vietnam Memoir*, 2011.

HQ PACAF, Project *CHECO Report, Operation Attleboro*. S. E. Asia Team: HQ PACAF, 1967.

Hughes, George W. *Always a Soldier*. Denver: Outskirts Press, 2009.

Isserman, Maurice, and Michael Kazan. *American Divided: The Civil War in the 1960s*. Oxford: Oxford University Press, 2008.

Jackson, Jerome J., and Constance Emerson Crooker. *Doc Jackson's Letters Home: A Combat Medic's 1968 Letters from Vietnam*. Beaverton: JayCee Publishing, 2015.

Jacobs, Rodger. *Stained with the Mud of Khe Sanh: A Marine's Letters from Vietnam, 1966–1967*. Jefferson: McFarland, 2013.

Johnson, Haynes. *The Best of Times: The Boom and Bust Years of America Before and After Everything Changed*. New York: Harcourt, Inc., 2002.

Johnson, Lt. Col. Richard M. *Lam Son 719: Perils of Strategy*. Carlisle: United States Army War College, 1996.

Johnson, Steven A. *Cammie Up! Memoir of a Recon Marine in Vietnam 1967–1968*. Jefferson: McFarland, 2012.

Jones, Greg. *Last Stand at Khe Sanh: The U.S. Marines Finest Hour in Vietnam*. Boston: De Capo Press, 2014.

Joyce, James. *Pucker Factor 10: Memoir of a U.S. Helicopter in Vietnam*. Jefferson: McFarland, 2003.

Just, Ward, ed. *Reporting Vietnam*. New York: The Library of America, 1998.

_____. *Reporting Vietnam: American Journalism 1959–1975*. New York: Literary Classics of the United States, 2000.

Kamps, Charles T., Jr. *The History of the Vietnam War: An Illustrated History of the War in South East Asia*. New York: The Military Press, 1988.

Kaplan, Fred. *The Insurgents: David Petraeus and the Plot to Change the American Way of War*. New York: Simon & Schuster, 2013.

Karnow, Stanley. *Vietnam, A History: The First Complete Account of Vietnam at War*. New York: The Viking Press, 1983.

Kelley, Michael P. *Where We Were in Vietnam: A Comprehensive Guide to the Firebases, Military Installations and Naval Vessels of the Vietnam War*. Ashland: Hellgate Press, 2002.

Kerry, Bob. *When I Was a Young Man: A Memoir*. New York: Harcourt, Inc., 2002.

Ketwig, John. *... And a Hard Rain Fell: A GI's True Story of the War in Vietnam*. Naperville: Sourcebooks, Inc., 2002.

Kimball, Jeffrey. *Nixon's Vietnam War*. Lawrence: The University Press of Kansas, 1998.

Kissinger, Henry. *Ending the Vietnam War: A History of America's Involvement in and Extraction from the Vietnam War*. New York: Simon & Schuster, 2003.

_____. *White House Years*. Boston: Little, Brown and Company, 1979.

Kitchin, Dennis. *War in Aquarius: Memoir of an American Infantryman in Action Along the Cambodian Border During the Vietnam War*. Jefferson: McFarland, 1994.

Krepinevich, Andrew F., Jr. *The Army and Vietnam*. Baltimore: The Johns Hopkins University Press, 1986.

Kurlansky, Mark. *1968, The Year That Rocked the World*. New York: Random House, 2005.

Kuzmarov, Jeremy. *The Myth of the Addicted Army: Vietnam and the Modern War on Drugs*. Boston: University of Massachusetts Press, 2009.

Langguth, A. J. *Our Vietnam: The War 1954–1975*. New York: Simon & Schuster, 2000.

Lanning, Michael Lee. *The Only War We Had: A Platoon Leader's Journal of Vietnam*. New York: Ballantine Books, 1987.

Larson, Mike. *Heroes: A Year in Vietnam with the First Air Cavalry Division*. New York: iUniverse, 2008.

Lawrence, A.T. *Crucible Vietnam: Memoir of an Infantry Lieutenant*. Jefferson: McFarland, 2009.

Lawrence, John. *The Cat from Hue: A Vietnam War Story*. New York: Perseus Books Group, 2002.

Lawrence, Mark Atwood. *The Vietnam War: A Concise International History*. New York: The Oxford University Press, 2008.

_____. *The Vietnam War: An International History in Documents*. New York: The Oxford Press, 2014.

Lee, J. Edward, and H. C. "Toby" Haynsworth. *Nixon, Ford and the Abandonment of South Vietnam*. Jefferson: McFarland, 2002.

Leppelman, John. *Blood on the Risers: An Airborne Soldier's Thirty-Five Months in Vietnam*. New York: Ballantine Books, 1991.

Lind, Michael. *Vietnam, The Necessary War*. New York: Simon & Schuster, 1999.

Logevall, Fredrik. *Embers of War: The Fall of an Empire and the Making of America's Vietnam*. New York: Random House Trade Paperbacks, 2013.

Loving, John C. *Combat Advisor: How America Won the War and Lost the Peace*. New York: Universe, Inc., 2006.

Loyte, Colonel J. F., Jr. *Project CHECO, Southeast Asia Report, Lam Son 719, 30 January–24 March 1971, The South Vietnamese Incursion into Laos*. 7th Air Force: HQ PACAF, 1971.

Luan, Nguyen Cong. *Nationalist in the Vietnam Wars: Memoirs of a Victim Turned Soldier*. Bloomington: Indiana University Press, 2012.

MacDonald, Peter. *Giap: The Victor in Vietnam*. New York: W.W. Norton & Company, 1993.

Maitland, Terrence and Peter McInerney. *The Vietnam Experience: A Contagion of War*. Boston: Boston Publishing Company, 1983.

Manchester, William. *Remembering Kennedy: One Brief Shining Moment*. Boston: Little, Brown and Company, 1983.

Maraniss, David. *They Marched into Sunlight: War and Peace Vietnam and America, October 1967*. New York: Simon & Schuster Paperbacks, 2003.

Mark, Roy. *Fixin' to Die Rag: Gooood Morning Vietnam... We've Just Had a Mid-Air Collision*. Charleston: CreateSpace, 2014.

Marshall, Tom. *The Price of Exit*. New York: Ballantine Books, 1998.

Mauldin, Bill. *Bill Mauldin's Army: Bill Mauldin's Greatest World War II Cartoons*. New York: Random House Publishing Group, 1944.

McCullough, David. *Truman*. New York: Simon & Schuster, 1992.

McKenna, Thomas P. *Kontum: The Battle to Save South Vietnam*. Lexington: The University Press of Kentucky, 2011.

McMasters, H. R. *Dereliction of Duty: Johnson, McNamara, the Joint Chiefs of Staff, and the Lies That Led to Vietnam*. New York: Harper Perennial, 1997.

McNamara, Robert S. *In Retrospect: The Tragedy and Lessons of Vietnam*. New York: Vintage Books, 1995.

Mertel, Kenneth D. *Year of the Horse: Vietnam, 1st Air Cavalry in the Highlands 1965–1967*. Atglen: Schiffer Publishing, Ltd., 1997.

Moore, Harold G., and Joseph L. Galloway. *We Are Soldiers Still: A Journey Back to the Battlefields of Vietnam*. New York: Harper Perennial, 2008.

_____, and _____. *We Were Soldiers Once ... and Young: Ia Drang, the Battle That Changed the War in Vietnam*. New York: HarperCollins Publishers, 1992.

Moore, Robin. *The Green Berets*. New York: Crown Publishers, Inc., 1965.

Morocco, John. *Thunder from Above: Air War, 1941–1968*. Boston: Boston Publishing Company, 1984.

Moyar, Mark. *Triumph Forsaken: The Vietnam War, 1954–1965*. Cambridge: Cambridge University Press, 2006.

Murphy, Edward F. *Dak To: America's Sky Soldiers in South Vietnam's Central Highlands*. New York: Ballantine Books, 2007.

_____. *The Hill Fights: The First Battle of Khe Sanh*. New York: Ballantine Books, 2003.

Murry, Gregory H. *Content with my Wages: A Sergeant's Story, Book I, Vietnam*. Austin: No End to Publishing Company, 2013.

Nelson, Deborah. *The War Behind Me: Vietnam Veterans Confront the Truth About U.S. War Crimes*. New York: Basic Books, 2008.

Nesser, John A. *Ghosts of Thua Thien: An American Soldier's Memoir of Vietnam*. McFarland, 2008.

Nguyen, Lien-Hang T. *Hanoi's War: An International History of the War for Peace in Vietnam*. Chapel Hill: University of North Carolina Press, 2012.

Nhu Tang, Truong. *A Viet Cong Memoir*. New York: Vintage Books, 1986.

Nixon, Richard. *No More Vietnams*. New York: Arbor House, 1985.

Nolan, Keith William. *Into Laos: The Story of Dewey Canyon II/Lam Son 719, 1971*. Novato: Presidio Press, 1986.

North, Oliver L. *Under Fire: An American Story*. New York: HarperCollins, Inc., 1991.

Novick, Peter. *That Noble Dream: The "Objectivity Question" and the American Historical Profession*. Cambridge: Cambridge University Press, 1998.

Oates, Stephen B., and Charles J. Errico. *Portrait of America, Volume 2*. Boston: Houghton Mifflin Company, 2007.

Oberdorfer, Don. *Tet! The Turning Point in the Vietnam War*. Baltimore: The Johns Hopkins University Press, 1971.

Okendo, Lawrence D. *Sky Soldier: 173rd Airborne Infantry Brigade Separate, Battles of Dak To Vietnam*. Lawrence D. Okendo, 1988.

Olson, Rocky. *Sgt. Rock: Last Man Standing*. Zeroed-In Press, 2010.

Palmer, General Bruce, Jr. *The 25 Year War: America's Military Role in Vietnam*. Lexington: The University Press of Kentucky, 1984.

Park, Stephen L. *Boots: An Unvarnished Memoir of Vietnam*. Boston: Writers Amuse Me Publishing, 2012.

Pezzoli, Rar, Jr. *A Year in Hell: Memoir of an American Foot Soldier Turned Reporter in Vietnam 1965–1966*. Jefferson: McFarland, 2006.

Pimlott, John. *Vietnam: The Decisive Battles*. New York: Chartwell Books, 1997.

Pisor, Robert. *The End of the Line: The Siege of Khe Sanh*. New York: W. W. Norton, 1982.

Prados, John. *In Country: Remembering the Vietnam War*. New York: Ivan R. Dee, Publisher, 2011.

_____. *Vietnam: The History of an Unwinnable War, 1945–1975*. Lawrence: University Press of Kansas, 2009.

Prochnau, William. *Once Upon a Distant War: Young Correspondents and the Early Vietnam Battles*. New York: Random House, 1995.

Project CHECO Southeast Asia Report. *Lam Son 719, The South Vietnamese Incursion into Laos, 30 January–24 March 1971*. HQ, PACAF, 1971.

Rawson, Andrew W. *Tet Offensive 1968, Battle Story*. Gloucestershire: The History Press, 2013.

Reynolds, David. *One World Divisible: A Global History Since 1945*. New York: W. W. Norton & Company, 2000.

Ricks, Thomas E. *The Generals: American Military Command from World War II to Today*. New York: The Penguin Press, 2012.

Rienzi, General Thomas Matthew. *Communications-Electronics, 1962–1970 (Vietnam Studies)*. Washington: U.S. Government Printing Office, 1972.

Rogers, Lt. Gen. Bernard William. *Cedar Falls–Junction City: A Turning Point*. Washington: Ross & Perry, Inc, 2001.

Roleff, Tamara. *The Vietnam War*. San Diego: Greenhaven Press, 2002.

Ronnau, Christopher. *Blood Trails: The Combat Diary of a Foot Soldier in Vietnam*. New York: Ballantine Books, 2006.

Rottman, Gordon L. *North Vietnamese Army Soldier 1958–75*. New York: Osprey Publishing, 2009.

_____. *Special Forces Camps in Vietnam, 1961–1970*. New York: Osprey Publishing, 2005.

Safer, Morley. *Flashbacks: On Returning to Vietnam*. New York: Random House, 1990.

Santoli, Al. *Everything We Had: An Oral History of the Vietnam War*. New York: Ballantine Books. 1981.

Schlesinger, Arthur M., Jr. *A Thousand Days: John F. Kennedy in the White House*. New York: Houghton Mifflin Company, 2002.

Schmitz, David F. *The Tet Offensive: Politics, War, and Public Opinion*. Lanham: Rowland and Littlefield Publishers, Inc., 2005.

Schulman, Bruce J. *The Seventies*. New York: Da Capo Press, 2001.

Schwarzkopf, General H. Norman. *It Doesn't Take a Hero: The Autobiography of General Norman Schwarzkopf*. New York: Bantam Books, 1992.

Scott, Leonard B., LTC. *The Battle for Hill 875: Dak To, Vietnam, 1967*. Carlisle Barracks: U.S. Army War College, 1988.

Scruggs, Jan C. *Dreams Unfulfilled: Stories of the Men and Women on the Vietnam Veterans Memorial*. Washington: Vietnam Veterans Memorial Fund, 2010.

Scruggs, Jan C., and Joel L. Swerdlow. *The Vietnam Memorial: To Heal a Nation*. New York: Harper & Row, Publishers, 1985.

Shapley, Deborah. *Promise and Power: The Life and Times of Robert McNamara*. Boston: Little, Brown, and Company, 1993.

Sheehan, Neil. *A Bright Shining Lie: John Paul Vann and America in Vietnam*. New York: Random House, 1988.

Shore, Moyers S. II. *The Battle of Khe Sanh*. Washington, D.C. History and Museums Division, Headquarters, U.S. Marine Corps, 1969.

Shulimson, Jack. *U.S. Marines: The Defining Year, 1968*. Washington, D.C.: History and Museums Division, Headquarters, U.S. Marine Corps, 1997.

Sigler, David. *Vietnam Battle Chronology: US Army and Marine Corps Combat Operations, 1965–1973*. Jefferson: McFarland, 1992.

Simmons, David B. *Our Turn to Serve: An Army Veteran's Memoir of the Vietnam War*. Lexington: Xlibris Corporation, 2011.

Singer, Daniel. *Prelude to Revolution: France in May 1968*. New York: Hill and Wang, 1970.

Sorenson, Theodore C. *Kennedy*. New York: Harper & Row, Publishers, 1988.

Sorley, Lewis. *A Better War: The Unexamined Victories and Final Tragedy of America's Last Years in Vietnam*. New York: Harcourt, 1999.

_____. *Honorable Warrior: General Harold K. Johnson and the Ethics of Command*. Lawrence: University Press of Kansas, 1998.

_____. *Thunderbolt: General Creighton Abrams and the Army of His Times*. Bloomington: Indiana University Press, 2008.

_____. *Westmoreland: The General Who Lost Vietnam*. Boston: Houghton Mifflin Harcourt, 2011.

Stanton, Shelby L. *Anatomy of a Division: 1st Cav in Vietnam*. Novato: Presideo Press, 1987.

_____. *The Rise and Fall of an American Army: U.S. Ground Forces in Vietnam, 1965-1973*. New York: Balantine Books, 1985.

_____. *Vietnam Order of Battle: A Complete Illustrated Reference to U.S. Combat and Support Forces in Vietnam, 1961-1973*. Mechanicsburg: Stackpole Books, 2003.

Summers, Harry G. *On Strategy: A Critical Analysis of the Vietnam War*. New York: The Random House Publishing Group, 1982.

Suri, Jermi. *Power and Protest: Global Revolution and the Rise of Detente*. Cambridge: Harvard University Press, 2003.

Tang, Truong Nhu. *A Viet Cong Memoir: An Inside Account of the Vietnam War and Its Aftermath*. New York: Vintage Books, 1986.

Taylor, K. W. *Voices from the Second Republic of South Vietnam (1967-1975)*. Ithaca: Cornell University, 2014.

Taylor, Maxwell D. *Swords and Plowshares: A Memoir*. New York: Da Capo Press, 1972.

Telfer, Gary L., Major. *U.S. Marines in Vietnam: Fighting the North Vietnamese, 1967*. Washington D.C.: History and Museums Division, Headquarters, U.S. Marine Corps, 1984.

Terry, Wallace. *Bloods: An Oral History of the Vietnam War*. New York: Ballantine Books, 1985.

Thao, Hoang Minh. *The Vietnamese Military During the Resistance War Against the U.S. for National Salvation and Defense*. Vietnam: The Gioi Publishers, 2014.

Thi, Lam Quang. *The Twenty-Five Year Century—A South Vietnamese General Remembers the Indochina War to the Fall of Saigon*. Denton: University of North Texas Press, 2001.

Tho, Brig. Gen. Tran Dinh. *Indochina Monographs: The Cambodian Incursion*. Fort McNair: U.S. Army Center of Military History, 1979.

Thomas, Evan. *Robert Kennedy: His Life*. New York: Simon & Schuster, 2000.

Tiffany, A. L. *Youth in Asia*. 2015.

Tolson, John J., Lieutenant General. Vietnam Studies Airmobility—1961-1971. Washington: Department of the Army, 1999.

Tram, Dang Thuy. *Last Night I Dreamed of Peace: The Diary of Dang Thuy Tram*. New York: Three Rivers Press, 2007.

Troung, Ngo Quang, IndoChina Monographs. Washington, D.C.: Center of Military History, 1980.

Tucker, Spencer C. *The Encyclopedia of the Vietnam War: A Political Social, & Military History*. New York: The Oxford University Press, 1998.

Uhl, Michael. *Vietnam Awakening: My Journey from Combat to the Citizens' Commission of Inquiry on U.S. War Crimes*. Jefferson: McFarland, 2007.

Van Atta, Dale, and President Gerald R. Ford. *With Honor: Melvin Laird in War, Peace, and Politics*. Madison: The University of Wisconsin Press, 2008.

Varon, Jeremy. *Bringing the War Home: The Weather Underground, the Red Army Faction, and Revolutionary Violence in the Sixties and Seventies*. Berkeley: University of California Press, 2004.

Veith, George J. *Black April: The Fall of South Vietnam 1973-1975*. New York: Encounter Books, 2012.

Vien, General Cao Van. *The Final Collapse*. Honolulu: University Press of the Pacific, 2005.

Vuic, Kara Dixon. *Officer, Nurse, Woman: The Army Nurse Corps in the Vietnam War*. Baltimore: Johns Hopkins University Press, 2010.

Westmoreland, William C. *A Soldier Reports*. New York: Doubleday & Company, 1976.

Whalon, Pete. *The Saigon Zoo, Vietnam's Other War: Sex, Drugs Rock 'n' Roll*. Conshohocken: Infinity Publishing Company, 2009.

Wheeler, James Scott. *The Big Red One: America's Legendary 1st Infantry Division from World War I to Desert Storm*. Lawrence: University Press of Kansas, 2007.

Widmer, Ted. *Listening In: The Secret White House Recordings of John F. Kennedy*. New York: Hyperion, 2012.

Wiest, Andrew. *The Boys of '67: Charlie Company's War in Vietnam*. New York: Osprey Publishing, 2012.

_____. *Vietnam's Forgotten Army: Heroism and Betrayal in the ARVN*. New York: New York University Press, 2008.

Wilensky, Robert. *Military Medicine to Win Hearts and Minds: Aid to Civilians in the Vietnam War*. Lubbock: Texas Tech University Press, 2004.

Willbanks, James H. *The Tet Offensive: A Concise History*. New York: Columbia University Press, 2007.

Williams, Kieran. *The Prague Spring and Its Aftermath: Czechoslovak Politics, 1968-1970*. Cambridge: Cambridge University Press, 1997.

Articles

"Battle of the Slopes." *Sky Soldier Magazine,* Autumn 2015, Volume31, Number 4, 11.

"The Battle of the Slopes." *2/503d Newsletter, Issue 29,* 22 June 2011.

"Dak To." *Vietnam Magazine,* April 2015.
"Excerpts from Talk by Westmoreland." *New York Times,* 22 November 1967.
"Inside the Cone of Fire at Con Thien." *Life Magazine,* 27 October 1967.
"The Invasion Ends." *Time Magazine,* 5 April 1971.
"A Look Down the Road." *Time Magazine,* 19 February 1965.
Prados, John. "Dak To: One Hell of a Fight." *VVA Veteran,* January-February 2012.
"Ten Great Battles of Vietnam." *Vietnam Magazine,* 2012.
"33 Days of Violent Sustained Combat." *Veterans of Foreign Wars Magazine,* March 2006.
"U.S. Troops Take Top of Hill 875 Defy Fierce Fire." *New York Times,* 22 November 1967.
"Win Bitter Viet Battle." *Washington Evening Journal,* Washington, Iowa, Nov 23, 1967.

Web Sites

2/503rd Vietnam Newsletter. www.corregidor.org/VN2-503/fbp/issue_29/index.html (last accessed on 12 March 2016).
4th Infantry Division. www.ivydragoons.org/afteractionreports.htm (last accessed on 28 March 2016).
American War Library. americanwarlibrary.com/vietnam/vwc24.htm (last accessed on 28 March 2016).
Army Publications. "Presidential Unit Citations." armypubs.army.mil/epubs/pdf/go6942.pdf (last accessed on 12 March 2016).
The Battle of Kontum. www.thebattleofkontum.com (last accessed on 28 March 2016).
Center of Military History. www.history.army.mil/art/A&I/vietnam/vn-inf.htm (last accessed on 28 March 2016).
Con Thien "The Hill of the Angels." www.vietvet.org/jhconthn.htm (last accessed on 28 March 2016).
Congressional Medal of Honor Society. "Archive." www.cmohs.org/recipient-archive.php (last accessed on 12 March 2016).
Dak To. www.history.army.mil/books/vietnam/tactical/chapter7.htm (last accessed on 28 March 2016).
National Archives. http://www.archives.gov/research/military/vietnam-war/casualty-statistics.html (last accessed on 28 March 2016).
The Official Home Page of the United States Army. www.army.mil/ (last accessed on 28 March 2016).
Sony Pictures Classics. www.sonyclassics.com/fogofwar (last accessed on 18 March 2016).
U.S. Army Center of Military History. www.history.army.mil/index.html (last accessed on 28 March 2016).
U.S. Defense Department. "Medal of Honor Recipients." valor.defense.gov/Recipients (last accessed on 12 March 2016).
Vietnam Veterans' Memorial. thewall-usa.com (last accessed on 28 March 2016).
Vietnam Veterans' Memorial. www.virtualwall.org/ (last accessed on 12 March 2016).
Wikipedia. en.wikipedia.org/wiki/Battle_of_Khe_Sanh (last accessed on 28 March 2016).

Television

Cronkite, Walter, *Vietnam War,* DVD, 2003.
National Geographic, *Inside the Vietnam War,* DVD, 2008.
PBS, *Vietnam: A Television History,* DVD, 1983.
The Battle of Dak To—The Lost Film, DVD, March 2014.

Unpublished Materials

Boedeker, Gene. Unpublished memoir.
Chang, Sa Won. Unpublished memoir.
DeRuggiero, Stanley J. Unpublished memoir.
Donahue, Paul. Papers. Unpublished memoir.
Edwards, John H. Unpublished memoir.
Eggleston, Michael A. Unpublished memoir.
Hale, Dennis. Unpublished memoir.
Luoma, Gary. Unpublished memoir.
Means, Tom. Unpublished memoir.
Moran, Irvin "Bugs." Unpublished memoir.
Placencia, Ed. Unpublished memoir.
Quintanar, Juan Alex. Unpublished memoir.
Robinson, John R. Unpublished memoir.
Stovall, Cliff. Unpublished memoir.
Vandenburg, Mercer. Unpublished memoir.
Vorthmann, Steven C. Unpublished memoir.
Walls, Gary. Unpublished memoir.

Public Documents

Department of the Army. *After Action Report—Operation Sam Houston Conducted by the 4th Infantry Division.* Office of the Adjutant General: 28 June 1967.
Headquarters, 4th Infantry Division. *Combat Operations After Action Report—Battle of Dak To.* Office of the Commanding General: 3 January 1968.
Headquarters, 4th Infantry Division. *Combat Operations After Action Report—Operation Francis Marion.* Office of the Commanding General: 25 November 1967.

Index

Numbers in ***bold italics*** indicate pages with photographs.

Abner, Sergeant 83, 84
Abrams, Creighton, Jr. 125, 131, 133, 139, 142, 144, 157, 163, 199, 206
Acheson, Dean 5, 9, 157, 183, 193, 198, 201
Adamson, James B. 33, 40, 121
advisors 3–4, 8, 16–17, 20, 23, 26, 35, 37, 43, 108, 113, 127–129, 133, 137, 139–141, 143–144, 149, 151, 157–159, 163, 165–166, 169–171, 194, 199, 201–202, 204
air strike 22, 24, 27, 46, 50–53, 75, 79–80, 82–84, 87–88, 90, 120, 124, 135, 15350, 3, 9, 80, 82, 83, 87, 124
AK-47 35, 50, 58, 109, 165
Albright, John **29**, **49**, ***51–52***, ***54***, 196, 201
Allen, Robert 43, 50–51, 63, 180
ammunition 10, 25, 33, 35, 39, 46, 53, 57, 63, 65, 75, 77–78, 79–80, 84, 94, 103, 118, 120, 132, 143, 148, 151, 168, 196
An Khe 12, 23, 33
Anderson, Charles R. 106, 201
anti-war demonstrations 44
Ap Bac 17, ***18***, 19–20, 23, 126, 132, 142, 163, 194
APC 17, 165
Arc Light 109
Arnett, Peter 20, 47, 48, 81, 91, 197, 201
Arnold, James 83, 175
ARVN 10, 17, 19–21, 26–28, 39–41, 43–44, 46, 92, 108–109, 111, 118–120, 125, 127–128, 130–135, 138, 142–144, 146, 148–149, 151–154, 165, 167–168, 173, 206

Atkins, Billy 86
Atwell, Michael 97
automatic weapons 38, 50, 73, 84, 96

B-40 59, 67–68, 93–94
B-52 62, 70, 104–106, 109, 121, 132, 143
backpack 35
Baird, Thomas 45, 49, 50, 51
Baldridge, George 45, 53, 54
Ban Me Thout 9, 124, 152, 165; *see also* Ban Me Thuot
Ban Me Thuot 7, 151–152; *see also* Ban Me Thout
bandages 56, 59, 67–68, 71, 80–81, 84, 91, 96
Bangalore Torpedoe 102
Bao Dai ***7***, 8, 12–13, 151, 157, 169
Barnes, John A. 59, 94, 95, 177
Barthelemy, John 70
Basecamp 61
Battle of the Slopes 35, 67, 195, 206–207
Baum, Douglas Bruce 66, 178
Belnap, Glen D. 46, 48, 183
Ben Hai 101
Ben Het 41, 45–46, 49, 58, 62, 80, 145
Bickel, Robert J. 53, 177
Bien Hoa 23, 25, 33, 66, 122, 128, 165, 169
Blackman 70, 71
Bodine, Phillip 63
body count 25, 27–28, 40, 43, 47, 51, 55, 60, 109, 121, 127, 137, 140
Boedeker, Billy E. ***70***, 73, 196, 207
Borowski, John 41, 176

Bronze Star 57, 72, 161, 196
Brooks, Rick ***61***
Brown, Charles 80
Bru 119–120
Burton, Michael D. 49–50

C-4 63, 119
C-130 63, 148
C-rations 33, 35, 60, 86, 90, 103, 105, 165
Calley, William 140, 157, 170, 171
Cam Lo 113
Cam Ranh Bay 25
Cambodia 13, 15, 17, 26, 28–30, 44, 55, 62, 75, 86, 101, 107–108, 128–130, 133, 135–136, 161–162, 165–166, 169, 171, 193, 206
Camp Carroll 113, 119, 143
Camp Enari 30, ***31***, 33
canteen 68, 85, 124
Capital Military Region 151
Caputo, Philip 137, 199, 201
Carmichael, Sam 68, 178
CAS *see* close air support
Catecka 33, 35
Cates, William 89, 179
Caulfield, Matthew 119
Cecil, Gerald 57
Central Highlands 9, 23, 28, 31–33, 50, 66–67, 91–92, 96, 122, 129, 142, 151–152, 165–166, 169–170, 178, 193, 195, 196, 202, 204
CH-47 *see* Chinook
Charlie *see* Viet Cong
Charmichael, Sam 57
Cheo Reo 9, 152, 153
China 8, 13, 141, 143, 157, 159–160, 162, 169, 194

209

Chinook (CH-47) 46, 55, 90, 128, 162, 165
CIA 124, 126, 152, 165–166
CIDG *see* Civilian Irregular Defense Group
Civilian Irregular Defense Group (CIDG) 28, 35–37, 39, 41–43, 49–50, 108, 113, 165, 173, 195
Claymore 33, 54, 66
Clifford, Clark 127
close air support (CAS) 38, 56, 62–63, 65, 69, 104–105
Coan, James P. 99, 101, 103–104, 194–195, 197, 202
Cobra gunships 131, 166, 201
Collins, William 50, 178
command post (CP) 36–38, 54, 67, 80, 87–88, 90, 104, 166
communism 5, 8, 10, 12–13, 19, 26, 28, 91, 124–126, 132, 135, 142–143, 152, 163, 165–167
Con Thien 28, 99, *100*, 101–106, 112–113, 118, 129, 170, 173, 194, 197, 202, 206, 207
Congress 7, 22, 72, 91, 97, 135, 141, 143, 150–151, 166, 170, 207
Connolly, William 45, 54–55, 58, 80, 81
Cooper-Church Amendment 129, 166
Corbett, John 118
CORDS 166
CP *see* command post
Cronkite, Walter 126, 207
cross-over point 22–23, 25
CS 36, 38, 119

Da Nang 23, 135, 153, 170
Dabney, William H. 110, 118
Dak Seang 43
Dak Sek 43, 174, 193, 195–198, 202, 204–205, 207
Dak To airstrip *64*
Darling, Robert 53, 177
Davidson, Gen. Philip 122, 124–125, 133, 194–195, 198–199, 202
Deane, Gen. John R. 30, 33, 40–41, 44
de Castries, Christian 10, 157, 158
Deeb, Michael 76
Deems, John M. 41, 43
Depuy, Gen. William E. 126
De Ruggiero, Stanley S. 82, 87, 89, 97–98, 197, 207
Diem, Ngo Dinh 8, *9*, 12–13, 15–17, 19–21, 154–161, 163, 166, 169, 170, 194, 199, 202
Dien Bien Phu 10, *11*, 12, 27–28, 106, 120, 157–158, 169, 193–194

Distinguished Service Cross (DSC) 69, 72, 73, 162, 166
DMZ 12, 26, 99, 101, 106, 112, 116, 124, 129, 134, 140, 142, 166
Dohrn, Bernardine 136
domino theory 13, 15, 135, 166
Donahue, Paul 38, *39*, 43, 195, 196, 207
DSC *see* Distinguished Service Cross
Duckett, Sam 57, 65, 68, 70, 72
Dunston, William 43
Duong, Van Nguyen 21, *114*, 135, 199, 202
dustoff 42
Dyer, Joseph F. 66, 178
Dyerson, Fred 63

Easter Invasion 121, *141*
Eggleston, John *100*, *107*
Eggleston, Mike 158, 194, 197, 199, 202, 207
Eigen, Darryl 102–103, 105–106, 197–198, 202
81-mm mortars 34, 53, 66, 101, 118
Eisenhower, Pres. Dwight D. 13, 15, 22, 151, 154, 166
elephant soldiers 34

Falcone, John 47–48, 183
Fall, Bernard B. 9, 158, 193, 194, 202
Feagin, John L. Jr. *45*
Felt, Adm. Harry D. 19–20
Ferrin, Robert 85
52nd Aviation Group 48, 173
fire support base 41, *45*, 46, 48, 50, 55, 62, 97, 113, 116
Fire Support Base Mary Ann 138
firebase 131, 140, 143
1st Air Cavalry Division 3, 12, 23, 26, 33, 41, 188, 190, 202
1/9 Marines 102, 119
1/12 Infantry 87, 89
1/503d Infantry 35–36, 44, 46, 55–57, 59, 65–66, 68–70, 75, 90–91, 196
1st Infantry Division 3, 25–26, 108, 206
Fladry, Leroy E. 59, 60, 179
flamethrower 80, 87–89
Fleming, Robert 78
Ford, Pres. Gerald 91, 147, 150, 152, 159, 200, 204, 206
Fort Benning 84–85, 163
4.2 inch mortars 101
4/503d Infantry 41, 43–45, 48, *49*, *51*–*52*, 57–59, *74*, 75, 80–82, 86–90, 195

4th Infantry Division (4ID) 3, 26–28, 30–31, 33, 40, 44, 46–48, 63, 87, 89, 90, 92, 94, 96, 121, 161, 165, 170, 180, 195, 197, 200–201, 207
fragmentation grenades 33
Freeman, Ray *61*
French 1, 3, 5, *6*, 7–9, 10–13, 15, 25, 27, 99, 101, 106, 108, 112, 121, 146, 157–160, 167–169, 192–193, 202
FSB 12 45–46, 49–51, 53, 58
FSB 15 48, 55–57; *see also* Hill 883
FSB 16 62–63, 80
FSB 46 62, 90, 138, 144, 166
Fulghum, David 131, 143, 199–200, 203

Gallup 44, 126, 196
Garcia, Raymond, Jr. 71, 178, 196
Geneva Accords 13, 160
Giap, Gen. Vo Nguyen 1, 10, 11, 12, 27, 91, 99, 111–112, 120–121, 133, 142, 145, 151, 158, 203, 204
Gio Linh 99, 101–102, 106, 112–113
Goins, Sergeant 58–59
Gove, Charles L. *64*
"Great Society" 127, 135, 166, 199
Green Beret 6, 31, 44, 109, 116, 204
Greene, Gen. Wallace M., Jr. 111
Greenfield, "Greeny" 84–85
grenade launcher 33, 35, 50, 59, 166, 167, 172; *see also* M79
Grosso, Joseph 80
Gulf of Tonkin 22, 170
Gulf of Tonkin Resolution 22

Haig, Gen. Alexander M., Jr. 1, 4, 158–159, 199, 203
Haiphong Harbor 141, 143
Halberstam, David 17, 19, 23, 203
Haldeman, H.R. 140, 142, 158, 199, 203
Hale, Dennis 79, 86–87, 90, 197, 207
Hanoi 7, 10, 12–13, 22–23, 25–28, 40, 99, 109, 112, 121–122, 124–126, 129–130, 133–135, 141–144, 149–153, 158–161, 169–171, 198, 205
Harkins, Gen. Paul D. 19–21, 121, 126, 159
Hartzel, Jack T. 104–105, 197, 203
HE 86, 148, 166
Henderson, Oran 159

Index

Herbert, Dave 56–57
Highway 9 101, 129; *see also* Route 9
Highway 14 10, 43, 92, 144, 152; *see also* Route 14
Highway 19 33, 152; *see also* Route 19
Hill 530 92
Hill 724 46, **47**, 48, 196
Hill 815 75
Hill 823 48, 49, 50, **51**, 52–57, 62, 75, 97; *see also* FSB 15
Hill 830 41–43, 46, 75, 121
Hill 861 112–113, 115–116, 118–120
Hill 875 61–62, 66, 70–73, **74**, 75–76, 78–82, 87, **88**, 89–91, 94, 97, 121, 196, 205
Hill 881 111, 113, 116
Hill 881N 112–113, 115–116, 118
Hill 881S 112–113, 115–120
Hill 882 66–71, 73, 75
Hill 889 56–57, 62, 64–65, 70–71
Hill 950 117
Hill 1338 36, 39, 41–42, 46, 92, **93**, 94, 121, 196
Hill 1416 92
Hill Fights 113, 116, 170, 198, 205
Hinh, Gen. Nguyen Duy 3, 130–131, 193, 199, 203
Ho Chi Minh 7, 8, 20, 27, 111, 135, 140, 157, 159, 169, 171
Ho Chi Minh City 125
Ho Chi Minh Trail 17, 20, 28, 43, 62, 111, **114**, 116, 117, 129, 130, 134
Hoang, Ngoc Lung 123, **130**
Hoffman, Phillip 137, 199, 203
Hood, Richard E. 37
Hue 5, 7, 112, 125, 157, 160, 170, 204
Huey 58, 82, 90, 128, 131, 166–167
Hughes, Wayne 203

I Corps 58, 99, 116, 120
I Corps Tactical Zone 165
Ia Drang Valley 23
II Corps 58, 144, 152–153, 165
II Corps Tactical Zone 165
II Field Force, Vietnam 165
III Corps Tactical Zone 165
III MAF 101, 103, 105
Indochina 3, 5, **6**, 132, 141, 143, 167, 193, 202, 206
infiltration 25, 194
IV Corps Tactical Zone 165

Jackley, Larry 41–43, 45, 195
Jacobson, Kenneth 6, 179, 197

Japanese 5, 7, 9, 160, 162, 169, 193
JCS *see* Joint Chiefs
Jesmer, David 56–57, 64–67, 69–72
Johnson, Gen. Harold K. 159
Johnson, James H. 45, 49, 50–52, 55, 80–81, 86, 91
Johnson, Pres. Lyndon B. 21–22, 24–25, 109, 111, 116, 125–127, 135, 160, 166, 170, 198–199, 201, 203
Joint Chiefs 13, 21, 101, 160, 167, 199, 203–204
Jordan, Danny 41, 176
Judd, Donald R. 37, 176

Karnow, Stanley 3, 19–20, 23, 125, 193–194, 198–200, 204
Kaufman, Harold J. 62, 75–76, 78, 179
Kelly, William 80, 90
Kennedy, Pres. John F. 16–17, 19–21, 155, 160, 169–170, 194, 201–202, 204–206
Kennemer, Larry 56–57, 68
Kent State University 136
Khe Sanh 10, 12, 27–28, 106, 109, **110**, 111–113, **115**, 116, **117**, 118–120, 124, 129, 131–132, 170, 173, 198, 201, 203, 205
Khe Sanh Combat Base 110–113, 115–121
Kiley, Michael J. 62, 75–77, 179
Kimball, Jeffrey 133, 199, 204
King, Martin Luther, Jr. 140
Kissinger, Henry 1, 4, 127, 129, 133, 141–142, 149, 151, 158–159, 171, 199–200, 204
Komer, Robert 125
Kontum 9–10, 28–29, 43, 96, 142, 144–145, **146**, 148–149, 152–153, 163, 165, 200, 204, 207
Koster, Samuel W. 159
KSCB *see* Khe Sanh Combat Base

Laird, Melvin R. 127, 130–131, 134, 160, 206
Lam Son 719 3–5, 129–135, 141–142, 148, 193–194, 199, 203–205
Lang Vei 113, 116
Langguth, A.J. 155, 194, 198–199, 200, 204
Laos 4, 10, 13, 15, 17, 26, 28, 33, 44, 58, 62, 86, 101, 111–112, 116, 129–133, 135, 166–167, 169, 193, 199, 204–205
Larsen, Gen. Stanley R. "Swede" 40

LAW 35, 66, 89, 167; *see also* M72
Lawrence, A.T. 44, 148, 195–197, 204, 206
"Leatherneck Square" 102
LeMay, Gen. Curtis 21, 160
lensatic compass 65
Leonard, Ronald R. 36–38, 40, 54, **69**, 80–81, 97, 195
Leppelman, John L. 32, 37–38, 40, 195, 204
Ligon, Peyton, III 42
Linn, Louis 104
LLDB 109, 167
Loc Ninh 28, **107**, 108–109, 170, 173
Lodge, Henry Cabot 21, 122
Lon Nol 160, 161, 162
Long, James **31**, 136
Long Range Reconnaissance Platoon (LLRP) 60, **61**, 62, 160, 167
Loving, John 16, 194, 204
Lozada, Carlos 76–77, 95, 179
LRRP *see* Long Range Reconnaissance Platoon
Luoma, Gary 63, 196, 207
LZ 32–33, 36, 38, 42–43, 50, 52–53, 57–58, 61–62, 76–77, 79–80, 82, 86, 104, 167, 195

M16 31, 33, 41–42, 56–57, 59, 65, 77, 79, 89, 98, 112–113, 172
M60 33, 37, 50, 59, 67–68, 76, 80, 97, 112
M72 66, 86, 89, 148, 167; *see also* LAW
M79 33, 50, 53, 55, 65; *see also* grenade launcher
MACV *see* Military Assistance Command, Vietnam
Madame Nhu 161
Main Supply Route (MSR) 102–103, 167
Mao, Zedong 8, 157
Marines 23, 26–27, 99, 101–106, 110–113, 115–120, 124, 132, 170, 198, 205, 206
Marshall, Tom 4, 193, 204
Martin, Graham 154
Mataxis, Gen. Theodore C. 137
Mays, Thomas C. 83–84, 179, 197
McCarthy, Joseph 8–9, 19, 193
McCoy, John 108, 198
McDevitt, C. Allen 63
McElwain, Thomas 56–57, 60, 64
McKee, Jack 124
McLaughlin **61**
McNamara, Robert S. 19, 21–23,

101, 126–127, 160, 194, 199, 204–205
McNamara Line 101
Means, Tom 66, 196, 207
Meatgrinder 101, 106
Medal of Honor 2, 59, 72, 76–79, 94, 174, 177, 179–181, 187, 202, 207
medevac 32, 42, 48, 60, 63, 68, 9, 81, 103, 106, 113, 118, 138, 148, 158, 167
Mekong Delta 23
Miles, PFC 58–60
Military Assistance Command, Vietnam (MACV) **15**, 19, 27, 106, 109, 124, 126, 166–167, 195
Military Region 1 (MR1) 26, 99, 101, 107–108, 129, 142–143, 148, 153, 165, 167
Military Region 2 (MR2) 9, 73, 107–108, 124, 137, 142, 144, **147**, 148, 151–152, 163, 165, 167
Military Region 3 (MR3) 16, 108, 122, 148, 167
Miller, Clarence A. 53, 177
Miller, Louis C. 53, 177
Milton, David H. 36–40, 195
Minh, Duong Van 21, 154, 170
monsoon 30, 32, 73, 99, 102, 105, 117, 130
Montagnard 31, 44, 49, 50, 75, 108, 112, 119, 142, 148–149, 158, 167, 195
Moore, Gen. Harold G. 23, 194, 204
Moorer, Adm. Thomas H. 160
Moran, Irvin "Bugs" 60, **61**, 161, 196, 207
Morse code 48
mortar 17, 20, 30, 33–34, 42, 44, 46, 48, 53–54, 56, 59, 63, 66, 68–69, 80, 82–84, 86–89, 93, 96, 101–105, 108–109, 113, 115, 118–120, 122
Moss, Charles E. 50
MR1 *see* Military Region 1
MR2 *see* Military Region 2
MR3 *see* Military Region 3
MSR *see* Main Supply Route
Muldoon, James J. 45, 54–55, 81, 83–84, 86
Murphy, Edward F. 1, 111, 193, 195–196, 198, 204
My Lai massacre 27, 121, 140, 157, 159, 161, 170–171, 203

napalm 38, 46, 67, 82, 86
National Guard 25, 136, 157
National Liberation Front (NLF) 13, 109, 167, 169

nationalist 3, 5, 7–8, 12–13, 20, 135, 157, 194, 204
NATO 8, 112, 158
NDP *see* Night Defensive Position
Needham, Thomas 64, 67
Newton, Leonard Lee 118
Ngok Kom Leat 48–49, 51, 54–55
Nguyen Cao Ky 154, 159
Nha Trang 40, 63, 152, 165
Nhu, Ngo Dinh 21, 158, 161
Nicholson, PFC 84
Night Defensive Position (NDP) 109, 167
1954 Geneva Accords 13, 101, 160, 167
9th Marines 113, 115
Nixon, Pres. Richard M. 1, 20, 127, 129–130, 132–136, 140–143, 147, 149, 150, 155, 157–160, 171, 199–205
NLF *see* National Liberation Front
Nolan, Keith William 138, 199, 205
Nolting, Frederick, Jr. 20
North Korea 8, 9, 162
North Vietnam 5, 17, 21–23, 25–27, 43, 46–47, 49–50 53–55, 57–60, 73, 91, 94–97, 101, 103, 106, 110–113, 118–121, 126–127, 129, 132–133, 137–138, 140–141, 143, 149, 152, 154, 160, 162, 165–167, 169–171, 194–195, 205–206
Nung 108
NVA 4, 10, 22, 24–28, 30, 33–73, 75–90, 92, 94, 99, 101–103, 105–109, 111–113, 115–121, 124, 127, 129–135, 140, **141**, 142–154, 158–160, 163, 165–168, 195–196, 198, 200
NVA Regiment 44, 92

Okendo, Lawrence 41–42, 45, 49, 75, 195–196, 205
Okinawa 25, 79
O'Leary, Bart G. 75–76, 79
101st Airborne Division 25, 140, 162
105 mm artillery 118
120 mm mortar 110
130 mm guns 120
152 mm guns 120
173rd Airborne Brigade 3, 23, 25–26, 30–33, 35–36, 39–41, 43–44, 46, 55, 57, 60, **61**, 62–63, 70, 75, 83, 87, 91–92, 94–97, 121, 124, 160–163, 170
174th NVA Regiment 63, 90

op 6, 104
Operation Francis Marion 30, 170, 195, 207
Operation Greeley 30, 170
Operation MacArthur 45
Operation Neutralize 104, 106
Operation Niagara 120
Operation Sam Houston 28–30, 170, 207
operations group 28, 168

pacification 27, 101, 111, 157–158, 163, 167
Palmer, Gen. Bruce 4, 125, 138, 161, 199, 205
Pan, Angla B. **175**
Paris Peace Accords 149–150, 171
Parkes, Jim 61, 62
Peebles, Lance D. 62
Peers, Gen. W.R. 28, 30, 44, 73, 121, 161, 203
Pentagon 1, 3, 22, 44, 91, 126, 135, 171, 202–203
Pham Van Dong 13, 142, 151
Phillips, Alan 41–42
Phu, Gen. Phan Van 151–153, 200
Phuoc Long Province 108
Placencia, Ed 76–77, 79, 161, 197, 207
Pleiku 2, 10, 12, 23, 28, 30, 33, 48, 128, 144–145, 148–149, 151–153, 202
Pol Pot 162
Ponting, John L. 53, 179
Presidential Unit Citation 96
Puff the Magic Dragon 55
Purple Heart 8, 60, 161
python 109

Quang Tin Province 138
Quang Tri 99, **100**, 112, 143
Quintanar, Alex 47–48, 196, 207

RC-292 110
rifle 10, 22, 25, 35, 39, 45, 50, 54, 66, 68, 70–72, 77, 84–85, 112–113, 115, 137, 165, 172, 196
Riley, Thomas J. 70–72, 178, 196
Robertson, Ed 56, 64–65, 71
Robinson, John R. 65–67, **69**, 70–73, 162, 196, 207
Rocket Ridge 144
Rogan, James P. 63
Rolling Thunder 25
Rosson, Gen. William B. 63
Rostow, Walt 109
Rottman, Gordon 108, 198, 205
Route 7 9

Index

Route 9 112–113, 117, 119, 131; *see also* Highway 9
Route 14 151–152; *see also* Highway 14
Route 19 12; *see also* Highway 19
RPD 35, 168
RPG 35, 58, 68, 87–88, 102, 168
RTO 41–42, 53, 56, 68, 84, 88
rucksack 33, 56, 58, 60, 65–66, 68, 84
RVNAF 3–4, 17, 22, 26, 159, 163, 165, 167–168

Sa Won Chang 56, 65, 68–69, 90, 158, 195–197
Saigon 1, 3, 5, 8, 12, 17, 19, 21–23, 25, 40, 48, 101, 109, 119–120, 122, 124–125, 127, 132, 134, 140, 142, 145, 149, *150*, 151–155, 158, 163, 170–171, 200, 206
Sandstrom, RTO 68
Saulsberry, Jerry N. 119
Schumacher, David J. 55–56, 59–60, 67, 121
Schweiter, Gen. Leo H. 44, 57, 162
2/3 Marines 113, 115–116
2/4 NVA 102, 104
2/8 Infantry 94
2/9 Marines 102–106
2/174 NVA 81
2/503d Infantry 32, 35–38, 44, 46, 62–63, 75–76, 78–80, 82, 86–87, 89–90 195, 197, 207
Severson, Daniel 41–42
Shapley, Deborah 19, 23, 126, 194, 198, 205
Sheehan, Neil 3, 17, 19, 20, 128, 139, 149, 193–194, 197–200, 205
Shipman, Frederick 87
Shore, Moyers S. *14*, *110*, *115*, *117*, 198, 205
Sihanouk, Norodom 161–162
Silsby, Art *61*
Silver Star 56, 97, 168
60 mm mortars 34
66th NVA Regiment 46, 55, 60, 62–64, 69, 73, 96
SKS semi-automatic rifle 35
Smith, Lloyd E 83
smoke grenades 33, 65
Soc Trang 79
SOG 28, 168, 195
Song Be 107–108, 170, 173
Sorley, Lewis 133, 144, 199–200, 206
South Korea 8
South Vietnam 3, 12–13, 15–17, 21, 23, 25–26, 28, 30, 90, 92, 99, 101, 104, 108, 111, 120–122, 124–125, 127, 129–130, 132–136, 138, 141–142, 144–145, 147–148, 151–155, 157–159, 160–161, 163, 165–172, 193, 195–200, 203–204, 206
Southeast Asia 13, 60, 167, 170, 204–205
Soviet Union 8–9, 13, 15, 140–141, 143, 151, 159, 168, 194
Special Forces 16, 23, 30, 35–37, 43, 45, 75, 101, 108–109, 112–113, 116, 131, 165, 167, 198, 202, 205
Stanton, Shelby 4, 12, 24, 193–195, 197–198, 200, 202, 206
Steverson, James R. 63, 75, 9, 81
Stiner, Carl 48, 202
Stovall, Cliff 75, 162, 196, 207
Strategic Hamlet Program 20–21
Sully, Francois 20, 128, 194

tactical area of responsibility (TAOR) 116, 168
Tactical Operations Center (TOC) 37–38, 108
Tan Canh 92, 144, 148
Tan Son Nhut 122
TAOR *see* tactical area of responsibility
Tchepone 129, *130*, 131–132
TCK/TKN *see* Tong Cong Kich, Tong Khai Nghia
Terrazas, David 50, 84
Tet 3, 40, 94, 99, 106, 111, 118, 120–122, *123*, 124–126, 131, 160, 163–164, 168, 170, 194, 198, 205–206
TF Black 56–59, 62, 64
TF Blue 56–58
Thanksgiving 82, 87–92, 97
Thieu, Nguyen Van 108, 124, 127, 129, 130–135, 140, 142, 149–152, 154, 159, 161, 170–171, 194
3rd Marine Division 99
3rd Marine Regiment 113, 115, 173
3rd Marine Tank Battalion 99
3/3 Marines 113, 115
3/8 Infantry 46, *47*, 48
3/9 NVA 102
3/12 Infantry 92, *93*
3/26 Marines 119
3/503d Infantry 44, 46
Thornton, Thomas W. 84
319th Field Artillery 50, 75
Thua Thien 99, 205
TOC *see* Tactical Operations Center

Tong Cong Kich, Tong Khai Nghia (TCK/TKN) 26, 99
trip flares 33
triple-canopy 28, 32, 81
Troung, Ngo Quang 141, *146*
Truman, Pres. Harry S 8, 169, 204
Tuy Hoa *39*, 44–46, 56, 61, 70, 72, 124
12.7 mm anti-aircraft gun 71, 130
20 mm cannon 65, 68–69
24th NVA Regiment 46, 92
26th Marine Regiment 116, 173
272nd VC Regiment 109

United Kingdom 8
United States 1–3, 5–6, 8–26, 28, 30, 32, 35–36, 40, 43–44, 47–48, 55, 60, 65, 72–74, 78, 82, 88, 90, 92–96, 99–102, 106, 108–113, 115, 117, 120–142, 144, 147, 149–152, 154–155, 157–164, 166–171, 175, 193–194, 197–198, 199, 201, 203, 205–207
Upsher, Ronald 88

Vandenburg, Mercer "Nick" 41, 82, *83*, 162–163, 195, 197, 207
Vann, John Paul 17, 19–20, 139, 144, *145*, 148–149, 163, 193–194, 199, 205
VC *see* Viet Cong
Versailles 5
Viet Cong (Charlie; VC) 16–17, 19–21, 25, 26–28, 32–33, 36–37, 44, 63, 91, 97, 105, 108–109, 111, 119, 121–122, 124–126, 134, 138, 140, 142, 149–151, 161, 165, 168–171, 194, 197, 205–206
Viet Minh 3, 8–13, 106, 160, 163, 168–169
Vietnam *14*
Vietnamization 3, 126–127, 129, 133, 137, 142, 144, 160, 171, 194, 202
Vorthmann, Steve 58, 80–81, 87–88, 124, 163, 196–198, 207

Wagner, Richard 67
Walker, Tom 41, 48, 176, 178, 190
Walls, Gary F. 33, *34*, 58–60, 163, 195–196, 207
Walt, Gen. Lewis W. 109, 111–112
Watters, Chaplain Charles J. 75, 78–79, 95–96, 174

Weathers, Lieutenant 87
West, David 85
Westmoreland, Gen. William C. 1, 3–4, 8, 22–23, 25–28, 40, **69**, 92, 101, 104, 106, 111–112, 117, 120–122, 124–127, 139–140, 157, 163–164, 193–194, 197–198, 202, 206–207
Weyand, Gen. Fred 122, 124
White House 3, 135–136, 140, 150, 152, 158, 194, 201, 204–206

Williams, Freddie **61**
Williams, Walter D. 41–42, 179
Wilson, Pres. Woodrow 5
Worley, Jimmy R. 50

York, Gen. Robert 20

www.ingramcontent.com/pod-product-compliance
Ingram Content Group UK Ltd.
Pitfield, Milton Keynes, MK11 3LW, UK
UKHW050528150426
5217IPUK00026B/1846